ROXY MUSIC

Both Ends Burning

ROXY MUSIC

Both Ends Burning

JONATHAN
RIGBY

Reynolds & Hearn Ltd
London

PICTURE CREDITS

Front cover and spine:

photography – Jonathan Fisher
cover girl – Ruta Mia
concept – Jonathan Rigby
design – Peri Godbold
crew – Jason Atomic, Renée Glynne, Michaela Greene

Back cover: Peter Mazel/London Features International

Page 1: David Redfern/Redferns (top); Rex Features (bottom left); Harry Goodwin/Redferns (bottom right)
Page 2: Brian Moody/Rex Features (top); Dezo Hoffman/Rex Features (bottom)
Page 3: Redferns (top left); Jorgen Angel/Redferns (top right); Alan Messer/Rex Features (bottom right)
Page 4: Angus Mayer/Rex Features (top); Peter Mazel/London Features International (bottom)
Page 5: London Features International (top)
Page 6: Peter Mazel/London Features International (top and bottom)
Page 7: Rex Features (top left); Peter Mazel/London Features International (top right)
Page 8: Amanda Edwards/Redferns (top); Richard Young/Rex Features (bottom)

First published in 2005 by
Reynolds & Hearn Ltd
61a Priory Road
Kew Gardens
Richmond
Surrey TW9 3DH

A CIP catalogue record for this book is available from the British Library.

ISBN 1 903111 80 3

Designed by Peri Godbold.

Printed and bound in Great Britain by Biddles Ltd, King's Lynn, Norfolk.

Contents

"There's this thing called Roxy Music which is bigger than all of us individually. You say 'Roxy Music' and your mind is free to wander into all sorts of areas and fantasies. When all these bands say they're influenced by Roxy, maybe they mean the idea of Roxy as well."

Phil Manzanera, July 2001

Introduction

Writing a history of Roxy Music is an intriguing exercise on several levels, but particularly so for me in that my first published work was an interview with Andy Mackay. This was way back in April 1981, when I proceeded, aged 18 and with considerable trepidation, to the plush address on Clapham Common North Side where Mackay then lived.

The trepidation turned out to be unnecessary, of course. Sitting in front of the colossal Eric Scott canvas that had done duty as the cover of his second solo LP, Mackay proved a model interviewee, happily giving me some three hours of his time when I had expected maybe 30 minutes. He spoke on a wide range of topics, from his earliest musical experiences to the composition of classic songs like *Love is the Drug*, from his satisfaction with the band's most recent album to his amazement at the Number One success of their latest single, together with an erudite aside regarding his disillusionment with the music press. He was an exemplar of the kind of poise and style that has always clung to Roxy Music in general, a band who from the outset had "determined to make it in as civilised a way as possible."

A wintery conversation, eight years on, with the equally approachable Phil Manzanera only intensified my interest in this unique band. It was an interest that had formed back in the mid-1970s, when it was my elder brothers who owned those exotic and enticing albums with the glossily laminated covers and the even glossier temptresses sprawled in erotic reverie across the gatefolds. Then, Roxy seemed like the progenitors of an entirely new kind of music, and indeed they very soon proved to be exactly that. From Cockney Rebel to Cabaret Voltaire, from Spandau Ballet, Siouxsie and the Banshees and Suede right up to Scissor Sisters, their influence has extended down the years in any number of surprising directions. Radiohead, The Human League, Garbage, U2, Japan, Talking Heads, even Chic – and, in the 21st century, the aptly named Ladytron and the meteoric Franz Ferdinand... The list goes on.

The extraordinary diversity of the bands whom Roxy Music have influenced is an index, of course, to the diversity of the Roxy sound itself. On their emergence in 1972, the shocking newness of their music owed a lot to the bewildering old-ness of some of the sounds and styles embedded within it. Here was a band that was unafraid to acknowledge the rich legacy of rock's past, and before even that, the pre-rock era of musical theatre and torch-song histrionics – cannibalising all these elements into a kind of retro-futuristic Pop Art collage unlike anything rock fans had ever heard. Even stranger, the whole thing contained a heavy admixture of irony, a slippery and virtually unheard-of notion in the area of early 1970s rock'n'roll.

On top of this came what the band's prime mover, Bryan Ferry, called "a complete package." The sound was indivisibly linked to the look, with the then-antithetical worlds of high fashion and popular music yoked together just as cavalierly as the musical melange. The effect, dismissed by many in 1972 as merely camp, was actually epoch-making – even to someone encountering Roxy Music at second hand on LPs owned by his brothers.

And the diversity was maintained throughout. The widespread notion that Ferry sold the band's avant-garde credentials down the river in exchange for a more Top 40-friendly sound seems to me simplistic; in its own way, their concluding album, *Avalon*, was as starkly experimental and as enduringly influential as their first, ten years before. The band's earliest albums – particularly the first two, when the mercurial stylistic innovator and self-described "non-musician" Brian Eno was still on board – will always remain the most critically venerated. Indeed, in June 2004, when the *Observer* polled several musicians, including Phil Manzanera, on their Top Ten British LPs of all time, The Smiths frontman Morrissey put down Roxy's 1973 album *For Your Pleasure* and left it at that; in parentheses appeared the editorial explanation, "Morrissey claims he can only think of one truly great British album and that this is it." But the later work has potent claims to importance too, with both ends of the Roxy trajectory burning just as brightly, though in radically different ways.

The received wisdom that Eno was the true instigator of the band's revolutionary approach, and that Roxy's music became considerably less interesting after his shock departure, took its cue from a pithy soundbite ascribed to Eno himself in 1975: "If I listen to the first album now, I still find it a bold statement. But what happened is what happens to most bands: they become successful."

Elsewhere, however, he downplayed his own contribution: "With Roxy, any time anyone heard a sound that they couldn't identify they assumed it was me. I actually got credit for a lot of things I didn't do." Even so, by 1982 Ferry was issuing tight-lipped statements along the lines of "Some fans believe Eno was the inspiration for the Roxy sound. They are wrong."

In the final analysis, the Eno-Ferry debate is likely to remain in the category of imponderables. What's much less debatable is the dazzling virtuosity of Roxy's musicians, from Mackay and Manzanera on woodwind and guitar to the multi-instrumental talents of Eddie Jobson, who took over from Eno for three albums. Paul Thompson, meanwhile – routinely dubbed 'The Great' by fans – remains the "wonder drummer" prescribed in the *Melody Maker* ad he answered back in 1971. It's noticeable, too, how the diversity of Roxy's sound is reflected in the constituent members: in 2005, Eno is a highly prized lecturer and all-round oracle, Mackay a Bachelor of Divinity and author of a benchmark tome on electronic music, Manzanera one of the world's foremost producers of Latin American music. From these ingredients comes the bizarre hybrid that is Roxy Music.

More than the resignation of Eno, what *did* dull Roxy's edge to some degree – blurring the band's outline in the eyes of posterity until a startlingly powerful reunion tour in 2001 brought the real picture back into focus – was Ferry's simultaneous pursuit of a solo career, the fruits of which would never be as arresting as his Roxy work. In this, however, he was hoist by his own petard, for it's his solo work – initially taking an ill-advised route down the MOR trail and then becoming creatively blocked by the labyrinthine possibilities of studio technology – that has fostered the lurking suspicion that Ferry failed to achieve his potential.

This is a familiar complaint, analogous, for instance, to the sighs of condescension directed at Richard Burton, who apparently could have been a great Shakespearean actor but threw in his lot with Elizabeth Taylor and the top-dollar blandishments of Hollywood. For his part, Ferry could have voyaged further into art-rock bizarrerie but was sidetracked instead by Jerry Hall and a fatal inclination to wear white tuxedos.

The man who could have propelled him further in an experimental direction, of course, was Eno, who in 2005 came up with a typically thoughtful response when faced head-on with the 'did Ferry fail to realise his potential' question. "No, but then neither did I," he answered. "This is a sad story, really, and I was talking about it with a chap I met on my run this morning. He told me about a friend who was a terrible alcoholic, came out of rehab, founded a make-up company and now he's a multi-millionaire. It's funny how people who have one tiny idea do a lot better than those of us who have plenty."

* * *

Both Ends Burning: The Complete Roxy Music aims to provide an insight into the band's remarkable body of work through a detailed account of their development and shifting dynamics, as well as scrutinising the back catalogue on a song-by-song basis. If Roxy's eight studio albums are the trunk, then the various solo LPs produced by Ferry, Mackay and Manzanera are surely essential branches of the Roxy tree. So they, too, have been considered in detail. Eno's solo career has also been evaluated, though only up to the point where he abandoned writing songs and therefore ceased to be in roughly the same ballpark as Roxy themselves.

In addition, 'side projects' like Mackay's *Rock Follies* score and Manzanera's 801 enterprise have been accorded their rightful place in the overall scheme. These satellite ventures are significant for the way in which the sheer variety of the band's extracurricular pursuits served to enrich the Roxy sound. In a *Rolling Stone* tribute written in 2005, John Taylor of Duran Duran emphasised the importance of every key Roxy contributor in vivid terms: "There were tremendous musical personalities in the band: Phil Manzanera, Andy Mackay, Paul Thompson. You could get your teeth into everybody; this is a band whose solo albums were worth getting. They all had quite interesting voices. And they were a band that you could argue about; Paul Thompson had a tremendous fan club, and he's the least-known of all of them."

Given Ferry's enduring fondness for recording cover versions of other people's songs, it's interesting to note that Roxy themselves have been subject to relatively few high-profile covers. What covers there have been are noted in the relevant song entries, though the contents of three multi-artist 'tribute' albums – *More For Your Pleasure*, *Roxy Re-modeled* and *Dream Home Heartaches*, the latter co-ordinated by John Taylor himself – have been excluded. For the record, these albums contain versions of the following songs not covered elsewhere: *Pyjamarama*, *Do the Strand*, *Beauty Queen*, *Street Life*, *Casanova*, *Just Another High* (performed by Taylor), *Angel Eyes*, *Same Old Scene* and *Rain Rain Rain*.

As for the song entries themselves, I have opted to rely on subjective responses rather than musicological analysis, the former being where Roxy's highly evocative soundscapes really 'get' to the listener. From beginning to end, the band's oeuvre is certainly capable of the latter kind of treatment; a book could easily be written that discusses the contrast of the opening of *Ladytron*, with its minor chord progressions, and the literally 'major' mood-shift initiated by the vocal. Or the suspended chords with which the synthesiser propels *Both Ends Burning*, or the drum kit's 'dotted' rhythm that becomes regularised in the choruses of *Ain't That So*. Or, for that matter, the way in which *Avalon's* suspended chordal notes are resolved on the word 'Avalon' itself.

But this book isn't that book, the author concurring with Eno in his assertion that "I know many theories about music, but I don't know the particular one that has to do with notation." For that approach, the reader is referred to Allan F Moore's brilliant anatomisation of early Roxy in *Rock: The Primary Text*, or Eric Tamm's equally erudite analysis of Eno's Progressive Rock in *Brian Eno: His Music and the Vertical Color of Sound*. In addition to Moore and Tamm, much else has been written about Roxy Music since their meteoric arrival in 1972. Latterday retrospectives like Rob Chapman's excellent *Mojo* piece 'They Came from Planet Bacofoil', together with the original blow-by-blow music press reports from Nick Kent, Ian MacDonald, Allan Jones, Richard Williams and others, have done much to fill in the numerous gaps in the band's long and complicated history. Similarly, no writer on Roxy can afford to ignore the pioneering efforts of Johnny Rogan, whose 1982 book *Style with Substance* laid the story out in admirably straightforward fashion.

A fuller list of sources is provided on page 294, but in the meantime I'd like to extend my gratitude to the following: Jason Atomic, Josephine Botting, Kate Brown, Jonathan Fisher, Renée Glynne, Peri Godbold, Michaela Greene, Marcus Hearn, Ruta Mia, Ian O'Sullivan, Richard Reynolds, Simon Sheridan, Paul Taylor and Pete Walker. Thanks, too, to Philip Spedding, who recklessly accompanied me on that original Mackay expedition in the role of cameraman, and to Rachael Hewer, without whom this book would have been finished in half the time.

Jonathan Rigby
London
August 2005

PART ONE

Roxy Rising

One: *Chance Meeting*

"We've got a lot of confidence in what we're doing and we're determined to make it but in as civilised a way as possible. The average age of this band is about 27, and we're not interested in scuffling. If someone will invest some time and money in us, we'll be very good indeed."

Bryan Ferry, quoted in Melody Maker 7 August 1971

Well, how are you? How have you been?

One day at the tail end of 1970, two men in their early twenties bumped into one another on the London Underground. They hadn't seen each other for a couple of years, but both were into avant-garde music and as students had organised musical events at their respective colleges.

In 1967, Andy Mackay had been part of Sunshine, a 'performance art' group from Reading University that had been invited to perform at Winchester School of Art, where Brian Eno was president of the Students' Union. In a reciprocal gesture, Eno had then made a guest appearance at one of the events organised by Mackay at Reading. The pair had even speculated, half-jokingly, on getting together a group called Brian Iron and the Crowbars.

Reunited with Eno on the Northern Line, Mackay had recently returned from a year spent in Florence, having become tired of interleaving his continued experimentation at London Arts Lab with tedious stints as a librarian and an English teacher. Eno, meanwhile, had moved to London from his native Suffolk in 1969, living in an arts commune and rapidly quitting a job as paste-up assistant on a local newspaper, instead beginning a sideline in refurbishing clapped-out stereo equipment for a coterie of like-minded friends.

Both men were adherents of John Cage, the US composer-philosopher who in the late 1930s had devised the so-called 'prepared piano' as a nascent version of the synthesiser. Both men, too, had used their time in higher education to gain an eclectic range of musical experiences. The classically trained Mackay had not only played oboe in the university orchestra but had also been saxophonist in an R'n'B combo called The Nova Express, while Eno had alternated his role in the avant-garde outfit Merchant Taylor's Simultaneous Cabinet with a position as lead vocalist in an improvisatory rock group called Maxwell Demon. By 1970, both men were tending to the view that rock music was where it was really 'at', agreeing on this point as they chatted in the tube train.

Mackay would later describe Cage as "a leading proponent of musical chance and indeterminacy," and on this cue Eno would build a whole philosophy devoted to chance events in recording and composition, even devising a set of epigrammatic playing cards to encourage lateral thinking in the studio. He was well aware, therefore, of the irony involved in his chance reunion with Mackay: "I was getting on a train on the Northern Line and there was a choice between one carriage and the next. I got in and bumped into Andy Mackay. If I'd got into the other one, I probably would have had a completely different life."

Rock music, too, would have taken a quite different course, for within a few months both men would be founder members of arguably the most innovative and influential band of the 1970s.

Kindred spirits

Hailing from Lostwithiel in Cornwall, Andy Mackay was some two years his friend's senior. Born on 23 July 1946, his time in the west of England was brief, the family moving to London in 1947. Four years later he was enrolled at St James the Less Primary School in Pimlico, and by 1960 he was a pupil at Westminster City School in Victoria. His father was an accomplished amateur pianist, and by the age of 12 Mackay had taken up the oboe ("only because the school band had enough clarinets"), studying under James McGillivray via a weekly scholarship to the Guildhall School of Music. He was soon proficient enough to take his place in the London Schools' Symphony Orchestra, as well as earning the distinction of being head chorister at St Margaret's Westminster.

Studying both music and English literature at Reading from 1965, Mackay temporarily set aside his classical leanings, coming under the sway of John Cage and his close associate Morton Feldman and indulging in what he would later call "very pretentious 'happenings'." "Attacking musical tradition seemed to appeal to me in those days," he recalled in 1981, "and at Reading University I was looked upon as a pretty suspect character, especially since I was in a rock band too." This was The Nova Express, its name derived from the William S Burroughs novel *The Naked Lunch*. Mackay's parallel enthusiasm for rock'n'roll had been fostered by close attention to Radio Luxemburg, but the band's Home Counties gigs were to become the scene of an ongoing battle between the jazz-influenced members and the out-and-out rockers, among whom Mackay counted himself.

In a bid "to revamp my musico-cultural orientation," Mackay migrated briefly to Italy in 1969. "I knew I had to be a musician, and I wanted to be a rock musician," he observed three years later. "I suppose I could've been a classical oboeist, but it didn't seem free enough. And I couldn't have supported myself by playing electronic music; also the audience is very limited. The only way I could be a musician was in rock – but with people who had a lot of ideas."

For the purposes of his riffing role in The Nova Express, Mackay had taken up the saxophone aged 18, acquiring his first alto by 'swopping' it for his beloved boyhood telescope. It turned out to be a worthwhile exchange; indeed, Mackay would later describe the transaction as his "defining moment." Self-taught, by 1981 Mackay modestly acknowledged his role in popularising the saxophone by saying that "The best thing about the sax revival is that they're used without reference to jazz." Reminiscent of the battle lines drawn up long ago in The Nova Express, this was nevertheless a surprising observation given the uniquely jazzy three-note riffs that would become his trademark on Top Ten hits like *Love is the Drug*, *Angel Eyes* and *Over You*.

Jazz was conspicuously absent, in any case, from the influences Mackay listed in a *Melody Maker* profile in 1972. These ranged from Beethoven, Chopin and Wagner to Smokey Robinson and King Curtis. His favourite single was *You Can't Hurry Love* by The Supremes, his most influential LP John Lennon's recently released *Imagine* (which featured the raunchy sax sounds of King Curtis), and his favourite singer Elvis Presley.

Mackay's po-faced avant-garde 'happenings' at Reading had been another matter altogether. "We would sit in silence for a long time," he remembered. "Someone would climb up a step ladder, then someone would make some funny electronic noises with a tape recorder. That sort of thing." His Reading associate Simon Puxley, a D.Phil who would later play a vital backstage role in the band for which Mackay was destined, was a party to these gnomic performance art pieces, also witnessing Eno's reciprocal performance. In conversation with Rob Chapman, he remembered that this "involved a tape recorder with a giant loop [and] tape wrapped round chair legs going round a huge hall. It kept breaking down."

Eno – full name Brian Peter George St John le Baptiste de la Salle Eno – came from East Anglia rather than the west of England. Born in Woodbridge on 15 May 1948, he was the son of a postman and was educated at a Catholic convent, providing the inspiration for future Prog Rock peculiarities like *Put a Straw Under Baby*. Further inspiration came from the proximity to Woodbridge of two US air bases and some 15,000 GIs, ensuring that he was exposed to a then-unusual pot-pourri of what he called "feeble, weedy English pop music and the American stuff, full of what I still find to be menace and strangeness." Doo-wop, in particular, he responded to as "Martian music": "It could have been from another galaxy for all I knew. I was absolutely entranced by it, from the age of seven or eight, when I first heard those early songs like [The Silhouettes'] *Get a Job*."

Initially intent on becoming a painter, the young Eno was discouraged by a spell at Ipswich School of Art, where he enrolled aged 16. The school's prime mover, Roy Ascot, proved an inspiration, however, particularly in his approach to behavioural psychology. The naturally extrovert Eno accordingly found himself cast as a follower rather than a leader, creating in him "a lasting interest in working with other people under what might normally be considered quite artificial restrictions."

Moving to Winchester, Eno was further inspired by personal contact with composer Cornelius Cardew (an influence, too, on Mackay), together with a reading of Cage's seminal 1961 tome *Silence*, stumbled upon, naturally, by chance. He also accumulated over 30 tape recorders, whose multi-tracking capabilities convinced him that traditional musical training was unnecessary. From all this sprang his 1968 pamphlet *Music for Non-Musicians* (privately published and amounting to no fewer than 25 copies), by which time his imagination had been further fired by The Who's *My Generation* and the example of The Velvet Underground, whose third album he nominated as "my favourite album ever," explaining that "it was a turning point in my appreciation of all kinds of music."

And here Eno expounded a vital tenet of his rapidly coalescing philosophy. "The thing that The Velvet Underground took from their whole experience with

[Andy] Warhol and The Factory," he told Ian MacDonald in 1973, "was that you didn't have to force things to happen – and you didn't have to think of music in terms of progressing ... Which is what Steve Reich and LaMonte Young and Terry Riley are completely hip to, and which is a cornerstone of their music: the fact of repeating something changes it."

In the same *Melody Maker* profile that laid bare Mackay's formative influences, Eno nominated Lou Reed as his favourite singer, Captain Beefheart as his favourite songwriter and, tellingly, in the 'favourite musician' category he inserted a producer, Phil Spector. His compositions to date were all fitted with titles that were to characterise his later preoccupations, from *Water Music* and *Delay and Decay* to the punningly titled *Sinister Dexter*. He also joined Cardew's coalition of untrained musicians, Scratch Orchestra, and the deliberately inept Portsmouth Sinfonia.

The fateful reunion of these two kindred spirits came, as it turned out, at an opportune time. Soon after re-encountering Eno on the Northern Line, Mackay became aware of advertisements in the 'Musicians Wanted' section of *Melody Maker* appealing for a keyboard player. Through artist Tim Head he was put in touch with the man who had been placing the advertisements, who was a graduate, like Head, of Newcastle University. "By then I had sold my sax to one of those seedy junk shops with bicycle wheels and old prams in the window," Mackay remembered, though this signal handicap, together with the fact that his keyboard skills were not especially noteworthy, didn't prevent him from fixing up to meet the mystery advertiser. His name was Bryan Ferry.

Just interested in the style

Born in Washington, County Durham on 26 September 1945, Ferry had begun taking piano lessons aged five, abandoning them in a fit of petulance when he realised his elder sister was more proficient. An aunt exposed him at an early age to the glamorous sound of artists like Nat 'King' Cole and The Inkspots (whose lead vocalist, he would claim in 1972, "has a vocal artistry comparable to Smokey Robinson's"), and later his first personally purchased EP would be by Charlie Parker. His first encounter with a bona-fide pop star came aged ten, when he ran through the streets to petition visiting US crooner Johnnie Ray (the so-called 'Prince of Wails') for his autograph.

"My working class roots are very strong and very much part of me and certainly nothing I've been ashamed of," he would later tell *Rolling Stone*'s Sylvie Simmons, "but I try not to wave them around too much because they can be very boring." Even as a boy, Ferry felt like an outsider looking in, somehow removed from the 'tin bath and outside loo' environment in which he was brought up – "an orchid born on a coal-tip," as he eloquently put it. His father Fred had moved on from being a farm worker to tending the ponies at the Glebe pit-head, and was venerated by his only son as "a throwback" and "a countryman at heart." "He wouldn't allow the men to swear in front of the horses," he remembered fondly in the glossy colour supplement pages of the *Sunday Telegraph* in 1982.

Ferry was educated at the Glebe School and then, from 1957, at Washington Grammar School. He was already fascinated by the Hollywood glamour on offer at Washington's two picture houses, the Ritz and the Regal, and was more enamoured of jazz than the burgeoning sounds of rock'n'roll, having been studiedly unimpressed on winning a competition organised by Radio Luxemburg. "The prize," he said, "was tickets for a Bill Haley concert. It was the first rock'n'roll tour in Britain. I looked down on it really. I was a musical snob." By the age of 15 he had affected a floppy-haired Bohemian look, Keats and Shelley uppermost in his mind, and was also making a conscious effort to lose his accent. Years later, he would tell fellow north-easterner Paul Thompson that this was because "You can't really read Shakespeare with a Geordie accent."

Cadences suitably adjusted, at Christmas 1963 Ferry appeared in a school production of *Twelfth Night* in the plum role of Malvolio, a pompous steward with romantic aspirations above his station, a performance that garnered him a write-up, and photograph, in the *Sunderland Echo*. It was a visit to the Theatre Royal Newcastle to see Puccini's *La Bohème*, however, that decided him on his next move. "Don't go down the pit, lad" has often been cited by Ferry as the best advice he ever received, and, indeed, his parents had high hopes of him joining the police force. They were understanding, however, when he elected instead to study Fine Art at Newcastle University.

A visiting tutor during Ferry's first year was Richard Hamilton, who in the early 1950s had been part of the so-called Independent Group at London's ICA, whose collective fascination for post-war consumer culture would lead one member, Lawrence Alloway, to coin the phrase Pop Art. Though Ferry quickly abandoned any serious aspirations to becoming a painter, he found Hamilton's example inspirational. As a key figure in the 'This is Tomorrow' exhibition of 1956, Hamilton had contributed the epoch-making 'What Is It About Today's Homes that Makes Them So Different, So Appealing?', which yoked together Hoovers, TVs, tape recorders, a well-muscled body-builder and a spangled stripper against an Outer Space backdrop.

Hamilton's enthusiasm for collage, the playful juxtaposition of apparently antithetical elements, all forms of Americana, and above all his blurring of the traditional divisions between 'high' and 'low' art – all these were to prove a seminal influence when Ferry set about applying the tenets of Pop Art to pop music in the early 1970s.

By the time he got to Newcastle, Ferry's interest in music had progressed well beyond his early exposure to the *Melody Maker* while on his paper-round. His former passion for cycling had thrown up the opportunity to front his first band, a cycling companion from way back having suddenly reappeared to invite him to join The Banshees, an amateur group working the club circuit. Once at university, he got together an eight-piece covers band (half the personnel given over to an impressive brass section) called The Gas Board, among whom were future collaborators Graham Simpson and John Porter, plus film-director-in-waiting Mike Figgis. Operative for two years, the band were a notable feature of a local scene centred on Newcastle's Club A-Go-Go and the chart success of local heroes The Animals.

In thrall to the gritty and heartfelt sounds of R'n'B – and blown away by a glimpse of Booker T and the MGs and other Memphis stars in the Stax package tour of 1967 – Ferry was now convinced that stage presentation was a key to success. "The music was good and we looked good," he told Jim Crace. "We wore American sweatshirts and white jeans. But when the rest of the band went professional, I ducked out. I couldn't have taken the guilt of not finishing my studies and not having a 'proper' job."

In the meantime, he had invested £60 in a second-hand Studebaker Champion, which would later receive a name-check in *Virginia Plain*. According to Ferry, "It had a beautiful shark-like quality and looked very good with my mohair suit, I thought. In those days looks were everything as far as cars were concerned. I never bought a car for its performance or anything; I was just interested in the style." A photo of man and machine taken by his college friend Nick de Ville would be used to illustrate a small exhibition of Ferry's work staged at Durham University in 1967. Sharp-suited and impeccably groomed, his clothes coming direct from Mod tailoring guru Marcus Pryce, it was clear that Ferry already had no truck with the encroaching fug of hippiedom or the brain-curdling experimentation of psychedelia.

It was a defiantly unfashionable figure, then, who collected his degree in the summer of 1968 and made his way down to London.

Dropped thirds and King Crimson

"1969 was a dull time," Ferry would later claim, "and I saw the gap in music." He was at first not in a very propitious position to fill it, being conspicuously free of music biz contacts other than his old Gas Board chum Graham Simpson, two years his senior and a competent violinist as well as bass guitarist. Having dropped out of university to play in a band called Cock-a-Hoop, Simpson had since fetched up in London and became a willing collaborator in Ferry's as yet rather sketchy plans. As well as taking odd jobs as a van driver and antiques restorer, Ferry added to his one-off childhood piano lesson a further ten, also shelling out £5 for a second-hand harmonium.

With Simpson's encouragement and advice, he began writing songs, inadvertently giving them a peculiar off-kilter quality by his elimination of the third chord in any given sequence, a habit his future collaborator Simon Puxley would call "Bryan's dropped thirds." Ferry later explained that "the songs had a very simple structure to them, and yet they had lots of changes of mood, which I like to do. The lyrics were strange, too ... I was using images, throwaway clichés and amusing phrases that you found in magazines or used in everyday speech – stylistic juxtapositions. But you have to do it properly – you can't just throw them together at random." Given the obviously Pop Art-derived nature of Ferry's writing process, it came as no surprise when he added: "I always thought of music as a visual thing."

In the meantime he had been engaged as a ceramics teacher at Hammersmith's Mary Boon Secondary School for Girls, often turning lessons into record-spinning sessions and finally getting the sack towards the end of 1970. Ferry's own ceramics – small but colourful affairs representing blancmanges and suchlike – were exhibited at the Piccadilly and Thomas Gibson galleries, indicating that he was still torn between apparently conflicting commitments to art and music. He had amassed quite a number of songs by this stage, but, isolated in his small Shepherd's Bush flat, seemed unsure how to proceed, daunted in particular by the notion of gathering together a band of like-minded individuals to express his ideas.

By the end of 1970, he was sufficiently discouraged to audition for another band altogether, namely the strife-torn King Crimson. Vocalist Greg Lake had moved on to Emerson Lake & Palmer, and his replacement Gordon Haskell had survived little more than six months. "What we really want is a bassist who sings," remarked Crimson's Robert Fripp in the 19 December edition of *Melody Maker*, "but we'd be happy with a bassist and a singer separately. They need to have very broad musical interests but the singer for instance might at this moment be a choirboy or even languishing in a hotel dance band."

Ferry was well aware that his inability to play bass might pose a problem, but he had been sufficiently impressed by the mystical soundscapes of Crimson's first album, *In the Court of the Crimson King*, to give it a whirl anyway. On the audition panel was Crimson's lyricist and sound effects man, Pete Sinfield, who would later play a decisive role in Roxy Music's career. Fripp noted later that among the other hopefuls was John Gaydon, the 'G' of Crimson's management company EG and formerly a vocalist with The Band of Angels. "Both were among the best although not suitable," he claimed. "I recommended Bryan to EG Management and some 18 months later they were handling Roxy Music. But this was a time of desperation and the auditions were quite awful."

By February Fripp had settled on Boz Burrell, circumventing the bass-vocals difficulty by teaching him bass personally. By that time, however, things were beginning to look up for Ferry, for this is where Andy Mackay and Brian Eno came in.

London 70-1

Mackay was by now a full-time music teacher at Holland Park Comprehensive School, and he turned up to his appointment without the hoped-for keyboard but with an oboe and a VCS3 synthesiser instead. For Mackay the latter contraption, popularly known as 'the Putney', turned out to be £350 well spent, for the prospect of a combined synth operator and Stax-style horn player was too good for Ferry to pass up. As a result, Mackay soon found himself collaborating with Ferry and Simpson in shaping the musical fragments built up so far. For Mackay, this seemed an ideal situation, based on his conviction that "the only way I could be a musician was in rock – but with people who had a lot of ideas."

"Andy brought in a more classical thing," Ferry told Rob Chapman. "He was a trained player. When I met him he didn't own a sax, but he had an oboe and a synthesiser." Ferry would later describe Mackay as "rather like an old school-teacher ... a bit fogeyish," a description at odds with Richard Williams' later assessment of him as being "almost over-endowed with cool." This dichotomy was presumably a reflection of the Jekyll and Hyde transformations undergone by all the group members when the time came to get up and perform. That was still some way off, however, so in the meantime Mackay and Ferry took it upon themselves to give the group a name, concocting to that end a long list of old-style cinemas, rejecting such monikers as Essoldo, Gaumont and Rialto and finishing up with the euphonious Roxy, which had the benefit of a pun on 'rock' similar to The Beatles' pun on 'beat'.

Mackay soon realised, however, that a separate operator for the VCS3, and all-round technical support person, would free him up considerably. It was at this point that he remembered his recent Northern Line meeting with Brian Eno. "I'll never forget the sight of Brian lugging in this enormous, German industrial tape recorder," Ferry told Michael Bracewell 25 years later. "You can imagine the scene: Andy and Brian making this extraordinary sound, and me pedalling away furiously on this old harmonium." The diminutive, almost gamine Eno, hair thinning already aged 22, was at this stage, like Mackay, a long way from the outrageous creature he would metamorphose into when Roxy started gigging. "He was more like a mad boffin," Ferry remembered. "With Eno, there were always wires everywhere and bits of old speakers all over the place. In terms of his appearance, he really blossomed once he was in Roxy."

Here already, in human form, was Richard Hamilton's playful Pop Art juxtaposition of apparently antithetical elements – Ferry with his grounding in slick and soulful R'n'B, Mackay with his avant-garde interests and classical training, Eno with his untrammeled zeal for sonic experimentation, Simpson keeping time meanwhile with his uniquely supple bass lines.

Even so, the band's lack of a guitarist and a drummer was a blind spot that could no longer be ignored. The first musicians to fill these gaps were Roger Bunn and Dexter Lloyd. Bunn had played with a group called Enjin and viewed his brief Roxy stint with no great enthusiasm, especially because Ferry had made it clear the person he was really after was David O'List. Unsurprisingly, by September Bunn would be gone, though he'd lasted several months longer than Lloyd, who departed in June. Ferry maintained that Lloyd, an American player late of the Cleveland Symphony Orchestra, "was the only drummer we tried who could play anything creative on the slow numbers." Even so, Lloyd's classically trained style simply didn't gell. It remains unclear, however, whether Eno's 1971 composition *Sinister Dexter* was a nod to Roxy's short-lived timpanist as well as a punning reference to 'left right'.

On the departure of Lloyd, the wording of Ferry's next emergency call in *Melody Maker* was "Wonder drummer required for avant-rock group." The successful applicant was fellow Geordie Paul Thompson, who had just turned 20 on his induction into the band. Born in Newcastle on 13 May 1951, Thompson was educated at West Simonside Secondary Modern in Jarrow and Hebburn Technical College, later becoming an apprentice at Palmer's Shipyard. Having been given the sack for moonlighting in a club band and for falling asleep on the job – which amounts to the same thing, given that one was a product of the other – he turned professional aged 17.

His first drum kit had been bought by his mother on hire purchase, the young Thompson putting it to good use with fledgling local bands like The Thyme and Johnny Blue and the Blue Boys. Having been tutored by a South Shields night-club drummer called Barry Black, Thompson rapidly totted up a formidable CV that included such outfits as The Influence, Yellow, The Urge, even a spell in Billy Fury's backing band. By this time, as Thompson put it, "I had become more influenced by 'underground' and 'progressive' music," adding, "that style didn't go down well at all in the clubs."

A short stint with Smokestack brought him south to London, where he answered both Ferry's ad and one placed by a group called Egypt. When Egypt didn't get back to him, he passed the Roxy audition with no difficulty, despite an initial hiccough when Thompson realised his drum kit was locked in a Denmark Street rehearsal room; happily, he was able to borrow an alternative kit from the friend he was staying with, who was a roadie for Matthews Southern Comfort. "Paul and I have a very good rapport," Ferry noted, "because he's a Geordie too, from Jarrow. He's very sensible and practical. When he joined us, he was working on a building site, getting up at seven o'clock in the morning and turning up for the gig in the evening still wearing his Wellington boots."

The earthy power of Thompson's percussion, providing a rock-solid base for the cerebral flights indulged in by the others, was a crucial addition to the burgeoning Roxy Music. His straight-ahead 4/4 rhythms earned him the sobriquet 'Blooter Blatter', but just because Thompson bucked the band trend by not having attended university or art school didn't mean that his musical influences weren't just as outré and eclectic as the others'. In a *Melody Maker* band profile, he would list Led Zeppelin, The Beatles and Frank Zappa alongside Beethoven, Dionne Warwick and the *Switched On Bach* Moog specialist, Walter (soon to be Wendy) Carlos.

"I'd always wanted to do something out of the ordinary," he claimed in 1972. "I can't stand the heavy bands that just play riffs – only Led Zeppelin are good enough to get away with it. I try to play melodically as well as rhythmically, and I try to create my own licks. For instance – when drummers go right round the kit, they almost always do it clockwise. It seems to be the natural way. So I sometimes try it anti-clockwise – and it sounds really interesting."

Here comes The Nice

By this time, Ferry had returned to part-time teaching and had moved in to Mackay's cramped Battersea residence. The new-to-London Thompson was staying, meanwhile, at Eno's place in Kilburn. Ferry had also begun the dispiriting process of hawking the band's demos (featuring the since-departed Dexter Lloyd and the soon-to-depart Roger Bunn) around various record companies, meeting with blank befuddlement wherever he went. One recipient, however, was *Melody Maker*'s Richard Williams, soon to compere the opening season of the seminal BBC show *The Old Grey Whistle Test* and already a highly influential voice. In his *Horizon* column of 7 August 1971 – subtitled 'New Names that could break the sound barrier: Roxy in the rock stakes' – he ensured that Roxy's first splash in print was an almost unqualified rave.

"Roxy," he wrote, "has produced one of the most exciting demo tapes ever to come my way. Although it was recorded on a small home tape machine in what sounds like a Dutch barn it carries enough innovatory excitement to suggest that Roxy may well be ahead of the field in the avant-rock stakes … The band's influences stretch from Ethel Merman to The Velvet Underground to jazz and they want to bring all these elements into the music, creating a very diverse approach.

The electronic thing is important to them, but they are also interested in the flash and style of rock – like wearing outrageous clothes and having some kind of act."

Williams would later tell Johnny Rogan that "It was quite a dull time and this was a very odd tape ... Parts of it had things overlaid on the tape so that you'd be hearing two things at the same time. And there was an oboe on there which was very unusual. Several of the tracks, like *The Bob (Medley)*, were vaguely recognisable on the first album. Some of it was pretty shitty in terms of playing and sound quality. It was a mess. It seemed like people mucking around ... But you could tell that this group, like the American Pop artists, weren't afraid to admire Coca-Cola bottles or American cars."

With Roger Bunn having departed by September, the business of hiring a new guitarist was to prove trickier than the earlier acquisition of a new drummer; indeed, Ferry's ad would read, "Wanted: Tricky Dick lead guitarist." Spencer Mallinson, a Kilburn restaurateur, was brought briefly into the fold by Eno but left when he decided the band had no future.

Meanwhile, the *Melody Maker* ad attracted an enthusiastic young applicant in the lofty and bearded form of Philip Targett-Adams, who was taller even than the lanky Ferry and Mackay. Not long out of Dulwich College, Targett-Adams had recently dissevered from a barely known Prog Rock combo called Quiet Sun and by now was thoroughly cheesed off with his nine-to-five job at Clarkson's travel agency. But before Phil Manzanera, as he was known, could be inducted into the group, Ferry had to get a nagging idée fixe out of his system. He was determined to find and hire an elusive guitarist whom he had seen play at Newcastle City Hall in 1968.

It was around this time that the man in question, David O'List, placed an ad of his own in *Melody Maker*, reading "Well-known guitarist seeking image-conscious progressive rock group with recording contract and agency." According to O'List, Ferry replied to it despite his lack of either a contract or an agency, and was thrilled to bits when he realised he was addressing the very man he'd been searching for for months. Thirty years later, O'List would point out on the vivaroxymusic website that "I had produced The Nice into recording stars from nothing and [felt that] perhaps I could produce and transform Roxy Music into a hit group, too."

The Nice – O'List, Keith Emerson, Brian Davison and Lee Jackson – had come into being in May 1967 after Immediate Records artist P P Arnold had scored with the Cat Stevens song *The First Cut is the Deepest*. They soon outgrew their role as Arnold's backing band, however, themselves signing with Andrew Loog Oldham's label and reaching number 21 in June 1968 with a grisly psychedelicised revamp of the *West Side Story* number *America*. This paved the way for Emerson's later keyboard excesses with Emerson Lake & Palmer, meaning that by summer 1971 O'List was at a loose end for the same reason that King Crimson had lent an ear to Ferry the previous December.

O'List was a uniquely innovative guitarist, however, having occasionally subbed for Syd Barrett in various Pink Floyd sessions. By his own (somewhat self-aggrandising) account, he consented to a meeting at the Mackay-Ferry HQ in Battersea and agreed to join the band, "amid," as he put it, "loud cheers from Bryan, Andy, Eno and Graham."

In a forecast of his bedazzlement by name session players in the latter part of the decade, Ferry reportedly agreed to all sorts of contractual minutiae, including a guarantee that O'List would write for and produce the band, as well as ensuring an outlet for O'List's solo work through whatever contract the well-connected guitarist managed to engineer for the band. O'List even foisted some of his own unrecorded songs on Ferry, among them *Green Willow Tree*, *White Indian Butterfly* and the modestly titled *O'List's Waltz*, whereupon rehearsals got under way in earnest at a photographic studio in Hampstead.

We are Rock'n'roll

Despite O'List's name value and the enthusiastic endorsement of Richard Williams, Ferry was still having no luck with the band's demo tapes, leading to the long-delayed decision to indulge in some discreet gigging. Beginning in November, the venues were carefully chosen to expose Roxy to a highly discerning, 'private functions only' sort of audience, Ferry having told Williams that "we're determined to make it but in as civilised a way as possible."

Here was a pronouncement that would soon raise hackles among the more fundamentalist members of the rock fraternity, but it was a view shared by all the founder members of the band and one based in part on their ages, which for a fledgling group were relatively advanced. "I realised that there were certain areas of music you could enter without actually learning an instrument," quipped Eno, "which at my age I certainly wasn't about to do." Mackay went further, noting that "Most people in rock music just leave school and go around the clubs playing with different bands until they make it. But when, like me, you're in your mid-twenties and have never played in a professional band before, the only way to get into being a rock musician is to form your own band."

And Ferry was more forthright still, stressing the fact that "the average age of this band is about 27" and that "we're all completely new to the scene. I think we're a different type of person to the normal group member in that we've been involved in completely different things over the past six years instead of spending it all gigging on the road."

By now the band's name had been adjusted to Roxy Music, a more imposing handle by far but motivated purely by the discovery that an obscure US band called Roxy had released an album on Elektra Records in 1970. According to O'List, the newly minted Roxy Music performed their first gig above an Olympia pub called The Hand & Flower. But Simon Puxley, a member of Mackay's performance art troupe at Reading and soon to become Roxy's Tricky Dick lead PR man, came up with a very different version in his 1976 book *The Bryan Ferry Story*.

"Christmas loomed and a top glamour photographer, who had earned a fortune in the previous ten glamorous years and bought a palatial penthouse to prove it, threw a party," wrote Puxley under his nom de plume of Rex Balfour. "Of course it needed some music, the real thing – and as it happened his cousin had a friend who had just joined a new group and being new had never played anywhere before and would do it for free … A handful of party guests who weren't overwhelmed by the hot punch and paperchains became curiously overawed by the motley crew of musicians – or rather by their spellbinding, atmospheric music, which somehow defied description … When one of the partygoers, driven to distraction by this unprecedented musical farrago, aggressively demanded that they 'play some rock'n'roll!', the singer just smiled and replied in cool, measured tones: 'We are *rock'n'roll*.'"

This, of course, is a tale told by a press agent, but nevertheless signifying something of the mystique that was building up around the half-heard name of Roxy Music. Ferry had by this time designed a gnomic promotional poster, showing a cartoon aeroplane whose vapour trail spelled out the legend 'Roxy Music' no fewer than 60 times. After their private party appearance (or Hand & Flower appearance, if you will), Roxy's next gigs came through contacts of Ferry and Mackay respectively – a gallery showcase as part of the 'Friends of the Tate Christmas Show' and a stint at Reading University's Christmas Student Union Ball.

Roxy's early gigging involved Mackay's acquisition of a beat-up Austin van from his father and the unusual procedure of Eno occupying a mixing desk in the middle of the audience, making it unclear whether he was a band member or a backroom technician. As well as transmuting the musicians' sounds through his Revox tape machines, Eno would also contribute backing vocals from his unusual vantage point, causing double-takes galore among the chicly accoutred onlookers, whom Richard Williams would later characterise as a presentiment of the New Romantics.

Like Williams, Puxley was present at a Roxy showcase at Oxford Street's 100 Club: "I was totally amazed. It was like what you had occasionally imagined might be possible – what you had always wanted to hear from rock'n'roll. It was a new sound, and it had to work."

Accompanying Eno at the mixing desk for Roxy's Christmas shows was Phil Manzanera, who had returned to his day job at Clarkson's travel agency after being passed over in favour of David O'List. He had not lost sight of Roxy in the meantime, however, having frequently bumped into them socially, notably at a Steve Reich concert at the Royal Festival Hall. Shortly before the Tate Gallery show, Roxy had lost their sound engineer and Manzanera had responded enthusiastically to Ferry's summons, joining the band's rehearsals at a dilapidated property in Notting Hill and addressing himself to a task he had no prior knowledge of, namely mixing the band's sound.

Our man in Havana

If Roxy had been a bizarre hybrid before, it would become yet more so with the dash of exotica brought it by Manzanera. Born Philip Targett-Adams in London on 31 January 1951, he had spent much of his early life in Cuba; his father was BOAC's very own 'our man in Havana', and as a result the young Manzanera would witness the Castro uprising at first hand.

"We were always on the move – Cuba, Hawaii, Venezuela – and this itinerant lifestyle not only taught me to cope but gave me an early insight into how different people live," he told the *Times* in 2004. "My father was very English, my mother Colombian and that duality has informed my whole life. I took my mother's name because it seemed a little more appropriate for a band member than Targett-Adams. I hate any dictator, of course. But I grew up in the midst of the Cuban Revolution, I experienced the shooting, the murders under Batista. I formed my left-of-centre political views from these experiences." Indeed, one of his later songs, *Rayo de bala*, would dramatise "the night during the Cuban revolution when our house and garden were used by the 'barbudos' (the bearded ones) to attack the dictator Batista's Chief of Staff's house."

Against this bloody backdrop, Manzanera was soon in thrall to British and American pop music. Aged six, he had been shown the rudiments of acoustic guitar by his mother, who taught him numerous Cuban and Colombian folk songs, and soon afterwards – the family having since moved to Caracas – he graduated to picking out Chuck Berry numbers on its electric equivalent.

Manzanera's father died when he was 15, by which time he was back in the UK and a pupil at Dulwich College in south east London. There, his musical experiences moved from a group reportedly known as Wing Commander Nixon and His Wheat-Eating Bees to a psychedelic combo called Pooh and the Ostrich Feather, formed with his school friends Bill MacCormick and Charles Hayward. Starting early in 1968, Pooh's repertoire consisted in the main of Cream and Jefferson Airplane covers, though there was a powerful influence much closer to home in the form of Soft Machine. Robert Wyatt was a close friend of MacCormick and his elder brother Ian (who, having changed his name to MacDonald, would eventually become assistant editor of *New Musical Express*), and the Wyatt-MacCormick axis would remain a pivotal one throughout Manzanera's career.

With Dave Jarrett attached, Manzanera, MacCormick and Hayward would form a new band called Quiet Sun, a somewhat po-faced assemblage of the Prog persuasion given, as Manzanera put it, to "playing insane 17/8 things at ridiculous speeds all the time." Despite interest from Warner Bros and some sporadic gigs, chiefly on the continent, Quiet Sun had folded by the time Manzanera came into Roxy's orbit, in part because MacCormick had joined Dave Sinclair and Phil Miller in Robert Wyatt's post-Soft Machine project, Matching Mole. Soft Machine figured, nonetheless, in the list of influences Manzanera would prepare for *Melody Maker* in 1972; others included Elvis Presley, Pink Floyd, The Beatles, Otis Redding, Spirit, The Velvet Underground and avant-garde composer Terry Riley. His favourite single at the time was The Beach Boys' *Good Vibrations*.

Confined for the time being to the humble role of part-time roadie, Manzanera found himself having to lug O'List's gear around; where the other band members gamely struggled with their own equipment, the former star player with The Nice was not one for mucking in. For the others, as Eno put it, "It was a case of just getting on with it – and we all did what we were best at: me doing all the soldering, Andy driving the van, etc."

According to O'List, Roxy played several further dates at this time, including stints at Bristol University, two London colleges and in a support slot to The Pretty Things. The next confirmed sighting of them, however, was at the BBC's T1 studio in Kensington House, Shepherd's Bush. A demo tape had reached Radio 1 producer John Walters, who among other things was intrigued by what he called Ferry's "Larry the Lamb" vocal technique. Accordingly, on Tuesday

4 January 1972 the band ran through five of the songs they were working on – *Re-make/Re-model, If There is Something, The Bob (Medley), Would You Believe?* and *Sea Breezes* – for BBC producer John Muir, the session going out on Friday the 21st in the 'Top Gear' section of John Peel's influential programme *Sounds of the Seventies*. By coincidence, the next 'Top Gear' showcase, the following Tuesday, featured another 'world premiere', that of Matching Mole.

In his 'This Week's Sounds' column, Richard Williams took the opportunity to introduce Roxy to the readers of *Radio Times*, rephrasing his first *Melody Maker* article in describing them as "a new band whose influences range from Ethel Merman to The Velvet Underground. You'll be hearing a lot more of them." Though *Sea Breezes* would be kept back for broadcast on 18 February, it was clear from Roxy's first 'Top Gear' stint that Williams' enthusiasm wasn't misplaced, with Ferry supplementing his worse-for-wear Hohner Pianet with one of the BBC's grand pianos and O'List contributing intriguing solos, albeit in strangely compartmentalised sections.

O'List's increasing distance from the band, his role devolving into that of specially showcased guitar god, was allegedly exacerbated by a drug problem. According to producer John Muir, "When the band came into the control room to listen back to the mix, I asked 'Where's Dave?' 'In the studio,' they said, and there he was, lying flat on his back." The BBC session would contain further disquieting indicators of future turbulence, with the sensitive Simpson, apparently overwhelmed by the sudden acceleration of the band's progress, crying his eyes out even while playing.

Bingo

With the patronage of Richard Williams and John Peel, it remained only for Roxy to finally get a management deal and a recording contract. And it was here that the problem with the once-so-prized David O'List came to a head. O'List was already fearful that Manzanera's mysterious arrival at the mixing desk was part of an Eno-engineered plot to oust him from the band, and a fortnight's illness had made him miss out on several rehearsals. Now, at an all-important audition for EG Management on the afternoon of Tuesday 1 February, an embarrassing alter-cation would break out between O'List and the hapless Thompson, an altercation that degenerated, according to some accounts, into a fist fight.

EG were a pair of trendy Old Harrovian bikers called David Enthoven and John Gaydon, under whose wing Emerson Lake & Palmer, T.Rex and King Crimson had all become thriving concerns. The team was bolstered by Mark Fenwick and Sam Alder, though it was Enthoven whose ears pricked up on hearing Roxy's demo tape; he would later liken it to the epiphany he experienced on first encountering King Crimson. Their initial interest reportedly centred on Ferry alone, but he held his ground on the principle, as he would put it later, that "I deliver a complete package."

It was therefore the entire band that turned up to the EG audition, which took place, appropriately enough, at a disused cinema, the Granada, on the Wandsworth Road in south London. Though O'List has since described the whole event as a formality, Richard Williams, who was present, felt there was a lot more riding on it than that. "They've done about 20 gigs so far," he reported in *Melody Maker*, "and only one of them has been anywhere near satisfactory." It went well, however, with Roxy's set making the hoped-for impact well before the arrival of Wandsworth's resident Bingo-fanciers. According to Williams, Roxy sounded "like the product of some weird meeting between The Marcels and one of the heavier German bands." Having championed King Crimson at an early stage, Enthoven was strongly attracted towards music of a spikey and uncompromising kind, so on Friday the 4th he made his move and signed the band up.

Come Monday the 14th, however, Manzanera, too, would be signing on the dotted line, O'List having finally been shown the door. Latterly, O'List has made large claims regarding his short-lived involvement with the band, telling John O'Brien of the vivaroxymusic website that "I completely rearranged the songs, rewrote parts of them and added new melodic sections to make the songs sound more fashionable. I added new beginnings, new middles, new endings and generally beefed up the sound as Bryan wanted me to. You can hear the evidence of all my work on Roxy Music's first album."

After a period in the doldrums, he would resurface in 1974 via a lacerating guitar break on Ferry's solo version of *The 'In' Crowd*, soon afterwards forming the short-lived Jet with vocalist Andy Ellison, a band that, if nothing else, confirmed the lingering impact on O'List of his brief flirtation with Roxy Music. "If Jet's first single, an O'List composition called *My River*, is anything to go by," commented David Fudger in *Disc*, "they have taken hold of the essence of *Virginia Plain* and added a dynamism sadly lacking in R Music's current output." Added Fudger with rather less conviction: "Jet will be the group you can't ignore, the promise of Roxy dreams fulfilled."

Manzanera's Valentine's Day gift of an EG contract meant that his patience had been amply rewarded; having given up a university place in order to devote himself to the ill-fated Quiet Sun, he was now convinced that Roxy "were going to be really big." A regular visitor in his role as sound engineer, Manzanera had been asked to do "yet another audition, which turned out to be the longest I've ever played. Lasted about three days. And then they said yes and I joined at exactly the right time, because all the hassling about contracts had been done by then and I didn't have to go through the Quiet Sun thing again." Manzanera would avoid the Quiet Sun thing in terms of repertoire as well as red tape: "Also, after playing very complicated time signatures, being with Roxy was like running through a Carole King number. Two chords? Great! Now I can relax!"

Having signed the band, and seemingly careless of continued resistance from the major record labels, EG acted quickly. With Manzanera on board – and Eno by now occupying an eye-catching position on stage – Roxy played a few further gigs, including a return visit to The Hand & Flower on Friday the 18th, Leicester University the next night and another college date, at Bristol, on Friday 3 March. Only now did Thompson abandon his day job on a Fulham building site; "goodbye cement dust, hello the road to stardom," as he later put it. Pupils at Holland Park Comprehensive, meanwhile, came back from half-term to find their young music teacher had gone for good. Instead, Mackay had joined Ferry, Simpson, Eno, Thompson and Manzanera at Piccadilly's Command Studios to record the band's first album.

Two: *The Roxy Music Album*

"This is so far and away the best, most original, most incredible album of the year that it makes the mind boggle … This album is so great I wanna turn the whole bloody world on to it. LISTEN, BROTHERS. THIS IS IT. THIS IS WHAT YOU'VE BEEN MOANING FOR SINCE 69 AND IT'S HERE NOW SO DON'T BLOW IT!!!"
Alan Niester, *Phonograph Record* December 1972

The *Roxy Music* album was recorded over ten days in March 1972 at a cost of £5000. Ferry has since grumbled that, let loose in a studio for the first time, the band adopted a scattershot approach to the fund of competing ideas they had accumulated over the previous 12 months, on the principle that they'd better express all the ideas right away just in case they never got the chance again. At the time, however, this eclectic approach was a source of pride. "The album is really kind of a tracer as to where we could go," Ferry claimed. "There are lots of different directions there, and deliberately so, because we never really did want to have one recognisable sound. Being elusive is one of the things we quite like, and being as varied as possible."

King Crimson's Robert Fripp had been tipped to produce the album, but the same band's Pete Sinfield got the job instead, with Andy Hendriksen on hand as engineer. The same year, Eno would add his VCS3 to the track *Gloria Gloom* on Matching Mole's *Little Red Record* LP with Fripp as producer, thus inaugurating a fruitful collaboration manifested later in records like *(No Pussyfooting)* and *Evening Star*. For the time being, however, Roxy's first album was recorded at Command Studios, a former BBC facility, in three blocks, running from Tuesday the 14th to Friday the 17th, Wednesday the 22nd to Friday the 24th, and Monday the 27th to Wednesday the 29th. *Would You Believe?*, *Ladytron*, *Chance Meeting* and *If There is Something* occupied the first phase, *The Bob (Medley)*, *Sea Breezes* and *2 H.B.* the second, and *Re-make/Re-model* and *Bitters End* the third.

The 28-year-old Sinfield had recently returned from a November/December stint in the USA, the New Year's Day edition of *Disc* explaining that "King Crimson's compulsive poet and one-man environment almost wishes he hadn't joined the group on the recent six-week US tour. 'It's not that we actually failed anywhere,' he says. 'We went down reasonably to very well but … I think I'd be happy to stay at home and write poetry.' The problems were manifold … and the resulting pressure on the group created much 'internal turmoil'. Sinfield returned a wreck." The same day's *NME* went further, reporting that "Pete Sinfield has left King Crimson. Pete played VCS3 and was responsible for the group's lyrics, lighting and sound. The band will continue as a four-piece but Sinfield's future plans are not yet known."

Sinfield, then, was at a loose end; he was certainly determined not to accompany Crimson on their next US jaunt, which stretched from the second week of February to April Fool's Day. This was the commitment that prevented Fripp from handling the Roxy debut, hence Sinfield's smartly stepping into the breach. "After leaving King Crimson I spent three months in the doldrums wondering what I was going to do with my life, and finding confidence," Sinfield told Chris Welch in May 1973. "I got involved with Roxy Music, who had come to EG Management with a dreadful tape. But I thought they had atmosphere and produced their first album. Bryan Ferry, I remember, wanted to be Noël Coward … They were not the world's best musicians, and I wouldn't let them sound like The Velvet Underground."

Sinfield may have curbed Roxy's Velvet Underground tendencies, but in the opinion of several early commentators he made them sound instead like a band much closer to home, with the album's extensive use of Mellotron tapes incurring unwelcome comparisons to the mighty, and mightily erratic, Crimson. "We'd never been in the studios before," Ferry had innocently pointed out, "and you can save an awful lot of money by having someone who'll get a certain type of sound. I always liked the clear sound of King Crimson albums, so we used him."

By December, however, Ferry was responding in no uncertain terms to Martin Hayman's queries regarding a possible Crimson 'taint'. "I would hotly deny it!" he insisted. "Obviously there are lots of sympathetic moments, but I thought it was so different from anything that King Crimson had done, apart from the Mellotron, which we use a lot, but I can't quite see the Pete Sinfield element. I have a great deal of respect for him, he has a great deal of experience, but he doesn't influence the music."

For his part, Sinfield has confessed to finding Eno a nuisance at first, only later realising the striking similarity between his own 'backroom boy' position in King Crimson and Eno's 'backroom boy brought out front' position in Roxy Music, pointing out also that Eno's use of the VCS3 was just as Sinfield-esque as the album's pervading Mellotron sounds. By the spring of 1973, after Roxy had turned to producers John Anthony and Chris Thomas for the *For Your Pleasure* LP, Sinfield was complaining that the band "thought I had over-produced the album. It's a matter of opinion. They thought I was doing too much on the album, but I don't mind. It's cool. I just wish they had been on the road for six months when I made the album." This last complaint was to become the governing theme of the anti-Roxy faction once the band had emerged into the media spotlight.

With reservations regarding the thin-ness of his production job becoming more persistent over the years, Sinfield noted the album's absurdly tight schedule and the inexperience of the band members, in particular Simpson's tendency to break down in tears on a regular basis, a reminiscence of his fragmenting behaviour at the band's BBC session and a portent of things to come. Ferry, however, seems retrospectively unconcerned by Sinfield's unfairly maligned pro-duction, wincing instead at the "too thin and too hard" sound of his own voice.

Producing Roxy's first album focused Sinfield's mind on his personal ambitions, prompting him to spend some £10,000 on *Still*, a 1973 solo album made under the stewardship of ELP's Greg Lake, the man who had sung Sinfield's lyric for *21st Century Schizoid Man* at the beginning of the first Crimson LP. "The LP may prove to people that perhaps a bit more of King Crimson was me and that it wasn't all Bob Fripp's vibes," Sinfield maintained, also noting that "I'm never going to produce an album again – it's insanity, exhaustion."

Sinfield would later rebuild his career (laid low by punk) through a diligent application to the craft of writing hit songs. Among these were *The Land of Make Believe* for Bucks Fizz, *Have You Ever Been in Love* for Leo Sayer, *Heart of Stone* for

Cher, *Peace in Our Time* for Cliff Richard and both *Call the Man* and *Think Twice* for Celine Dion, all of which sold in millions, *Have You Ever Been in Love* and *Think Twice* garnering him two Ivor Novello awards to boot. All a world away from Crimson's *21st Century Schizoid Man* – or, for that matter, the first Roxy Music album.

For Ferry, the packaging of the LP was almost as important as the music. With its lightly scowling covergirl suggesting a slimline Betty Grable and the design itself echoing the mildly salacious sleeves of jazz records from the 1950s and 60s, the *Roxy Music* album was calculated to offend rock'n'roll purists from just about every angle. Among many other crimes, it was the first rock LP to credit a fleet of high-fashion names, giving due deference to designer Nicholas de Ville, photographer Karl Stoecker, couturier Antony Price and hairstylist Keith Wainwright.

This was a stellar crew. Wainwright had been in charge of the chic Knightsbridge salon Smile since the late 1960s, Stoecker would also shoot the covers for Lou Reed's *Transformer* and Sparks' *Kimono My House* (as well as marrying Errol Flynn's troubled daughter Arnella), while Ferry's university friend de Ville later became Professor of Visual Arts at Goldsmith's College and author of the coffee-table tome *Album: Style and Image in Sleeve Design*. Price was at the time operating out of Stirling Cooper in Wigmore Street, an emporium described by Ferry as "really the 'in' place, with new weird clothes and designs. Tight trousers, big shoulders, a very sexy sort of look."

With input from all these key collaborators, the inner fold-out of the album's gatefold sleeve presented Roxy Music in their mid-1972 pomp: Eno in leopard-skin and a tumbling oil-slick of blond hair; Manzanera and Mackay in black leather, the former sporting a pair of bug-eyed shades reportedly stumbled upon on Antony Price's floor; Ferry in black tee-shirt and tigerskin jacket, topped by a gravitationally improbable quiff. Thompson and particularly Simpson look slightly out of kilter by comparison (the former, according to the *NME*'s Tony Tyler, "looks like a member of Black Sabbath"), but four potential rock gods out of six was an impressive score by any standards.

"I deliver a complete package," Ferry pointed out at the time. "Something not only has to sound good but also has to look good and feel good." In fact, the band's outrageous costuming (which counted as another black mark against them for the denim-clad fundamentalists of the day) was not merely an attempt to give the whole Roxy enterprise an alluring visual appeal to match the accompanying music. It was also a device to give the naturally shy band members alternative personae – and, through them, the nerve to get up on stage. The off-duty Bryan Ferry, for instance, was entirely different. "Bryan didn't make much of an impression on me," said *Roxy Music* covergirl Kari-Ann Moller in 1981. "All I can remember is that he looked very neat, very clean and rather straight. He was just a nice, poor young man in blue jeans and tennis shoes. Compared to most of the men I knew he looked like the boy next door."

"But it was great watching them being turned from boys next door into superstars," she added in 1990. A former consort of both Keith Richard and Vidal Sassoon, in 1972 Kari-Ann was an aspiring actress whose modelling work was centred around St Martin's School of Art. "Bryan saw me doing a fashion show and decided he wanted to use me," she recalled. "I got a meagre £20, as Roxy were unknown at the time and had no money. Ironic, isn't it, that it would be voted the best record cover of the decade?"

The cover's pink-and-white cheesecake impact was so hopelessly retro as to appear futuristic, a postmodern sleight-of-hand confirmed not only by the startling band photos but also by the music on the accompanying album. Discovered sprawled among white satin sheets, a pink rose in one hand, a prophetic gold disc impudently nestled among the folds of her *Baby Doll* train, Kari-Ann's expression is that of a genteel vampire floodlit by blue eye-shadow and frosted pink lipstick. "I felt like I could eat somebody up," she stressed. "I felt strong enough to take someone on."

With the traditionally submissive cheesecake pose subverted by the unreadable come-hither promise in her eyes, Kari-Ann's parted lips and clenched teeth were sufficiently like Ferry's stage persona to induce some fanciful viewers to speculate on whether she was, in fact, Ferry in drag. "I just got out there and did what I felt," she continued. "It was very glamorous, very sexy, or at least I felt that way. It was very ice-creamy in a way. The colours remind me of a marshmallow, like something really delicious. Fleshy, in a word."

For Antony Price, the cover provided an opportunity to indulge his fantasies of 1950s cheesecake as exemplified by the *Esquire* artwork of Alberto Vargas and the Sunset Strip photography of Bruno Bernard, what he would call "the *Girl Can't Help It* look." Though the pneumatic Jayne Mansfield references would only come to full fruition on the cover of *Stranded* (which looks exactly like a Bruno Bernard photograph), Price would become Ferry's designer of choice not only for Roxy's covergirls but also for his own couture. The other band members, meanwhile, would turn for their increasingly outlandish costumes to designers like Jim O'Connor, Pamla Motown (graduates, like Price, of the Royal College of Art), Wendy Dagworthy and Eno's then girlfriend, St Martin's graduate Carol McNichol.

"The dressing up was always part of the fun of Roxy. People tend to overlook the humour that was there," Manzanera informed Chris Roberts in 2001. "It also gave us something to do to conquer the nerves and feelings of amateurishness before we went on. It'd be: yes, *more* make-up, *more* outrageous costumes! We had lots of friends in fashion. It was never pre-arranged, we never saw each other's stuff until five minutes before the set, so we'd turn up and freak each other out."

Later in 1972, the band would be amazed not only by the success of their first album (and, more particularly, their first single), but also by the degree to which the 'look' they'd been devising for 12 months or more suddenly caught the popular imagination. Marc Bolan had donned sequins and satin to propel Tyrannosaurus Rex from small-time hippy cultdom to teen-appeal chart domination as T.Rex, and David Bowie had adopted the forbidding glam persona of Ziggy Stardust for an epoch-making LP released a mere fortnight ahead of *Roxy Music*. But Roxy took the process several stages further, particularly once their sartorial aspirations were bolstered by an advance from Island Records.

"There was a definite Janus feeling abroad at the time," Eno told Michael Bracewell 25 years later. "Looking to the past in a kitsch way, and imagining the future as it might be – but perhaps in an equally kitsch way. Our costumes were quite deliberate takes on those Fifties versions of space nobility – the masters of the Galactic Parliament and so on." Roxy's exaggerated costuming therefore encapsulated the dizzyingly strange stew of music they purveyed – it was a forecast of the future mediated through the past. Not for them the realistic costumes of recent science fiction films like *Planet of the Apes* and *The Andromeda Strain*. Roxy reached back instead to *The Day the Earth Stood Still* and, before even that, *Buck Rogers* and his near relation *Flash Gordon*.

Inevitably, the band's look foregrounded the science fiction soundscapes to be heard on their debut LP, but closer inspection would reveal a pot-pourri of musical styles far exceeding the eerie atonalities of *It Came from Outer Space*. Among myriad others, there was Country & Western in there (*If There is Something*), Kurt Weill (*Sea Breezes*), doo-wop (*Bitters End*), warped rock'n'roll (*Would You Believe?*), musique concrète (*Chance Meeting*), even, on *2 H.B.*, a fleeting echo of *As Time Goes By*. And most of the songs passed through several different phases, with a corresponding number of allusions and influences. Though a novice effort, with the rough edges inseparable from a first trip to a recording studio, it was nevertheless a heady hybrid brew, unlike anything previously heard in 1972.

Before all this, however, there were a few minor technicalities to be sorted out. The bald fact remained, for instance, that EG had yet to secure their protegées a record deal. "We did the record," Manzanera pointed out, "and the management took it around the record companies as a complete package – cover and everything. They took an incredible risk." It was a risk that, come July, would pay off handsomely for all concerned.

* * *

Re-make/Re-model
(Ferry) 5:14

The first Roxy Music album fades up on an advancing tinkle of cocktail glasses. Is that the band members who can be heard conferring, and laughing, against a generalised burble of partygoers? An ominous undertow is provided by an almost subliminal bass guitar, thrumming its way through the bass line that's soon to propel the entire track. On top of which, we can just about discern a manic voice chanting its own response to the empty charade: "Talk talk talk, talk talk talk..."

Though eventually positioned as the opening track on Roxy's debut album, *Re-make/Re-model* was the last to be recorded, alongside *Bitters End*, in a studio schedule that wound up on 29 March. It had already featured in Roxy's first BBC Radio session on 4 January, at which point David O'List was still on board as the band's guitarist. O'List would later claim that the track's working title had been the rather less memorable *CPL* and that, though Ferry modelled the eventual title on a 1962 Pop Art canvas by Derek Boshier called 'Re-Think/Re-Entry', the song itself had a more mundane inspiration: merely Ferry's memory of a pretty girl he had once caught sight of in his car, hence the song's bizarre use of a shouted car number-plate instead of a chorus.

No less bizarre is that high-society opening, impudently positioning Roxy as the kind of band more likely to be found performing at a private view in an art gallery (as indeed they had in December 1971) than in conventional rock venues. After some 30 seconds of this strangely muffled banter, Ferry's honky-tonk piano suddenly cuts across the hub-bub, itself superseded by the pounding assault of Thompson's drums and the fractured wailing of Ferry's voice.

It's a masterstroke of disorientation: the in-your-face, hard-rock onslaught of the track proper immediately translates the preceding cocktail party ambience into a wicked joke. Manzanera's jagged guitar noodlings erupt stage right, Mackay's droning sax riffs stage left, and Ferry spells out a puzzling 'party' manifesto regarding the "next time" – with the disturbing proviso that there may be no next time. To complete the listener's confusion, there are references to "the sweetest queen", clearly a 'she' but teasingly referred to in car number-plate terms as "CPL593H". In this enervated party atmosphere, is Ferry's ideal a woman, or a woman objectified as an automobile, or the automobile itself – or possibly some freakish fusion of woman and machine?

Richard Williams would later complain that "*Remake* has nothing like the energy of the take they did for 'Top Gear'" – but this is hard to substantiate from a comparison of the two versions. Here, the track's pile-driving force just doesn't let up. In a madly energised middle section, Mackay unleashes a thoroughly demented sax solo, following no discernible pattern but, accompanied once again by increasingly savage improvisations from Manzanera, sweeping the track forward on an exhilarating head of steam.

Ferry returns to restate his previous sentiments, only this time with an even more manic intensity, and joined now by wildly erratic washes of Eno electronics. The driving instrumental stew that rounds off the track finally stutters to an exhausted close, but not before a witty passage showcasing a phrase from each musician, including in-joke snatches of Eddie Cochran's *C'mon Everybody* (Manzanera), The Beatles' *Day Tripper* (Simpson) and even Wagner's *The Ride of the Valkyries* (Mackay). It was here that Roxy set out their iconoclastic stall. These were fragments of a musical past (samples, in today's terminology) thrown carelessly into the air and therefore up for grabs by anyone daring enough to re-make/re-model rock and pop into something rich and strange – and, above all, new.

Sinfield has noted that *Re-make/Re-model* was the track he had earmarked for single release, but it proved too unruly a beast to mould into the kind of shape suitable to the Top 40. As for the track's opening Hooray Henry buzz (which reappears at the opposite end of the album in *Bitters End*), it bears a striking resemblance to the credits sequence of Bob Fosse's *Cabaret*, in which the eerily blurred faces of the Kit Kat Klub's patrons are juxtaposed with an expectant ambient burble. Poised precisely between the recording and release of the *Roxy Music* album, Fosse's film had opened in London on 31 May; the similarity may be coincidental, but the association with what Liza Minnelli's Sally Bowles calls "divine decadence" is certainly an apt one.

As well as being the subject of a student film shot at the Royal College of Art in June (qualifying, more or less, as Roxy's first promotional video), *Re-make/Re-model* would resurface in September for the band's *In Concert* radio showcase and in November for BBC TV's live arts marathon, *Full House*. Here, the band belted out the song over the programme's opening credits, coming to a sudden, and highly effective, halt at the conclusion of the first verse. Their set proper, comprising *For Your Pleasure, Ladytron* and *The Bogus Man Part II*, followed an hour later.

The seismic impact of *Re-make/Re-model* was reflected in occasional references to it that surfaced in the band members' extracurricular activities. Mackay would develop his *Die Walküre* quote into a rocked-up Wagnerian extravaganza on his first solo album, as well as recycling Siegfried's call as the opening fanfare of *Lorelei*, debut single of his 1984 Manzanera collaboration, The Explorers. Manzanera himself made teasing reference to the CPL593H mantra on the *Numbers* track of his second solo collection, *K-Scope*, while Ferry went further, re-recording the song for use as the flip-side of his June 1975 single, *You Go to My Head*, the track reappearing the following year as B-side to the US single *Heart on My Sleeve*.

Funked up 100 per cent (and, according to Ira Robbins, "too revisionist for words"), this version is a short and sweet 2:43 and benefits from the muscular contributions of Roxy alumnae Phil Manzanera, Eddie Jobson, Paul Thompson and Johnny Gustafson, together with a blaring Stax-style horn section and sassy shrieks of "CPL593H" from 'Sirens' Jacqui Sullivan and Doreen Chanter. Having done duty on 45, it joined four other madeover Roxy tracks on the slung-together Ferry solo album, *Let's Stick Together*. Two decades on, the song was covered by former Pixies front man and long-time Roxy enthusiast Frank Black for use as the B-side of his 1995 single *Men in Black*, later turning up on the 2001 anthology *Oddballs*.

Ladytron
(Ferry) 4:26

Following the thunderous conclusion to *Re-make/Re-model*, *Ladytron* begins with perhaps the creepiest soundscape Roxy Music ever created – Eno's fluttering atmospherics underpinning a baleful oboe motif that sounds as if Mackay is issuing a call to prayer from atop some intergalactic minaret. Here, in musical form, is the abiding Pop Art preoccupation with science fiction, whether the chilly monochrome of *It Came from Outer Space* or the lurid Technicolor of *Forbidden Planet*. "*Ladytron* is a sort of sci-fi lunar landscape with the oboe playing what I call 'The Haunted Landscape Theme'," Ferry explained in the *NME*, "before I come in singing like a cowboy with castanets. About half the album I sing in an American voice because most of the culture I like comes from the States."

How far Ferry sounds American in this or any other of the *Roxy Music* tracks is open to debate; indeed, 25 years later Mackay would make the interesting observation that the sheer Englishness of Ferry's vocal style would constitute a profound influence in itself. Basically, as on so much of the album, Ferry's *Ladytron* vocal sounds like nothing on earth, though perhaps a faint whiff of Transylvania is detectable in his vampire's croon.

Against an entrancing melange of shimmering castanets, atonal piano runs and the metronome throb of Simpson's bass guitar, Ferry laments the humiliations attendant on pursuing a high-maintenance lover, eventually adopting a vaguely vengeful tone. The ambiguity remains tantalising as Mackay launches into a hectic, hyped-up oboe break, Thompson galloping below with a breathless tom-tom beat and Manzanera letting loose isolated guitar chords in metallic counterpoint. Ferry's final observations shift from vengeful to borderline sadistic, then a Mellotron power surge causes Manzanera to go wild, Mackay matching him with the inexorable rise and fall of a honking four-note tenor riff. Then guitar and sax spell out a sublimely tuneful motif in unison, the tom-toms return with a vengeance and Manzanera's final guitar freak-out is hedged about by Eno's space-age sound effects, crazing and disintegrating into a thoroughly brain-reeling fade.

Clearly shattered by the *Ladytron* listening experience, US critic Alan Niester observed in *Phonograph Record* that "This is the most painful yet psyche-grabbing moment in rock this year." The song's disorientating shifts in tone confounded any critics tempted by the previous track, *Re-make/Re-model*, to dismiss Roxy as mere retro-rockers. Here was a bizarre soundscape suggestive of the Theremin fantasies of *The Day the Earth Stood Still*, yet the listener couldn't be sure whether the 'Ladytron' of the title was a shimmering robot, as per Brigitte Helm in *Metropolis*, or a thigh-slapping cowgirl like Doris Day in *Calamity Jane*; that's how freakish and uncategorisable this music sounded.

The track's shock tactics were aptly summarised by Eno himself in the 1 July edition of *Sounds*: "There's a 50s spaceship-type opening, then a cowboy song, then a kind of Phil Spector thing with an oboe solo like one of those organ solos they used to do, and [finally] a piece with synthesised guitars." He also pointed out that the album's two opening cuts constituted a kind of multi-faceted musical manifesto: "I think what might happen is we'll get two nice directions together – one the *Re-make/Re-model* direction where you have a continuous wedge of sound with a lot of complexity inside it, and the other the *Ladytron* direction, which moves through a whole set of changes in four and a half minutes." In *Disc*, Mackay was more laconic about the futuristic vistas being opened up by Roxy Music. "Lennon describes his music as seventies rock," he opined. "Ours is fifties, seventies and eighties."

Ladytron was showcased on Roxy's BBC Radio session of 23 May, the result broadcast on *Sounds of the Seventies* on 23 June (the same day the *Roxy Music* album was released); it also figured on two of the band's appearances for BBC TV, first in *The Old Grey Whistle Test* on 20 June, then in their live *Full House* set on 25 November. It was also a highlight of their 1972 stage act, with Nick Kent reporting from Newcastle on 18 November that "*Ladytron* is simply the best psychedelic song since *I had too much to dream last night* by The Electric Prunes, and the band know it, beating it out complete with Manzanera's apocalyptic guitar thrashing."

The track was rumoured to have been among the songs toyed with by David Bowie during his July 1973 stint at the Château d'Hérouville, sessions that resulted in the all-covers album *Pin Ups*. In common with other mooted titles like The Stooges' *No Fun*, The Beach Boys' *God Only Knows*, The Velvet Underground's *White Light/White Heat* and Lovin' Spoonful's *Summer in the City*, *Ladytron* would have disrupted Bowie's stated intent for the collection, which was to pay tribute to the mid-1960s Britpop that had inspired him as a teenager. (Among others, The Pretty Things, Them, The Yardbirds, Pink Floyd, The Who and The Kinks.) If

Ladytron had indeed ended up on *Pin Ups* (or even, as suggested by Bowie-philes, a projected *Pin Ups II*), it would have made for a fetching irony, given Ferry's indignation at what he perceived as a rip-off of his own *These Foolish Things* collection.

In 1997, Mackay would form part of a one-off 'supergroup', The Venus in Furs, for Todd Haynes' overblown celluloid glamfest, *Velvet Goldmine*; among the Roxy tracks Mackay got to reinvent was *Ladytron*. A year later, the song received a different kind of tribute when keyboardists Daniel Hunt and Reuben Wu joined with vocalists Mira Aroyo and Helena Marnie to form Ladytron; subsequent recordings like the *Commodore Rock* EP and *Light & Magic* album established them as seminal figures on the turn-of-the-century electronica scene. After a hiatus, in December 2004 they switched record labels to Island, the formal announcement pointing out that "It is with great pleasure they now join the likes of Roxy Music, Sparks, B-52's, Pulp, P J Harvey, and countless other acts they love on this label."

If There is Something
(Ferry) 6:34

The fourth track to be recorded for the *Roxy Music* album, *If There is Something* wound up the band's first week of recording in mid-March 1972. By October, Ferry was confiding to Steve Turner of *Beat Instrumental* that "Every song is a little kind of play. There is a strong idea behind every song."

If There is Something is an obvious exemplar of this, being constructed, like the traditional well-made play and the majority of film scripts, in three distinct acts. But these separate movements – ranging through introduction, development and finally resolution – are presented in such radically different styles that they seem to come from entirely different plays. "What interests me, far more than ambiguity, is juxtaposing things so they shock. I like surprise," Ferry explained.

The first section is a hokey love song in mutated Country & Western vein, Ferry detailing his search for love against a richly confected mesh of supple percussion, whimsical 'walking' bass, honky-tonk piano and Manzanera's cotton-pickin' guitar twang. Mackay's saxophones surge in to signal the onset of Phase Two, spelling out a uniquely mournful motif in unison with Manzanera prior to an impassioned peal of courtly-love phrase-making from Ferry. Here, Ferry's cracked vibrato moves from outright cliché to arrant absurdity, his offer to suffuse his loved one with home-grown potatoes being almost, but not quite, matched for bathos by the offers of fish and candy in the 1980 B-52's track *Give Me Back My Man*. Backed by Thompson's brilliantly funky timekeeping, Mackay then holds sway for over two minutes, his sax solo divided, appropriately, into three sections, shading from piercing to querulous to soaringly romantic in a seamless progression that remains one of the supreme moments in Roxy's repertoire.

Initiated by Ferry's piano, the third section is augmented by ethereal Eno-Mackay backing vocals and an otherworldly wash of Mellotron strings. Here Ferry is at his most forlornly nostalgic, mourning a ponytailed lost love in a backward-looking litany commemorating lost youth. The complex weave of guitar, Mellotron and backing vocals sends the song out on a genuinely epic note, yet the extensive use of Mellotron would be a source of regret to several critics. Though tireless in his self-appointed role as chief Roxy cheerleader, *Melody*

Maker's Richard Williams conceded that it was "an obvious mistake," while the *NME*'s Tony Tyler pointed out that *"If There is Something* is less successful [than *Ladytron*] and I wish it weren't there because there's too much Crimson-quoting."

The Mellotron had indeed been a vital constituent of such earth-shaking King Crimson epics as *Epitaph* and *In the Court of the Crimson King*, both of which had been recorded under the EG aegis in July 1969. The instrument had formed part of the explosion of new technology that transformed rock music in the late 1960s, as Mackay would explain in his 1981 book *Electronic Music*: "Although many of the instruments developed were synthesisers or organs, there were one or two interesting hybrids. The Mellotron ... was a keyboard instrument using pre-recorded tapes. In effect it was a multiple tape recorder, each key activating a tape. Instrumental sounds were on the tapes, the flutes and strings having a particularly distinctive, eerie quality (heard on The Beatles' *Strawberry Fields Forever*). Other sounds could be recorded and added at will."

Despite the misgivings of contemporary critics, the prominent use of Mellotron on *If There is Something* seems in retrospect less like plagiarism than just another of Roxy's playful gestures towards pastiche. Here was a sound characteristic of their distinguished EG stablemates King Crimson, a sound propagated by the very band Ferry had unsuccessfully auditioned for in December 1970, a sound all too familiar to Roxy's ex-Crimson producer Pete Sinfield. A spot of "Crimson-quoting" was too good a gag to miss – yet, true to Roxy's perplexing knack of combining the tongue-in-cheek with sincere emotion, its inclusion doesn't compromise the elegiac power of the track as a whole.

With David O'List still in place on guitar, *If There is Something* had been one of the five tracks Roxy taped for John Peel back on 4 January. Then, some three weeks after the album's release, the band recorded a third Peel session on 18 July, juxtaposing an extended *Virginia Plain* with a massively extended *If There is Something*. Clocking in at just under 12 minutes, this version seems to have been influenced by Richard Williams' caveat regarding the song in his *Melody Maker* review of 24 June. But, instead of making the song sound less like King Crimson, the band perversely increase its Crimson soundalike qualities by several hundred per cent, the slather of Mellotron dominating the middle section as well as the end, the feverish buzz of the saxophone more like *21st Century Schizoid Man* than ever.

The song would be developed further as a multi-faceted centrepiece of Roxy's contemporary stage act. "When we do *If There is Something* live," Ferry observed, "people always seem startled by the juxtapositions – it's tilting along pleasantly and suddenly this agonised voice bursts out. I find doing it quite embarrassing sometimes, because it's just raw emotion and you can't be in 20 different moods in one night. You have to be an actor, project yourself into it." Eno was more enthusiastic, noting that the stage version of the song had expanded beyond the two directions (exemplified by *Re-make/Re-model* and *Ladytron*) he had previously identified as the band's antithetical mainstays. "*If There is Something* has become a strange creature," he maintained. "It's modified into something else completely which isn't either of those two, and isn't a cross between the two either. It's Grand Music, if you know what I mean, it's got a feeling of grandness about it which is hinted [at] on the album but which has developed even more now."

Nineteen years later, David Bowie resurrected *If There is Something* for his ill-received Tin Machine project. Having covered John Lennon's *Working Class Hero* on their first album, Bowie and US guitarist Reeves Gabrels added Ferry's song to the line-up of their second, *Tin Machine II*, released in September 1991; unfortunately, the industrial thrash implied by the band's name makes a risible backdrop to Ferry's whimsical lyric. A different version, recorded for the BBC on 13 August, subsequently surfaced on the band's *Baby Universal* single, after which the song formed part of the Tin Machine 'It's My Life' tour and accordingly appeared a third time on the live *Oy Vey, Baby* album, issued in July 1992.

2 H.B.
(Ferry) 4:30

Anticipating the hip title notations of Prince by some ten years (and the pidgin English of text messaging by more like a quarter of a century), *2 H.B.* is an ode 'to Humphrey Bogart' that also references, for no good reason other than Ferry's addiction to puns, a grade of pencil.

Fifteen years after his death in January 1957, the Bogart mystique had reached the proportions of a fully fledged cult, perhaps the most conspicuous feature of an early 1970s 'nostalgia craze' that, in film alone, had thrown up delicacies as diverse as Liza Minnelli in *Cabaret*, Vincent Price in *The Abominable Dr Phibes*, Twiggy in *The Boyfriend* and Woody Allen's own hymn to Bogie, *Play It Again Sam* (the latter making it to UK cinemas, incidentally, in September 1972). Ferry claimed, however, to have conceived the song as a tribute to Hollywood in general, the dreamworld of Art Deco picture palaces that had given Roxy its name, rather than Bogart in particular.

"*2 H.B.* was written sitting at the piano with the typewriter balanced on my knees," he noted. "It wasn't that I have a thing about Bogart, it could have been any popular idol of the period, or later, James Dean or somebody, and it's not that Bogart was a very tragic figure anyway. It was just that line, 'Here's looking at you, kid', from the film *Casablanca* and coming out of the cinema remembering all those great scenes: the cigarette smoke in the nightclub, and Peter Lorre in a white jacket … The song was written around a period … as captured in that one picture."

Despite Ferry's protestations, it's hard to imagine him fashioning a musical tribute to the rootless teen rebellion of James Dean, notwithstanding the very fleeting reference to Dean that would soon pop up in *Virginia Plain*. Bogart's compromised anti-hero in Michael Curtiz' 1942 film, relinquishing his cynical pose when confronted with a lost love, is much more Ferry's style; indeed, his eventual acquisition of the iconic white tuxedo in autumn 1973 is predicted here in his reference to Bogart's dinner-jacketed Rick Blaine persona.

In typically convoluted style, Ferry invokes 'wings' not merely in terms of winged collars but also aeroplanes, explicitly evoking *Casablanca*'s climactic airstrip dilemma and Bogart's self-sacrificing gesture of allowing Ingrid Bergman to take flight with Paul Henreid. Ferry's final paean to lingering memories also contains multiple meanings, applying equally to Bergman as seen by Bogart,

Bogart as seen by Ferry, and a vanished world of Hollywood glamour as seen by the nostalgic patrons of 1970s repertory cinemas.

Though suffused in a backward-looking haze, Ferry's intoxicating celluloid fantasy is realised with thoroughly modern means, the Eno-heavy soundstage incorporating tape loops and delay systems. The dreamlike oscillations of the opening keyboard motif suggest a daydreamer emerging from some prolonged Tinseltown reverie, while the intriguing agglomeration of Mackay's saxophones in the middle, dozily wending their way through the tune of *As Time Goes By*, was to be perfected later in the Eno-Mackay collaboration *Time Regained*, and later still in the tranquilised woodwind ambience of Roxy tracks like *More Than This*. Thompson's syncopated drum patterns are delightful throughout, while the self-effacing Manzanera contributes only a few discreet chords to what pass in this stream-of-consciousness context for choruses.

2 H.B. was previewed alongside *Bitters End*, *Chance Meeting* and *Ladytron* in Roxy's *Sounds of the Seventies* broadcast of 23 June. In September of the following year, a Ferry cover of the song was used as the B-side to his first solo single, *A Hard Rain's a-Gonna Fall*. A fairly straightforward rendering, even down to Ferry repeating his glottal-stopped 'k' on "smoky nightclub situation," it loses some of the original's edge with an overly saccharine soundstage and a Ferry vocal more starry-eyed than sleepy-eyed.

In 1995, *2 H.B.* was covered by R Stevie Moore on one of his multiplicity of 'homemade' albums, *Unpopular Singer Vol 4*. The song was also referenced by Madness, briefly resurrecting themselves as The Madness for an album of the same name in 1988. The final track (written by resident saxophonist Lee Thompson), it wittily turned 'to Humphrey Bogart' into 'for Bryan Ferry' via the title, *4 B.F.*

The Bob (Medley)
(Ferry) 5:48

After *2 H.B.*, Ferry pulled out another punning acronym with *The Bob (Medley)*, the title referring not only to a hairstyle of the period but also spelling out 'Battle of Britain'. The wide-ranging triptych of *If There is Something* is here trumped by a soundscape that passes through at least six different phases, less a 'suite' than a thing of shreds and patches analogous to Pop Art's enthusiasm for collage. As such, it allowed Mackay and Eno to let rip with the kind of avant-garde strategies they'd absorbed at Reading and Winchester respectively. As Mackay informed Michael Bracewell in 1997, "Interpreting a piece by John Cage gives you enormous confidence to do something on a pop record that other people might think was weird."

Ferry's impressionistic collage of wartime Britain provided Mackay and Eno with an opportunity to introduce 'systems music' into a rock'n'roll context. According to Eno, "each musician plays a simple part over and over again so that the different parts overlap in a different phase relation at any given time. It gives the appearance of a complex piece of music progressing, when it is really very simple. The changes are not in the music, but in the perception of the listener, whose ear picks out more and more detail."

There's plenty to pick out in *The Bob*. The baleful drone of Eno's synths, together with a mesmeric pulse of electronic percussion suggestive of a mad scientist's laboratory, gives way to arguably Ferry's least listenable vocal on this or any other album, a strangulated wail completely at odds with the winsomely romantic lyric. First surprise: the thickly pasted melange of guitar, saxophone and bass suddenly switches to a delicate oboe theme, a motif echoed later in the Ferry-Mackay composition *Bitter-Sweet*. Eno conjures a cloud of anti-aircraft guns, spiralling V.1 rockets and jangling fire engines from his VCS3, Mackay switches to a lugubrious tenor melody that sounds like Glenn Miller's brass section with a severe hangover, and from the warning tinkle of Ferry's piano the song leaps athletically into a bubblegum singalong.

Ferry's shouted vocal here is succeeded by a gaily skipping synth and Manzanera's sub-Hendrix guitar improvisation. With Mackay's *Ladytron*-style oboe chirruping in hot pursuit, the mixture soon curdles into a mesmeric whirlpool of sound, arbitrarily cut off by the airy beauty of a classical piano and oboe duet. Ferry's disembodied voice issues from the ether in a spoken aside, and the soundstage suddenly lurches back to the opening blur of musique concrète, Ferry sadly acknowledging that his dream of love was a tragic over-simplification of life's complexities.

The whole thing winds up on an absurdly grandiloquent guitar chord and ceremonial drum pattern, a blaze of pomp and circumstance conjuring images of Bombardier Billy Wells striking the Rank gong, not to mention memories of David Bowie's recently released *Life on Mars?*

Three versions of *The Bob* were heard on BBC Radio 1, featuring on *Sounds of the Seventies* in January and November together with an *In Concert* broadcast in September. The first of these, featuring David O'List on guitar, sees Eno bringing in the eerie wail of air-raid sirens at the beginning rather than in the middle, evoking an image of search-lights scouring the night sky above St Paul's far more effectively than the album version; it also benefits from a slightly more comprehensible vocal and a considerably more swinging backbeat.

Presumably to warn audiences at the outset of Roxy's unusually high unpredictability factor, *The Bob* was chosen as the opening number for the band's autumn tour. The evening would kick off with a lengthy stretch of Pachelbel's *Canon* being pumped through the PA (reportedly one of Eno's favourite compositions), prior to the arrival of what Richard Williams called "that nightmarish warping and woofing noise which introduces *The Bob (Medley)*." At the opposite end of the set, the band launched, inevitably, into *Virginia Plain*. Audiences were clearly getting the message by this time; as Eno reported, they turned up "with just the right amount of expectation about it – they know the numbers aren't going to be the same all the way through, most of them chop and change quite often, so the thing that used to happen doesn't any more, where people used to start dancing and then an oboe and piano bit would come, and they'd be left hanging over the edge."

In 1976, Mackay would revisit the Battle of Britain via the scabrous satire of Thames TV's *Rock Follies*, in the concluding episode of which – titled *The Blitz* – girl group The Little Ladies are cajoled by a monomaniac Greek entrepreneur into purveying 'austerity rock' under the name The Victory Gals. Songs like *Glenn Miller is Missing* and *War Brides*, set to lyrics by playwright Howard Schuman, remain among the most memorable in the series – though a great deal more mellifluous than the dauntingly experimental sound of *The Bob*.

Chance Meeting
(Ferry) 3:08

"Some of my lyrics are pure throw-away, while others are of vital relevance," Ferry announced, tongue firmly in cheek, in November 1972. "I think *Chance Meeting* is of great social importance." Having handled *Casablanca* on *2 H.B.* and, roughly speaking, *The Way to the Stars* on *The Bob (Medley)*, Ferry ventures further into the 1940s here, invoking the tight-lipped territory of Noël Coward and David Lean. The stiff-upper-lip angst of the 1945 film *Brief Encounter* was the inspiration, Ferry conjuring familiar images of snatched tête-à-têtes in a Home Counties railway buffet through a halting and inarticulate monologue that lasts a mere eight lines.

In this short space, Ferry's one-sided conversation progresses from standard-issue stuffed-shirt banalities to something more specific yet still strangely ambiguous. The tongue-tied lack of elaboration points forward to the next album's *Strictly Confidential*, in which the anguished narrator insists that there are some topics too dark to be openly discussed. Appropriately, Eno lards this drama of emotional inarticulacy with a jumbled blur of sound synthesised from the hard-to-separate contributions of Mackay and Manzanera, whose instruments seem to be speaking in unaccustomed tongues as an anguished parody of Ferry's stumbling recitation.

Dispensing with Thompson's percussion altogether, the track kicks off with a bashfully atonal piano motif, accompanied only by the high-thrummed ruminations of Simpson's bass; then, on a vibrato cue from Ferry, Mackay and Manzanera start struggling for utterance against a discordant wash of Eno treatments. "At the moment, I'm mostly interested in modifying the sound of the other instruments," Eno told Richard Williams on the album's release. "You get a nice quality – the skill of the performer, transformed by the electronics. Neither the player nor I know what each other is going to do – which means you get some nice accidents."

In September, Manzanera explained something of the process to the *NME*'s Ian MacDonald. "On the album I got the chance to prepare some stuff beforehand on my Revox but even then a lot of it was improvised on the spot," he observed. "On *Chance Meeting* they wanted me to play backwards, or rather play forwards while the tape went backwards. When that failed dismally I tried feedback which meant playing so loud I couldn't hear Bryan singing, only the chord changes. Eno likes that a lot – randomness. Taping one track and then sticking another one over the top without listening to the first one. And with *Chance Meeting* it was singularly appropriate."

For all its cacophony, the result is strangely moving, especially during a protracted fade in which bass and piano mark time undeviatingly through an increasingly agitated wall of Eno sound. The thickly clotted layering of instruments here is arguably the closest Roxy ever got to so-called Prog Rock; indeed, as late as 1980 the extreme nature of *Chance Meeting* was used to incur a bit of middlebrow Middle England outrage in, of all things, the BBC sitcom *Butterflies*. The noise-like thrash of punk had come and gone by this stage, yet *Chance Meeting* was the 'not in front of the parents' track chosen for Wendy Craig to grimace at as she ventured into the bedroom of her troglodytic teenage son.

Chance Meeting figured in Roxy's Radio 1 performances in both June and August of 1972, with Eno's experimentation reserved for a prolonged fade, the body of the song given over to a sensitive oboe meditation from Mackay. A similar approach characterised its final live performances in autumn 1973, one of which (from the Apollo Glasgow in November) is preserved on the *Viva! Roxy Music* album.

In 1996, a cover of *Chance Meeting* appeared on the Mike Rep and the Quotas album *A Tree Stump Named Desire*. Twenty-two years earlier, Ferry had concocted a *Chance Meeting* cover of his own, first unveiled as B-side to his May 1974 single *The 'In' Crowd* and then added to the odds-and-sods stew that was the *Let's Stick Together* album in 1976. This version is notable for the presence of Roxy's pre-Manzanera guitarist, David O'List, as well as a gorgeously spectral synthetic soundstage dominated by the band's post-Eno synth specialist, Eddie Jobson. The only thing letting it down is Ferry's vocal, which replaces the glazed neurosis of the original with a rather self-conscious attempt at spell-stopped spookiness.

Would You Believe?
(Ferry) 3:53

Described by *Sounds'* Penny Valentine as a "nostalgic thumper," *Would You Believe?* was one of five tracks recorded for John Peel's *Sounds of the Seventies* on 4 January, subsequently being broadcast on the 21st. Some seven weeks later (by which time David O'List had been replaced by Phil Manzanera), it became the first track laid down during the *Roxy Music* sessions.

A relatively un-selfconscious rockabilly pastiche, it would cause the more cloth-eared sections of the music press to brand Roxy as cynical rock'n'roll revivalists and, together with the band's camped-up stage appearance, inspire unwelcome comparisons to US pasticheurs Sha-Na-Na (who, by unhappy coincidence, were making a heavily publicised assault on the UK at the time). Stung, Ferry was more or less disowning the song within a week of the album's release. "There's one track on there," he told Steve Peacock on 1 July, "which is a kind of rock revival thing, but we're not a rock revival band – not that at all. That's just a very straightforward track, a period piece, and I think we'll get further away from that in the future if anything."

Roxy would later turn their hands to several other generic pastiches, ranging from Country & Western (*If It Takes All Night*) to R'n'B (*Cry, Cry, Cry*) and disco (*Angel Eyes*). As the first track in this vein, *Would You Believe?* has youthful energy to spare and remains an impressive showcase for Mackay in particular. Cued in by a very strange wheeze of heavily treated saxophone, and an even stranger clustering of Eno-tweaked percussion, Ferry sashays into view as if direct from the Senior Prom, crooning a brief but oddly convoluted lyric.

In full-fledged teen balladeer mode, Ferry is well matched by Simpson's gently bubbling bass line and the warm smooch of Mackay's alto, as well as his own relaxed piano improvisations. But then comes the characteristically Roxyfied volte-face: Thompson suddenly goes into percussive overdrive and Mackay unleashes a honking fanfare reminiscent of his Wagner quoting on *Re-make/Re-model*. As the rocking middle section takes flight, Ferry breaks out into a yodelled refrain so painfully strident it obscures some of the most cynically amusing lines in his entire repertoire. Nevertheless, this section boasts a tearing guitar solo from Manzanera, nicely juxtaposed with Mackay's riffing alto, and some exuberantly hammered Jerry Lee Lewis piano chords from Ferry himself. And, as Ferry warbles a repeated "Woh-woh" against Eno's energetic "bow-wows," Mackay cuts loose with a blistering sax solo that modulates seamlessly into a reprise of the original theme.

Ferry, however, was soon dissatisfied with the song even as a live proposition. "Actually, *Would You Believe?* is the most restricting thing we do – far less satisfying than the rest," he told the ever-supportive Richard Williams, "because it's a very set thing, a little cameo with no room for improvement or interesting improvising. It's very much something that we have to act through, and if we're not in the mood there's not much we can do."

Even so, the song's rock'n'roll flavourings helped the band perfect the kind of tongue-in-cheek retro stage routines that would distinguish all their live appear-ances, reaching an apotheosis with Mackay's absurd *Editions of You* duck-walk. Reporting on Roxy's Crystal Palace performance at the end of July, the *NME* noted that "Visually, Andy Mackay and Phil Manzanera (reeds and guitar respectively) are the focal point on stage. They work together on step routines à la 50s, and play lines in unison." "Oh, they're very simple," Manzanera explained in a later issue, "though we do tend to bump into each other now and then. One night Andy had something on his mind and forgot where he was, and I found myself mincing about on my own. I felt such a fool. And another time we got entwined in our leads and couldn't get out – stuff like that."

Despite its theatrical possibilities, Ferry was still keen to explain the track away to the fleets of rock journalists who were by now queuing up for interview opportunities. "I don't think a group so much into advanced music has ever used these old sources so obviously before. It's our adolescent streak, really," he told the *NME's* Ian MacDonald. "Besides, that use of past music was really to do with the way I first planned the album, which goes back to 1970 – and I don't expect we're going to do too much more of it in the future. *Would You Believe?* is about the end of that line and there's no scope for development there; it's like a gem, or a lump of coal. A rough diamond."

Even so, Ferry already had a song up his sleeve called *The Bogus Man Part II* (later to surface on the *For Your Pleasure* album as *Grey Lagoons*), which would prove, if nothing else, that there really was "no scope for development there."

Sea Breezes

(Ferry) 7:03

Midway through the band's second week at Command Studios, the mesmerising soundscape of *Sea Breezes* was committed to tape in tandem with *2 H.B.* The emotionally constipated quaver of *Chance Meeting* flowers into naked vulnerability in this gorgeous lament. In the *NME*, Tony Tyler heaped high praise on the result, drawing attention to the song's "superb lyrics, sung with a metre and a feel that I thought was gone forever since Dylan chose the path of least resistance."

The opening is stark in its stripped-down simplicity: a subliminal wash of lapping waves, a plaintive keyboard melody, the extraordinary fragility of Ferry's voice, the discreet accompaniment of Mackay's oboe. The voice, in particular, is thoroughly desolate, even otherworldly. Speculating on the possibility that love doesn't come easily even in Heaven, Ferry's last phrase spirals back into the mix on a sublimely attenuated echo, Manzanera then making a belated entrance in delicate counterpoint to the sombre sonority of Mackay's oboe.

"Roxy Music can bring pictures to your head like no one else and they've only just begun," enthused Richard Williams in his *Melody Maker* album review. *Sea Breezes* remains the most intensely visual of all the tracks on Roxy's debut, conjuring a cold and forbidding mood, the narrator lovelorn and stranded, the soundstage painfully evocative of rainswept out-of-season seascapes. It's like Morrissey's 1988 single *Every Day is Like Sunday* but without Morrissey's trademark lugubriousness. In its place is a hesitant, pain-wracked appeal to the highest power – not to rain retribution on Morrissey's braindead seaside resort, but instead to provide some relief from the curse of loneliness.

This theme is introduced by an unassuming piano figure, itself swept away by the sudden onslaught of Thompson's hitherto silent drum-kit. Thompson and Simpson do amazing work here, laying down a rivetingly out-of-kilter, stop-start staccato backbeat suggestive of a rhythm section that's recently undergone a lobotomy. Appropriately, Ferry's anguished vocal takes on a robotic quality as Manzanera's heavily Eno-treated guitar starts to craze in from stage right. Mackay's oboe reappears too, only to be snatched up by Eno and converted into an asthmatic fuzz of electrical static. Inevitably, the dissonant squall cooked up by Mackay, Manzanera and Eno, together with the disorientating lurch of bass and percussion, is just as summarily curtailed for a restatement of the original theme, the song ending on a repetition of Ferry's plangent speculations regarding angels in Heaven.

Back on 18 February, *Sea Breezes* had been heard on John Peel's *Sounds of the Seventies* as a stand-alone hold-over from the session of 4 January, the other four tracks having already been broadcast. This early version of *Sea Breezes* is graced by a wonderfully doleful guitar solo from the soon-to-be-deposed David O'List, as well as surprisingly ritzy back-up vocals from Eno and Mackay. Later, with Manzanera on board, the song was resurrected as one of six items featured in the band's *In Concert* radio special in September.

Also in February, Richard Williams had dubbed *Sea Breezes* "a little bit of *Brighton Rock* mixed up with *The Dream of Olwen*," while Eno gave him an explanation of his all-pervading wave effects: "Actually, we were doing that before King Crimson – it's the first thing anyone does when they get a synthesiser, make the sound of waves. After I heard them do it, I though we'd carry on with it and treat it as a kind of pun." This somewhat disingenuous claim sounds almost as if Eno was anticipating the adverse reaction to the "Crimson-quoting" on *If There is Something*.

In September 1974, *Sea Breezes* became the first Roxy track to be 'covered' by another artist. Famous for his collaboration with Roger McGough and John Gorman as part of The Scaffold, Paul McCartney's younger brother, Mike McGear, used Ferry's song as the opening cut on his second solo album, called simply *McGear*. It was recorded at Stockport's Strawberry Studios, with McCartney as producer and two other Wings members, Linda McCartney and Denny Laine, among the personnel. Thirteen years on, the song formed part of the all-covers Siouxsie and the Banshees album, *Through the Looking Glass*, an intriguing collection that also paid tribute to Kraftwerk, Sparks, The Doors, Iggy Pop, Bob Dylan and John Cale – the latter represented by *Gun*, the original of which had featured Phil Manzanera.

Ferry's own cover version appeared as the B-side to his June 1976 smash *Let's Stick Together*. Garnished with lovely keyboard work from Eddie Jobson, together with Thompson's familiar percussive power, it has windswept atmosphere in abundance, but Chris Spedding's guitar solo, accomplished though it is, cannot compensate for the lack of Eno's sound manipulation.

Bitters End
(Ferry) 2:03

Shortly before leaving Roxy Music, Eno was still able to bamboozle passing journalists with enigmatic interpretations of Ferry's songs. "I suppose you could describe it [our music] as luxurious decadence. It upsets some people," he announced in *Sounds* in April 1973. "We wrote a song called *Bitter End* [sic] which is just about a cocktail, that's all. All we are saying is at least enjoy the luxury before it's too late."

Polished off alongside *Re-make/Re-model* in the band's final three-day stint at Command Studios, *Bitters End* would later be recorded for the BBC on 23 May. When the *Roxy Music* LP came out a month later, Ferry found himself trying to explain his motives to mystified album buyers in the pages of *Melody Maker*. "Only two songs on the album – *Would You Believe?* and *Bitters End* – really use elements of Fifties and Sixties music," he told Richard Williams. "And *Bitters End* is quite serious – there's the ambiguity of the doo-wopping singers in the background, which gives people a certain image, against the words, which are strange and not at all the kind of thing you'd usually find in that musical context."

While the musical backdrop is, as Ferry put it, a "sort of Inkspots, Platters thing," the lyric is a sustained purple passage that sounds far from serious: more like Noël Coward enunciating the self-important windiness of Prog Rock. Amusingly, Roxy's producer, Pete Sinfield, had been responsible for his fair share of the latter as lyricist for King Crimson. Here, Ferry employs his best supper-club tones in transmuting the gnomic occultism of Crimson into a ludicrous ode to over-indulgence in cocktails.

With Ferry's nonsense lyric taking in scraps of off-the-wall humour (the dilettante narrator coming to at cock-crow after a night of debauch and sparing a thought for the soon-to-be-slaughtered cockerel), it soon becomes clear that the narrator is drinking to forget. Mackay and Eno, meanwhile, can be heard happily doo-wopping away in the background as an ironic counterpoint to his drink-addled desolation.

Dispensing with guitar and drums, the soundstage is busy enough in their absence, with a rambling piano figure shadowed by the tuneful resonance of

Simpson's bass, a battery of castanets and other percussive devices suggesting the flutter of cocktail-shakers, and a honking sax sound introduced on Eno's tongue-in-cheek announcement of "bizarre…" "I can understand anybody hating the two verses at the beginning and the one at the end," Ferry conceded, "but I think the middle bit's good, especially the Earl Bostic saxophone … That's the whole album, really. A party-piece. Parti-coloured."

With a title seemingly cannibalised from the antithetical repertoires of Noël Coward and Bertolt Brecht (Coward: *Bitter-Sweet*, Brecht: *Happy End*), *Bitters End* would later find an echo on Side Two of the *Country Life* LP. And if it seems like a surprisingly lightweight conclusion to so revolutionary an album, at least it closes the circuit with a satisfying symmetry. As the *Re-make/Re-model* cocktail party re-emerges at the end, Ferry adopts his most portentous vibrato for a fantastically impudent envoi of "Should make the cognoscenti think…"

And so, of course, it did.

Three: *Part False Part True*

"We just want to get used to playing with each other, really. I mean, we rehearsed the album, recorded it, rehearsed the set, and went on the road and I still haven't been introduced to the drummer."

Phil Manzanera, quoted in *NME* 23 September 1972

Situation vacant

A s mixing got underway in the first half of April, the band members plunged into intensive rehearsals, at Jubilee Studios as well as Wandsworth's familiar Granada Bingo Hall. Also brought on board at this time was Mackay's university friend, Simon Puxley, who would handle the band's PR, become popularly known as 'Dr' Puxley and remain a trusted Ferry lieutenant for close to 30 years.

The band's anxieties were relieved on Tuesday 2 May with the long-awaited announcement from EG that Island Records had agreed to release the album. Despite the support of marketing men Tim Clark and Dave Betteridge, the opposition of the label's chief A&R man, Muff Winwood, had weighed heavily until label boss Chris Blackwell sanctioned the contract on seeing the pre-prepared album visuals.

With the relief of one set of anxieties, however, came another. Bill MacCormick, bass player with Manzanera's old band Quiet Sun, takes up the story: "One of the first breaks Roxy got, apart from a rather over-the-top review of their demos by Richard Williams of the *Melody Maker*, was at a big festival somewhere in Lincolnshire in May '72," he told Stephen Yarwood. "They'd recorded the first album and this was to be their first high-profile live appearance after the sessions, but with about a week to go [actually, more like a fortnight] bass player Graham Simpson had a nervous breakdown. Apparently they phoned me but I was in Paris with Matching Mole. That was that, I was in the wrong place at the wrong time, but who knows? With their track record with bass players I might have only lasted a couple of weeks."

The departure of Simpson marked the beginning of Roxy's "track record with bass players." Increasingly withdrawn, Simpson had become an adherent of Sufism, which eventually drove him to India and complete oblivion as far as rock music was concerned. Hindsight grants his photo in the *Roxy Music* album's gatefold a perhaps unwarranted significance; though fixed directly at the camera, the gaze nevertheless seems strangely remote, even vacant – and, of course, he has obviously resisted all appeals to drag himself up like the other members. (Even Thompson, never very enthusiastic in submitting to the prevailing dress code, sports a cartoon leopard epaulette, as, indeed, would Ferry at the band's Great Western Festival appearance.) When Simpson's withdrawal became literal – he began to fail to show up for rehearsals – Ferry bit the bullet and sacked him, leaving others to speculate on whether Simpson's apparent 'nervous breakdown' was brought on by a horror of the success which now seemed guaranteed.

With a BBC session at Kensington House booked for Tuesday 23 May, the search was on for a replacement. As we have seen, Bill MacCormick's commitment to Matching Mole made him miss the crucial phone call (presumably from Manzanera), after which Ferry's Gas Board friend, John Porter, was passed over too. An extremely fleeting appearance by Peter Paul was followed by the arrival of the Sinfield-recommended Rik Kenton. Born in Nottingham on 31 October 1948, Kenton was a veteran of such forgotten outfits as Woody Kern, Armada and the splendidly named Mouseproof, with whom he had made his professional debut at David Bowie's Beckenham Arts Lab in 1969. He was a friend of former King Crimson percussionist Mike Giles, and through him Pete Sinfield.

His initial enthusiasm for Roxy makes mournful reading given that he, too, would be judged surplus to requirements within eight months. "I'd heard the album," he told Richard Williams, "and I liked Bryan's songs and voice, and Andy's oboe-playing. So when Graham left, I joined ... From the outside it may not look like a musicians' band, but it is," he remarked. "In Bryan's voice we've got something that's identifiable straight away – so we haven't got to keep the music straight in order to retain a 'Roxy sound'. That's one of the reasons why there's plenty of room for the band to grow. It's very exciting and stimulating."

The speed with which Kenton had to learn his parts must certainly have been stimulating; only a matter of days elapsed between the band's latest *Sounds of the Seventies* stint (in which *Bitters End* was given an extremely rare live outing alongside *2 H.B.*, *Chance Meeting* and *Ladytron*) and their slot at the Great Western Festival on Saturday 27 May, which qualified as their first 'official' public appearance.

Staged at Tupholme Hall outside Bardney by Welsh film star Stanley Baker, film producer Michael Deeley and British Board of Film Censors president Lord Harlech, the event was a predictably mud-soaked one. The presenter was John Peel, Bob Harris having handled the Friday roster. Also advertised for the main stage that day were Nazareth, Locomotive GT, Ry Cooder, Head Hands and Feet, Steve Goodman, The Persuasions, Stone the Crows (with vocalist Maggie Bell), Helen Reddy, The Strawbs and The Faces. Roxy's set seems to have made more of an impact on the music press than the benighted rock fans out front, with *Disc* observing that "Despite their outward flamboyance, it was a quietish and reasonably self-conscious set – yet there was something lurking behind it all that suggests we might do well to keep tabs on this band."

The best 'first'

In June, Roxy were committed to film for the first time. As well as performing *Re-make/Re-model* for student filmmakers at Antony Price's alma mater, the Royal College of Art, they also made their television debut on the BBC's flagship rock showcase, *The Old Grey Whistle Test*. Broadcast on Tuesday 20 June – starting at 10.00 pm, it was the last programme in the BBC2 schedule that evening – Roxy shared the bill with The Sutherland Brothers; their eerie performance of *Ladytron* under a multi-faceted glitter ball has since been preserved on the 2003 DVD release *The Old Grey Whistle Test Volume 2*.

The presenter was none other than Richard Williams, who took the opportunity to give the band a major send-off in the normally staid pages of *Radio Times*. "Quite simply," he wrote, "Roxy Music are destined to save the world, through the articulate, atmospheric songs of Bryan Ferry, the lunatic pre-recorded tapes of Captain Eno, the honky sax of Andy McKay [sic], their sparkling lamé uniforms, etc... and they're also on Peel's *Sounds of the 70s* on Friday (10.00 pm Radio 1)." This was the session Roxy had recorded back on 23 May, the programme being trailed as "two hours of progressive pop, with JSD Band, Roxy Music, Jellybread, [and] Ralph McTell."

Friday 23 June was also significant in that it was the day on which the band's debut album was finally released. "In my opinion, Roxy Music – the newest band in the EG stable and by far the best – are a potentially enormous musical influence," raved Tony Tyler in the *NME*. "They've still to develop but their ideas are already well-formed and come together very nicely, thank you, on this excellent first album." Tyler's final observation could hardly have been bettered by Dr Puxley himself: "Altogether, this is the finest album I've heard this year and the best 'first' I can EVER remember."

In *Melody Maker*, the indefatigable Richard Williams was equally complimentary: "Roxy Music is a concept which not everyone will latch onto at first, but which is as rich in performance as in promise, carefully calculated yet simply oodles of fun. Despite their general Fifties orientation, the result is thoroughly contemporary, and they use their awareness of earlier modes to inform and reinforce their own unique ideas." *Disc*'s Caroline Boucher wasn't too keen on the album's more electronic cuts (what she called the "hoot-at-intervals numbers") but concluded with: "I still reckon this band will be a monster."

Other reviewers ranged from disappointed to merely gobsmacked. Floundering in a morass of comparisons, the *Record Mirror* critic finally resorted to: "What I'm really trying to say is that they're indescribable." In the *Evening Standard*, however, Andrew Bailey claimed that "the LP is rather disappointing. After hearing so much about the group's exciting concept of combining electronics with rock'n' roll, it was a let-down to discover that they are little more than average in the conventional areas, and not all that advanced in the electronic department either."

As well as its alluringly laminated cover art and band photos, the album came complete with ludicrous liner notes by Puxley; consciously ludicrous, but no less unreadable for that. According to Puxley, Roxy's sound constituted "rock'n'roll juggernauted into demonic electronic supersonic mo-mo-momentum – by a panoplic machine-pile, hifi or scifi who can tell? ... mixed/fixed/sifted/lifted to driving, high-flying chunks & vortices of pure electronic wow – gyrating, parabolic, tantalising (oh notes could not spell out the score)." AAnd much more in similar faux-Beat vein. Just as the cover shot carried kitsch echoes of antiquated jazz LPs, so Puxley sought to put a 1970s spin on the gushing sleeve notes of a bygone age. Though delivered tongue-in-cheek, his style of art-school hyperbole no doubt contributed mightily to the suspicions of Roxy's denim-clad nay-sayers.

They have been to the moon

As the album entered the charts, there was precious little art-school hyperbole in Mackay's down-to-earth observation that "My mum sells records for us all the time by talking to people about the group. Really – she's always going into the newsagent and they'll tell her if there's a story about us in the papers that week." Though no longer driving around in Mackay senior's van, the band had already gone back on the road, starting on Wednesday 21 June at Sheffield and, in the weekend immediately following the album's release, playing at the University of East Anglia on the 24th and supporting David Bowie at the Croydon Greyhound on the 25th.

Roxy were so unclassifiable that they began to experience a 'strange bedfellows' problem that would reach critical mass on their US tour come December. "We've often played with bands that have a very specific appeal, like Quintessence or Rory Gallagher," Ferry told Steve Peacock at the end of June, "and their audience come prepared for that sort of music, so to have us as a filler is a bit strange. We don't keep a coherent mood long enough for the audience to get into any particular frame of mind." Indeed, at one gig impatient fans of guitar hero Rory Gallagher reportedly regaled Roxy with a shouted fusillade of "Poofters!"

This kind of response typified the profound resentment and incomprehension Roxy aroused in much of the rock community. Who were these gilded upstarts? And, more to the point, who the hell did they think they were? They'd apparently come out of nowhere, backed by shadowy public school types and without having 'paid their dues' with year on year spent on the club and college treadmill. Yet they'd become superstars over night. Their peacock plumage, meanwhile, reeked of a cynical 'style over content' masterplan, a mere spangled smokescreen to disguise instrumental skills that were no more than competent. 'Hype' was the hated hippie buzz-word, just as 'sell-out' would be to a later generation.

On top of all this, Roxy's showbiz playfulness, in their music as well as their presentation, was anathema to the more self-important rock fundamentalists, for whom 'irony' was a dirty word – possibly, in fact, an unknown quantity – and 'sincerity' was the only acceptable artistic criterion. "It seems impossible to believe now," Richard Williams commented ten years later, "but there was a really strong feeling about this. If you'd polled the music business and asked 'Should this band be a success?', 99 per cent would have said, 'No, they should be liquidated tomorrow.' They were really hated because they hadn't been like Hawkwind or Family, slogging away at the college circuit."

The irritation only increased with some of the prestigious showcases the band were beginning to enjoy. Dates at Walbrook College and Lancaster preceded a major support slot at Wembley's Empire Pool on Friday 30 June. The J Geils Band having pulled out at the last minute, Roxy found themselves opening for the outrageous US import Alice Cooper in all his self-guillotining pomp. In the *Guardian*, Robin Denselow dismissed the attention-seeking headliner in favour of "an outstanding new British band, Roxy Music ... playing the oddest, most exciting music I've heard in months."

Though facetious, the programme notes for Roxy's Alice Cooper appearance offer as cogent a sketch as any of the band's futuristic impact in summer 1972, complete with a joky reference to Manzanera having replaced former Nice guitarist David O'List. Referring to Eno, crystal-gazing clairvoyant Mme Acacia observed that "His face is clear. He has long flowing silver hair. The faces of the other young men are distinct also. They are called Bryan Ferry and Andy Mackay. They are both very tall and thin – perhaps eight foot tall. They have been to the moon. The faces of the other three are less clear: they merge with the features of ... No, this one is distinct. They call him Paul Thompson. He is only three foot tall, unless ... Yes, he is seated. He is seated before a drum kit. The young man with the guitar and the enormous crystal eyes comes from another land, or perhaps another planet. He is called Phil Manzanera. He is not Nice ... Now I see them all together. They have a name. They are called Roxy Music."

Apart from Thompson and Kenton, the touring experience was a quite new one for the band; "just going up and down the M1 for the first time is very enjoyable," Ferry observed. "It's strange to do something and be cheered for it, when you're used to a cool reaction to anything that you've ever done before [ie, ceramics exhibitions]. It's much nicer this way, and the audiences really do seem to appreciate the fact that we perform, rather than just play." Four years later, Mackay would point out that "It was exciting for all of us because it was all so new. We were also proving to be a great success. We had hit records, and it didn't matter that we were still losing money like mad, or that we were, in effect, being paid only about £15 or £20 a week ... That's all we took then, because we knew we were running up big debts and we didn't want them to get any bigger."

After the Alice Cooper event, there were humbler engagements at Halifax, Wood Green, Leytonstone and Chippenham. Then on Sunday 11 July a so-called 'Electric Mecca' multi-band extravaganza at the Bristol Locarno saw Roxy second-billed to Hawkwind. The next day, they re-entered Piccadilly's Command Studios to cut their first single.

* * *

Virginia Plain
(Ferry) 2:58

Along with its B-side, *The Numberer*, Roxy's first single was recorded at Command Studios from 10 to 12 July, Pete Sinfield again in place as producer. In conversation with Richard Williams on Wednesday the 19th, a somewhat harried Ferry passed off *Virginia Plain* as merely "a bid to get on *Top of the Pops*, actually – just a way to get to meet Pan's People," as well as confiding his fear that "It could be much stronger. We did a live version for the BBC yesterday which was full of power – thick and rough. But the record has some fine bits. Oh, I don't know what to think of things any more."

The "fine bits" referred to by Ferry were crowded into a little under three minutes and constitute a veritable torrent of verbal and instrumental invention. Ferry's gibberish lyric, a riot of unrelated thoughts and ideas in classic Pop Art mould, seemed nevertheless to follow some unguessable internal logic. The soundstage, meanwhile, resounded to a dissonant clash of instruments unlike anything previously heard in what was then still known as 'the Hit Parade'.

On top of all this, there was the band's genuinely seismic debut performance on the BBC's Thursday night treat for teens, *Top of the Pops*. In retrospect, the spectacle seems almost comic: pasty-faced hippie chicks in pastel colours, bespectacled boys in brown tank-tops, all of them shuffling uncertainly to the racket whipped up by the strangest-looking combo the programme had ever encountered. Manzanera in spangled red, eerily unidentifiable in his trademark 'Human Fly' sunglasses. Mackay in lurid green and yellow, hair whipped up into strange arabesques, Ming the Merciless with a cor anglais. Ferry in his best Elvis in Transylvania mode, grimacing suggestively from behind an upright piano with, strangely, a blue-check tablecloth tacked on to its back. Another homely touch: Thompson lurking behind his drum kit, looking less than comfortable in leopard-skin. And, contrary to popular legend, Eno is more than just a befeathered hand manipulating the joystick of his cumbersome VCS3. That kind of egregious oversight on the part of the BBC's cameramen would be reserved for *The Old Grey Whistle Test*; here he's clearly visible, hunched vulture-like over his banks of electronics.

The triumph of *Virginia Plain* was its effortless expansion of Roxy's target demographic; with a hit album to their name and a growing army of earnest musos rallying to their cause, Roxy proceeded to capture the teeny-bopper audience in one dazzling manoeuvre, doing so, what's more, with a track noticeably denuded of any of the conventional verse/chorus structures deemed indispensable to the Top 40. As Ferry himself put it: "We want to get through to different people on different levels, so that whereas one person, maybe a Hampstead intellectual, would say: 'How camp!', a kid would respond by saying 'That's weird!' The kid would probably get the bigger kick."

The track was also a dazzling vindication of Ferry's determination to cut a stand-alone single in the first place, a determination that flew in the face of prevailing rock snobbery regarding the 45rpm format. "I think a single is necessary – after all, most of the best things in pop have been done in that medium," he claimed. "We've always wanted to make them, and I don't want people to think it's a cop-out – that's silly." Even here, though, Roxy couldn't resist topping and tailing the track with a couple of tricks calculated to give the average disc jockey a minor cardiac arrest, first via a half-heard piano and guitar opening, then by a teasingly unexpected a capella ending. As John Peel put it in *Disc*: "It starts very quietly, then seconds after you've turned up the volume, comes tearing in like the terror of the Rue Morgue. It ends very precipitously, and has caught me unawares both times I've played it on the air so far."

Virginia Plain teems with detail, from the great looping arcs of Eno's synth to the primitive clang of Manzanera's guitar, from the metronomic throb of Rik Kenton's bass to the propulsive St Vitus Dance gibber of Mackay's oboe. There are subliminal electronic hand-claps in the closing section and, before that, a revving motorbike no less, presumably thrown in as a back-handed compliment to 'Shadow' Morton, the Svengali producer behind The Shangri-Las' 1964 hit *Leader of the Pack*. This last was achieved by the cumbersome expedient of sending a suitably mic'd-up roadie scooting up and down Piccadilly.

And in the middle there's a spikey Manzanera guitar break, assailed by the disorientating foghorn interpolations of Mackay's saxophone, that was memorably apostrophised 25 years later by Will Sergeant of Echo & the Bunnymen. "Phil Manzanera definitely influenced my playing," he told *Uncut*'s Dave Simpson. "Those mad swishy chords he used to do, like [on] *Virginia Plain*. Daaaa-daaanng! Funnily enough, in those weird enveloping shades he used to look like a bluebottle, and the guitar sound was like a bluebottle in a biscuit tin. So maybe there was some subtle conceptual thing going on even there, that he didn't let on."

What Manzanera did let on, even while the song was still in the charts, was the totally improvisatory nature of his contribution. "Frequently the group go into the studio to do a new number without telling me how it goes so that I'll play with the spontaneity they like," he told Ian MacDonald. "Like for *Virginia Plain* I got into the studio and set up my amp and the time was getting closer and closer to my solo and I still hadn't the faintest idea what I was going to do. And the break arrived and I just went blam! I mean, I could've put my fingers anywhere. I've since tried to reproduce that solo and I can't work it out at all."

For Ferry, *Virginia Plain* was an unexpected outcrop of a canvas of the same name he had painted during his first year at art school back in 1964. The picture, "a sort of throwaway watercolour," showed a desert expanse punctuated by a monolithic cigarette packet, itself adorned by a glamorous girl. Typical of Ferry's fondness for ever-multiplying puns, 'Virginia Plain' therefore connoted all three – desert, cigarette brand and, of course, girl. "I don't know why I remembered the painting so clearly," he told Caroline Boucher. "It was a part of the whole early Warhol movement of the time – of wanting to have a huge studio and live in New York. The face of the girl in my painting was based on one of Warhol's stars at the time, Baby Jane Holzer – she's referred to in the lyrics."

The prodigiously beehived Holzer, still only 31 when Ferry immortalised her in song, had been a key figure in Warhol's Factory set, appearing for him in experimental films like *Soap Opera* and *Batman Dracula*. In *Virginia Plain*, she's just one of numerous scattershot references to what Ferry called the "whole American Dream thing." Though the opening lines refer directly to recent wrangles with Roxy's legal representatives, Ferry leaps from them directly to namechecking Robert E Lee, hero of the South in the American Civil War and himself a Virginian. And if that reference reminded contemporary listeners of NBC's long-running TV series *The Virginian*, cancelled by 1972 but still omnipresent on British screens, then so much the better.

Elsewhere, he conjures up American movies both new (Peter Bogdanovich's bitter-sweet 1971 drama *The Last Picture Show*) and old (Thornton Freeland's *Flying Down to Rio*, the 1933 debut of Fred Astaire and Ginger Rogers), together with a brief nod to James Dean on the line "teenage rebel of the week." And the Americanisms proliferate, ranging from Havana and rollercoasters to Acapulco and plane rides; there's even a namecheck for the ostentatious Studebaker Ferry had owned back in Newcastle. "It's about driving down the freeway," he elucidated, "passing cigarette ads on vast billboards. And Las Vegas casinos..." With Ferry's disconnected Pop Art epigrams given an extra kick by his bravura rendition of them, *Virginia Plain* is a Technicolor splurge of Americana later refashioned in sprawling CinemaScope for the *Country Life* track *Prairie Rose*, but without the teeming fecundity of Ferry's stream-of-consciousness lyric.

One of the beauties of the song is the tension between its aspirational origins – recalling the time eight years before when "I was up in Newcastle, living with a guy who'd helped Warhol to make the Marilyn [Monroe] silkscreens ... living up there yet constantly thinking about Warhol's Factory and Baby Jane Holzer" – and its playful mood of nose-thumbing arrogance now that those aspirations were close to being realised. (Ironically subverting industry scepticism regarding Roxy's meteoric rise, Ferry refers early on to the band's lengthy attempts to make an impression on their peers.) In tribute to its origins, Ferry considered preparing a new version of his 1964 painting for use on the single's picture sleeve, but pressure of time precluded this; probably also the fact that, by 1972, picture sleeves were hardly ever bothered with by record companies.

On 18 July, less than a week after recording had been completed, Roxy went to the BBC's Maida Vale studio to tape two songs for John Peel's *Sounds of the Seventies*; one was an 11-minute version of *If There is Something*, the other a *Virginia Plain* lasting a good minute longer than its vinyl counterpart. This was now set for release on 28 July but mixing problems delayed it by a week. The first version lacked the motorbike sound effect, while the third and final one was prepared by Sinfield alone, the band having returned to their erratic gigging schedule, starting at Dunstable Civic Hall on Saturday the 22nd.

"Under normal circumstances I run and hide when someone tells me about a group that is 'intelligent'," commented John Peel in the singles review column of *Disc*. "However, Roxy rock like hell on this one; Bryan Ferry sings like some crazy, ruined angel, and the record is full of twists and turns that'll rip the top off your fool head."

With endorsements like this, by 15 August *Virginia Plain* had entered a singles chart dominated by Alice Cooper's *School's Out*; from its starting point of number 46, it rose rapidly to 26, 18, eight and finally – on 12 September – number four. "I thought maybe it would have got to 19 or something," Ferry admitted soon afterwards. "I was quite surprised it went as high as it did."

After a further fortnight in the Top Ten, the single finally left the chart on 31 October, having enjoyed a run of 12 weeks. In the meantime, it had seen four further Number Ones come and go – Rod Stewart's *You Wear It Well*, Slade's *Mama Weer All Crazee Now*, the David Cassidy ballad *How Can I Be Sure?* and Lieutenant Pigeon's freak novelty item *Mouldy Old Dough*. Hardly surprising that, on 9 October, *Guardian* critic Robin Denselow should refer to "that moribund institution, the Top Ten" while simultaneously nominating *Virginia Plain* as "the best single I can remember since The Who's *I can see for miles.*"

In 1977, with EG's catalogue by then transferred from Island to Polydor, *Virginia Plain* was reissued as a double A-side with a remixed version of *Pyjamarama*. The idea was to boost the newly released *Greatest Hits* album, and the strategy worked a treat. The single entered the chart at number 29 on 18 October, reaching a high of 11 three weeks later and leaving the chart on 22 November. At its peak, it was positioned just ahead of The Bee Gees' *How Deep is Your Love* and (bizarre pairing) The Sex Pistols' *Holidays in the Sun*. In a chart landscape also featuring Elvis Costello's *Watching the Detectives*, The Boomtown Rats' *Mary of the Fourth Form* and The Stranglers' *No More Heroes*, it sounded as crazed and prescient as ever.

Two years later, Spizzenergi (nom de plume for Kenneth Spiers, also operative under such variant monikers as The Spizzles, Athletico Spizz 80 and Spizz Oil) provided a rare punk rock acknowledgment of Roxy's enduring influence by attaching a *Virginia Plain* cover as B-side to Spiers' *Soldier Soldier* single. The track resurfaced on a 2002 Cherry Red compilation of Spiers' finest moments, named after his most famous single, *Where's Captain Kirk?* Another version, performed live by The Metal Gurus (aka Goth band The Mission in T.Rex reference mode), appeared on their 1990 10" EP *Deliverance*. Three years after that, prolific production outfit Stock Aitken Waterman produced a *Virginia Plain* of their own. The Svengalis behind monster 1980s hits for Sinitta, Pepsi & Shirlie, Mel & Kim, Rick Astley and Kylie Minogue, among others, they made Slamm's version of the song available in four different mixes, the longest of which (the 'La Camorra Headless Pigeon Mix') clocked in at nearly eight minutes. The single reached number 60 in the UK charts.

Back in 1972, the belated US issue of the *Roxy Music* album had interpolated *Virginia Plain* into the track listing between *If There is Something* and *2 H.B.*; though the song sits decidedly uneasily in this context, it was an arrangement followed years later by the UK CD release.

The Numberer
(Mackay) 3:40

Recorded in the same three-day stint that threw up *Virginia Plain*, this was the first instance of Ferry delegating songwriting duties to other members of the band, albeit confining them for the time being to B-side status. The working title for this one, *First Kiss*, gives a better picture of the kind of 'teen angst' 1950s instrumental sound Mackay was aiming at, though its gnomic substitute, *The Numberer*, better fits the characteristically mutated, Roxyfied version of it that resulted.

Writing of his 1974 solo LP *In Search of Eddie Riff*, Mackay observed that in the course of the album "I acknowledged my love of classical music, Motown, Fifties rock and roll instrumentals, film music, electronic effects and, partly for my wife Jane whom I had recently married, Country & Western." Acting as an *Eddie Riff* trial run, in the space of *The Numberer*'s three-and-a-half minutes Mackay packs in skewed fragments of all these, with the possible exception of country and with the movie soundtrack leanings reserved for further development on his next

B-side. In the meantime, he alternates smoochy supper-club sax with the kind of 'dirty' bray characteristic of rockers like Jackie Kelso, sax man with the 'Stone Age' instrumental combo The Piltdown Men.

The track opens to a muted Manzanera motif and showcases Thompson at his most fruitily inventive, Eno meanwhile sending chromatic synth twiddles zinging around the mix in a foretaste of the Morse Code signal he would later apply to *Pyjamarama*. Mackay's sax shifts from an infectious honking riff to a romantically phrased interlude in which he audibly loses his thread; modulating back to a strident clarion call, he's joined by a whimsical Manzanera solo and an eleventh hour intervention from Ferry's squalling harmonica. Kenton's bass improvises tunefully under all this, and the whole thing ends on a sustained caterwauling from all concerned, Thompson extemporising wildly and Mackay seemingly spluttering for air.

Though recorded several months after the debut album, the band sound here exactly the way they look on the album's inner sleeve, a look memorably summarised by Angus McKinnon as "Johnny and the Hurricanes in claustrophobic dereliction, marooned somewhere beyond Andromeda." And in its wholly surprising shifts of mood, *The Numberer* anticipates the more airbrushed sound of *Pyramid of Night* (the epic centrepiece of the *Eddie Riff* album), as well as equalling in eclectic unpredictability anything Ferry had concocted up to this point.

That unpredictability was in part a product of the riotous atmosphere in which the track was recorded. "That was an amazing session," Manzanera claimed in September. "We were all capering around in there during *The Numberer*, shouting silly things which eventually had to be edited out." Though it's a shame that the shouted ribaldries remembered by Manzanera failed to make it onto the final cut, *The Numberer* remains a stand-alone moment of improvisatory weirdness unlike anything else in the Roxy oeuvre.

The track's original title, *First Kiss*, was later appropriated for the most comprehensive of the several bootleg collections of Roxy's 1972-3 BBC Radio sessions. Others turned to album tracks (*Re-make/Re-model*, *Chance Meeting*, *Bitter-Sweet*) and even refrains (*When We Were Young*) for their collective titles. Still others went out on a limb of their own devising, notably the mind-boggling *Absinthe Makes the Heart Grow Fondle*.

*   *   *

Here's one for all you sailors

Straight after recording *Virginia Plain*, Roxy resumed their gigging schedule, encompassing Salisbury, Northwich, Dunstable, Bexley, Hornchurch, Liverpool and Abbey Wood in the fortnight beginning Friday 14 July. As already noted, on Tuesday the 18th there was a spell at Maida Vale for *Sounds of the Seventies*, *If There is Something* and the freshly minted *Virginia Plain* the chosen tracks and Tuesday 1 August the eventual transmission date.

Saturday 29 July, meanwhile, had been given over to a major showcase at a 'Special Summer Garden Party at the Crystal Palace Bowl'. The fourth such

Crystal Palace event, Roxy went on first, shortly before mid-day, as part of a bill comprising Arlo Guthrie, Osibisa, Stone the Crows, Edgar Winter and Loggins & Messina. (Compere: Pete Drummond; tickets: £1.25 in advance, £1.50 on the door.) This latest batch of gigs concluded at Stoke on Monday 31 July, with the Crystal Palace performance receiving a notice from the *Croydon Advertiser*'s Barry Shinfield that was typical of the suspicion Roxy aroused: "Dressed like Sha-Na-Na," sniffed Shinfield, "they put plenty of embellished icing on the cake of their music, but the centre is sterile."

The success of *Virginia Plain* inevitably pushed the *Roxy Music* album further up the charts; having arrived on 29 July, it eventually hit number ten, only departing in November after a run of 16 weeks. Ferry, meanwhile, moved out of Mackay's Battersea home to take up residence in Redcliffe Gardens, a chic address poised between Earl's Court and the King's Road. Much later, he would pass the flat on to Thompson, but in the meantime he sounded bullish when interviewed by Caroline Boucher early in September. "Four months on we're a lot wiser," he told her. "One feels a bit smug, although I shouldn't say so I suppose, because people said to us, 'Oh, you can't do that, it takes three years to get a band off the ground,' but we've done it. It proves that record companies haven't a clue. It's like everything we wanted to happen has happened right down to the month."

Ferry was fresh from Roxy's most prestigious showcase yet, the band having played their final support gig on the weekend of 19 and 20 August to David Bowie at Finsbury Park's Rainbow Theatre. This was the apotheosis of Bowie's *Ziggy Stardust* tour, with his mentor Lindsay Kemp bringing his mime troupe to bear on what Charles Shaar Murray would call "the most consciously theatrical rock show ever staged." Roxy had to pull out all the stops in order to compete, and they succeeded; in the estimate of *Record Mirror*, "Roxy Music no longer deserve to be a support band, and Bowie is one of the few performers who can follow them."

The *NME*'s facetious gig guide adopted a limp-wristed tone in previewing the concerts: "Hello handsome, my name's David and I'm going to be at the Rainbow in lovely North London with The Spiders from Mars, some very pretty people called Roxy Music and a gorgeous butch blues singer called Lloyd Watson this Saturday and Sunday. It would be just too, too divine if you could make it there – and if you can't make it there just be there hmmm? It's going to be the most exquisite concert of the year. I wish Lou would come." Lou Reed did indeed turn up, though Ferry, for one, was too overawed to talk to him.

According to a correspondent for *Gay News*, Ferry acknowledged the triple-strength array of campness represented by Bowie, Kemp and Roxy by prefacing *Sea Breezes* with "Here's one for all you sailors." Roxy Music did indeed qualify as "very pretty people," with all the band members being unusually dishy in their different ways. Even Bowie was startled by them, particularly Eno, with whom he would collaborate some four years' hence: "The first time I met him I thought he looked more effeminate than I did. Really quite a shock."

In fact, Eno's experimentation with cross-gender clothing was nothing new, stretching back to his time at art school. "For me there was no sexual aspect to it – I was not gay or anything, and never have been – but I just wanted to look great," he remembered. "And looking great meant dressing as a woman! Or at least as some kind of weird new hybrid." Though not responsible for Eno's stage clothing, Antony Price was nevertheless a keen observer of the impact the band made, telling Rob Chapman in 1995 that "They were all raving heteros, of course. But Bryan had a big gay following from very early on. Andy too. He looked like a male model."

Roxy's air of sexual ambivalence, though playfully deployed, was enough to complete their demonisation in a male-dominated rock culture still caught up in the denim-clad tailwinds of hippiedom; those Rory Gallagher fans who had yelled "Poofters!" at them were by no means alone.

The Roxy member least likely to be mistaken for a "poofter" was Paul Thompson, whose approach was always uncompromisingly down to earth. Known to fans, quite rightly, as 'The Great Paul Thompson', he recalled in 2001 that "I was only 21 or 22 and success was pretty quick. I knew I had arrived when I came back to Tyneside. I went to see a mate of mine playing at a social club in Gateshead. I didn't have my club card and I expected a grilling from the door-man. But he looked at me and said: 'It's all right son, you can go in. I saw you on *Top of the Pops!*'"

Dodgy tonsils

The contempt in which Roxy were still held by 'serious' musos wasn't alleviated by dilettante pronouncements like these, delivered by Manzanera in September: "Well, we're not solemn about our music. We like to give people a good show, dress up and that sort of thing. Have a laugh." (Have a laugh? Shock! Horror!) "Towards the end of our last tour, things were getting very silly indeed. Eno had a giant pair of plastic knives and forks and was playing the synthesiser as if it were a plate of biriani or something. But it's natural and, although as a group we tend to laugh a lot, we don't believe in hammering phoney humour. In fact we play rather badly if we're giggling. So, if everybody's in high spirits in the dressing room we usually have to insult each other before we go on stage. All our best gigs have happened when we've been in filthy tempers."

In the aftermath of their Rainbow engagements, Ferry seemed unaffected by Bowie's ardent championing of the band, telling *Sounds*' Steve Peacock that Bowie's Kemp-devised show was "all sort of 1964/65 pseudo avant-garde American Happening, eight years out of date and rather embarrassing." He would also observe that "Bowie seemed to push all the band back; props in their little boxes" – an ironic complaint given future Roxy developments. Mackay, however, made a similar point in *Music Scene*: "His records are very good, some of his music is very strong, a lot of it comes from his band. I just think he uses people as a buffer. Although the theatricality is good, it's almost too theatrical ... He is an excellent saxophone player. A frustrated serious artist." It was left to Manzanera to extol Bowie from the pages of the *NME*: "David Bowie's songs I like a lot," he claimed. "His management were rather disagreeable at the Rainbow, but Bowie and the Spiders are very nice people and I enjoyed what they were doing."

Another BBC engagement followed, this time a Radio 1 *In Concert* special broadcast on Saturday 16 September, with Bob Harris introducing a live set comprising *The Bob (Medley)*, *The Bogus Man Part II*, *Sea Breezes*, *Virginia Plain*, *Chance Meeting* and *Re-Make/Re-Model*. Also on the bill were Irish folk-rock duo Leo O'Kelly and Sonny Condell, collectively known as Tir Na Nog. *The Bogus Man Part II*, which Harris announced as being played live for the first time, would be renamed *Grey Lagoons* on Roxy's second album.

But, if Puxley's florid account is to be believed, Roxy's triumphal progress, and Ferry's self-congratulatory tone in interviews, concealed a brief bout of 'what to do next' depression: "Bryan would sit silently, gazing at the silent TV image, brooding, oppressed in spite of the last year's dreamlike success." Perhaps as a result, Ferry suddenly lost his voice, his always dodgy tonsils being identified as the culprit and having to be summarily removed. It had been hoped that the operation could be delayed until January 1973, but in the event it caused the cancellation of 25 gigs and a loss of some £10,000.

Manzanera put a brave face on the situation, calling it "our summer recess." "We're going to spend the next four to five weeks playing about with the ideas the rest of us have got, irrespective of whether we eventually utilise them or not," he claimed. Ferry, too, appeared raffishly unconcerned when addressing Ian MacDonald from his hospital bed in October: "As soon as these crooning tubes are repaired, we're all going to be working like mad, putting together a short set of fast numbers for the States in December. It's a drag about this throat, because I'd like to have gone and done something in Holland and Belgium for a month. I see the album and the single are doing well over there. And I imagine we might score heavily in Paris, there being a certain chicness in our ensemble which the French would appreciate."

On tour and on TV

Roxy's ensemble chicness was visited instead upon Weston-super-Mare, where the band's delayed autumn tour began on Saturday 28 October. After this they trooped through highly successful dates at Reading, Chatham, Rugby, Coventry, Birmingham, Liverpool, Manchester, Sheffield, Newcastle, Redcar, Nottingham, Leicester (sharing the bill on this occasion with Fleetwood Mac), Croydon, Guildford, York and Hanley. The Croydon date transmuted into two shows on the same night thanks to an unprecedented demand for tickets. Yet, despite the band's meteoric success, Ferry was still too unsure of himself to come front and centre, instead singing from his keyboard stage left, with Eno balancing him stage right and Mackay and Manzanera doing their chintzily co-ordinated stuff stage centre. All this would change, however, in the new year.

As already noted, the band's autumn dates commenced with a ten-minute-plus excerpt from Johann Pachelbel's Canon in D Major, an Eno favourite. Eno himself seemed increasingly to be a fan favourite, as Richard Williams' report from Manchester's Hardrock venue makes clear: "Shadowy figures took the stage, the greatest response being reserved for the lad with the dye in his hair and a twinkle in his fingers. 'Eno! Eno!' they roared. And the odd thing is that the loudest roarers were thickset bearded lads who looked as though they'd just come from thrashing the All Blacks on the rugby field. To see them yelling for this slight blond youth was, indeed, strange."

In the midst of their first headlining tour, the band recorded another Peel session on Monday 6 November, the selected tracks – *The Bob (Medley)* plus the as-yet-unrecorded *For Your Pleasure* and *The Bogus Man Part II* – going out three days later. The final tour date was at Lancaster University on Friday the 24th, with an immediate follow-up the next day in the shape of BBC2's arts showcase *Full House*. This "live entertainment for Saturday" took the form of a TV magazine programme lasting a bum-numbing two hours plus. The live experience, to judge from the surviving tapes, seems to have been particularly daunting for actor Joe Melia, who came to life when he got to perform in specially devised sketches but had trouble in the unaccustomed role of arts presenter.

Following a talking-head comic monologue from *Monty Python* star Eric Idle, Roxy played a truncated version of *Re-make/Re-model* over the opening credits, after which an hour elapsed devoted to Australian artist Sidney Nolan, the London Saxophone Quartet playing Jean Françaix's *Petit Quatuor*, and a Pinteresque playlet by ace TV dramatist John Bowen with former Rank film star Michael Craig heading the cast. When the time finally came for Roxy to do their set, Melia – apparently having swallowed Dr Puxley's PR promptings wholesale – came out with a bizarrely self-reflexive introduction that's worth reproducing in full for its garbled account of the kind of nostalgic associations Roxy were trading in.

"In the background you hear some very strange sounds," he began, referring to various space-age Eno noodlings. "I wonder what the word 'Roxy' means to you, at home or in the studio. When I was at school we had a cinema called The Roxy. I don't know if it's still there in Leicester; it may have been pulled down. And I remember very well in the '40s going to the movies every Saturday night, packed up to the ceiling – those old cinemas with Egyptian façades and curly columns, all kinds of glamour. Roxy is a good name for a pop group, especially a pop group which has some roots in nostalgia and mixes its styles. We have Roxy Music in the studio tonight, six of them. Bryan Ferris writes and sings most of the numbers. [An affronted spot of feedback is unleashed in response to this gaffe.] They're going to do three numbers straight off for us. The first is called *For You Pleasure* [sic], the second is – what is it called? *Try-Out Girl* or something like that. And the third one is *Bogus Man Number II*. Ladies and gentlemen: Roxy Music!"

Roxy's 12-minute set moved from a rather tentative preview of *For Your Pleasure* (ghostly "ta-ra's" supplied by Mackay and Kenton) through a blazing version of *Ladytron* (not, as Melia surmised, *Try-Out Girl*) to a slick run-through of what would later stand revealed as *Grey Lagoons*. Ferry was resplendent in matador glam, Mackay in what looked like a green romper suit, and Manzanera in trademark Venezuelan duds. Strangely, Eno was barely visible at all, though a silver lamé shimmer was occasionally discernible stage right. (Contrary to received opinion, it was on this TV show and *The Old Grey Whistle Test* – not *Top of the Pops* – in which Eno, so prominent on stage, was virtually ignored by the BBC cameramen.) Even when their set was over, Roxy were not forgotten; US artist Robert Cottingham showed off a painting of an LA cinema frontage and Melia observed: "Interestingly, it's called Roxy, in unconscious homage to our group tonight."

This engagement was an important one, revealing Roxy to a (presumably gob-smacked) television audience somewhat wider than that of *The Old Grey Whistle Test* as well as fostering interest in their current tour dates, not to mention the still-selling *Roxy Music* album. The *Ladytron* performance here was subsequently featured in the *Total Recall* video compendium (though with Mackay's mesmerising oboe prologue inexplicably chopped off), while in 2001 the nascent *Grey Lagoons* was repeated on *TOTP2* in anticipation of Roxy's reunion dates.

Strange bedfellows

By Wednesday 6 December, the band were in New York for a press reception organised by their US record label, Warner Bros. The ensuing US tour started (by all accounts disastrously) at Athens, Ohio the following day, after which it was straight back to New York on the 8th for another gig supporting Jethro Tull, this time at Madison Square Garden. They then visited Chattanooga, Charleston, Philadelphia and Detroit prior to a five-day spell in California, comprising two nights in Los Angeles, one each at Fresno and Bakersville, then a return trip to LA for a performance at the Whiskey a Go Go.

The run-up to Christmas featured two nights in Milwaukee and two in San Francisco, then the band were in Florida for appearances at Tampa and the Miami Speedway. 1972 wound up with dates in Charlotte, Fayette, Augusta, and, on New Year's Eve, Chicago's Kinetic Playground. "I remember sitting next to Bryan on a Roxy Music tour when our plane was struck by lightning between Chicago and Washington," Manzanera recalled 30 years later. "That taught me the power of prayer." Arriving intact, the band wound up their tour with three nights at Mother's Place in Washington, after which they flew back to the UK on Friday 5 January.

Among the acts Roxy were supporting on this 30-day jaunt were Humble Pie, The J Geils Band, Ten Years After, Wild Turkey, The Steve Miller Band, Edgar Winter, Jo Jo Gunne, The Allman Brothers and Dr John. The match in each case was not a favourable one, and straight-ahead US rock fans were for the most part mystified by these peacock-plumed art-rockers from London. Sold in cack-handed fashion by Warners as an Anglo counterpart to Alice Cooper, Roxy suffered a number of humiliations in the course of their itinerary, notably at Miami's Speedway Stadium, which was one of several gigs where the band had things thrown at them.

The result was that Roxy soon became as disgruntled as their audiences. "We've been playing short sets to large places, and that's annoying," maintained Eno. "You have to condense, so we can't do long slow things. It's difficult to generate a mood. It's amazing how quickly 35 minutes goes." And, according to Ferry, "The only time we play really well is when we're top of the bill. Our equipment is complicated so we need [sound] checking beforehand. Now we're just being thrown on and having to make do." Mackay, too, was just as incensed: "People tend to underestimate how much failures of equipment can affect you on stage – coupled with nervousness and inexperience and a very difficult audience. It also needs to be said that some bands treat their support band very badly.

From whatever motives, I always felt on those early gigs that Jethro Tull were to some extent sabotaging our act."

Mackay's impression of Jethro Tull was confirmed by the constituent members of Mott the Hoople, who 'came round' after the Madison Square Garden fiasco to commiserate with Roxy about their having been denied a sound check. Mott's Ian Hunter published his recollections of the event two years later in his *Diary of a Rock and Roll Star*: "By the time the sound was right they were wilting under pressure, although I thought they held on extremely well. To my mind doing Madison Square Garden without a sound check is like Marc Bolan fighting Joe Bugner for English heavyweight title."

When not performing in front of 15,000 indifferent Tull fanatics, Roxy scored one or two bullseyes, generally on the rare occasions when they were billed by themselves, notably at LA's Whiskey a Go Go on Tuesday 19 December. A more typical US response, however, came from *Chicago Sun-Times* critic Dick Saunders, whose bamboozlement was aptly expressed in his word-picture of Mackay and Eno at the Kinetic Playground: "a Flash Gordon type with two-toned hair who made a few good sounds on the saxophone, and one little thing in black feathers and thinning blond pageboy [hair] who occasionally removed his hand from his hip to flip some electrical switches and add to the noise."

There were compensations for the band in the form of a trip up the Empire State Building and the view from their LA hotel of Kari-Ann stretched across a colossal Hollywood billboard, a sight described by Ferry as "by far the nicest thing there." There was also an LA encounter with John Cale, who nominated himself as producer of their next album. Ferry was clearly wounded, however, and on returning to the UK was pretty unsparing in his opinions, maintaining flatly that "the American audience isn't as intelligent as the British. We've been playing with some very basic bands ... It could be we're too subtle for most Americans, maybe you need to be English to get into our humour. I think an Englishman would appreciate us more."

Roxy could take solace in the music press Readers' Polls that greeted them on their reappearance in England. Already the readers of *Melody Maker* had voted them 'British Brightest Hope'; now they were the 'Most Promising New British Name' in the *NME* (as well as second most promising internationally), while *Virginia Plain* was voted second best UK single and tenth best 'world' single. *Disc*, too, had them down as the 'Brightest Hope for 73' and *Virginia Plain* as 1972's fourth best single.

If the alien flash and filigree of their stage presentation had been a stumbling block for them in the USA, Roxy certainly weren't about to alter it. Much of their early impact, after all, came from the strangely sinister vibes they gave off in performance, a frisson of unease shared out equally between Ferry, Eno, Mackay and Manzanera, and aptly summed up by bedazzled US critic Lisa Robinson when she had first encountered them in Guildford on 20 November. In Robinson's account, they would begin "by just standing there, swaying in unison – a sort of deadly, ritualistic, unified gesture, and then ... perform their alternately shattering and rocking music, bathed in the tackily dramatic, vulgar green, red and purple lights."

Ferry, in particular, would remain a sneering fusion of two horror archetypes, his less-than-graceful stage deportment being compared by many to

Frankenstein's monster and his vampire's croon making him seem like Laurence Harvey auditioning to play Count Dracula – or, as Ian Hunter put it at the time, "a Dracula-type Presley." (It's all there in Roxy's contemporary TV appearances: the slicked-back hair, the bat-like ears, the half-closed eyes, the permanently clenched teeth.) Though apparently using the camp appurtenances of horror and science fiction as mere set decoration, Roxy would reconvene in February to record an album that transmuted these trimmings into a proto-Goth soundscape that remains genuinely disturbing.

Four: *The Second Roxy Music Album*

"There are a large number of people in the music business who would be delighted to hear that Roxy Music had blown it ... Happy to state, they gonna have to close down operations for some little while, because the new Roxy album is here, and it's a staggeringly fine piece of work, easily outstripping the first album: For Your Pleasure *it's called, and damn if it ain't just that."*

Charles Shaar Murray, *NME* 24 March 1973

For the *For Your Pleasure* album, Roxy headed down Regent Street, at John Cale's suggestion, from Command Studios at Piccadilly Circus to George Martin's Air Studios three floors above Oxford Circus. When Cale proved unavailable to produce them, the band brought in John Anthony to oversee the beginning of the sessions. Anthony had begun his musical career as vocalist with Windsor band Hogsnort Rupert, then acquired a formidable reputation through his production work for Yes, Van der Graaf Generator, Rare Bird, Genesis and Lindisfarne; he would later produce Queen's first album. With Roxy, he polished off five tracks, two intended for the band's next single release and the other three comprising Side Two of the eventual LP.

The tracks on Side One were all new pieces, perfected by Ferry during a self-imposed exile at the Derbyshire cottage of designer Nick de Ville and entrusted to resident Air producer Chris Thomas. Just turned 26, Thomas was already a sought-after name thanks to his work with Climax Blues Band, Badfinger, Procol Harum and Pink Floyd; later he would forge an epoch-making alliance with The Sex Pistols. Collaborating with Roxy, he was aware from the start of the tensions already at work within the band, specifically between Ferry and Eno. "I was always caught in the middle and it was driving me nuts," he claimed in 1974. "I just wanted to make a record. Everyone was taking sides."

Mackay viewed the tensions in a more creative light. "At one stage we were thinking of producing it [the album] ourselves," he told Caroline Boucher, "but then we thought we'd like a producer. It's a difficult job. I wouldn't want to produce us; we're all far too arrogant about what we're doing. With six people all saying things, it's not at all easy – we've too many ideas, our problem has always been to reconcile the diverse elements."

Oddly, John Anthony's role in reconciling the band's diversities would end up rather grudgingly acknowledged. Though the label copy on both the LP and accompanying single accorded him a proper credit, the album's gatefold inner sleeve contained only the legend 'Produced by Chris Thomas and Roxy Music' followed by a mere 'Special thanks to John Anthony.'

The album sessions occupied the first two weeks of February, with Rik Kenton being summarily dismissed from the band just days ahead of the start date. Ferry's old Gas Board confrere, the impressively sideburned John Porter, was drafted in instead, having himself been pipped at the post by Kenton the previous May. Porter's credit on the album sleeve as 'Guest Artiste' would set in stone the Roxy tradition of fly-by-night bass guitarists, though Ferry was unstinting in his praise for his old chum, claiming in 1974 that "he's amazing. The guy lives music and never gets the credit he deserves. Ridiculously underrated." This injustice would be rectified in the early 1980s, when Porter's work as producer for The Smiths climaxed with the shattering *How Soon is Now?*

Kenton's expulsion seems to have been brought about by something Ferry couldn't stick at any price, namely songwriting ambitions; worse, a desire for his songs to be incorporated into the Roxy repertoire. (This, of course, was a fatal error previously perpetrated by David O'List.) A devotee of John Lennon, Kenton had produced demos that made it clear his efforts would never fit within the Roxy framework. Conceding that "the end was inevitable," Kenton pointed out that "We had to work within a very narrow line. Because they're Bryan's songs, he always wants to know what everyone is playing, but even then the numbers managed to change on stage."

Ferry's control freakery was less stringent where the permanent band members were concerned. "I know a couple of them want to do their things," he commented in January. "Andy's done some. If anybody comes up with something I think is terrific and which I can relate to, then it'll go on the album." In practice, however, this vaguely democratic impulse would have to wait until August to be put into effect.

Faced with a high level of anticipation from the music press, Ferry was studiedly evasive regarding the new LP, only volunteering the observation that "Side Two has much longer tracks [than Side One]. I wish we could make everything as long as that. I mean, we had to cut the last track on Side One [*In Every Dream Home a Heartache*] to a third of its length because … if you start cramming more onto an album you lose out in sound quality. But that track is the best thing I've ever done." Elsewhere he was more facetious, proposing that the new album, and all subsequent ones, would repeat the tracks from the first collection only in ever-more economical versions. "Norris McWhirter would start checking us for world records: 'This year they've got *Re-make/Re-model* down to two minutes forty-five – how far can this band go?'"

There followed the gruesome notion that "The cover would be Kari-Ann one year older, and trying to adopt the same pose. Each year we'd do the same numbers, and the lines would start appearing on her face." In fact, Ferry had determined to supplant Kari-Ann's marshmallow vision of cream and pink with a cover redolent of the profound darkness at the heart of the new album. He certainly wasn't about to go down the skittish route with which Eno regaled Nick Kent on 3 February. "Oh God, I'm really fed up with all this thing about glamour," moaned Eno. "We had to get a girl in to pose for the cover of the new album, which I thought was a drag because it's all becoming too stereotyped.

Personally I'd prefer a nice unpretentious unglamorous picture of the band, wearing false beards and denims and standing around a tree with 'Support Ecology' on the back of the sleeve."

The girl Eno referred to was Amanda Lear, a mysterious figure reputed to have previously been a boy. But as Jonathan Meades later reflected, "Her multiple pasts are to be believed at will; their different facets are parts of a kit from which you build your own Amanda (if you want to – and she can't believe that anyone could fail to want to)."

The Amanda built by Ferry was a sneering dominatrix in pill-box hat and midnight-blue leather dress, teetering on impossible heels against an inky-black Vegas skyline and holding a snarling black panther on a tight leash in front of her. Where Kari-Ann recalled a piece of Alberto Vargas cheesecake and Marilyn Cole would resemble a Bruno Bernard photograph, Amanda was an absurdly articulated fantasy straight out of the glossy Pop Art canvases of Allen Jones. The rumours that she had been the subject of a sex change financed by her ancient and impotent companion, Salvador Dalí, only added further spice to an already dangerous image, as did the notion that Ferry had a brief fling with her in the wake of the photo session.

"Bryan and Antony Price thought I'd be the right girl with the right attitude, because the girl had to be way before her time," Lear recollected. "1973 was too early for the black leather dominatrix look. They wanted a girl who looked like a Hitchcock movie, a little bit dangerous but arrogant at the same time. I had to be able to carry off that ridiculous shiny dress look ... Bryan was very charming. He took me out and offered me the job, but never mentioned the black panther. They overdid the valium though, and the poor animal couldn't get up, poor thing. It was lying flat on its stomach. I was looking fierce though. When it came to it, they had to paint the [panther's] eyes open on the sleeve."

In fact, the entire panther, never mind its eyes, seems to have been painted in, the cover as a whole counting as another triumph for the *Roxy Music* team of Ferry, Price, Karl Stoecker and Nicholas de Ville. Lear herself went on to become a suitably ambiguous queen of Euro-disco, with record titles like *Incredibilimente donna* (Unbelievably Woman) designed to fan the flames of her perceived trans-sexual status. In 1990, however, she stated incontrovertibly: "That was bullshit, a phony publicity stunt in order to sell records. No one wanted a boring girl like any other. But it was the time of *The Rocky Horror Show*, and I was around, looking glamorous, and people always dream, don't they? The lady is a girl, and that's it."

For the band, the album's back cover sparked more controversy than any genetic question marks attaching to its front, a controversy that paved the way for the crisis to come in the summer. As Manzanera put it the following year, "I remember the first actual blow-up occurring when Bryan held back on telling us that he'd designed the album sleeve of *For Your Pleasure* – which resulted in a huge argument on our coach."

Given that Ferry had openly 'art directed' the previous album, it seems that what Manzanera meant by "designed the album sleeve" was "designed himself onto the album sleeve." There, on the rear of the gatefold sleeve, chauffeur's cap tilted at a rakish angle, is Ferry himself, leaning on the kind of ostentatious automobile referred to in *Virginia Plain* and ready to whisk Amanda, and presumably the panther too, to some unspecified nocturnal rendezvous. The signal thus given out was all too obvious, and the luscious inner-sleeve shots of the band in their outlandish stage costumes seemed insufficient to reverse it.

Karl Stoecker's group photos of the band decked out in what the PR machine dubbed "flamboyant luresque" were widely disseminated, however, making the cover of *Disc* on 24 March. For all the lurid extravagance of these images, Mackay and Eno, in particular, were being courted as new-found rock intellectuals. Their joint interest in 'systems' music was glossed by Eno as "that sort of music constructed to a strict and fairly simple system which is concerned with the phasing of sets of musical events over one another. A good example is *In C* by Terry Riley, where a number of musicians move independently from repeating separate bars moving in and out of phase with each other and thus creating an infinite variety of combinations within a finite piece.

"Right now I'm very interested in Muzak as a form," he added. "I used to suffer from long stretches of insomnia and was forced to construct a piece using tape-loops that took the form of Muzak which, in turn, was conducive to sleep." Mackay was more laconic, pointing out that the goal was a kind of music that "you can listen to from point to point and let it come and go." Musings of this sort would not only leave their mark on hypnotic album tracks like *The Bogus Man* but also profoundly influence the course of Eno's post-Roxy recordings.

On Monday 5 March, the band recorded their fifth and last Peel session, broadcast three days later and featuring all-new tracks *Pyjamarama*, *Do the Strand*, *Editions of You* and *In Every Dream Home a Heartache*. The new bass guitarist for live purposes was towering (6'4") New Yorker Salvatore Maida. Bolstered by support acts The Sharks (including Chris Spedding and Andy Fraser) and stand-alone slide guitarist Lloyd Watson, the band's latest tour began on Thursday the 15th in Nottingham, with two nights at London's Rainbow Theatre preceded by dates in Manchester, Bracknell, Birmingham, Leicester, Plymouth, Torbay, Stoke, Sheffield and Newcastle.

"What's new?" asked Martin Kirkup in *Sounds*, reporting from the Nottingham debut. "Well, Eno's had a haircut, Bryan sports a guitar, and the audience is full of Andrew Mackay lookalikes. The music? Ah, it's about twice as tough and strong as it was even three months ago, and most of it's new. There aren't many bands who'd chance playing nearly an hour of new songs, and then throw in their hit singles as encores. Of course, there aren't any bands like Roxy." Meanwhile, critics fell over themselves trying to describe the band's visual impact. For one, Ferry "clutches a big white guitar and looks just like Eddie Cochran"; for another, "Eno looked like a redundant peacock as he fiddled with his knobs and gadgets"; for still another, "Andy Mackay [appeared] in a riot of bobbled green satin like a humanoid plant from an early horror film."

The Rainbow extravaganza took place over the weekend of 31 March and 1 April, with Elton John attending on the Sunday and a chorus of praise issuing later from the press. Amanda Lear herself introduced the band "for your pleasure"; as *Melody Maker*'s Chris Charlesworth described it, "slinking from behind the curtains comes this peroxide blonde with awfully long legs and I'd swear she hadn't a stitch on under that black brocade creation." Later, the matador-clad Ferry crooned *In Every Dream Home a Heartache* to her. Elsewhere there were four rather less classy dancing girls in denim and red T-shirts, "hopping about," according to one critic, "like Pan's People without a routine."

The new live act was conspicuously more self-possessed, more showbiz than before, with Ferry even occupying the centre mic for several songs, notably the rabble-rousing opener, *Do the Strand*. Noting that the band's stage costumes were "for the most part exaggerated versions of dandified Teds with various Frankenstein-like additions," the *Observer*'s Tony Palmer assured his readers that "on stage, the group is demonic, sinister, apocalyptic, monstrous, dazzling, flashy – what opera might have been in the 1970s before it lost its nerve." Palmer was well qualified to make such a judgment, his later work as a film and TV director encompassing portraits of Puccini, Chopin, Wagner, Handel, Stravinsky and Shostakovich.

The Rainbow showcase was followed by dates in Preston, Liverpool, Glasgow, Edinburgh, Leeds, Brighton, Southampton, Bournemouth, Bristol and Cardiff, after which there was a week's breather prior to a brief European tour commencing on Monday 23 April. Several of Ferry's stage costumes had been stolen during the UK itinerary (allegedly by future Sex Pistol Steve Jones), and the group were thoroughly exhausted by the end of it; "I wish I could get the acclaim and the money without having to go out and do the work," quipped Eno.

In the midst of all this, the band reappeared on *The Old Grey Whistle Test*, sharing the bill with Allan Taylor and performing *Do the Strand* and *In Every Dream Home a Heartache*. The result went out on Tuesday 3 April, the show now compered by Bob Harris, who certainly wasn't about to replicate Richard Williams' enthusiasm for the band. His soft-spoken but adamant dissociation of himself from Roxy's appearance has since gone down in television legend, but by this time his 'hype'-fixated views were sounding distinctly passé.

The album reviews had come in on 24 March and were almost uniformly positive: "a huge and lovely improvement on their first album" (*Disc*), "better than anybody could have dared hope" (*NME*), "a vastly better album that Roxy's first" (*Sounds*). A sour note came from the USA, however. "If *Do the Strand*, *Pyjamarama* and *Virginia Plain* were all on a maxi-single it would be one of the buys of the year," commented Paul Gambaccini in *Rolling Stone*. "But the bulk of *For Your Pleasure* is either above us, beneath us, or on another plane altogether."

Though climbing only to 193 in the US, *For Your Pleasure* entered the UK chart on 7 April and hit number four, staying in all for 27 weeks. Pointing out that the first Roxy album had been an embarrassment of riches ideas-wise, Eno added that the new one "might be criticised for not showing enough ideas, but the ideas in there have been investigated much more thoroughly."

* * *

Pyjamarama
(Ferry) 2:52

Variously reported in the music press pre-release as either *Pyjama Amour* or even *Pyjama Armour*, Roxy's second single was cut at the beginning of the *For Your Pleasure* sessions with John Anthony as producer and John Porter hurriedly drafted in as substitute bass player. In *Disc*, John Peel would extol the result, with good reason, as "Another dandy pearl from the boys."

Talking to Ian MacDonald from his hospital bed the previous October, Ferry had contradicted his pro-singles stance with the pronouncement that "We're not a singles group really. I certainly don't want to find myself sliding down that Slade/T.Rex corridor of horror." Nevertheless, Island were anxious for a *Virginia Plain* follow-up, so *Pyjamarama*'s impending release was announced on 10 February, only a matter of days after the LP sessions had begun. It was rushed out a mere fortnight later, a hasty move that was to be castigated by at least one member of the band.

"About their music Roxy are frank," noted *Sounds'* Barry Dillon on 28 April, while *Pyjamarama* was still riding high in the charts at number ten. "If it's good they say so without ego-tripping, and if it's bad they put it down. Eno, for example, thinks *Virginia Plain* is a classic single, but [along] with the others he dislikes *Pyjamarama*, despite its commercial success. 'We should never have put it out as a single. We did it in a rush after our American tour. We were still musically disorientated at that time. *Do the Strand* would have been far better, but we hadn't recorded it at that time. We will never rush a single like that again.'"

Perhaps because of the band's own dismissive attitude towards it, *Pyjamarama* has been unfairly overshadowed by its predecessor ever since, its also-ran status exacerbated by a persistent refusal to append it to subsequent reissues of the album that spawned it. (It would certainly seem no more incongruous in the context of *For Your Pleasure* than *Virginia Plain* does on *Roxy Music* – probably less so.) It also quickly dropped out of Roxy's live repertoire, featuring on both 1973 tours and a smattering of the band's 1975 dates but disappearing thereafter. And yet there was no shortage of praise for it in the music press of the day; *NME* called it "very clever," *Record Mirror* dubbed it "the big hit sound," and, in *Disc*, John Peel described it as "another case of don't know-what's-coming-next-but it's-bound-to-be-good."

After *Virginia Plain*, of course, the fans didn't know what was coming next either, and certainly *Pyjamarama* caught them on the hop with a much less stridently in-your-face sound, its subtler charms perhaps accounting for its rather less robust chart performance. "The whole thing is that we change from one record to another," Ferry would claim in the 9 June edition of *Sounds*. "We could have brought out a *Virginia Plain Part 2* instead of *Pyjamarama*, which was very different." Ferry's approach to writing it was different, for a start – it was his first experiment in writing a tune on guitar, and he duly made his rhythm guitar debut on the final recording.

The tone is frothy and the lyric uncomplicatedly starry-eyed, as well as containing ghostly foretastes of two future Roxy tracks, *Just Like You* and *Angel Eyes*. Ferry's lunatic phrasing of the line "How could I apologise for all those lies?" – attenuating the final vowel of "apologise" into a shape previously unheard by man – is almost, but not quite, as authentically berserk as Mackay's sax break, which takes its cue from Ferry's antiquated promise of billing and cooing and is so thoroughly off-the-wall even John Peel had trouble identifying it. ("There's a kazoo-like flurry from the synthesiser – or it could even be a synthesiser-like flurry from the kazoo," he wrote. "Whichever it be it is a handsome row.")

Thompson, meanwhile, romps playfully all around the soundstage, Manzanera opens with a "daaaa-daaanng!" familiar from *Virginia Plain* prior to winding things up with a gaily energised solo, and Eno peppers the mix with an intriguing range of Morse Code signals.

Though Mackay's sax break sounds uniquely strange, it's worth noting that, while making the *For Your Pleasure* album, he made time to do some session work for Mott the Hoople, whose album *Mott* was also being recorded at Air Studios. His contributions can be heard on the tracks *Honaloochie Boogie* and *All the Way from Memphis*, both of which became hit singles, the latter graced by some saxophone histrionics in much the same demented mould as *Pyjamarama*.

On 5 March, *Pyjamarama* was one of five songs recorded live for BBC Radio 1's *Sounds of the Seventies*; the result was broadcast three days later. The single had already been issued back on Friday 23 February, entering the singles chart at number 45 on 6 March. Making it into the Top 40 at 31 the following week, by 10 April it had reached number 10, just behind The O'Jays' Philly soul classic *Love Train*, and it stayed there for three weeks, during which time Dawn's *Tie a Yellow Ribbon Round the Old Oak Tree* succeeded Gilbert O'Sullivan's *Get Down* in the Number One slot. It slipped out of the chart on 22 May after a run of 12 weeks.

In 1977, *Pyjamarama* was reissued as a double A-side with *Virginia Plain*; true to its 'second banana' reputation, however, the single was principally sold on the latter. It was slightly remixed for the occasion, with Mackay's awesome sax break smoothed out into a much more romantic, but in its way equally awesome, sound. This was the version that appeared the same year on the *Greatest Hits* collection and subsequently on the *Street Life* double album. The track's undeserved obscurity was only made worse, of course, by the decades-long unavailability of the original, crazier mix – though, subsequent to its revival in 1995 for the *Thrill of It All* box set, it has since been included on both the *Early Years* and *Best of Roxy Music* compilations.

The Pride and the Pain
(Mackay) 4:14

During Ferry's tonsil crisis in October 1972, the other band members took the opportunity to work on musical ideas of their own, with Mackay proving the most productive. "I work differently from Bryan; since I was trained as an Academy musician I'm able to write my own arrangements and I can work away from the piano and write down tunes from my head, which is an advantage as it means I can write anywhere," he explained to *Disc*'s Caroline Boucher. "I've got a lot of songs that aren't suitable for Roxy, and I'd very much like other people to do them. I'm handing some over to the publishing company to hawk around. Some of them are almost Tom Jones type of things. I've got a lot of things that are partly finished, things that I may work into music at some stage."

The Pride and the Pain was presumably not one of the items Mackay had earmarked for Tom Jones; instead, its swirling vistas would provide the taped introduction to Roxy's stage act on their 1973 spring tour. Rescued from oblivion 22 years later on the *Thrill of It All* box set, the track remains Roxy's most substantial and beguiling instrumental flip-side.

The very title here puts one in mind of swollen cinematic excursions like *The Pride and the Passion* (Cary Grant, Frank Sinatra and Sophia Loren in a Napoleonic intrigue) or *The Agony and the Ecstasy* (Charlton Heston and Rex Harrison in a Michelangelo biopic). As per *Pyjamarama* and the second side of the *For Your Pleasure* album, *The Pride and the Pain* was produced by the band in collaboration with John Anthony, the result sounding like a freak collision between the exotic film scores of Mario Nascimbene and a road company version of *The Desert Song*. "I love the film music type thing," Mackay informed *Disc*'s Caroline Boucher at the time.

Whether Nascimbene was a direct influence or not, he was clearly a composer after Roxy's own mix-and-match heart, eager as he was to use any 'found objects' – most famously, garden rakes – to punch up his soundtracks for films as genuinely groundbreaking as *Room at the Top* and as irretrievably outré as *The Vengeance of She*. Mackay's sprawling canvas for *The Pride and the Pain* falls firmly into the latter camp, conjuring images of solar-topee'd adventurers stumbling across ancient civilisations in uncharted climes.

The soundstage here is redolent of cold and arid desert plains at dusk, with Eno's opening wash of wind effects joined by the eerie fluting of watchful night birds. (Mackay would recycle the latter effect in 1984 via the lyricon-flavoured owl hoots featured on The Explorers' *Falling for Nightlife*.) A stately piano figure is introduced just ahead of Mackay's lovely, yet forbidding, oboe melody, which is in turn taken up by Manzanera's strident yet spidery guitar break. Then the percussive lashings of a whip are heard, with Mackay adopting his best John Wayne-style "Truly this man was the son of God" accent in order to shoo away various underlings at the approach of the Emperor.

The chill sonority of Mackay's oboe suggests that maybe this is a funeral procession, and with Mackay himself having bagged the role of tight-lipped, sweat-stained slave driver, Eno and Ferry then chime in as a chorus of poker-faced, basso-profundo High Priests. Manzanera's guitar takes a mournful downturn, Mackay starts speaking in tongues and the receding procession is finally screened from view by Eno's aural sand storm.

Of course, Mackay's spoken passages, together with the whip-cracking sound effects and rumbling backing vocals, elevate *The Pride and the Pain* to the giddiest heights of high camp. But the trick here – as in Mackay's later score for *A Song for Europe* – is that the whole thing is played with such a completely straight face that the track takes on a genuinely icy grandeur to match the melodramatic sweep of its title. It's a shame that the British film industry was by this time no longer making exotic fantasies of the Rider Haggard variety; a shame, in fact, that it was no longer making too many films of any description. Had it been doing so, Mackay could have cornered the market in pith-helmeted expeditionaries, ageless Ice Queens and flames of Eternal Youth.

Do the Strand
(Ferry) 4:00 / single edit 3:19

In conversation with *Rolling Stone*'s Cynthia Dagnal in 1974, Eno pointed out that "One of the recurrent themes of rock music is a preoccupation with new dances. And it's taken by intellectuals as the lowest form of rock music, the most base and crude." With *Do the Strand*, Ferry had clearly decided to reverse this notion, bringing a dazzling torrent of erudition to bear on a bogus dance craze conceived as the quintessential St Vitus Dance, the irresistible expression of an age-old imperative.

He nevertheless erected a familiar smokescreen of flippancy around the song, stating flatly that *Do the Strand* was "purely a dancer" – "I think it's nice to write a dancer, don't you?" – and informing *Melody Maker*'s Roy Hollingsworth that "We were going to get Lionel Blair to work out some dance routines for it." The same tongue-in-cheek attitude characterises the whole song, providing an inexhaustible index of dance crazes down the ages together with a litany of all the improbable historical figures who preferred instead to do the Strand. Amid all the camp humour, there's also the lurking suggestion that a wild and uninhibited submission to the dance is the dilettante's only means of coping with life's essential hollowness. Given the beguiling, and thoroughly decadent, sheen of Roxy's proposed dance craze, it's hardly surprising that Hollingsworth was moved to suggest that "before you know it, the whole country will be Stranding like buggery."

After referencing the waltz and the quadrille, Ferry casts his dance-craze net yet further, taking in South America (tango, fandango, samba), the Caribbean (the beguine) and the rock'n'roll heartlands of the USA (the Madison, the mashed potato). The Madison, connoting as it does New York's Madison Avenue, is presumably close kin to Ferry's Strand, with its multiple associations of 'doing' the fashionable thoroughfare that connects Charing Cross to the Aldwych, strolling along a beach (this connotation picked up, of course, in the next album's title, *Stranded*), or pulling on a cigarette. Hazy memories of the latter's old advertising campaign (a solitary, trenchcoated man accompanied by the slogan "You're never alone with a Strand") threaten to tip the multi-faceted imagery into sensory overload, as well as recalling the US cigarette brand immortalised some six months earlier in *Virginia Plain*.

But there's more. Subscribers to the Strand include a stellar array of artistic icons, even a kingly one. Toulouse-Lautrec's capacious model LaGoulue, legendary ballet dancer Nijinsky, Nabokov's alluring nymphet Lolita – all sign up for the Strand. Even the famously inscrutable Egyptian Sphinx and her Renaissance descendant the Mona Lisa cannot remained unmoved by so-called "Strand power." In thrall to the heady intoxication of the Strand, all human life seems to be here. In England, it demolishes class barriers at a stroke, being popular at both high-class restaurants and low-grade cafés; worldwide, it convulses everyone from the Arctic Circle to the Great Wall of China.

The song begins with a rousing rallying cry that nevertheless contains a disturbing notion, that the Strand could be some Orwellian government measure designed to keep the rowdier elements of society in a state of anaesthetised unawareness: "a danceable solution to teenage revolution." And a similarly apocalyptic note is sounded at the end: even the massacred inhabitants of Guernica (immortalised in Picasso's 1937 painting of the same name) are apparently swept up in the global exhilaration. Six years on, Ferry would unequivocally state in *Manifesto* that "I am for the revolution's coming," glossing the line as "I'm for whatever the new thing is." Not necessarily a dance, the Strand is exactly that – a state of mind, "the new thing" – but a bogus new thing imposed from above to stifle revolutionary impulses.

Or maybe not. At least as fecund as those of *Virginia Plain*, Ferry's word pictures here are dazzlingly inscrutable as well as dazzlingly inventive. "I quite like the lyric," he conceded modestly in 2001. "I was trying to do a modern Cole Porter thing really, trying to use lots of different images. And it works better than most of them."

If Ferry's words are of staggering virtuosity, the spectacular riot of competing instruments that surrounds them is no less so, making the track a take-no-prisoners rocker even more pile-driving than the previous album's opener, *Re-make/Re-model*. Ferry's opening four lines of Pop Art sloganeering are set against the shuddering weight of Thompson's percussion, the Jerry Lee Lewis-style hammering of an electric piano and the molten flares of Mackay's tenor saxophone; the latter wraps up King Curtis and Junior Walker in one explosive sound, surging irrepressibly out of the mix on a note of genuinely hair-raising intensity.

With Porter's bass rolling gymnastically below, Manzanera steps forward for an extended instrumental break in which his hypnotically repeated guitar motif is Eno-melded with Mackay's tenor to create a dizzying cacophony of trance-like sound. On Ferry's re-entrance, a submerged Eno burble underpins the music almost as persistently as Mackay's oboe did on *Virginia Plain*, and the thundering final chord leaves the listener in no fit state to encounter the grimmer fantasies soon to saturate the very grooves of the *For Your Pleasure* album.

Pre-release, *Do the Strand* was previewed along with three other new songs (*Pyjamarama, Editions of You* and *In Every Dream Home a Heartache*) in a live performance for John Peel's *Sounds of the Seventies*, broadcast on Thursday 8 March; in preparation for the upcoming *For Your Pleasure* tour, Salvatore Maida was drafted in on bass for this session. It subsequently received its television premiere, courtesy of *The Old Grey Whistle Test*, on Tuesday 3 April.

In *Rolling Stone*, Paul Gambaccini was baffled by the album as a whole, but warmly endorsed *Do the Strand* as "the cleverest use of language and rhyme since *I Am the Walrus* … By the time the band has taken off on its mid-flight solo, the listener desperately wants to do the Strand, whatever it is. Turns out it isn't anything, which enhances the magic of what is a total performance." Indeed, the infectious brilliance of *Do the Strand* made it an obvious contender for release as a single – as Eno put it apropos *Pyjamarama*, "*Do the Strand* would have been far better, but we hadn't recorded it at that time" – but Ferry's singles policy was still stubbornly in place. "But that would be cheating kids," he told Roy Hollingsworth, "putting a single out from an album. That's cheating."

Admirably high-minded, this attitude would nevertheless be revised in short order, starting with the very next album. It didn't apply in Japan or mainland Europe anyway, where *Do the Strand* was duly accorded single status with *Editions of You* as its B-side. In performance, the same combination would turn up in Roxy's *Siren* itinerary of 1975, where the two songs formed a medley, with *Editions of You* sandwiched between opening and closing slivers of *Do the Strand*.

Finally, in January 1978 Polydor looked at the healthy sales of the previous October's *Virginia Plain-Pyjamarama* double A-side and put out *Do the Strand* in tandem with, again, *Editions of You*. Sadly, it failed to chart, despite a fetching red-and-black picture sleeve showing a Pop Art dance matrix complete with swivelling footprints. *Do the Strand* endures, nevertheless, as the classic Roxy anthem and the natural climax to pretty much every live performance the band has given since its release.

Beauty Queen
(Ferry) 4:36

In the brief interval between his long-delayed tonsilectomy and the band's ill-fated assault on the US in December 1972, Ferry speculated on the possibility of having a *Virginia Plain* follow-up on the singles market by Christmas, nominating "a ballad called *Beauty Queen*" and promising that it "will be grandiose and heavy in the Walker Brothers tradition."

Though a seasonal single release failed to materialise (*Pyjamarama* eventually filling the breach in late February), *Beauty Queen* nevertheless made it onto the ensuing *For Your Pleasure* album. Ferry's estimate of the finished product was rather more flippant. "This one has a distinct Northern working men's club feel to it," he told *Melody Maker*'s Roy Hollingsworth during an exclusive sneak-preview of the new LP conducted in EG's King's Road offices. Hollingsworth, too, adopted a facetious tone: "On this slow, droopy ballad, Ferry sounds like a mutated cross between Gene Pitney and Engelbert (whoops) ... It creeps, and groans a little – groaning so much after a minute that you wanna laugh."

Perhaps what Ferry had in mind with his reference to Northern working men's clubs was merely the echoing organ sound that leads off the track, for the song's multiplying accretions of Pop Art imagery would almost certainly have disqualified it from inclusion in the contemporary TV showcase, *The Wheeltappers' and Shunters' Social Club*. Against a Thompson-Porter rhythmic backdrop that is at once resonant yet understated, Ferry delivers one of his most impassioned love songs, brimming with melodramatic flourishes yet sincere in its sighing conclusion that life's convulsions are no more substantial than sand on a beach.

The mood is soulful and resigned from the start, with Ferry apostrophising the beauty of a lost love in a dazzling string of swooning metaphors, among them a charmingly self-reflexive reference to the previous album's *Sea Breezes*. In a typically arch piece of rug-pulling, Ferry follows this high-flown Pop Art litany with the workaday observation that his loved one is "the pride of [her] street." The 'Valerie' invoked in the opening line was reportedly a Newcastle model operative in the latter part of the 1960s, making the song's luxuriously upholstered imagery seem like a sustained dream of wishful thinking.

The dream takes flight in a swirling, Eno-treated instrumental break. Here, Ferry's chattering piano motif races along beneath two energised extemporisations from Manzanera's guitar (the pair laid side by side in exhilarating counterpoint) before the track modulates back to the mordant tone of the opening. In a final section that enshrines some of his most beautiful lines, Ferry concludes with the melancholic realisation that even soulmates must learn to get by without each other.

Presumably taking a well-earned breather after his heart-stopping contributions to *Do the Strand*, Mackay appears to have been out of the studio when

Beauty Queen was recorded. Nominated by Eno as "my favourite Roxy track" (a magnanimous judgment, given that "Bryan did [it] practically by himself"), it would turn out, ironically, to be the agent of his resignation from Roxy Music. As Richard Williams reported, in performance Ferry's "vocal control on *Beauty Queen*, with its brilliant lyric, is stunning." This cut no ice, however, with Eno's more voluble fans, whose disruptive heckling during this very Ferry-centric song would assume 'last straw' status at the York Festival in June.

Strictly Confidential
(Ferry) 3:44

Ferry reportedly wrote this one at dead of night in Derbyshire, hardly surprising given the end-of-the-line despair in which every line is steeped. Here the *For Your Pleasure* album starts to reveal the profound blackness at its heart, with a guilt-ridden protagonist eager to pass on various unspecified secrets while composing what appears to be a suicide note. The climactic arrival of ghostly inner voices, eerily eager to fold the expiring confessor in their embrace, provides a spine-chilling index to his passing over into (as Ferry would put it in the next album's *Psalm*) Death's vale.

Mackay's funereal tenor sax sets the sombre tone, joined by the plaint of synthetic strings that morph imperceptibly into Manzanera's guitar as Ferry's recitation begins. There's an agreeable dislocation in Ferry's vocal style here, lending the prim and pious tones of a parish priest to a deeply disturbed character whose soul seems curdled by some unspecified, but presumably atrocious, burden of guilt. To point up the mortal agony entailed in the unburdening process, Mackay's oboe chimes in with unaccustomed asperity; similarly, bass and drums are only introduced to provide an instrumental counterpoint to Ferry's falsetto admission that he cannot sleep. And as Ferry warms to his theme, Manzanera's guitar unleashes a series of lacerating improvisations that eventually crowd out Mackay's keening oboe.

A later song, *The Thrill of It All*, refers to the needling nocturnal questions posed by "preying shadows," aptly summing up the chill of fear invested in the *Strictly Confidential* dialogue that follows. Here, those preying shadows are clearly sitting in judgment on their benighted victim, and the grim outcome is a fore-gone conclusion if their whispered insinuations are anything to go by. The agony over, Mackay's droning sax returns to complement a less-than-cheering Ferry coda, which acknowledges the breaking of the nocturnal spell but ends on the despairing observation that it provides no key to relieving the narrator's pain.

"It leaves one feeling quite emotionally wasted," enthused Roy Hollingsworth. "Most enjoyable." Even so, *Strictly Confidential* was never likely to become a con-ventional crowd-pleaser, being granted its only live performances during Roxy's *Siren* itinerary in 1975, and even then only occasionally. Though unrelentingly bleak, it would nevertheless sire several successors in the Roxy canon. The insidious urging of an inner voice was a device retooled at least three times (on *Mother of Pearl*, *Sentimental Fool* and *Still Falls the Rain*), while *No Strange Delight*, from the otherwise anodyne *Flesh + Blood* album, seems like a *Strictly Confidential* remake with the nightmarish fade of *For Your Pleasure* tacked on at the end.

71

Editions of You
(Ferry) 3:45

From its opening Doors-style keyboard parody to its exhilarating sax-driven conclusion, *Editions of You* is up there with *Do the Strand* as one of Roxy's classic rockers. With Ferry offering a breathless word picture of disposable high-life party-going and the band firing on every conceivable cylinder, the song lends a giddily apocalyptic edge to Ferry's agitated paean to "modern times the modern way."

The tone is studiedly camp from the word go – more specifically, from the self-satisfied "mmm…" which Ferry purrs over that opening keyboard motif. The soundstage resounds to Thompson's tub-thumping drums, Porter's chugging bass and Manzanera's needling guitar runs as Ferry yodels his way through a fairly tricky Pop Art analogy, likening the ephemeral nature of 'picture frames' to the similarly disposable debs populating the narrator's nocturnal world. On the next track, he will confess to an ability to throw away his favoured darling, for all her apparent disposability, but in *Editions of You* he has yet to reach that nightmarish endgame; instead, he describes his favoured 'edition' as "a pin-up done in shades of blue."

This prescient forecast of the blue-tinted *Siren* cover is given added emphasis by an explicit reference, just before the instrumental break kicks in, to the mythological sirens. Here, the absurd Lorelei trilling of "wooo!" is matched for campness by Ferry's fleeting reference to the sailors intoxicated by it, whereupon a suitably crazed instrumental section gets into gear with an incandescent rock'n'roll sax break from Mackay. Grammatically adjusted, this honking tenor outburst precisely embodies the "slinky siren's wail" Ferry has just mentioned, and in performance it would be accompanied by one of the live Roxy Music's most indelible signifiers: Mackay's splendidly ludicrous imitation of Chuck Berry's trademark 'duck-walk'.

The instrumental rave-up here seems to career out of control but is nevertheless neatly divided into three sections: Mackay's saxophone histrionics done with, Eno takes over for a dazzlingly squiggly synth solo prior to handing the baton to Manzanera for a guitar break that crazes across the stereo image seemingly from nowhere. Though for the most part reserving his synthesiser for use as a sound source-cum-manipulator, when Eno deigned to use it in more straightforward keyboard fashion he could still produce staggering effects, his solo here remaining the last word in 'freakish' synth noodling. And through all this – the hard-edged, very nearly demented interchange of sax, synth and guitar – we can begin to hear Roxy, for all their glam accoutrements, fashioning a sound that anticipates punk by several years. Appropriately, Eno himself would furnish further pointers to rock's future in the more manic cuts on his *Here Come the Warm Jets* album.

Ferry returns to administer a few more louche lifestyle tips, by turns savoir-faire and laissez-faire, and including a regretful reference to decimalisation that would be expanded upon by the *Country Life* track *Three and Nine*. Ferry then throws in a cheesy organ solo, Mackay's baritone riffing ritzily in the rear, and the lyric ends, ironically, on a dire warning regarding the mortal dangers of the lifestyle just celebrated. On this cue, the track punches its way to a shattering climax, leaving only a quivering, half-heard question mark from Porter's bass guitar to herald the grim onset of *In Every Dream Home a Heartache*.

This is Roxy at their unpredictable best, dovetailing a wildly energised hard-rock workout with lyrics that, absurdly, drag in a reference to badgers as well as the mythical Lorelei. Indeed, so fecund was Ferry's lyric writing at this time that a single phrase from *Editions of You* would provide the title of a whole LP, *Quiet Life*, by turn-of-the-decade Roxy soundalikes Japan.

More straightforward tributes would come in the form of two cover versions. *Editions of You* was recorded by Canadian band Men Without Hats, best known for their 1982 hit *The Safety Dance*, for inclusion on the 1984 album *Folk of the '80s (Part III)*, but in the end was withheld until their *Greatest Hats* [sic] appeared in 1996. Seattle grunge specialists Mudhoney performed the song for the BBC's *Evening Session* on 24 May 1995; this version surfaced five years later on the album *Here Comes Sickness: The Best of the BBC Recordings*. A studio take, meanwhile, was used as the B-side of their *Butterfly Stroke* single in 1999 and subsequently appeared on the three-CD career retrospective *March to Fuzz*.

In Every Dream Home a Heartache
(Ferry) 5:23

Ferry's definitive Pop Art statement, *In Every Dream Home a Heartache* is a flesh-crawling monologue in which a glaze-eyed recitation of consumer luxuries finally reveals the deadening, nightmare vacuity at its heart. Despite a tremulous query regarding Heaven, the song actually charts a latterday descent into Hell, the fetishistic protagonist so obsessively addicted to his material possessions that all human contact has been lost, his atrophied emotions focused only on a mail-order blow-up sex doll. The London *Times*, no less, described the result as "laconic, sinister, brilliantly observed and nuanced to perfection ... a modern masterpiece." Praise indeed, though slightly compromised by the fatuous generalisation: "Ferry is the first man to bring a real intelligence to bear on pop."

Whether one envisages the song's braindead narrator as a figure from Richard Hamilton's 1956 collage 'What Is It About Today's Homes that Makes Them So Different, So Appealing?' – or places him instead among the Bel Air palm fronds and luminescent swimming pools favoured by David Hockney – it's clear that *In Every Dream Home a Heartache* takes the familiar Pop Art obsession with postwar luxury living and infects it with a devouring worm of sexual obsession and incipient madness.

Is the narrator already dead, as well as braindead? He may as well be, Ferry investing his probing questions with a quasi-religious solemnity that mocks the squeaky-clean detritus of his existence. His total reliance on fashionable accoutrements is mirrored by his total dependence on his "disposable darling," a rubberised grotesque which, ironically, he finds impossible to throw away. She's described in suitably affirmative ad-mat terms but turns out to be an ungrateful amoureuse who is incapable of returning her owner's passion. It's a uniquely frightening parable of the objectification of existence in general and women in particular, of 'love' parceled up and commodified in the jet-set dreamhomes of the 1970s.

The music is as spare and stripped down as Ferry's robotic vocal is glacial and emotionless. Against a twinkling, Eno-programmed Mellotron haze, the metronome imperturbability of Porter's bass is closely shadowed by Manzanera's subdued, metallic whisperings, while Mackay's jazzy saxophone interjections are strangely hushed, weirdly hesitant. With the final admission that the narrator's mind has been blown just as surely as his vinyl companion has, Manzanera tears into an orgasmic and heavily phased solo, blistering with West Coast pyrotechnics even as it fades inexorably out, only to craze back in again for a final spasm as the protagonist's psyche flies apart once and for all. As Charles Shaar Murray observed in his *NME* review, "It ends with a slightly modulated ring and leaves your sound system emitting small plumes of smoke. Fun and jollity time is definitely over." The disorientating false fade-out would be replicated on The Smiths' magisterial 1985 track *That Joke isn't Funny Anymore*, though in homage, apparently, to Elvis Presley's *Suspicious Minds* rather than Roxy Music.

In Every Dream Home a Heartache bears a superficial resemblance to a David Bowie track released the following month. Rounding out Side One of Bowie's *Aladdin Sane* album, *Cracked Actor* is a savage indictment of a faded Hollywood star, cruising hungrily up and down Sunset Boulevard, strung out on a killer combination of drugs, fellatio and recreational S&M. But where Bowie's protagonist is a forgotten heart-throb fancying himself as an autumnal Harry Reems in *Deep Throat*, Ferry's has lost even the capacity for human contact required to sexually abuse a Sunset & Vine prostitute.

He's no better, in fact, than the blow-up doll to which he's enslaved. By this time, articles were appearing in the music press with titles like 'Roxy Music: Terror in the Rue Morgue'. And, yes, it's tempting to see *Dream Home*'s narrator as a contemporary version of the manic-depressive neurasthenics that populate the Gothic vignettes of Edgar Allan Poe. Congress with an immobile, vinyl-skinned, uncomplaining facsimile of womanhood is, after all, interchangeable with Poe's governing theme of necrophilia. He could be a 1970s update of the insane narrator of Poe's 1835 story, *Berenice*, a man so fixated by his consumptive girlfriend's teeth that he digs up her body (and, inevitably, it turns out she's been buried alive) prior to removing all 32 of them with a pair of pliers. "All other matters and all different interests became absorbed in their single contemplation," he babbles, exactly anticipating the fetishistic absorption of *In Every Dream Home a Heartache*.

What *Melody Maker* would later call Roxy's "exotic, Poe-like quality" is also contained in Ferry's horrifying image of the doll being dressed up on a daily basis and lovingly preserved "till Death sighs." This isn't so far from Robert Bloch's Poe update, *Psycho*, with the mummified Mrs Bates preserved, not in the fruit cellar, but in the cool-blue waters of the madman's Hockney-esque swimming pool; fitted, not with a lacerating butcher knife, but a vinyl orifice in which her owner's sanity was long ago subsumed.

"I allow that it approaches the very verge of bad taste," a penitent Poe informed his panicked editor after the teeth-wrenching horrors of *Berenice* had inspired a record number of complaints, "but I will not sin quite so egregiously again." Nor, as it happened, would Ferry; he would never sound quite as seriously unhinged as this on any future recording. Even so, *In Every Dream Home a*

Heartache rapidly became a live favourite, though sometimes keel-hauled by the, as it were, overblown metallic thrash of Manzanera's solo. Its final lines – a facetious reworking of a similar passage in The Rolling Stones' *Honky Tonk Women* – were nevertheless guaranteed to be echoed by appreciative fans.

If the song's Poe-like whiff of necrophile corruption conjures images of famously castellated, billionaire recluses like Howard Hughes or William Randolph Hearst, it was intriguing to find an equally atmospheric follow-up of sorts on Ferry's 2002 album, *Frantic*. Set to music by former Eurythmic Dave Stewart, *San Simeon* turned out to be a section of *Dream Home*'s lyric discarded some 30 years earlier. "It was twice as long when I first wrote it," Ferry had told Roy Hollingsworth back in 1973, "but with it being a recitation rather than a song I had to cut it quite a bit."

Dusted off after nearly three decades, these 'out-takes' from Ferry's cutting-room floor were retooled to suggest a spooky snapshot of the 1930s rather than the 1970s, but nevertheless added numerous dreamhome design features: curving driveways, canvas-studded walls, leather upholstery, even crazy paving. Ferry was right to ditch this material in 1973 for 'too much information' reasons, but its restoration helped make the *Frantic* album qualify as a long-awaited return to form. On top of this, the track opens with a footsteps-on-flagstones sound effect that seems to translate the snazzy opening of *Love is the Drug* to the sepulchral environs of Castle Dracula.

Remakes of *In Every Dream Home a Heartache* have been particularly popular with artists purveying gloom and/or noise. The song received an atmospheric makeover at the hands of Stevenage Goth-rockers Fields of the Nephilim as the B-side of their 1987 *Blue Water* single; it resurfaced posthumously as part of a two-disc retrospective, *Revelations*, in 1993. David Bowie also had a crack at the song, occasionally cross-fertilising bits of it into his own *Heaven's in Here* during the Tin Machine 'It's My Life' tour of 1991/2, a set that also included a fully fledged version of *If There is Something*.

A further Goth reading followed from Rozz Williams and Gitane Demone, previously the mainstays of Christian Death, on their 1995 album *Dream Home Heartache*, with the Ferry song topping and tailing the disc and a Hendrix cover, *Manic Depression*, thrown in for good measure. Four years later, Jared Louche (former frontman of US machine-rock pioneers Chemlab) enlisted another industrial icon, Jim Coleman of Cop Shoot Cop, to collaborate on a *Dream Home* cover that led off Louche's *Covergirl* album. Finally, Ferry himself would reinterpret the song as a duet with Jane Birkin on her 2004 album *Rendez-vous*, a spellbinding version in which the love object comes to disconcerting life.

The Bogus Man
(Ferry) 9:20

Talking to long-time Roxy supporter Caroline Boucher during the making of the new LP, Andy Mackay pointed out that "Most of the tracks on the album are a bit longer than tracks on the first album – obviously we feel freer now. With the first one we were a bit more tentative. We've done one very weird thing with a reggae drum beat and completely atonal sax; I stopped myself playing in key."

The Bogus Man is very weird indeed and, as Mackay also intimated, of pretty epic duration. It's a thickly textured wall of sound founded on Thompson's funkily rhythmic percussion and a churning, undeviating riff from Manzanera, recalling the freeform psychedelic experimentation of so-called Krautrock and anticipating the metronomic pulse of disco. Over it, Ferry intones a genuinely frightening five-part monologue, intensifying the mood of alienation already brought to a high pitch by *In Every Dream Home a Heartache*, while Mackay's strident sax breaks blare out at entirely predictable yet strangely disorientating intervals. And, as Ferry's vocal drops away and the band wend their way through an inexorable, trance-like instrumental section, contemporary listeners could have been forgiven for checking that the record label really did say 'Island' rather than 'Brain', 'Pilz' or 'Kosmische'.

Unsurprisingly, the track seemed to make a big impact on all concerned. "For me it's probably the most successful track because it's the one on which the band is most obviously working together, and it's also got a lot of discipline," claimed Eno. Manzanera, meanwhile, observed that "There is one particular track on the new album which is incredible. It is called *The Bogus Man* and I never dreamed it would turn out the way it did when we started doing it in the studio."

Ferry's lyric alternates three verses delivered in an insidious sotto voce croon with two that are pitched on a kind of hi-falutin' falsetto. The first delivers a rasping warning against the so-called bogus man, who might be exhausted but is still intent on homicide. It sounds as if some sleazy urban character, a natural denizen of the rain-slicked city streets depicted on the album cover, is buttonholing a wet-behind-the-ears, up-from-the-country greenhorn (ie, the listener) who doesn't realise just how dangerous those streets are. The prissily falsetto interpolations are harder to call; are they the inner thoughts of the speaker or of the person he's speaking to? The ambiguity is deeply unsettling, with only the terrible underlying sense of threat assuming any concrete form. And the threat seems all the more potent when the opening lines are repeated at the end, but with the horror of the bogus man's gun supplanted by an even nastier promise of some unspecified 'fun'.

Pre-release, Eno gave a blow-by-blow account of the recording of the track (still called *The Bogus Man Part I* at that stage) to *Sounds'* Steve Peacock: "We had an undeveloped idea of making something that had a sinister feeling to it, but with … a fairly happy-sounding riff; it was just meant to sound uneasy. But the problem until about a week before we did the album was that it was tending to sound a bit 'let's do something sinister' … Then Paul started playing this kind of reggae beat to it, a very bland sort of thing, and John Porter joined in, which put a totally different face on it, and it gradually developed parts that were completely incongruous but worked because they were held together by sheer willpower. Andy was playing a kind of atonal saxophone part that had nothing particularly to do with the song – the same 12 notes over and over again in different times and inversions, a kind of Schoenbergian thing … I played a thing on synthesiser that was derived from the sound of a steel band, and Phil played a very simple thing based on echo guitar, repeated. All the elements are very strange but they do work together to give this feeling of something very uneasy proceeding in a direction it's not quite sure of."

The result is mesmerising in its intensity, with the lobotomised drone of Porter's bass hedged around by eerie Mellotron strings and the choppy extemporisations of Manzanera's guitar. Mackay, in particular, is on top form here, his channel-hopping sax breaks exactly echoing the sleazy insinuations of Ferry's vocal, finally being subsumed in Eno's all-pervading, viscous sludge of treated sound. For his part, Ferry redoubles the horror of the line "He's scratching at your throat" by putting a really nasty, plosive emphasis on the 't' of 'throat', later garnishing the mix with phonetic 'chi-kaa' sounds that would be replicated in Siouxsie and the Banshees' 1979 single, *The Staircase (Mystery)*.

Clocking in at over nine minutes, *The Bogus Man* is a track that has always divided opinion. Back in 1973, *Disc's* Caroline Boucher was so overwhelmed that she forgot Ferry's vocal entirely, referring to "an instrumental called *The Bogus Man*, which I thought the weakest track on the album, a lot of basic rhythm but uninspired embellishment." Jonh Ingham was closer to the mark in the *NME*, asking "Is there any Stranding kid on your block who doesn't groove to *Bogus Man*? Yet everyone is working entirely at odds to everyone else and, even more importantly, the music doesn't go anywhere ... That they can make all the discordant factors work as a song is a tremendous step – but that it also succeeds as Hammer-esque creep and clunk, rather than a song trying to sound scary, is a tribute to Roxy as a unified band."

Other contemporary estimates ranged from Charles Shaar Murray's, also in the *NME* ("*Bogus Man* is Roxy's *Midnight Rambler*, a long, funky workout which should leave you in a state of trembling paranoia"), to Paul Gambaccini's in *Rolling Stone*: "Side Two drones on with a nine-minute instrumental that sounds like a rip-off of The Doors' *Alabama Song*." The latter was unlikely, given Ferry's less-than-flattering comments about the track in his recent contribution to the *NME's Whatever Turned You On* column.

By 1977, Eno, too, had changed his tune regarding the effectiveness of the track. Though noting approvingly that "*Bogus Man* was almost like some of the things Can were doing at the time – you know, open-ended, improvisatory, and not just thoroughly rehearsed peformances with bits for the band to fiddle around in," he concluded that it "could have been really good, but it was just left as it stood."

It's hard to see how a track as intricately wrought and teeming with detail as *The Bogus Man* could be said to have been "left as it stood." It aims to convey a mood – in this case, one of flesh-crawling horror – and succeeds all too well. Indeed, the paranoid chill of unease is the overriding concern here, making any interpretation of Ferry's creepy and inscrutable lyric purely subjective. Interpretations are nevertheless many and various, ranging from 'urban sex-crime scenario' to 'Art Rock repositioning of *Invasion of the Body Snatchers*'. The former pegs the song as a forerunner of Talking Heads' *Psycho Killer*, the latter sees the speaker as a soulless doppelgänger, one of a whole race of metropolitan dupli-cates struggling to give a seamless impersonation of humanity.

It's worth noting, however, that 'bogus' seemed to be something of a buzz-word for Ferry at the time, cropping up in interviews on a regular basis; on one occasion, discussing the band's struggle for recognition, he remembered "carrying tapes around to all the record companies and trying to find a manager. After meeting a lot of bogus people I met EG Management." From that, one could easily cook up a theory that *The Bogus Man* is a robot composite of all the music industry yes-men and Jobsworths Ferry had encountered in his time.

But, of course, it would be no more persuasive, or absurd, than any other.

Grey Lagoons
(Ferry) 4:13

Under the title *The Bogus Man Part II*, this received its broadcast premieres via Roxy's *In Concert* radio set in September 1972 and *Full House* TV appearance the following November. It made it onto the *For Your Pleasure* album more or less unchanged save for a title switch to *Grey Lagoons*, though a tenuous (possibly bogus) link to the previous track was maintained by bringing in the song's opening piano figure right on top of Ferry's laboured *Bogus Man* breathing. Similar slight-of-hand, giving the impression that certain songs are part of a greater tapestry rather than stand-alone items, would be employed on the *Stranded*, *Country Life*, *Siren* and *Flesh + Blood* albums.

If *Grey Lagoons* is in that respect something of a trailblazer, in most others it gives the impression of recycled goods. A bluesy ballad that tears into a knock-'em-dead rock'n'roll middle section before modulating back into ballad country, it's *Would You Believe?* all over again, and to bolster the impression it's positioned in pretty much the same place (midway through Side Two) that its progenitor occupied on the *Roxy Music* album. Disorientating gear changes of this kind are typical of Roxy's approach at this time, of course, but *Grey Lagoons* boils down to little more than a showcase for one of Ferry's more purple lyrics and a starburst of instrumental pyrotechnics.

Fortunately, both are of a sufficiently high order to maintain interest. Ferry's supper-club croon is at its schmaltziest as he reels off a series of florid, courtly-love promises in the style of *If There is Something*, cynically juxtaposing "satin teardrops on velvet lights" with "morning sickness on Friday nights." He's supported by little more than a muted chorale of heavenly voices, the track only sparking into life with a sudden acceleration of Manzanera's guitar.

In a further echo, this time of *Editions of You*, the ensuing instrumental workout follows a set pattern, progressing from saxophone to heavily Eno-treated harmonica and finally to a recurrence of that recklessly speeding guitar. (And in a charming gesture to Roxy's loose and accident-prone stage act of the time, at least one bum note is allowed to stand in the midst of Mackay's blazing alto squall.) Entertaining though these individual outbursts are, the transitions between them are by no means as neatly contrived as those on *Editions of You*; indeed, the gear changes are sometimes grindingly audible. Eventually, the track reverts to schmaltzarama mode, with Ferry backed up by some very droll contributions from the Eno-Mackay barbershop duo. The querulous coda is nicely done, dovetailing a lovely glissando of Thompson's cymbals with a final spasm from Porter's superbly funky bass.

If Eno resisted the temptation to reproduce his quirky *Editions of You* synth solo in its allotted space – settling instead for manipulating Ferry's intriguingly double-tracked harmonica – it may well have been because of his dismissive attitude to the track as a whole. "I thought *Grey Lagoons* was a very trivial track, our Fifties gesture type of thing," he would confide to Ian MacDonald in 1977. A 'Fifties gesture' in itself would be welcome enough, but, given that Ferry had been uncomfortable about *Would You Believe?* more or less from the moment it came out (the track giving rise to his adamant contention that "we're not a rock revival band"), it seems strange that he should do it all over again with *Grey Lagoons*. Perhaps tellingly, both songs were omitted from the track listing of the *Thrill of It All* box set in 1995 – *Grey Lagoons*, in fact, qualifying as the only *For Your Pleasure* track not to make the cut.

It did, however, make it onto the album *Wall of Noise* as a cover version. French synth-punk pioneer Eric Débris, here styling himself Doctor Mix & the Remix, included it alongside madeover tracks from The Stooges, The Velvet Underground, The Kinks, David Bowie, The Seeds and The Troggs.

For Your Pleasure
(Ferry) 6:53

The *For Your Pleasure* LP ends on a psychedelic descent into the maelstrom in which the album's entire dramatis personae – the crazed rock'n'rollers, the lovelorn depressives, the suicidal insomniacs, the reclusive perverts, the predatory night stalkers – are finally flushed unresistingly down a kind of cosmic plughole. That's a crude way of expressing the uniquely haunting atmosphere in which the album's title track is steeped, an atmosphere redolent of passing over, piercing the veil, traversing the River Styx, of the final dissolution.

The track had received its broadcast premiere on *Sounds of the Seventies* on 9 November 1972; taped three days earlier alongside *The Bob (Medley)* and *The Bogus Man Part II* (ie, *Grey Lagoons*), this performance is Roxy's only BBC session that appears not to have survived. It was also performed on TV, rather cack-handedly, during the band's *Full House* stint on the 25th of the same month. A much more persuasive live rendition from 1975 – founded on the eerie, atonal panting of 'Sirens' Doreen Chanter and Jacqui Sullivan, together with Thompson's characteristically muscular drum patterns – was issued in December of that year as B-side to *Both Ends Burning*. Though a natural for inclusion on an expanded reissue of *Viva! Roxy Music*, this five-minute version of the song remains the only Roxy track never to have made it to CD. The song would later make a surprise reappearance as the powerful coda to Roxy's reunion dates in 2001, an unplugged version appearing the same year on Simple Minds' all-covers album *Neon Lights*.

As its broadcast history makes clear, *For Your Pleasure*, like the other tracks on the album's second side, was an old piece that could just as easily have fetched up on the *Roxy Music* album. It's a kind of mirror-reverse of *Sea Breezes*, repeating the phrase "in our present state" and with the earlier song's hesitant enquiries regarding Heaven translated into the rictus grin of a narrator all too well acquainted with Hell.

A cryptic recitation in which the speaker seems to be bidding farewell to an expiring older man, the lyric abounds in ambiguous statements of vaguely sinister import. Everything stops for the hushed sobriety of Ferry's final envoi, after which a borderline-ludicrous refrain of "ta-ra" is endlessly repeated as a Mellotron chorale chimes in and the instrumentation gears up for a mind-bending swirl of Eno-manipulated atmospherics.

Thompson has introduced the track with a stately flurry of tom-toms suggestive of an impending ritual sacrifice, while the chill sonorities of a heavily reverbed electric piano have been supplemented by a loftily elegiac guitar solo from Manzanera. Now, at the haunting echoes of "ta-ra," Manzanera's guitar sound and the otherworldly wheezing of Mackay's oboe become indistinguishable (another reminiscence of *Sea Breezes*). The multiplying "ta-ra's" are juxtaposed against a night sky rich in reverb and delay effects, and Thompson's percussion keeps up a hypnotic rolling and turning before petering out in a dissonant splash of cymbals. A strange galloping of electronic percussion suggests the watchful presence of the four horsemen of the Apocalypse, a wash of spectral voices arises as some hellish vista opens up before the victim, and – in a truly spine-chilling touch – a mellifluous female voice croons "Don't ask – don't ask why…" Then a final subdued death rattle issues from Mackay's oboe (or is it Manzanera's guitar?), there are four delicate brushes at a cymbal, and it's all over.

There are further touches of Krautrock here, together with a dab or two of the avant-garde effects beloved of Mackay and Eno (that final female croon of "Don't ask why" might owe its inspiration to a 1972 Eno piece called *You Don't Ask Me Why*), and finally an immaculate production job from the barely credited John Anthony. The finished product left some commentators cold, however. "The title tune ends the album, but is it a tune?" asked Paul Gambaccini in *Rolling Stone*. "It sounds like dogs barking repetitively for minutes on end. Maybe it is Eno's genius at work, but if so you've gotta be Mensa level to understand him or be so stoned you still think the drum solo on *In-a-Gadda-da-Vida* is a tour de force."

Discussing Roxy's early Heath Robinson approach to electronics, Manzanera told Rob Chapman that the track "has this thing called Butterfly Echo which involved putting some sticky tape on the capstan of a tape recorder so when the tape went over it made a sort of wobble noise." Whatever the crudities of its methods, the track is an exemplar of Richard Williams' dictum that "Roxy Music can bring pictures to your head like no one else."

Entirely subjective, those pictures are likely to change from one listen to another. *For Your Pleasure* might on one occasion throw up images of the demonic master-race imagined by H P Lovecraft, patiently awaiting the chance to resume dominion over mankind; perhaps these are the disembodied voices that issue from the Pit in the final fade. Another time, the roiling murkiness of the soundstage might recall the climactic horror of Marlowe's Dr Faustus – "See, see, where Christ's blood streams in the firmament!" – when Mephistopheles calls him down to Hell after 24 years of high-living debauch. While for Charles Shaar Murray of *NME*, the track was more in the *When Worlds Collide* vein of science fiction: it "leaves you," he wrote, "with the tailwind of passing asteroids buffeting your ears."

Whatever the mental pictures it throws up, few listeners are likely to be as unmoved by the track as Johnny Rogan, who in *Style with Substance* made the perplexing claim that "In common with their debut album, Roxy chose to end

For Your Pleasure on a trivial note. The title track has some of the camp finery of *Bitters End* and creates a sense of anticlimax in its lack of musical adventure." He must have been mixing it up with a throwaway B-side like *Hula Kula*, for, on the contrary, *For Your Pleasure* is Roxy's most complex and thoroughly wrought piece so far, offering a suitably grim and uncompromising end to a grim and uncompromising album. Though Sphinx-like in its inscrutability, it seems to offer a glimpse of a netherworld horror profound in its implications.

Five: *The Pride and the Pain*

"Bryan never faces you with this kind of thing. It's not part of his character … So eventually I just stood up, said 'OK, fuck it, I'm leaving' – and walked out. And, as soon as I'd done it, a great weight lifted and I felt so exuberant … I went straight back home and started writing and wrote Baby's On Fire, *in fact, on that same day – 21 June 1973."*

Brian Eno, quoted in *NME* 26 November 1977

Montreux, Meurice, Musikladen

The band's first continental tour, which started in Italy on Monday 23 April 1973, subsequently ranged through France, Germany, Sweden, Denmark, Belgium, Switzerland and Holland. The response was ecstatic, much enhancing the sales of both *For Your Pleasure* and its companion Euro single, *Do the Strand*.

At the Golden Rose Festival in Montreux on Sunday 29 April, Roxy were awarded the Grand Prix du Disque for *For Your Pleasure* and wowed an audience previously regaled by the likes of Ralph McTell, Johnny Rivers, Maggie Bell, Focus and Tir Na Nog (with whom the band had been paired in the BBC's *In Concert* the previous September). The following week, a live TV appearance in Paris saw a rabble of ticket-less Roxy fans literally smash down the studio doors in their eagerness to attend; according to the excitable Dr Puxley, the mob numbered at least a thousand.

It was also in Paris that Roxy's newest covergirl, Amanda Lear, arranged an unusual photo opportunity for the band with her dessicated companion, Salvador Dalí. Limbering up for a showcase gig at the Olympia the same evening, the band members trooped into Dalí's domicile at the Hôtel Meurice and took afternoon tea with the Surrealist icon. The TV crew Dalí had organised failed to show up, however, and Ferry was later less than charitable towards their bug-eyed host. Mindful of the fact that the ageing artist had also recently encountered Alice Cooper, Ferry observed that "Dalí seems to have deteriorated into someone who hangs around with bands just to get publicity," adding airily: "His current outpout is quite meagre – certainly nothing to talk about over dinner."

A characteristic of Roxy's continental itinerary was their insistence on staying only in the plushest accommodation, the better to build up their hi-falutin' mystique; in Paris it was the Ancienne Regime luxuriance of the George V Hôtel. Their post-Dalí performance at the Olympia saw Ferry supplementing his stage wardrobe, depleted by thieves on the British leg of the tour, with a brocaded Musketeer-style frock coat hired from a local costumier. Years later, it was suggested that the thief was the future Sex Pistol Steve Jones, who in 1973 had allegedly looted various items from his idols – Rod Stewart and Ronnie Wood as well as Roxy – prior to delivering his pièce de résistance by swiping the entire PA intended for David Bowie's 'farewell' concerts at the Hammersmith Odeon. The 'borrowed' equipment and costumes were intended for Jones' fledgling band – called, aptly enough, The Strand.

The band's European jaunt also included a broadcast on Wednesday 30 May for *Beat-Club*, now rechristened *Musikladen* and with Manfred Sexauer joining longstanding *Beat-Club* host Uschi Nerke. With the Bremen TV crew requiring three run-throughs prior to filming, it was a punishing engagement, particularly after a gruelling tour that had started in mid-March. "I didn't realise at the start how all-consuming the whole machine would be," Ferry reflected. "This business of touring seems terribly old-fashioned … I think the answer must be more TV and less live gigs. We were playing to 10 or 15 million people the other day on this syndicated programme, which is the successor to *Beat-Club*, and that would save about 50 live gigs. That would give me more time to write stuff."

The band's carefully nurtured image, meanwhile, was being widely imitated, leading Ferry to institute a radical overhaul in the autumn. And it wasn't just workaday glam rockers like Gary Glitter and The Sweet who were, as Ferry put it, "debasing the look"; the band were well aware that even the famously magpie-like David Bowie was beginning to look increasingly like Andy Mackay, not only sartorially but follically, too.

Roxy's hairstylist, Keith Wainwright of Smile, had been responsible for Scott Walker's feathered look in the late 1960s and now relished the way in which Roxy were in at "the beginning of music as a part of fashion." Mackay's green-striped hair, which reportedly stopped the traffic when he left Wainwright's chic Knightsbridge emporium, was first seen on the band's *Full House* TV showcase in November 1972 and would be memorialised on the inner sleeve of *For Your Pleasure*. "Gary Glitter and Bowie both took a lot from Roxy," Wainwright recalled in 1980. "Bowie knew what was going on – he's always been that kind of great entrepreneur – and he started off all that stuff with dyed hair *after* they did. Andy Mackay's hair with the white stripe is a classic that was the beginning of coloured hair, revolutionary … And when the LP came out we were absolutely inundated with people wanting Andy's and Bryan's haircuts."

The Refreshing Experience

Though his hair was on the sparse side, it was nevertheless Eno who, as far as costuming and visual magnetism were concerned, represented the focal point of the band to many fans. "I do love the whole costume bit," he told *Sounds'* Steve Peacock in March, facetiously assuring him that "it's very important to me musically, not a superfluous thing in any way." Ferry, however, was beginning to consider Eno's peacock posturing decidedly superfluous.

Relations between the pair had been steadily worsening since Roxy's abortive US tour, at the end of which Ferry had reportedly determined on removing Eno from the band but had been dissuaded by EG. The enthusiasm of American journalists for accounts of Eno's more left-field experiments (including a proposed project to exploit the musical potential of earthworms) was, in Ferry's estimation, a serious impediment to Roxy's already problematic Stateside acceptance. And, to combat Eno's legendary loquacity, Ferry shot himself in the foot in spectacular style by affecting a Garbo-esque inscrutability in the few interviews he gave. Intended to increase his mystique, this tactic only sent disappointed journalists rushing all the more gratefully to the ever-spouting oracle that was Eno.

On top of all this, Eno was keen to draw the other band members' attention to what he called the unfair division of Roxy's spoils, with Ferry reportedly receiving over 70 per cent of the band's earnings. It was this disquieting ratio, as much as creative frustration, that would prompt Mackay and Manzanera to demand co-writing credits on Roxy's third album.

"Some of the papers seemed to think that I was the leader of the group, which was very embarrassing and quite unjust to Bryan," Eno pointed out four years later. "But then he went and started doing interviews where he'd try to re-establish the real position and started saying completely over-the-top things like 'This band is my baby and I could have done the same thing with any other group of musicians' – which was blatantly untrue."

As well as the eye-catching stage antics that had made him a fan favourite and the playful intellectual theories with which he was ever ready, Eno made good copy for the way in which his interest in the more out-there forms of pornography kept pace with his own, reportedly prodigious, sexual athleticism. As Cynthia Dagnal put it, Eno was "the man that groupies of three continents have come to know as The Refreshing Experience," a typical piece of fan mail reading: "Hi, am 18 years old and a good screw." Eno's enervated response? "I wish these girls would send photographs."

Early in 1974, he would suffer a collapsed lung brought on in part, so the music press intimated, by a 30-hour session involving six women. "The reason it fell apart, I think, is that Bryan was doing all the work and Eno was getting all the glory," David Enthoven confided to the *Independent* in 2001. "It was Eno who got to shag all the girls, and I think that drove Bryan completely bonkers. I mean, Eno was literally shagging non-stop; he was on for it all the time, like a fucking rabbit."

"And then there were the 'Eno!' shouters in the audience," Eno observed. "Because, you know, in the quieter, slower numbers in the set the audience would always shout my name. And I could understand exactly how Bryan felt. He'd be singing this beautiful, quiet song and some pranny at the back of the hall would bellow 'Eno!' Obviously, he got progressively more pissed off." The crunch came at the York Festival in June, when Eno prefaced Roxy's performance by clowning around on stage with his deliberately out-of-tune protégées, The Portsmouth Sinfonia, after which *Beauty Queen* was completely wrecked by the "Eno!" shouters. In a well-meaning attempt to give Ferry the spotlight, Eno promptly left the stage, which had the unfortunate effect of inflaming the Eno faction even further. At the end of the set, Ferry reportedly stumbled off ashen-faced, vowing never to share the same stage with Eno again.

Reflecting on the situation, Eno told Lisa Robinson that the early Roxy set-up "was one of the most interesting experimental situations that could have existed.

Just the idea that we didn't really want to have a focus on stage, it could have been Andy or me or Bryan … And for a time there really was a triple ambiguity. But apparently Bryan didn't want it that way and he conned us, really." Manzanera's recollection was more temperate, conceding that Ferry had been under intolerable management pressure to assume centre stage: "He was pushed to do it, definitely. By the management and by everyone. The message was, 'You've got to have someone, a focus, in the middle, otherwise the band won't be successful.'"

Two non-musicians is one too many

Eno's departure from Roxy Music – and in the event, Ferry's pathological fear of confrontation meant that he more or less had to sack himself – became perhaps the most hotly debated music press story of 1973, with *Melody Maker* first breaking the news on 21 July. It remains hotly debated to this day, with some regretting the consequent removal of Roxy's more extreme experimental edge, others applauding the more tuneful and Ferry-centric Roxy that resulted.

At the time, Ferry's summary of the situation was a terse one – "Two non-musicians in a band is one too many," he deadpanned. And by 1982 he was responding to the growing Eno cult with a categorical statement of "Some people believe Eno was the inspiration for the Roxy sound. They are wrong." He has since expressed regret, however, that some third party couldn't have stepped in to resolve this classic clash of youthful male egos, thus ensuring that Eno could have been kept on longer.

According to EG's official press release, "clashes of personality and ideology led to incompatibility," with Eno leaving Roxy in order "to pursue his own inter-ests." This was a prophetic statement if ever there was one, as Eno's subsequent career would turn out to be as wildly idiosyncratic as it was influential. Liberated from Roxy Music, he immediately plunged into a slew of alternative projects; indeed, the centrepiece of his first solo album, *Baby's On Fire*, was written on the very day he left. "Then EG called me to tell me how my finances were after Roxy," he remembered. "I was £15,000 in debt. That's what you get for trying to be a rock star." Though EG would lower the debt to a more manageable £5000, much of Eno's workaholic activity was motivated by a grotesque irony: while venerated as one of the most photogenic cover-stars of 1973, he was actually living a flyblown, hand-to-mouth existence in Ladbroke Grove.

Prior to his resignation from Roxy, Eno had been moonlighting with both Robert Fripp and Andy Mackay. He had first met the King Crimson frontman when contributing to Matching Mole's 1972 album *Little Red Record*, which Fripp produced. Their collaborative LP, *(No Pussyfooting)*, was a budget-priced guitar-and-tape-loops experiment consisting of two long pieces, *The Heavenly Music Corporation* and *Swastika Girls*. His work with Mackay at Island's Basing Street studio had resulted in two tracks so far, according to Nick Kent, "one, a tasteful rock-a-ballad with Eno's likeable wheeze embellishing the track on harmonies and yearning lead vocal, the other a new dance sensation with agitated shuffle beat and neat synthesiser trickery." A mooted single release, *Never a Light Without a Shadow*, failed to materialise, however.

Of Eno's other projects, some were real enough, such as his contributions to the Kevin Ayers-produced LP *Lady June's Linguistic Leprosy* and the Robert Calvert solo album *Captain Lockheed and the Starfighters*, in which he shared the bill with other 'one-offs' like Arthur Brown and Vivian Stanshall. Further work with Portsmouth Sinfonia, plus collaborations with such disparate characters as Magic Michael and Lynsey de Paul, also have a ring of plausibility. Others, however, can best be attributed to Eno's highly individual sense of humour, notably the so-called Plastic Eno Band, a projected album entitled *The Magic Wurlitzer Synthesizer of Brian Eno plays 'Winchester Cathedral' and 14 other Evergreens* and a girl-group project called Luana and the Lizard Girls (apparently "a daring move to turn launderettes and massage parlours into rock 'n' roll venues").

In all these side projects Eno identified himself as more a facilitator than a star, pointing up the irony of Ferry's conflict with a man who had always conceived of himself as an anti-star, whose stage shenanigans were no more than a pose, and who had already lost interest in the remorseless grind of touring. "What we were doing was taking up 85 per cent of my time, but actually occupied only 25 per cent of my interest," he informed *Melody Maker*, the clear implication being that he'd had his fill of Roxy Music in any case.

Ferry, however, didn't have the benefit of hindsight, and in the wake of Eno's resignation he grew more and more disconsolate. "I'm the most misunderstood man in the business," he complained to Ian MacDonald in September. "Some of the misinterpretations of me I've seen in the press have made me almost physically sick." His mood can hardly have been lightened by the news that Warners had summarily dropped Roxy's contract, temporarily leaving the band without a US record label.

How can anyone replace Eno?

On 28 July, just one week after Puxley's announcement, the *NME* carried the following baleful story: "In the wake of Eno's sudden departure from Roxy Music, strong rumours developed this week that saxman Andy Mackay is also about to quit – and that if Mackay leaves Roxy, guitarist Phil Manzanera will follow. The rumours began when this week Eno – who is to form a new group called Luana and the Lizard Girls – told *NME*'s Nick Kent that Andy Mackay was determined on leaving if plans to include violinist Eddie Jobson come to fruition."

Eno himself did what he could to calm the situation, telling Kent in the same issue that "My thirsting for revenge has died down somewhat over the last few days … I started off by wanting to call a press conference so that I could state my case, but that's all so pointless. Another reason for my reticence is because I don't want to damage Roxy for the sake of the other people in it. I mean, I really like the other members, and I [pause] really like Bryan in a funny way."

Of the other members, Mackay, for one, had determined to put his foot down. "It's not true – Eddie is *not* joining," he insisted, again in the same action-packed issue of *NME*. "What may have caused the confusion is the fact that I'm changing my name to Eddie Riff. Eddie [Jobson] might be playing on a couple of tracks on the next album, but any addition to the band must be agreed by all members." "How can anyone replace Eno?" he added indignantly.

Though by no means as outré as Prince's subsequent determination to rename himself as an unpronounceable heiroglyph, Mackay's quixotic resolve to change his name seems, at this stage in the game, utterly inexplicable. Mackay explained himself so: "The actual name comes from the days of my first band at college, The Nova Express. At that time there was a big conflict in the group between the jazzers and the R'n'B rockers, and I was amongst the latter. We never really had a good vocalist, so we'd rely on instrumentals, and every time we got towards the middle of a song, the jazzers would always want to take solos. I was never allowed one, so I used to just riff in the background all the time. So Eddie Riff (Edward is also my middle name) became my personality as a saxophone player."

As alter-egos go, Eddie Riff seems to have been Mackay's very own Ziggy Stardust, but in the event he did the sensible thing and confined the Riff moniker to the title of his upcoming solo album, *In Search of Eddie Riff*. It's intriguing, however, that in the midst of Roxy's personality crisis Mackay should seemingly suffer a personality crisis of his own, perhaps as a means of dissociating himself from the bloody business in which he'd become unwittingly embroiled.

The conflict of loyalties was indeed a bloody one; Manzanera and Mackay had become good friends of Eno's and felt a strong kinship with him. Twenty years on, Manzanera observed that, initially, "everybody was aiming towards one thing – success – and there was no power struggle to become leader of the band to start with. It's always the people behind the scenes, the managers and agents, who stir things up. When Eno left, we were in great danger of imploding completely."

The threat of implosion was made worse by Ferry's circuitous tactics in securing a replacement for Eno, which, unknown to the other band members, long predated Eno's departure. In fact, the flashpoint performance at York had been clandestinely attended, at Ferry's invitation, by an 18-year-old virtuoso called Eddie Jobson.

"I think Bryan sensed that Eno was going to leave, even if Eno didn't," Jobson later maintained, diplomatically. "I enjoyed the concert, but the ridiculous thing was that Eno was then told that I was there when he came off. That seemed strange, of course, and reflected badly on me, as though I was spying on Eno and trying to find out what he was up to." At the time, Eno himself had been under no illusions regarding the mysterious arrival of this musical prodigy. "I know both Andy and Phil are very annoyed about that," he pointed out. "One thing I'm personally very annoyed at is that when Eddie Jobson was brought up to York to study my style and form, Bryan didn't tell anyone up until the last minute."

Ferry and Jobson had previously met in Newcastle – their sisters Enid and Ann had been room-mates at university – and the acquaintance was renewed during the *For Your Pleasure* sessions. According to Jobson, Ferry suggested he join Roxy even at that early stage, but Jobson demurred thanks to his commitment to Curved Air. On Eno's resignation, Ferry went incognito to Colchester to see Curved Air in action, soon afterwards asking Jobson to play on his upcoming solo LP and reaffirming the Roxy offer. Initially hesitant, Jobson then discovered that two other members of Curved Air were about to jump ship, which prompted him to accept.

Mackay and Manzanera, by all accounts, gave him the frostiest welcome imaginable. "They didn't like it because they hadn't been consulted," Jobson realised. "Naturally they thought, 'Stuff this.' Andy wanted to exert his authority, to show he and they weren't just going to sit there and take it." Tensions, however, had simmered down somewhat by the time Jobson attended his first rehearsal: "I think that in the end all the words were really a demonstration of what they *might* do. I jammed, and, as it happened, they seemed quite happy."

Like Ferry and Thompson, Jobson was from the north east, having been born in Billingham on 28 April 1955. His prodigious achievements on violin and piano as a schoolboy had marked him out for a classical career until he was blown away by a Curved Air concert at Newcastle's Mayfair Ballroom. Fascinated by Darryl Way's use of classical violin in a rock setting, he snapped up the band's *Air Conditioning* album and learned all Way's solos, which turned out to be a self-fulfilling prophecy. After a spell with Fat Grapple, in October 1972 he was asked by vocalist Sonja Kristina to join Curved Air; Way had departed, as had keyboard player Francis Monkman, and Jobson filled in for both of them on the band's *Air Cut* album, foregoing a place at the Royal Academy of Music in the process.

For Ferry, Jobson offered the double attraction of remarkable musical dexterity coupled with a complete absence of Eno's incorrigible grandstanding; though Jobson had an elfin teen presence all his own, it would pose no threat to Ferry's centrality. In addition – and it was this precaution that may, in part, have been responsible for Mackay and Manzanera's acceptance of him – Ferry was careful not to make the new recruit a full member of the band. This was fine by Jobson, relieving him of a fifth share of the debt Roxy had so far accumulated, but it was a fact cannily concealed from the general public. "It didn't really matter; it was a technical thing," Jobson revealed in *Trouser Press* magazine. "I just wasn't part of their company, which meant that I didn't get record royalties. It also meant that I didn't have that much say in the way the band went."

'My Way' – certainly

At the height of the Roxy discord Ferry retired to Corfu for a short holiday; as Puxley would put it in his characteristically purple 'Rex Balfour' prose: "For two brief weeks, in a villa couched between a deserted mountain and an isolated beach – between the Devil and the deep blue sea – he pondered the future." In fact, the immediate future was carefully mapped out. On his return at the end of June, Ferry repaired to Air Studios to start work on his first solo album. "I don't want to spend too much time on it," he told *Sounds'* Martin Hayman. "The whole nature of it leaves me open to criticism because it will be all old classics. I don't want to compromise the next Roxy Music album."

Of course, the mere fact that he was making a solo album was seen as compromising the next Roxy one, only adding fuel to the doom-sayers convinced that Roxy were no more. Ferry, however, had been regaling music journalists with his plans for the LP long before the 'Roxy Split!' headlines started to appear.

The selected songs, as he told *Spectator* music critic Duncan Fallowell, were "clear-cut like Roy Lichtenstein pictures." The selection process, however, was by no means as clear-cut. The Beach Boys' *I Get Around* was discarded in favour of its flip-side, *Don't Worry Baby*, while Leiber & Stoller's *Baby I Don't Care* was preferred over their *Hound Dog*. Burt Bacharach was up for inclusion but didn't make the cut, nor did Cole Porter's *Ev'ry Time We Say Goodbye*. "Oh, *My Way*, certainly," Ferry had teasingly assured Nick Kent, but this too failed to appear. As for his Goffin & King selection, he plumped for *Don't Ever Change* over his perennial favourite, *Will You Love Me Tomorrow*; that one would have to wait two decades before featuring on Ferry's *Taxi* album.

The musical personnel included old Roxy hands John Porter and Paul Thompson (with Manzanera guesting on Ferry's Beatles selection), new Roxy recruit Eddie Jobson, pianist Dave Skinner (later to join Roxy for their 1979 comeback dates), and a brass section consisting of trumpeter Henry Lowther and Average White Band saxophonists Roger Ball and Malcolm Duncan. To produce, Ferry called on his old friend Porter and the similarly named John Punter, who had engineered the *For Your Pleasure* album. Punter had begun his career at Decca in 1967, subsequently joining the newly launched Air Studios aged 20 and working with the likes of Climax Blues Band, Procol Harum and The Strawbs. He would later produce Sad Café, Boomtown Rats and The Tourists, among others, as well as overseeing the classic 1979 album *Quiet Life*, much the best LP by the Roxy-inspired Japan.

"The trouble with doing something like *Tracks of My Tears*," Ferry pointed out, "is that the original was so brilliant it's hard to touch it." If this hinted at the self-defeating nature of the whole enterprise, Ferry was to be staggered by the negative response to the first fruits of his work. Issued as a single, his radical recasting of Bob Dylan's *A Hard Rain's a-Gonna Fall* entered the chart on 25 September, reaching a high of number ten on 23 October and enjoying a run of nine weeks. Despite, or perhaps because of, this gratifying commercial success, it was greeted with almost unanimous horror and disdain in the rock fraternity, which viewed its big-band theatrics as little better than an act of sacrilege.

True, Ferry was blithely unconcerned by the song's political content ("I can't be bothered with all that Cuba Crisis stuff," he claimed), but his intentions, he insisted, were completely sincere. Dylan's original, he pointed out, "was a poem with a guitar backing. But there are a hell of a lot of images in that song that I wanted to emphasise musically. And I thought it would sound good as a rock number … But the simple fact that it was controversial was a good thing."

Not everyone was scandalised by Ferry's presumption, however. "He makes it sound like Marc Bolan doing *Sugar Sugar* for Jonathan King; in short, this old warhorse has never come across better," enthused Greg Shaw in *Phonograph Record*. Ferry also received a telegram that read: "Congratulations on your record *A Hard Rain's a-Gonna Fall*. Fanfuckingtastic!!!" The sender, whom Ferry had yet to meet, was Ringo Starr.

In 1973, the very idea of an all-covers album was considered a heresy in the more po-faced climes of the rock community; indeed, the collective title, *These Foolish Things*, seemed in itself to betray Ferry's alien flippancy. His appropriation of Marcel Duchamp's phrase 'ready-mades' and mining of rock's past (even, horror of horrors, the utterly forgotten world of pre-rock show tunes) qualified as postmodernism before the concept was properly understood, and as a result Ferry's album soon trailed a flotilla of negative crits behind it. Even so, it hit number five in the album charts on its release in October, its progress much enhanced by the success of the accompanying single.

Hard Rain itself, with its fusillade of storm effects, rhythmic country fiddling, clod-hopping beat and exhilaratingly camped-up vocal, leads off the album on a high note that is repeated only twice. By his own account, Eddie Jobson was responsible, along with Paul Thompson, for the arrangement on both *Hard Rain* and the hypnotic closer, *These Foolish Things*, in which a fagged-out supper-club ambience gives place to a gently reggae-fied rendition of an antiquated tune dating from 1935.

Even better is a genuinely staggering remake of *Sympathy for the Devil*, one of four Rolling Stones items considered for inclusion. Here, Ferry's moustache-twirling aristocrat of evil sounds like he's auditioning for a Hammer horror film. Spitting out the Jagger-Richard litany against an awesome hard-rock backdrop, his demonic laughter peals insanely through the mix in a sustained ending that prefigures Ferry's scary version of *The 'In' Crowd*. Like *Hard Rain*, *Sympathy for the Devil* also benefits from the back-up vocals of former 'Ikette' Robbie Montgomery and her Dr John colleague Jessie Davis.

Ferry made promotional films for both *A Hard Rain's a-Gonna Fall* and *These Foolish Things*, accompanied by a piano-playing glamour girl on the latter and three Warhol-type backing vocalists on *Hard Rain*. In shades, black plastic macs and frumpy headscarves, this vocal trio looks sufficiently like three dragged-up blokes to suggest that Dr Puxley was getting his promos crossed when he claimed that *These Foolish Things*' "marvellously camp replica of Diana Ross" was "actually photographer Eric Boman in wig, in drag." Puxley also pointed out that "these two films have hardly ever been shown, considered too outré or outrageous for public taste." More to the point, prior to the appearance of Queen's *Bohemian Rhapsody* video, broadcasters didn't really know what to do with films like Ferry's.

The rest of the album has a kind of buoyant, even boyish lustre that disarms criticism, though the highlights are easily enumerated: the twinkling harpsichord sound of *I Love How You Love Me*, Ruan O'Lochlainn's charming alto solo on the same track, schmaltzy but highly engaging remakes of *Don't Worry Baby* and *Loving You is Sweeter Than Ever*, plus a stormingly camped-up rendition of the old Lesley Gore hit *It's My Party*. The latter Ferry identified as a "tribute to the gay side" of Roxy's fanbase, for whom he was careful not to change the song's addressee from 'he' to 'she'. *River of Salt*, too, is an intriguing choice intriguingly interpreted. Ferry himself described this forgotten Ketty Lester flip-side from 1962 as "a dark horse; I'm probably the only person in England with a copy of that. It reminds me of when I used to be in Gasboard in Newcastle – in fact, this whole LP does."

Essentially light in tone, *These Foolish Things* gave Ferry the opportunity to loosen his stays a little, most of Roxy's material having been comparatively forbidding up to this point. "One thing I learned," he told Nick Kent, "is that most of the classics I was reshaping were remarkably simple three-chord efforts and that what I'd been doing was, in effect, more complex." The album would not only have a far-reaching effect on his own approach to songwriting, but also on rock music as a whole, with covers albums soon ceasing to be considered anathema. Indeed, somewhat to Ferry's chagrin, David Bowie would record a collection of his own favourite oldies, *Pin Ups*, soon after *These Foolish Things* had been completed.

As a one-off exercise, Ferry's first solo LP remains a delight. Unfortunately, its success convinced Ferry that his beloved 'ready-mades' were the way to go for almost all future solo outings. This helped preserve the individuality of his Roxy recordings but resulted in increasingly bland and faceless solo ones. It was hard and unyielding terrain that Ferry would still be plugging away at 30 years' hence.

PART TWO

Roxy Rule

Six: *The Third Roxy Music Album*

"Roxy Music evoke on this album an impression of lush melancholy, full of elusive bitter-sweet fragrances. I can see why some critics find it hard to like them while appreciating what they do. Their music isn't warm or embracing; here, it's suffused with an exotic, Poe-like quality that distances the creators from their listener, while Ferry's strange voice lends it the chill bloom of the corpse."

unsigned review, Melody Maker 10 November 1973

Seemingly undaunted by recent traumas, not to mention a staggering workload, Roxy regrouped at Air Studios to start work on *Stranded* in the third week of August. The removal of Eno ensured that Ferry was now the group's undisputed focus, but, aware of the lingering rancour caused by the Eno debacle, he was sensible enough to bring a new element of democracy into the group. Emerging from the B-side gloom, Manzanera and Mackay would be responsible for co-writing a track apiece on the new album. "The others – Andrew and Phil – want to contribute," Ferry observed. "That's fine, as long as I have control over the material that goes in. I feel the need to guide the course of an album; they bring their songs or ideas – and I choose what I can best employ myself in."

With Eno gone, Ferry deeply affected by his work on *These Foolish Things* and both Mackay and Manzanera bringing their own sensibilities to bear on composing as well as performing, the Roxy sound underwent a profound change. Roughly speaking, the shambolic, scattershot creativity of earlier albums would be replaced by a more classically consonant approach, swopping the sonically unexpected for well-crafted melodies and an increased professionalism in the playing.

With Eno's old 'treatments' role now shared out between Manzanera and Mackay, the texture of the sound was also enriched by the appointment of teen virtuoso Eddie Jobson. As Manzanera put it, "We've got so many more possibilities in the sense that we've got a violin and a keyboard player. I'm not putting Eno down, because what he did was incredible, but I think it's going to be equally incredible with Eddie. If you like, this is the second phase ... The strange thing is that we would have changed anyway for this album. I suppose people will think we've changed because Eno left, but we were preparing for quite a dramatic change anyway."

Chris Thomas was again in place as producer, this time overseeing the entire album. Reflecting on the now Eno-free Roxy in the November 1974 issue of *Phonograph Record*, Thomas was philosophical: "Obviously, these things happen. It's nothing rare. It happens in every band ... Andy was so upset when we did *Stranded*, about Eno leaving, that there was a tension there between Andy and Bryan. Andy was telling me this and Bryan was telling me that and I was always in the middle. But they're all right now. I think they are all right now. I hope they are all right now."

Though co-writing one of the album's most magisterial songs (and one other that was discarded owing to lack of time), Mackay's continued disgruntlement is audible on the finished album, where he only really lets rip on three tracks, *Psalm, Serenade* and his own *A Song for Europe*. Elsewhere, notably on *Street Life*, he merely burbles in the backbeat in 'Eddie Riff' mode, or else he 'treats' his own contribution to such a degree that it all but disappears (eg, *Amazona*). Though deciding against changing his name, as he had threatened to do in the last week of July, Mackay seems to have used his 'treatments' role as a subtler means of self-effacement.

Establishing a pattern that would apply equally to *Country Life* and *Siren*, the *Stranded* album was made under considerable record company pressure. "We're having a bit of a panic stations," Manzanera admitted in early October, pointing out also that "we want to make sure the album comes out at the latest in the second week of November, or it would go back to February [1974], and I don't think we could stand that."

For Ferry, there was also the grave responsibility of coming up with a cover image to equal those of *Roxy Music* and *For Your Pleasure*, on which both Kari-Ann and Amanda seemed to be saying, among other things, "Follow that." Discussing the genesis of Roxy albums, Ferry pointed out that "The idea comes first and the cover then has to express the idea. You have to find the right chick for it." The "right chick" this time around was pneumatic Marilyn Cole, who had occupied the *Playboy* centrefold for January 1972 and subsequently been named 'Playmate of the Year'. Formerly a partner of Hugh Hefner himself and by now consort to *Playboy*'s UK boss Victor Lownes, she would enjoy a brief fling with Ferry just as Amanda had before her and Kari-Ann would later.

Devised by the now familiar team of Ferry, designer Nicholas de Ville, photographer Karl Stoecker and stylist Antony Price, the *Stranded* cover offered a memorable embodiment of the album's title, with a bronzed, Amazonian beauty sprawled in eroticised abandon on an exotic and palm-fringed strand. With wet-look crimson dress artfully rent to permit glimpses of nipple, Cole here looks like a 'Penthouse Pet' version of Fay Wray in *King Kong*, exhausted after a plunge in the tropical waters of Skull Island and ready for ravishment by the square-jawed Bruce Cabot – or possibly the sizeable Kong himself.

Despite felicitous details like a creamy orchid clutched in Cole's left hand just as Kari-Ann previously dandled a pale pink rose, Ferry confessed himself slightly disappointed with the end product. "There should have been more jungle and not so much girl," he told *Record Mirror*'s Roger Greenaway. "I wanted to create the steamy feel of the jungle. That's where the music of much [of] *Stranded* is. We built this fantastic jungle in the photographer's studio but somehow that final shot didn't quite make it." If Ferry's desire for "not so much girl" concealed a suspicion that Roxy's album covers were edging further from the kitsch pastiche of yore and closer to the legs-akimbo aesthetic of 1970s soft porn, it was a suspicion quickly forgotten, as the next Roxy sleeve would confirm in no uncertain terms.

Ferry's attitude to his covergirls is ultimately less mystifying, however, than his allusion to *Stranded* as 'jungle' music. Steeped in the songsmith perfectionism of

These Foolish Things, he brought to the album a chilly European grandeur redolent of Luchino Visconti's *Death in Venice* rather than Johnny Weissmuller's *Tarzan Escapes*. The proto-punk onslaught of *Street Life* is a many-tendriled riot, the funky dazzle of *Amazona* is literally steamy in places. But the album otherwise is about as far from 'jungle' music as it's possible to get. "I wonder whether Bryan at the time was really aware of what he was doing," Mackay mused during a 1997 conversation with Michael Bracewell. "I think he thought he was singing one thing, but because he was English, it came out differently."

Selected to play bass on the new album – a role he would fill on *Country Life* and *Siren* too – was 29-year-old Johnny Gustafson, formerly of Quatermass, The Merseybeats and The Big Three. Though his studio tenure with Roxy was an unprecedentedly consistent one, he would never rise above the level of hired hand, in part because Roxy's music wasn't to his personal taste and in part because he could command substantial session fees elsewhere. "Roxy was puzzling initially as nobody seemed to be directing it," he told Rob Chapman in 1995. "Bryan would have little more than a chord sequence. It was often a complete shambles … All Bryan would say was, 'Make it sound black.'"

Bass guitarist for the accompanying tour, as on the previous one, was the lofty Sal Maida. The itinerary kicked off at the Queen's Hall in Leeds on Friday 19 October, subsequently taking in Birmingham, Sheffield, Bradford, Liverpool, Manchester, Leicester and, on Friday 2 November, Glasgow. (The performances of *Pyjamarama* and *Chance Meeting* during this latter gig would eventually turn up on the *Viva! Roxy Music* album.) Dates in Edinburgh, Newcastle, Bournemouth and Swansea preceded Roxy's triumphal appearance at London's Rainbow on 10 and 11 November, after which a European tour ranged through Denmark, Germany, Italy, Austria, France, Belgium and Holland. To compensate for a cancelled Bristol date earlier in the schedule, the tour wound up with dates in Bath and Bristol on 16 and 18 December respectively.

Just ahead of the Roxy tour, Mackay had limbered up for it with a brief diversification into Deep Purple territory, giving two performances of Jon Lord's *Gemini Suite* at Munich's Circus Krone alongside Roger Glover, Pete York, Ray Fenwick, vocalist Yvonne Elliman and conductor Eberhard Schoener. This can hardly have prepared him, however, for the incredible scenes that greeted the Roxy concerts. Paradoxically, the retirement of the ultra-theatrical Eno acted as the trigger for an astonishing outbreak of Roxymania, complete with baying mobs, beseiged hotels and police escorts. Indeed, at Glasgow on 2 November, fan adulation was so ardent that Manzanera emerged from the melée with a broken leg, forcing him to adopt a Robert Fripp-like sitting posture for much of the remainder of the schedule. This is how he can be seen on the group's *Musikladen* performance for German TV, taped in Bremen on the 19th, during which the band gave storming renditions of new numbers *Street Life*, *Amazona* and *Psalm*.

The removal of Eno also prompted Ferry to finally take charge in performance and move to centre stage, where audiences and critics alike were knocked out by his newfound charisma. The absence of Eno's ostrich feathers, meanwhile, coincided with a complete image rethink; out went the flash and filigree, in came a more mature and forbidding look. "All those glitter groups sprang up and debased the look," grumbled Ferry. "Now, for me, it's the *Casablanca* look, which

I feel much better in anyway." Recalling his ode to Humphrey Bogart's Rick Blaine in *2 H.B.*, Ferry's soon-to-be-iconic white tuxedo was balanced by Mackay's Teddy Boy version of Wyatt Earp (or, as one contemporary critic had it, Kentucky's own Colonel Sanders).

And yet the tuxedo's maiden voyage was oddly underwhelming. At Leeds on 19 October, Roxy topped an all-night bill that also included the Elkie Brooks-Robert Palmer combo Vinegar Joe. Writing in *NME*, Bob Edmands was perplexed: "Ferry used to sport epaulettes, at the very least, as was only befitting a man of his status. Now he's chosen a white dinner jacket ensemble, complete with black bow tie, making him somewhat less chic in appearance than the crumpled Mr Robin Day. The former robot saxophonist Mr Andy McKay [sic] has also dispensed with fashion accessories. Gone is the white boiler suit and tinted hair. He, too, has opted for the colonial governor look, with minor variations, such as a string-tie ... Even Phil Manzanera wore bugged eye glasses with distinction, but he now evidently thinks his naked face has more impact ... Dear, oh dear. Boys, consider please. There is absolutely no mileage to be gained from looking drab."

Reporting from Manchester in the same paper, Tony Tyler accurately observed that "The trash element – an important part of Roxy's earlier breakthrough – is now Out of Favour with Mr F; suitings and clothings ranged from Ferry's own Lower Deck Lothario look (a cruise ship white tux ensemble) to Jobson's March Hare tailcoat ... Andy Mackay appeared in ... a distinguished suit of broadcloth with a string tie that gave him an undeniable air of fried chicken emporiums."

Mackay himself was unsure of the new direction, suggesting to Caroline Boucher in the first week of the new year that "the change of image we had on the last tour may have confused a lot of people. I think we may have deglittered a bit too rapidly. It wasn't something we'd cooked up purposely, it was just the way we felt ... I think we're all aiming at different people anyway. Paul, for instance, plays for other drummers as much as the rest of the audience, and I think Bryan plays across to a different section. It's good – it gives us individual identities as opposed to a row of friendly moptops." Though uncertain about the 'deglittering' process, Mackay nevertheless chose this juncture to make a decisive adjustment to his own image, affecting stylish pointed sideburns borrowed from the crew members of the Starship Enterprise – and, before them, silent screen heart-throb Rudolph Valentino.

Jobson's Roxy debut was met with plaudits for his instrumental virtuosity but qualms regarding his efficacy in reproducing Eno's sonic mischief of old. Commented Tyler, "his mutation of the Phil Manzanera power smashes during *Ladytron* were feeble and left Manzanera somewhat out on his own with an empty chord ringing embarrassingly in his sideboard-smothered ears." Surviving footage of Roxy's Rainbow dates show something similar happening during Eno's trademark synth squall in *Editions of You*, Jobson waving a hand in mock exasperation when the machinery fails to come up with the goods.

Support act on the tour was Adam Faith protégé Leo Sayer, done up like Jean-Louis Barrault's Pierrot in *Les Enfants du Paradis* and soon to have a substantial hit with *The Show Must Go On*, which far outstripped Roxy's own *Street Life* in its eventual chart high of number two. "Our first gigs were in support to Bowie," Ferry reflected in January 1974. "Now on this tour we took

Leo as support and the same thing seems to have happened to him." Sayer himself found this support slot a turning point in the use of his Pierrot disguise. "A strange thing happened," he told *Rolling Stone*'s Richard Cromelin. "When we were touring with Roxy Music the audiences were all kids. The kids love it, even the tiny tots, because they love the clown. But when we got to the Rainbow, which is the big gig in England, the critical, proper rock audience came along and *they* really got into it. I was surprised."

Stranded was finally released halfway through the tour and the music press, setting aside their post-Eno prophecies of doom, responded ecstatically, estimates ranging from "*Stranded* is the Roxy sound almost to perfection" (*Record Mirror*) and "a monumental improvement on Bryan Ferry's solo album" (*Disc*) to "*Stranded* is Roxy's third album, and immeasurably the best so far" (*Melody Maker*). In *NME*, meanwhile, Ian MacDonald was emphatic, asserting that "*Stranded* is a classic, the album Roxy have been aiming at for two years." The album also served to dismantle the lingering suspicions of 'hype' that had surrounded the band, Al Clark describing himself in *Time Out* as "another sour old sceptic turned true believer": "*Stranded* is a record which makes reservations evaporate and shows Bryan Ferry's writing to have substance as well as style. More importantly perhaps, it is evidence of a group (delete Eno, insert Eddie Jobson) in complete command of their increasingly accomplished material."

Buoyed by these responses and the simultaneous eruption of Roxymania, the album rocketed to Number One and stayed there for close to two months; having entered the chart on 1 December, it had a total run of 17 weeks. Taken up by Atlantic Records early in 1974, the LP was embraced Stateside, too. "*Stranded* is an eloquent statement that there are still frontiers which American pop has not explored," wrote Paul Gambaccini in *Rolling Stone*, while *Phonograph Record*'s Ken Barnes summarised the album as "definitely a treat; effete but quite neat, and with a beat."

Lester Bangs, influential editor of *Creem* magazine, went wild, insisting that "once you let Roxy Music work their venal magic on your inner ear canals you'll know why I'm frothing." Just in case he hadn't got his point across, in a later issue he went further: "You can throw all that other crap out – Dylan, Bowie, Clapton – it may be nice in its place but Roxy Music is the only music that says anything new or reflects the spirit of '74 with any accurate passion. If you still haven't bought *Stranded* GO GET THE GODDAM THING and wolf it down, it'll only leave you hungry for more."

* * *

Hula Kula
(Manzanera) 2:32

Anticipating the release of *Stranded*, this was the B-side to *Street Life* and the first exposure Roxy fans had yet received to the composing talents of Phil Manzanera. Rather than coming up with something dauntingly convoluted in the Prog Rock style of his pre-Roxy band Quiet Sun, Manzanera here confounded expectation with a simplistic and consciously absurd flight of fancy. His own biographical details in press releases of the period described it as "a clever dance-along guitar instrumental with a strong Brazilian flavour." Indeed. Tipping his hat to his Latin American upbringing, Manzanera chose to do so in thoroughly camped-up style, and, as unhinged novelty instrumentals go, *Hula Kula* is a hoot.

Front and centre, of course, is Manzanera himself, a Latino Duane Eddy twanging tunefully across a soundstage inhabited elsewhere only by a gently funky bass and the muttered nonsense of Ferry and, presumably, Mackay, who as backing vocalists seem to be having at least as much fun as they did while recording *The Numberer*. Ferry's whistled improvisation over Manzanera's initial phrases is soon dispensed with in favour of a ludicrous agglomeration of "oohs", "aahs", "zum-zums" and what sounds like a bumblebee playing a comb through tracing paper. There even seems to be a sotto voce conversation going on deep down in the mix. Finally, Ferry extemporises a few wordless yodels and, in one of the most delightfully unbuttoned moments in the Roxy repertoire, dissolves into disbelieving laughter having done so. "Si, si, señor," nods Manzanera reassuringly, and the whole thing ends on a sustained twang irresistibly reminiscent of the "That's all, folks!" conclusion to post-war *Loony Toons*.

Hula Kula is one of Roxy's most engaging throwaways, conjuring visions of dazzling tropical sunsets, South Sea island belles oscillating in grass skirts, Carmen Miranda in fabulously fruity headgear and Edmundo Ros on acid. And, in light of that concluding comedy twang, it's hard not to visualise Bugs Bunny, or possibly his lisping nemesis Elmer Fudd, shimmying to and fro with a Hawaiian guitar.

Street Life
(Ferry) 3:29

Another in the lengthening line of Roxy's classic rockers, *Street Life* was pithily apostrophised from a US perspective by Gary Sperrazza in *Shakin' Street Gazette*: "*Street Life*, a top British single, is punk-rock in space: excellent trebly guitar playing a four-chord riff with Mackay and Jobson overlaying their touches and Ferry slashing out the confusions of a night of slinking."

For new recruit Eddie Jobson, it provided the opportunity to show that anything Eno could do he could do, if not better, then certainly as well. And he makes a highly convincing case, creating a genuine climate of eeriness with the track's introductory advance of metallic dissonances, half-heard but weirdly inexorable, suggesting the awakening hum of some malevolent machinery. Simultaneously alluring and sinister, this peculiar overture acts as the perfect intro-duction to Ferry's cynical snapshot of the bright young things of contemporary glitter culture, alternating uneasily between fascination and withering contempt.

The heart-quickening oscillation of Thompson's cymbals is then added to Jobson's off-kilter Mellotron woodwinds and the band are off, Manzanera repeating a great zig-zagging riff throughout and Mackay's baritone sax underpinning all with a thickly clotted riff of its own. There are insanely energised hand-claps, a reappearance of those disquieting Mellotron figures between each phase of Ferry's vocal, and some super-cool finger-popping to reintroduce the main theme after a riotous instrumental break. Here, Jobson has thrown down the gauntlet in the most melodramatic way possible, whipping up a cacophonous storm of violin pyrotechnics that almost overwhelms the soundstage, the whole thing bizarrely transmogrified, appropriately enough, by Eno's old synthesiser of choice, the VCS3.

Through all this, Ferry warbles a lyric steeped in watchful, world-weary ambivalence yet delivered with an unaccustomed savagery. Rebelling at the telephone-jangling incursions of the outside world, he simultaneously celebrates the fact that the modern 'scene' has thoroughly kicked over the traces of the old. He reaches an early crescendo in a sneering aside about the intrusions of the gutter press, his fragmenting mania acting as the perfect cue for Jobson's explosive outbreak of treated strings. Elsewhere, Ferry shows off his erudition with references to Harvard, Yale and the onetime all-female college, Vassar, repudiating all three in one of his wittiest lines: "the good life's never won by degrees." (This section "may draw a few Ivy League smiles," quipped Paul Gambaccini in *Rolling Stone*.) Finally there's a magical namecheck for the album itself in a closing line that perfectly distils Ferry's ambivalent attitude towards the 'scene'.

Street Life was the first Roxy single to be excerpted from an album rather than being exclusive to the 45rpm format, Ferry's explanation for this volte face sounding just a little disingenuous: "I have relatives who are poor, and they say why don't I bring out a certain song as a single because they can't afford the album. People now aren't forced to buy both." Whatever the reasoning behind its release, *Street Life* was showcased on the 22 November edition of *Top of the Pops*, in which Roxy's dazzling turn wiped the floor with fellow performers Mud, Donny Osmond, Alvin Stardust, Gary Glitter, Cliff Richard, Wings, The New Seekers, and Barry Blue. The show's 500th edition, this was a special celebratory instalment fronted by Jimmy Savile and graced, of course, by Roxy favourites Pan's People.

The single had entered the Top 40 two days earlier at number 21, the highest of five new entries, among them T.Rex's *Truck On (Tyke)* and Mott the Hoople's *Roll Away the Stone*. It reached a peak of number nine on 10 December, hung on at number ten for three weeks over the festive season (with Slade's *Merry Christmas Everybody* all-conquering at Number One), and finally dropped out of the Top 40 on 21 January. The single's rapid rise naturally increased interest in the accompanying album, and Roxy accordingly received a pre-Christmas treat when *Street Life* entered the Top Ten in the same week that *Stranded* climbed to Number One on the album charts.

With its half-fearful, half-fascinated outlook and berserk instrumental middle section, *Street Life* would be updated some five years later in the slighter form of *Trash*. The impression it gives of a man under seige – from fans and journalists alike – would also find an echo in *She Sells* and the bitter solo single *Kiss and Tell*. In the meantime, it provided a heady adrenaline rush as opening number on the band's autumn tour of 1973, reappearing in the *Country Life* and *Siren* shows but then dropping out of sight until 2001. Coming hot on the heels of opener *Remake/Re-model*, this latterday version deleted the fourth and fifth verses, dispensing with Ferry's charming references to American temples of higher education.

Back in 1986, the track lent its name to a top-selling, two-LP compilation that cravenly mixed together a majority of Roxy cuts with a smattering of Ferry solo items. By this time, the youthful ferocity of the song itself seemed so much a thing of the past that Nick Kent's *NME* review could pooh-pooh the *Street Life* tag as a "ridiculous title for a Ferry retrospective."

Just Like You
(Ferry) 3:36

After the sonic assault of *Street Life*, the faltering grace of *Just Like You* provides the first indication of the impact upon Ferry of recording *These Foolish Things*, and specifically his enduring passion for Cole Porter and songsmiths in similar vein. Six years later, he told Nick Kent that "these people in fact had a far more direct effect on me than the so-called avant-garde. So straight after *Foolish Things* – which I now actually consider the third Roxy album in a way due to the influence it had on my writing – I made a very conscious attempt to compose conventional but strong, classy songs. *Just Like You* was certainly written in that style. The whole album was, in fact."

Here, then, is an early attempt at a straightforward love song, stark in its simplicity and all the more affecting for it. This transition to a more structured form of songwriting was not without its rigours, however. "I scratch away for hours, like an old-style lyricist," Ferry pointed out at the time, "because things don't come to me very easily. I find it much easier to write sad things."

Just Like You is intensely sad, reflecting on the inevitability of change in the outside world then, inevitably, zeroing in on Ferry's own microcosmic concerns regarding a departed lover. The lyric is reminiscent of *Beauty Queen* in its enumeration of florid romantic clichés, all of them harping obsessively on the theme of mutability. Indeed, the very era in which the song was written is castigated as an "alter-style age" in which high-maintenance mistresses tumble over each other to acquire the latest fashions. Introduced by a really lovely piano figure, the soundstage embraces the sad sobriety of Jobson's string section, a charming rhythmic interplay between Gustafson's bass and Thompson's sensitive percussion (no trace of tub-thumping here), and a sublimely brittle guitar break from Manzanera. Only Mackay seems out of sorts, his oboe barely registering on the couple of occasions it emerges from the mix.

In terms of emulating his Tin Pan Alley forebears, *Just Like You* indicates that there was still some Ferry homework to do in the verse-chorus department; rather like *Psalm* and *Mother of Pearl* to follow, the song remains more of a self-absorbed monologue than a conventionally structured pop song. (Much of this homework will have been done by the time we get to *A Really Good Time* on the *Country Life* album, a track which is in many ways an elaboration of the melody featured here.) In the meantime, Ferry manages to round off the song with a wonderfully schmaltzy invocation of the title as piano notes tumble gracefully around the final strains of Jobson's strings.

Just Like You failed to make it onto the set list for Roxy's contemporaneous tour, or indeed any other for some three decades. It was finally performed live for the first time in Basel on 29 September 2002, as part of Ferry's *Frantic* tour.

Amazona
(Manzanera-Ferry) 4:16

Amazona could well be the name of the strapping Amazonian beauty stranded on the front cover of the song's parent album. Then again, Ferry's lyric identifies

Amazona as a 'zone' (whether geographical or erogenous is unclear), presumably some fantasy Shangri-la, the attainment of which requires a leap of faith and a trip through the looking glass. And if the song's blazing fusillade of instrumental exoticism is anything to go by, the process of getting there is at least as intoxicating as the final destination.

As his first co-writing credit on a Roxy album, it's appropriate that Phil Manzanera should straddle the *Amazona* soundstage like a colossus, gilding the introductory passages with a wealth of chicken-lickin' noodlings prior to sending out an amazing shower of metallic sparks in the hell-for-leather middle section. The effect was to make many listeners sit up and pay closer attention to Roxy's self-effacing guitarist. Speaking to *Phonograph Record*, producer Chris Thomas explained that, once the band had laid down skeletal backing tracks, "Phil would ... take the tape home and work out his guitar part, and he would transform those tracks so much, it was totally amazing ... I really think Phil's given an awful lot to both the Roxy albums that I've worked on."

Powered by some charmingly nonchalant Thompson percussion, together with the treacly resonance of Gustafson's syncopated bass line, the opening of *Amazona* is funky in the extreme. Ferry indulges in a bit of cod-Latino phrasing, his high-flown monologue delivered later into the warm embrace of Jobson's synthesised strings as Mackay burbles sonorously below, occasionally hissing out across the stereo image but otherwise subordinated to some dazzling special effects.

Gustafson's bass goes into a delightful stop-start rhythm as wheezing escapes of gas bring to mind the pistons of some massive, Amazona-bound juggernaut. And then Manzanera is off, his guitar howling wildly against a seething backdrop of treated voices, Mackay racing in pursuit but soon submerged in Thompson's expertly accelerated backbeat. Another disorientating switchback and Ferry's original theme is restored, signalling the traveller's long-awaited arrival (again begging the question, what kind of zone was he heading for?), prior to a concluding splutter of synthesised static, an effect replicated on one of the next album's Manzanera compositions, *Out of the Blue*.

The sonic trickery of *Amazona* shows Mackay and Manzanera relishing their new-found control over the 'treatments' department formerly occupied by Eno – though it could be argued that Mackay goes overboard and 'treats' his own contribution virtually out of existence. The result, however, is an exotic and beguiling oddity, for sheer funked-up pyrotechnics a stand-out on the otherwise stately *Stranded* album. Ferry's decision to delegate composing duties to Manzanera and Mackay was bearing immediate fruit, as *A Song for Europe* would underline all the more firmly. "I think he's realised that he can only do so much," Manzanera suggested in typically understated fashion, "and that some new ideas – at least, say, melody-wise – are called for."

Psalm
(Ferry) 8:04

By his own account, *Psalm* was the first song Ferry ever wrote, finally finding its way onto the *Stranded* album as a highly peculiar example of 'God rock'. Most reviewers were perplexed by this one, one being reminded by it of Blackpool pier and even its most fervent admirer, writing anonymously in *Disc*, admitting to its "distinct shades of Jess Yates' *Stars on Sunday*" – though adding the crucial qualification, "but that is intentional, I think."

Judging from the steadily building swirl of the instrumentation, *Stars on Sunday* is exactly the area *Psalm* inhabits, the cheesy, showbiz end of religious devotion that proved a weekend winner for Yorkshire Television from its inception in 1969. What Ferry was actually aiming for was presumably the hothouse atmosphere of a Deep South revivalist meeting, the kind of gospel emotionalism that was the seed of so much secular soul music. But the cherubic shade of Jess Yates (hotly contested father of Paula) remains hard to shake.

The genius of *Psalm*, however, is that the Bible-thumping pastiche of the sound-stage is offset by a Ferry lyric that seems completely sincere, with wink-tipping irony kept firmly at arms' length. Reflecting on this track and the upcoming album's *Triptych*, contemporary critics saw deep significance in Ferry's nomination of John Donne as his favourite poet. "His admiration of the metaphysical strain made me remember a conversation I once had with Eno," noted the *NME*'s Nick Kent, "when the latter stated his contention that our Mr F would reach a peak of creativity and then crack and become totally committed to some organised religion."

In the meantime, the devotional phrases of *Psalm* are pretty much inter-changeable with the devotional phrases of Ferry's more 'straightforward' love songs. His dream of a domestic idyll in *If There is Something*, sitting in the garden and cultivating potatoes, is here exchanged for a cod-ecclesiastical one in which the narrator waits patiently for God's signal in the hope of eventually walking in His garden.

The track fades up to a cheesy shimmer of faux-church organ, a lurid stained-glass glow of yellow and purple already infusing the music even before Ferry's opening salvo. In lines reminiscent of *Chance Meeting*, he depicts a beaming countenance as something that has to be assumed in the same way one puts on one's clothes – a brief reminiscence, too, of the hollow pieties of The Beatles' most tragic churchgoer, *Eleanor Rigby*, whose face is described as some-thing to be put on only for special occasions, residing otherwise in a make-up jar. Ferry then offers his vision of a transcendant faith with all the buzz-words of the itinerant Evangelist. All the boxes are ticked – there's a coat of many colours, a ritualistic cup to drink from, the inevitable approach of Death, and finally a deliverance into God's domain which, like any properly enraptured lover, Ferry suspects he won't be worthy of. Unlike the exhilarating odyssey undertaken in *Amazona*, this is a journey of which the conclusion is darkly in doubt.

As well as the virtually subliminal presence of The London Welsh Male Choir, Ferry's song of praise is supported by dazzling contributions from all concerned, notably Thompson's subtly hesitant drum patterns, Ferry's own rambling harmonica break and Manzanera's discreet country stylings. For Mackay fanciers, the track no doubt came as something of a relief after the fairly slim pickings of *Stranded*'s opening side up to this point; by the end, he's whipped up a gorgeously impassioned storm of evangelical soprano that matches Ferry's anguished litany step for step.

The longest track in Roxy's repertoire bar only *The Bogus Man*, *Psalm* is likely to strike some listeners as an acute case of generic pastiche long outstaying its welcome. This was certainly the opinion of contemporary reviewers in *Time Out* ("for all the grandeur of its crescendo, [it] takes too long to develop too little") and *Melody Maker* ("it's hard to sustain interest over eight minutes on the strength of bizarreness alone"). But it remains proof of the fact that Roxy were now able to turn their hands to virtually anything. In any case, for Ferry eight minutes presumably qualified as 'cutting to the chase' in what he called "the gradual process a lot of poets go through. Like intense love poetry, over 20 years or so it can become stronger and stronger, and more introspective, until it reaches this amazing religious intensity."

Though unconvinced by the track, Ian MacDonald suggested in *NME* that it was "probably dynamite live." Augmented at Roxy's Rainbow dates by the serried ranks of the London Welsh Male Choir, immaculate in their scarlet blazers, no doubt it was. Even without them, it packs a real punch on Roxy's contemporary (and now much bootlegged) *Musikladen* TV performance.

Serenade
(Ferry) 2:59

Though smoother, *Serenade* is as short and sharp, and thoroughly infectious, as both *Virginia Plain* and *Pyjamarama*. Indeed, in 1995 *Mojo*'s Rob Chapman was moved to nominate it as "the best single Roxy never released (and criminally omitted from the forthcoming Virgin box set, *The Thrill of It All*)."

This is high praise, given that *Do the Strand*, no less, was never issued as a UK single during the band's lifetime. And though *Serenade* is not on quite that level, it's still a breathtaking blast of adrenaline in the stately midst of *Stranded*, containing scraps of word-play in the *Do the Strand* tradition and a tearing pace carried over from *Virginia Plain*. In the *NME*, Ian MacDonald spotted another derivation traceable to one of the songs Ferry had recently covered: "*Serenade* shows how much Ferry got out of doing *These Foolish Things*, charging along in a manner very reminiscent of *Loving You is Sweeter Than Ever* (with which it shares a number of tell-tale intervals; *Street Life* likewise)."

Like *Virginia Plain*, *Serenade* starts with a bit of 'do not adjust your set' misdirection, a musical undertow that seems to be hurtling at speed towards the listener but at a volume hardly decipherable to the human ear. Ferry's vocal then crashes in at top note, painting the now-familiar picture of a man watching as night encroaches outside his window and pondering on the imminent collapse of yet another love affair. The darkness is, of course, a metaphor for the slow extinction of the relationship, just as the narrator's guttering candle is analogous to the fitful flickering of the affair that's soon to wind down. After this, Ferry's 1974 Jerome Kern cover (with its memorable refrain, "When a lovely flame dies – smoke gets in your eyes") was presumably a foregone conclusion.

If this all sounds very gloomy, Ferry's wildly flippant reading is far from it, and the band's hell-for-leather instrumentation even less so. Thompson packs an amazing punch with some thrillingly gymnastic drum patterns, while Mackay's clarion-call oboe soars vaultingly over the entire mix. A bit of sneering Ferry product-placement, namechecking G-plan fittings and Everglo fires, is juxtaposed with starry-eyed romantic imagery to underline the 1970s adulteration of love into just another commercial undertaking, and on this cynical cue comes a brief but dazzling starburst of Manzanera pyrotechnics, Jobson scraping tunefully away below. The whole thing sprints insanely over the horizon on a fusillade of Ferry's most florid imagery since *Beauty Queen*, rounding up weeping willows and mirrored dew-drops with gay abandon prior to disappearing from view altogether.

Transposed to the box-office of an old-time cinema, the "courtly love to costly game" theme would be picked up in more nostalgic vein on the next album's *Three and Nine*. In the meantime, *Serenade* only added weight to the impression that Roxy were going to get along just fine, thank you, in Eno's absence. And that a track as accomplished as this could be polished off as if it were a mere throwaway remains a sign of how formidable a unit Roxy had become by the autumn of 1973.

A Song for Europe
(Mackay-Ferry) 5:46

The arrival of *A Song for Europe* coincided not only with Britain's enrolment in the Common Market but also Ferry's acquisition of the iconic white tuxedo. The tux crystallised for all time his world-weary image in the eyes of the general public, while the song did so in more detail for purchasers of *Stranded* itself. And, given the album's Number One status, there were plenty of them.

Here is Ferry stranded at a waterfront café in the enveloping shadow of Notre Dame; here he is too, marooned in a Venetian gondola and ruefully acknowledging that "the bridge, it sighs." It's Ferry's Byronic pose at its most concentrated, the song's pan-European scope neatly evoking the kind of 'Grand Tour' which eventually caused the undoing of the original Byron. It's a pose involving the straightest of straight faces but flirting with camp on a truly epic scale, Ferry's lamentations finally breaking out into muttered Latin and anguished French.

However overwrought, it has a genuine gravitas missed by several miles in imitations like Ultravox's 1981 hit *Vienna*. There, the pomp-synth stylings are merely self-important, and in the video Midge Ure (complete with Andy Mackay sideburns, Bryan Ferry 'tache and *2 H.B.* trenchcoat) looks merely callow. *A Song for Europe*, by contrast, remains a sweepingly romantic achievement that even Roxy would risk emulating only once.

And it was recognised as a classic from the moment it came out. "Andy Mackay, whose searing sax made Mott the Hoople's *All the Way from Memphis* an American favorite, has written the tune for *A Song for Europe* – the most impressive track on the album," enthused Paul Gambaccini in *Rolling Stone*. "Here is emotion without lack of control. Ferry's tortured recitation is supported by an eerie, pained musical backing. Mackay's sax is mournful, Phil Manzanera's guitar lines are expressive, and the drumming of Paul Thompson is dramatic."

Mackay's melody – which would strike most critics as sounding like a transmogrified take on George Harrison's *While My Guitar Gently Weeps* – struck Ferry himself rather differently. "I had the title for it a long time ago," he explained in *Melody Maker* soon after the album's release. "I was going to do a song myself using lots of different languages – originally I wanted to do Italian, German and Spanish as well – but Andy came up with this song and wanted me to do the words for it. It sounded very European to me, so I thought I'd do it as *A Song for Europe*." Peppering his lyric with some of his choicest puns, Ferry ensured that his most sardonic gag was reserved for the song's titular evocation of the Eurovision Song Contest, which he accurately described as "one of the more bizarre events on the calendar."

There's nothing *Boom Bang-a-Bang* about *A Song for Europe*, however. Instead, it takes a dash of supper-club lounge, an ample helping of Phil Spector-style 'wall of sound' melodramatics, even a flavour of the kind of Frenchified pop chansons exemplified by Billy Fury's 1965 hit *I'm Lost Without You*. On top of all this is Ferry's dazzling lyric, his nuanced rendition of which reaches sublime heights on the realisation that youth's sense of wonder and enchantment can never be retrieved. Here's a man so thoroughly self-absorbed that he reverses the usual 'all this will still be here when I'm gone' routine, stating with incontrovertible arrogance that Europe's grandest cities will pass away before his obsession does.

The swirling soundstage starts out beguilingly low-key, with Jobson's stately piano figure joined to delicate brushes of Thompson timpani and Manzanera's gently churning guitar. It builds to exhilaratingly muscular choruses, Jobson's classical piano remaining serene and unruffled beside the pounding improvisations of Thompson and Mackay's surging saxophone riffs. The latter steps forward for a sweetly contemplative tenor solo, subsequently letting rip with an impassioned alto squall in support of Ferry's climactic lapse into Latin and French, which faithfully transcribes the terms of his previously stated idée fixe.

The translation work here was done by Ferry's scholarly right-hand man, Simon Puxley, though he seems never to have taught Ferry the correct pronunciation of "reviendront", which comes out charmingly mangled both here and on every subsequent live rendition of the song. And at the end, in a never-to-be-repeated apotheosis, Ferry delivers King Lear's nihilistic "Never, never, never, never, never" in the keening style of Edith Piaf: "Oh jamais – jamais jamais jamais jamais jamais!" After that, he makes an exit custom-built for arena theatrics, whistling dolefully in a style far removed from *Hula Kula* but not unlike the later *Jealous Guy*.

Though the tune would be likened to George Harrison, and Ferry's vocal style (by one critic at any rate) to Jim Morrison, *A Song for Europe* found Roxy perfecting a magpie synthesis of disparate styles and creating something uniquely their own, something redolent of, as *Melody Maker* would head their *Stranded* review, 'An Air of Lush Decay'. The decay, though cold and crumbling and European, is, indeed, somehow just as lush as the lurid blooms in which Marilyn Cole lies sprawled on the album cover. And Ferry's final peals of "jamais" remain among the most indelible moments in 1970s rock.

A Song for Europe immediately became a staple of Roxy's live act, recurring on every succeeding tour bar the 1975 one, when the *Stranded* album was represented only by *Mother of Pearl*. As an obvious showcase for its composer, it gave Mackay a blistering extended outro, most memorably during Roxy's tour dates in 1980. In 2001, it was fitted with a gorgeous piano prologue played by tour MD Colin Good, as well as benefiting from Ferry's restoration of the Latin phrases long since abandoned for live purposes. Ferry also took the opportunity to dedicate the song to Roxy's shadowy eminence grise, Simon Puxley, who had recently died.

In the same year, Ferry told Nicky Parade that the new Roxy regime of sharing songwriting duties "worked very well with Andy, because he had more musical training than anybody, including me. So he would produce [songs] where the chords were a bit more unusual and developed. And that produced good things like *A Song for Europe* and, later, *Love is the Drug*. Andy had this European music background, where my background was much more American: black singers and blues and various other forms of 20th century music. It actually made for a good combination."

With so uniquely magisterial a product of that combination, it comes as a surprise to find that *A Song for Europe* has been covered even once; however, US indie band Superconductor gave it a go, using the result as B-side to their 1995 single *The Strip Oracle*.

Mother of Pearl
(Ferry) 6:52

In the bewitching *Mother of Pearl*, the schizoid unpredictability of Roxy's first two albums is corraled into a song of two distinct, and seemingly unrelated, halves. There's no build-up to the manic, hard-rock release of the opening; it comes out of nowhere and knocks the listener for six after the sombre fade of *A Song for Europe*. Rather than a build-up, there's a long and hypnotic comedown instead – the hedonistic splurge followed by the grimly exhausted, yet wryly philosophical, morning after; the climactic spasm followed by the jaded post-coital cigarette.

As Ferry himself put it in *Melody Maker*, "the first part of it's this very physical thing, which describes a party situation – the story of my life [laughter] – and the second is 'The Party's Over', like the blue period after the red, sitting back and thinking, 'What's it all about, Alfie?' It's very inward-looking."

Given the song's dualistic structure, it comes as no surprise that the party animal of the opening section is beset by a demonic inner voice seemingly carried over from *Strictly Confidential* (and later to resurface on both *Sentimental Fool* and *Still Falls the Rain*). Here, however, the satanic tempter is placed front and centre, exulting in the crazed melée while his timorous alter ego shrills in out-and-out panic. The raging metallic backdrop features a heavy Manzanera riff describing threatening circles around the alarm flares of Jobson's keyboards, the guitar going into shrieking hyperdrive when the beleaguered background voice is finally trounced by its leering counterpart. The effect is scary and exhilarating in equal measure.

Suddenly, however, Manzanera's manic assault gives place to a delicate piano melody and the gently funky rhythm of Thompson's drums. It's a magical moment, upon which, with Gustafson's eloquent bass line brought well forward in the mix, Ferry embarks on an extended sprechgesang litany that doesn't let up for a good five minutes. The story behind this *In Every Dream Home a Heartache*-style rap has long since passed into legend, the flames initially fanned by Roxy's wily publicist, Simon Puxley, in his slim 1976 volume, *The Bryan Ferry Story*. In common with the band's normal practice, the song existed in more-or-less finished form as a somewhat long-winded instrumental, only awaiting Ferry's vocal (and as-yet-unwritten lyric) to make it complete. All concerned were reportedly blown away when Ferry strolled in one morning and sang the enormously long and complex

Mother of Pearl lyric in one uninterrupted take. "*Mother of Pearl* was really just a sequence that went round and round and round," observed Mackay in 2002. "I remember we were all amazed that Bryan could come in and do that."

Whatever its origins, the effect remains mesmerising. Ferry's multi-faceted word-pictures are of an astonishing breadth and intricacy (he has since acknowledged the assistance of Dr Puxley in crafting some of them), and his vocal performance is sardonic and self-amused from the start. Cynically bemoaning the unavailability of true love in a shallow world devoted only to appearances, he introduces something of the quasi-religious intensity of *Psalm* via his musings on an ideal woman who'll bring a touch of divinity into his stale existence. Though fully aware that objectifying women as goddesses leads only to disappointment, he remains hopelessly caught on a perfectionist treadmill.

Manzanera's muted guitar lines twinkle like stars over Ferry's darkling monologue, tambourines and other percussive elements chatter away in the backbeat, and Mackay's baritone arrives at a late stage to punch up the steadily building momentum. Chris Thomas, meanwhile, adds a number of clever production touches: a flicker of castanets here, a bit of kissy-kissy purse-lipped percussion there, even hand claps at Ferry's Nietzschean nod to Zarathustra. The whole structure is finally stripped away to leave Ferry's hesitant vibrato standing stark and unadorned, only to be gently superseded by the opening piano chords of *Sunset*.

The press response to *Mother of Pearl* was instantaneous and incandescent. Manzanera's old chum Ian MacDonald, writing in the *NME*, was typical: "This is it, folks: Magnum Opus Time," he began, subsequently comparing the song to Dylan's *Sad Eyed Lady of the Lowlands* and The Beatles' *Hey Jude*. Another review nominated it – somewhat prematurely, given that 1973 was not yet out – as the greatest song of the decade. Across the Atlantic, critics were more keenly alive to the sepulchral undertow in even a melody as beautiful as this. "Added to the thick mix is the unique voice of Bryan Ferry," wrote Paul Gambaccini in *Rolling Stone*, "who sounds ... [as if he's] about to sink his teeth into your neck [on] *Mother of Pearl*." Ken Barnes of *Phonograph Record* was more skittish, noting that the track's opening phase sounds "like a modern-style followup from Bobby 'Boris' Pickett & His Crypt-Kicker Five (in some strange sense one of Roxy's spiritual ancestors)."

After its debut on the band's *Stranded* tour, *Mother of Pearl* was resurrected for the three subsequent ones but disappeared after 1979. It went out in style, however, Nick Kent observing in May of that year that "Ferry knows this is one of his two or three finest ever songs – possibly the finest of all – and his performance at Liverpool was powerfully affecting, reminding me of Dylan's reshaping of *Tangled Up in Blue* at Earl's Court last year." It was finally restored to the Roxy repertoire in 2001, augmented now by the husky maturity of Ferry's vocal and a sparkling guitar dialogue between Manzanera and Chris Spedding.

In 1995, a cover version of *Mother of Pearl* was recorded by Wall of Voodoo's Marc Moreland in collaboration with Johnette Napolitano (who, as part of Concrete Blonde, had previously covered Roxy's *End of the Line*). Under the collective name Pretty and Twisted, the Moreland/Napolitano version deleted the song's manic first section and also truncated some of the remainder. Several years later, Ferry himself recorded a belated solo cover of the song, included on the soundtrack album for the 1998 gangster film *Ordinary Decent Criminal*.

Sunset

(Ferry) 6:04

With its stately opening piano figure introduced even before Ferry has concluded his final invocations to *Mother of Pearl*, *Sunset* is a sombre paean to the close of day that makes an intensely beautiful coda to the *Stranded* album.

The lyric is one of Ferry's best – simple and heartfelt, just like the sparse, close to 'unplugged' instrumentation. Ferry watches the setting of the sun with much the same pangs of loss as he might the departure of an intimate friend. He sees the onset of darkness, lit only by the fitful effulgence of the moon, as a depressive slide finally arrested by the dawn chorus. He permits himself only one of his tricksy double-meanings (conflating 'mind's eye' with 'minds I') and only one borderline-baroque flourish, in which the flamingos previously referenced in *Virginia Plain* make a memorably poetic comeback. Elsewhere, he pictures the evening sky stained crimson by the bleeding heart of the declining sun. The imagery is florid, for sure, but *Sunset* remains a word-picture of extraordinary grace, with a delicate and unhurried melody to match. As in the later *End of the Line*, where night has already encroached and rain is tumbling down outside, the impression is of a man wrapped in a familiar melancholy that's cosy and somehow comforting, a mantle worn to fend off the kind of dangerously self-destructive nocturnal reveries dramatised in *Strictly Confidential*.

Chris Laurence's string bass lends a mournful gravitas to the skeletal sound and dovetails beautifully with Ferry's piano, which itself goes into a gorgeous descending melody following the realisation that these rarefied feelings might actually be commonplace, even banal, scattered about the "cutting room floors" of dreamers everywhere. This freefall instrumental section features delicate percussive interpolations and even the subliminal sound of Ferry breathing a desolate sigh, as heard previously in *The Bogus Man* and later (coupled with a dragged-on cigarette) *Dance Away*. The resumption of Ferry's vocal is accompanied by the distant keening of Mackay's oboe, after which the track winds down on a throbbing bass/piano coda introduced by a shimmer of sleigh bells. The effect is hypnotic, elegiac, genuinely moving.

A few months after the release of *Stranded*, Mackay went into Island Studios to cut his first solo LP, including on it a saxophone instrumental that could almost have been intended as a follow-up to *Sunset*; called *The Hour Before Dawn*, it concludes with the very dawn chorus specified by Ferry. An unofficial *Sunset* sequel may have been quick to arrive, but the song's first live performance had to wait for over a quarter of a century, the song forming part of Ferry's 1999 *As Time Goes By* tour. Chris Laurence, too, emerged after a long absence as one of the musicians on the accompanying album.

Seven: *This Alter-Style Age*

"I think Stranded *is a very cautious album, I don't think it breaks very much new ground … Strangely, as you improve as a band – and we have – you do become more cautious, without noticing it. I start thinking about musicians listening to*

our work, rather than the general public. And the final product is always so very different from the unmixed one."

Andy Mackay, quoted in *Disc* 19 January 1974

The real bizarro warp factor for 1974

As *Stranded* continued to bestride the UK album chart, Eno's first solo LP, *Here Come the Warm Jets*, appeared in the nation's record shops in January 1974. It had been recorded at Majestic Studios in a tight 12 days the previous September, its 16 musicians including King Crimson's Robert Fripp and John Wetton, the Hawkwind rhythm section of Paul Rudolph and Simon King, Roxy support acts Chris Spedding and Lloyd Watson, Roxy's own Manzanera, Mackay and Thompson, plus Manzanera's Quiet Sun companion Bill MacCormick. Eno was concerned to get together thoroughly disparate, even incompatible musicians prior to standing back and watching the fireworks, on the assumption that "there might be accidents, accidents which will be more interesting than what I had intended."

"My role is to co-ordinate them [the musicians], synthesise them, furnish the central issue which they all will revolve around, producing a hybrid," Eno told *Rolling Stone*'s Cynthia Dagnal. His role, according to the sleeve notes, was to provide "simplistic keyboards, Snake guitar, electric larynx and synthesiser, and [to treat] the other instruments." Here began Eno's longstanding habit of cooking up whimsical appellations of his own for his sometimes unspecifiable grace notes. Snake guitar, it transpired, was so named because the sound "reminded me of the way a snake moves through the brush," while electric larynx was mysteriously glossed in an Island press release as "bondage meets electronic music."

On top of all this, Eno's voice, no longer confined to backing vocals as it had been in Roxy Music, was revealed as a beguilingly off-key instrument in itself, smacking of English eccentrics like Syd Barrett and Ray Davies, occasionally providing a souped-up parody of Bryan Ferry, and frequently sounding, as Chrissie Hynde put it in *NME*, "not unlike the shriek of a hare that's just caught an air-gun pellet up the ass."

Perhaps afraid that the uninitiated might think the album's title was a reference to some mythical bunch of glam rockers in the style of Elton John's *Benny and the Jets*, Eno assured Hynde that it was a nod to his boundless zeal for pornography, a passion outlined in detail to the future Pretenders frontwoman in a piece she aptly entitled 'Everything You'd Rather Not Have Known About Brian Eno'. The 'golden showers' referenced in the title are even visible, albeit discreetly, on the sleeve, in which one of Eno's reportedly extensive collection of Edwardian dirty postcards is frowned down upon by a framed portrait of the man himself.

The music inside turned out to be every bit as beguiling a blend of ancient and modern as Roxy's first two albums. *Blank Frank*, for example, exactly anticipates the noise-like ferocity of punk, with a sneeringly vindictive Eno vocal and Fripp's guitar spraying awesome machine-gun sparks across the soundstage – yet its rhythmic foundation is derived from Bo Diddley's *Who Do You Love*. The ecclesiastical solemnity of *Some of Them Are Old* (much enhanced by Mackay's droning 'saxophone septet') melds into a woozy, calypso-flavoured middle section similar to Kraftwerk's contemporaneous *Ananas Symphonie*. The sunnily melodic 1960s textures of *Cindy Tells Me* are sandwiched between the relentless Prog pulse of *Baby's On Fire* and the brain-curdling musique concrète melée that is *Driving Me Backwards*, while Eno's ambient experiments are prefigured by the instrumental flow of the hypnotic title track and the moving *On Some Faraway Beach*.

With distortion and feedback well to the fore, Eno's trademark sound manipulation creates an alluring paradox; each track seems like a neatly constructed vignette that may yet break out into the kind of chaotic din encouraged by Eno's accident-prone working methods. Even more alluring, Eno's cast of psychotic or merely tragic characters ranges from the demonic suburban bomber of *Blank Frank* to the insanely laughing, spontaneously combusting glamourpuss of *Baby's On Fire*, from the stir-crazy middle-class housewives of *Cindy Tells Me* to the hapless, Ferry-soundalike job applicant of *Dead Finks Don't Talk*. Not forgetting, of course, *The Paw Paw Negro Blowtorch*, an ode, as Eno put it, to a Michigan man "with a strange ailment – his breath caused things to ignite."

The word-pictures that bring these freakish protagonists to life were wrought from Eno's own version of 'automatic writing', the medium, more often than not, being his nightly dreams, which he considered "much more brilliant in their construction than anything I consciously think of." He had no desire to write love songs, nor to pluck themes from his own experience, noting that "Bryan's an extraordinary lyric writer, but in a style that I could never do. That kind of verbal imagery doesn't really come from me very much. I have no pretensions to poetry at all. The deciding factor about what words I use is what vowels they have in them – what their phonetic structure is."

With all of Roxy present bar Ferry, the album provides an intriguing indicator of the direction Eno might have propelled the band in had not the classical graces of *Stranded* supervened. As co-writer of both *Cindy Tells Me* and the dazzling opener, *Needles in the Camel's Eye*, Manzanera is the most central of the Roxy members present, though Eno circumvents the danger of the record coming across as merely ersatz Roxy Music by never using more than one band member on any given track.

The media interest in Eno had in no way abated since his resignation from Roxy; his torrential loquacity was still avidly sought after by the music press, while the sessions for *Here Come the Warm Jets* were even made the subject of a 24-minute short, bluntly entitled *Eno*, by Alfons Sinniger of Teamwork Films. The finished album climbed to number 26 in the UK (its fortnight in the chart beginning on 9 March) and was hailed by *Record Mirror* as "one of the finest British albums in months."

In the USA, Gordon Fletcher sniffed in *Rolling Stone* that "the listener must kick himself for blowing five bucks on baloney," but *Creem*'s Lester Bangs was rabid in the album's praises, variously describing it as "solid and throbbing primitivo all the way" and "a precisely orchestrated cauldron of terminal hysteria muchly influenced by though far more technologically advanced than early Velvet Underground." "This guy is a real sickie, bubs," he added, "sick as Alice Cooper once was s'posed to be, sicker by far than David Bowie's most scabrous dreams ... Don't tell me about the sleaze in your *Silverhead* – Eno is the real bizarro warp factor for 1974." With panegyrics like this, *Here Come the Warm Jets* reached number 92 in the *Billboard* chart.

Jock the Rock

For all the cult cachet of Eno's solo debut, at the beginning of 1974 Roxy's pre-eminence seemed unassailable, with their latest album hitting Number One, a highly lucrative single still in the charts and a sell-out tour only just concluded. "Yet in all this lay the roots of discontent; in the roses of fame, critical acclaim and commercial success, the invisible worm had burrowed," Mackay noted some 25 years later. "In short, things were not as much fun any more. I needed a break, and as seemed entirely normal at the time turned once more to the recording studio."

In other words, Mackay, too, was preparing a solo album, writing the bare bones of it during a New Year stint in Devon and his first thoughts on it constituting the cover story of the 19 January edition of *Disc*. By April he could reveal that "It's called *In Search of Eddie Riff* and should be released any day now, once the vinyl crisis has been settled. Actually I wanted to call it *À la Recherche d'Eddie Riff* after being inspired by this piece I read which stated that David Bowie was the Jean-Paul Sartre of rock. I decided that I wanted to be the [Marcel] Proust of rock."

On this hopefully tongue-in-cheek note, Mackay managed to slip his solo debut into Island's release schedule six albums ahead of Ferry's new one. Looking back, he claimed that *In Search of Eddie Riff* arose "from a desire to play some relatively uncomplicated saxophone with friends – a kind of musical autobiography (which now seems pretentious since I was only 28)." At the time, however, it was widely seen as a tit-for-tat gesture of the 'if he can do it then so can I' variety, and Mackay more or less admitted as much, though in rather tortuous syntax. Solo albums, he told *Sounds'* Jonh Ingham, had "always been in the backs of our minds, because Roxy is that sort of people and that sort of band. Obviously, it was given a much more urgent reaction when Bryan established the two careers thing where, to maintain the status quo of Roxy, it was important that we were all seen to be solo musicians of one sort or another, so Roxy came across as the band we were in from choice rather than necessity."

Issued on 14 June, the result received a mixed reception, and, indeed, Mackay himself was clearly not entirely satisfied with it, as the following year it was issued in the US with two vocal tracks deleted in favour of a storming remake of *Wild Weekend* and a heavily Eno-ised cover of *The Long and Winding Road*. This version eventually superseded the original in the UK too, Mackay maintaining that the new running order was closer to his original intentions. "It's like a new car," he explained in a fan club bulletin. "The first model is tried and tested, then you know you can turn out the GT model with air-conditioning."

On the cover, Mackay appears in full teen-idol glam, auburn-locked and open-collared, reaching for a tenor saxophone as a fluffy black-and-white cat looks on. The back cover is a witty Cape Canaveral-type shot in which a space rocket and a super-sized soprano saxophone are lined up together against Wagnerian skies. If this suggested that Mackay's solo career was ready for lift-off, most critics tended to demur. Ingham himself was typical, claiming to have "had trouble associating with it emotionally. Apart from a Johnny and the Hurricanes treatment of

Wagner's *Ride of the Valkyries*, it seemed like Muzak, an idea [I] appreciated intellectually but found hard to consciously listen to. Perhaps if he could persuade supermarkets and Wimpy bars to play it over their music systems..."

That the LP is a kind of MOR precursor of Eno's later ambient experiments ("an easy-listening album for the thinking man," as Mackay himself put it) is true enough; indeed, his second solo album would suffer similar jibes regarding its suitability for use in Chinese takeaways. The set kicks off with an inspired rocked-up rendition of *Ride of the Valkyries* (issued also as a single, and a nice nod to Mackay's use of the same motif on *Re-make/Re-model*) before moving through an engaging remake of the Doris Day classic *End of the World* and a dreary one of Jimmy Ruffin's *What Becomes of the Broken-Hearted*.

In addition, there's a fairly unlistenable oboe-plus-country-guitars makeover for Schubert's *An die Musik* (presumably included for its punning title: 'Andy Music') and a delightful treatment of the old Roy Rogers horse-opera favourite, *A Four-Legged Friend*, previously heard in the Bob Hope comedy *Son of Paleface*. Full of naïve rustic charm, this is one of the two vocal tracks Mackay would later get rid of. The other, *Summer Sun*, is an original composition, a glammed-up riot of massed oboes and energetically riffing rock'n'roll tenor, only let down by Mackay's diffident vocal – which, in any case, is recorded as if from within a shoe-box several studios away.

The other originals are all instrumentals. *The Hour Before Dawn* is a graceful, and beautifully performed, saxophone meditation, accompanied again by country guitars and reaching the sort of bird-twittering coda Roxy themselves would add to the later *Nightingale*. *Walking the Whippet* is a euphoric and splendidly catchy rave-up, with rinky-dink synths pealing across the soundstage and an extended pause for Manzanera to do his stuff.

The album's filmic centrepiece, *Past, Present and Future*, would be renamed *Pyramid of Night* on the US edition, presumably to avoid confusion with The Shangri-Las' 1966 teen-trauma epic. (The new title was lifted, instead, from Shelley's *Prometheus Unbound*.) This is a multi-faceted tapestry in Roxy mould, starting out on a twangly mediaeval note, shifting into bombastic tenor outbursts, incorporating folksy violin from Eddie Jobson and concluding on a stately wash of heavenly harmonies. *Time Regained* is an extraordinary Mackay-Eno collaboration, a longer version of which appeared as the B-side to *Ride of the Valkyries*. It anticipates the soothing ebb and flow of Roxy's own *More Than This* in its thickly carpeted interplay of multi-tracked saxophones and oboes and is an undoubted gem, despite its title providing a worrying reminder of Mackay's contemporary interview quotes re Marcel Proust.

Of the tracks added in 1975, *Wild Weekend* was issued as Mackay's second single and dedicated to longtime Roxy supporter Richard Williams. The Rockin' Rebels' original, masterminded by producer Tom Shannon, had been a big hit in December 1962, reaching number eight in the US charts. With the vogue for brassy rock'n'roll instrumentals long gone, Mackay's version got nowhere but is nevertheless a screeching hoot, garnished with 'breaking glass' percussive effects and the stellar contributions of Manzanera, Jobson, Thompson, Gustafson, and Deep Purple bass guitarist Roger Glover. Finally, *Long and Winding Road* must be one of the weirdest Lennon-McCartney covers ever, an Eno collaboration in which Mackay's dyspeptic baritone and multi-tracked oboes suggest the sustained mewing of several thousand cats on several thousand hot tin roofs.

Mackay's solo album also gave him the opportunity to indulge his penchant for female vocalists (a penchant that would reach an apotheosis the following year, courtesy of Thames Television), with much of the heavenly voicing being supplied by 'Countess' Sadie Mackenzie, of whom Andy said, "I have known for quite some time that she will astonish the world." This didn't happen, but in the meantime, Mackay recorded three songs for John Peel's *Sounds of the Seventies* on Wednesday 26 June, the results (*The Hour Before Dawn*, *Ride of the Valkyries* and *Walking the Whippet*) going out on 16 July.

Tonight Southport

Eddie Riff may or may not have been out of his system, but Mackay was still not through with pseudonyms. Having contributed to Mott the Hoople's *Mott* album under his own name, he now graced three tracks on their follow-up LP, *The Hoople*, under the absurd monikers Rockin' Jock McPherson, Jumpin' Jock and Jock the Rock; the tracks were *The Golden Age of Rock'n'Roll*, *Marionette* and *Pearl 'n' Roy (England)*. By a strange quirk, the cover girl here was Roxy's own Kari-Ann, her tousled fright-wig accommodating the saturnine faces of Ian Hunter and his motley crew. "When that came out," she confided to the *Sunday Mirror's* Danae Brook in 1981, "Bryan Ferry insisted that I didn't do any more album covers for other people. I suppose he was being possessive but he didn't openly admit it."

It was also during this halcyon period that three of the five Roxy members got married, leaving Ferry a more eligible bachelor than ever. Manzanera wed school sweetheart Sharon, a Londoner working at the time in a property company, while Thompson's bride, Susan, was a 17-year-old Roxy fan from Glasgow whom he had met at the Speakeasy Club. Ferry himself introduced Mackay to his wife Jane, who hailed from South Shields, had studied Graphic Design at Leicester College of Art and had previously been married to Lee Jackson, bass guitarist with David O'List's old group, The Nice.

In March, Southport's Floral Hall was chosen as an unusually discreet means of limbering up for a handful of Roxy dates in the US. "Well, we originally wanted a secluded venue as a sort of public rehearsal ground for the American tour," Mackay assured Nick Kent. "It was sort of a 'Tonight Southport, tomorrow The World' manoeuvre. But then the American tour was postponed so we thought, 'Well at least, tonight, Southport can be ours!'" The northern coastal resort was treated to Roxy's clandestine shows on 4 and 5 April, with Ella Fitzgerald performing elsewhere in the town at the same time. And by Saturday the 20th, Puxley and Ferry were en route to the USA for a whirlwind, five-day promotional stint in which they took in Detroit, Cleveland, Chicago, Philadelphia and Boston.

"The important thing about this tour is that we'll be playing to an audience who have paid to come and see *us*, not another act further up the bill," Ferry was pleased to announce in *Melody Maker*. The schedule was a brief one, running from Saturday 25 May to Sunday 2 June and comprising dates in all the cities reconnoitred by Ferry and Puxley, together with Boston and a climactic concert at the New York Academy of Music. Sal Maida was on bass and the support group was again the Chris Spedding-Andy Fraser combine The Sharks. The final show was followed by a lavish party thrown by artist Larry Rivers in his loft apartment, with the band fêted by, among others, David Bowie, Amanda Lear and various Warhol types. Commented Ferry, "We've been amazed at the depth of fan appreciation over here. So many people travelled so far to see us. We had kids driving 500 miles to get to the gigs, and in Philadelphia, one guy even flew in from California!"

The *New York Times* described Roxy's set as "an arresting, if not exactly consoling, experience," also pointing out that Ferry was "looking for all the world like Desi Arnaz playing Brighton." After the disastrous nature of Roxy's first assault on the US 18 months previously, this mini-tour was designed as a toe in the water to stir up interest in a more extensive itinerary at some future date. "It was a short tour but we did it on our own terms," enthused Manzanera. "Last time we went there, we were put on a tour with a blues band and obviously we can't support someone like Steve Miller in Chicago. This time we had our own lighting and PA and we were top of the bill in small theatres, 3000-seaters which are small by their standards. And the people who were coming came to see us. We didn't sell out every place, but we felt we were making progress."

José by the pool last summer

Though there were niggling queries in the rock press regarding Roxy's apparent unwillingness to mount an all-out assault on the US (an assault of the kind King Crimson spent most of their time engaged in), it was a noticeably bucked-up Ferry who guested on Radio 1's *My Top 12* on Sunday 12 June. Seven years later, he would concoct another list of his all-time favourites for a similar Radio 1 show, *Star Special*, with three tracks remaining constant from 1974 to 1981: The Shirelles' *Will You Love Me Tomorrow*, The Beatles' *A Day in the Life* and Ike & Tina Turner's massive Spector canvas, *River Deep Mountain High*.

Bryan Ferry's all-time favourites seemed an apposite theme given the imminent release of his second solo album. "It seems a pity not to do another solo," he had told *Record Mirror*'s Roger Greenaway in January. "There are thousands of other songs I'd like to have a crack at destroying."

Issued in the second week of July, *Another Time, Another Place* was recorded at Island and Ramport studios as well as Air and was produced by Ferry and John Punter. The title was taken from a Paramount romantic melodrama of 1958, directed by Lewis Allen and starring Lana Turner and the young Sean Connery. Though the film had been made in the UK, the nostalgic ring of its title dove-tailed nicely with Ferry's Hollywood obsessions, which were further reflected in the instantly iconic cover photo.

This had been taken by *Vogue* photographer Eric Boman beside a Bel Air swimming pool in May, with Ferry in the white tux and red cummerbund familiar from Roxy's last tour, right hand nestled nonchalantly in his pocket and left hand dandling a half-smoked cigarette. It's Bogart's Rick Blaine yet again, this time transplanted to a Hockney-esque haze of LA opulence, with four indolent onlookers (among them the celebrity shoe designer Manolo Blahnik) miasmically visible on the rear of the gatefold. Though a truly startling statement to make in the denim-clad world of 1970s rock'n'roll, this cloying vision of newly monied luxuriance didn't fool everyone. In *Melody Maker*, Caroline Coon commented that "It misses that listless, aristocratic *Last Year in Marienbad* touch by a mile. 'José by the Pool Last Summer in Benidorm' is more like it."

Whether one 'bought' the look or not was immaterial, however, for it was now that Ferry's tuxedoed image really hit home. In Roxy, it had made an impact on young music fans and a vaguely indifferent music press; now – attached to an unashamedly middle-of-the-road album and with Ferry making various 'light ent' TV appearances – it made a far wider audience sit up and take notice of this highly unusual rock star.

This crossover effect had been foreshadowed in February when Ferry appeared on Cilla Black's television showcase *Cilla*. Broadcast on Saturday the 23rd as the eighth programme in a nine-strong series, this was produced by future *Top of the Pops* man Michael Hurll and musically directed by Ronnie Hazelhurst. BBC1 viewers who had sat through the Doctor Who story *Death to the Daleks*, Jimmy Savile's Eurovision preview *Clunk-Click* and the antiquated cop show *Dixon of Dock Green* were next treated to the sight of Ferry lounging nonchalantly over a cocktail bar as he crooned *These Foolish Things*.

Ferry's fellow guests on this occasion were smoothie thespian Gerald Harper and ever-smiling DJ Tony Blackburn; musical guests elsewhere in the series included such less-than-cutting-edge names as Joe Brown, The Sweet, Vince Hill, Mary Hopkin, The Shadows, even Kenneth McKellar. As these names suggest, Ferry's new-found MOR status would in the long run have a malign effect, seriously undermining his 'credibility' (as he would be reminded in no uncertain terms when punk came along a few years' hence) and simultaneously putting his much more formidable achievements with Roxy Music in the shade.

Musing on the origins of his white tuxedo look, Ferry admitted to Duncan Fallowell 16 years later that "I was sitting around with Antony Price saying we've done leopardskin jackets etc, so we were trying out various things and he said let's do one in [a] white tuxedo like Bogart in *Casablanca*. It looked so right on me – frighteningly so – and the image burned itself through all the subsequent years of other photographs and I got lumbered. In fact it's my least favourite album." At the time, however, he was more cocksure, asserting that "*These Foolish Things* was the prototype; this is the deluxe model."

'Twiggs' meets Byron Ferrari

The LP cost £23,000 to make and was dismissively reviewed, nevertheless making number four on the album chart and remaining in place for several months. It had been trailed by a blisteringly effective single, a black-hearted revamp of Dobie Gray's 1965 mod anthem *The 'In' Crowd*. In one of his several high-handed pronouncements of 1974, Ferry explained to Nick Kent that "One should never underestimate one's fans because they do appear to be smarter – at least my fans or the group's fans are. They're the crème de la crème, which is a very fortunate thing. That's why I did *The 'In' Crowd* – as a kind of gift to them really. So they could play it at home."

Undaunted by Ferry's lordly and patronising tone, the fans did indeed play *The 'In' Crowd* at home, and in gratifyingly large numbers. Backed by a solo remake of Roxy's *Chance Meeting*, it entered the singles chart on 21 May, a few days ahead of Ferry's departure for Roxy's select series of US dates, and remained there for six weeks, hitting a high of number 13 on 4 June. The *NME* review of it was something of a classic in its own right: *"The 'In' Crowd* of 1974 is a very different kettle of caviare from that of 1965 ... The whole thing sounds like it was yanked off a New York subway whilst fixing an overdose of heroin and then ground between the sides of two collapsing skyscrapers."

Powered by a splendidly viscous John Wetton bass line, a honking horn section and the metallic mushrooming of David O'List's guitar chords, the track is so thoroughly rethought as to leave Gray's original for dead, with Ferry on particularly splendid, teeth-baring form. And the demented, disintegrating racket cooked up by O'List makes for an astonishing climax. "The backing tracks were finished, with all the horns etc, and Bryan had done a guide vocal by the time I arrived at the studio," O'List told the vivaroxymusic website in 2004. "We recorded it at Pete Townsend's studio, Ramport, which was hidden beneath a tower block in Battersea. Townsend had recorded *Quadrophenia* there. There was an amazing atmosphere to the place."

On its release, the album turned out to be book-ended by *The 'In' Crowd* and the title track, which was the only self-penned song included. This is a really beguiling and bracingly schizophrenic piece, worthy of Roxy Music, in which Ferry swims up from the depths of a self-reflexive dream to unleash a tearing tirade complete with country-guitar trimmings and a chintzy organ solo. Then, with Thompson's drums rolling contemplatively below, Ferry's coda shifts into 'another place' entirely, taking on an almost cosmic grandeur. The woozy fade-out is reminiscent of Bowie's *The Man who Sold the World*, and very nearly as effective.

The rest of the album, however, is at best a curate's egg. There are well-muscled and reasonably engaging translations of Willie Nelson's *Funny How Time Slips Away*, the Joe South country-rock classic *Walk a Mile in My Shoes*, Ike & Tina Turner's *Fingerpoppin'* and Sam Cooke's *What a Wonderful World*, plus a touching version of Dylan's *It Ain't Me Babe*. But somehow they don't add up to much, lacking the joie de vivre that gave cohesion to Ferry's previous solo album. And to make matters worse there are covers of Kris Kristofferson's *Help Me Make It Through the Night* and the 1930s chestnut *You Are My Sunshine* that are definitely of the 'Don't do it, Bryan' variety. The latter, in fact, is a bona-fide abomination, and lasts nearly seven minutes to boot.

After *The 'In' Crowd* and *Another Time, Another Place*, the only real standout is Ferry's take on the Jerome Kern evergreen *Smoke Gets in Your Eyes*, which would be issued as a single and enter the chart on 27 August. Staying there for eight weeks, it rose to number 17 on 24 September. A really delicious confection, this benefits from a discreet garnish of faux-harpsichords, a sweet and soulful Ruan O'Lochlainn alto solo (somewhat in the style of Bowie's contemporaneous sax playing) and a lachrymose vocal performance that smacks of the weeping willows referred to on the recent Roxy track *Serenade*. "Does he want you to laugh at the singer's pain instead of share it?" asked Richard Cromelin in *Phonograph Record*, accurately catching the tone of ambiguity that Ferry was still sometimes capable of carrying over from his Roxy work.

More often than not, however, Ferry mislaid his tongue-in-cheek credentials and sounded merely self-important. In another pronouncement calculated to antagonise his contemporaries, Ferry remarked on Kern's "incredibly clever lyric," adding, "It's a piece of poetry in a way. The people who did the best songs were, for me, pre-Beatles. After '64, and The Beatles and Dylan, it became more or less obligatory for performers to write their own songs, whether they could or not. And most often they can't, in my opinion."

In virtually the same breath he consented to appear on pappy television shows that may or may not have mortified his fellow Roxy members but definitely dismayed the more hardcore Roxy fans. After the Cilla Black embarrassment, his rendition of *It Ain't Me Babe* for Russell Harty's LWT talk show on Friday 4 October was forgivable enough, and came with a typically dry introduction from Harty himself: "My next guest used to dress himself up in leopardskins, singing avant-garde songs with a group called Roxy Music. And then he chose a touch of Rudolph Valentinos to promote his next image. Last week I saw him dressed up like a gaucho. I don't know what he's come as tonight..."

Less forgivable, however, was a stint on BBC2's *Show of the Week: Twiggs* on Thursday 17 October, a musical revue presented in previous weeks by Nana Mouskouri and Lulu but here built around the former model Twiggy. The producer, as on *Cilla*, was Michael Hurll and Ferry's fellow guest was Motown legend Jimmy Ruffin. This involved Ferry duetting with Twiggy to the MOR strains of Ronnie Hazelhurst and His Orchestra; *What a Wonderful World* was the chosen song and the pair appeared, hard to believe though it may seem, togged up as cow-eyed schoolchildren sitting at schooldesks. Ferry had long ago expressed his desire to circumvent the grind of touring via saturation television coverage, but *Cilla* and *Twiggs* were hardly the best vehicles.

Unsurprisingly, it was at this point that the music press decided to terminate the honeymoon period and turn on Ferry instead, with the *NME* declining to use his real name virtually as a matter of policy. The variants were seemingly legion: Byron Ferrari and Biriani Ferret were perhaps the most popular, with Bryatollah Ferrani being added to the arsenal later in the decade. Unfortunately, Ferry was not the man to just laugh this nonsense off – to take it, in fact, in the playful spirit in which it was intended. And the fact that it so obviously got under his skin only made the nicknames proliferate.

Systemically, of course

Eno, meanwhile, had sobriquets of his own, ranging from "electro-wizard in peacock feather radiance," "the Scaramouche of the synthesiser" and "the sultry Marlene Dietrich of rock'n'roll" to "the cadaver we've all come to love and recognise." After the enthusiastic reception accorded *Here Come the Warm Jets*, he encountered a pub band called The Winkies – comprising Phil Rambow, Mike Desmaris, Guy Humphreys and Brian Turrington – and with them cut his first single, *Seven Deadly Finns*, a shambolic sex farce that presages the onset of punk even more stridently than *Blank Frank*.

The opening verse is a four-pronged classic of scatological invention, Eno allowing pearl necklaces, country joys and daisy chains to speak for themselves but thoughtfully informing interviewer Chrissie Hynde that "a burning shame" is "a pornographic term for a deviation involving candles." Anticipating *Tokyo Joe* (Ferry's 1977 ode to an Oriental call-girl), *Seven Deadly Finns* depicts a bordello-full of Gallic hookers invaded by seven sex-crazed Finnish sailor boys, dissolving into a crazily yodelled fade after Eno has slipped in a double-entendre reference to his own musical philosophy: "Simplicity's the crucial thing, systemically of course."

The single failed to chart, however, and worse was to come when Eno embarked on a tour with The Winkies as his backing band. After only five dates he was hospitalised with a collapsed lung, some commentators attributing his condition to his Finns-style sexual appetite. Prior to this, however, the Eno-Winkies combine had recorded a Peel session on Tuesday 26 February, including *The Paw Paw Negro Blowtorch*, *Baby's On Fire* and a riveting rendition of the Peggy Lee classic *Fever*. The Winkies themselves would land a record deal with Chrysalis that got them nowhere, though Rambow would subsequently write *Young Lust* for Ellen Foley and *There's a Guy Works Down the Chip Shop Swears He's Elvis* for Kirsty MacColl.

The Winkies experience forcibly reminded Eno of his distaste for touring and unfitness for 'frontman' status. "I decided that I didn't want to be a star, the kind of figure Bryan became," he would tell Ian MacDonald three years later. "I knew that becoming that would only inhibit what I really wanted to do." His true métier became clear soon afterwards, when he and Manzanera were co-opted as executive producers of John Cale's *Fear* album, a paranoid masterpiece that was the first of three LPs Cale put out on Island Records. Cale's Velvets confrere Lou Reed having recently fallen in with David Bowie, it was only natural that Cale should gravitate towards the Roxy camp, using Eno and Manzanera again on the second of the trilogy, *Slow Dazzle*, then Eno and Mackay on the third, *Helen of Troy*.

The results on *Fear* – dubbed "a 24-carat chimera" by *Time Out* – are the most remarkable. The accreditation 'Guitars: Phil Manzanera' is balanced by the gnomic 'Eno: Eno', the latter larding Cale's mournful lament to *Emily* with his old *Sea Breezes* wave effects. On the title track, Cale utters funereal epigrams over a relentless Eno-Manzanera sound collage, later allowing *Gun* to run on for eight minutes to the noisy assault of a bone-crunching, Eno-warped Manzanera solo, as well as bringing his sepulchral Welsh baritone to bear on deceptively tuneful tracks like *Buffalo Ballet*, *You Know More Than I Know* and *Ship of Fools*. The latter title would prove a durable one, incidentally, other songs of the same name cropping up as the opening tracks of both Robert Calvert's *Lusty Leif and the Longships* album, produced by Eno in 1975, and Manzanera's 1985 post-Roxy project, *The Explorers*.

Eno's work on *Fear* set the pattern for many of his future collaborations. "I play much less than Phil because that wasn't the role I was fulfilling," he told Lisa Robinson. "John was using me to bounce ideas off and get reactions from. It was a very intense month … I wasn't sort of putting hot licks on the album [but] it was interesting – being this sort of consultant, ideas consultancy. It was very pleasant and the album is tremendous; I think it's the best John Cale album really."

Soon afterwards, Cale utilised Eno and Manzanera again on the Nico LP *The End*, which Cale produced. "Nico was a big figure for those who knew about The Velvet Underground and the whole Warhol scene," Manzanera later recalled. "So I jumped at the chance to work with her." These Velvet Underground associations crystallised around a project organised by Richard Williams, now on the Island payroll and the man responsible for getting together Cale, Nico, Eno and Kevin Ayers (ex-Soft Machine) for a Rainbow concert subsequently issued on record as *June 1, 1974*. With one fan applying the unfortunate acronym ACNE to this fleeting supergroup, the song selections included Eno's *Driving Me Backwards* and *Baby's On Fire* plus riveting covers of *The End* (Nico) and *Heartbreak Hotel* (Cale). Robert Wyatt and Mike Oldfield were on hand to fill out the musical backing; Manzanera, too, had been asked to join in but demurred thanks to the impending sessions for Roxy's fourth album.

Eight: *The Fourth Roxy Music Album*

"I have never found the noisy collision of musical devices (though they are always expertly constructed) which make up Roxy Music any more entertaining than the hype and hysteria which have persistently surrounded them (they arose in one of the industry's troughs, and good luck to them). I do not, however, find the artwork for Country Life **in any way offensive.***"*
John Collis [complete album review], *Time Out* **20 December 1974**

W ork on Roxy's fourth LP began on Monday 1 July, with all ten backing tracks laid down, in skeletal form, within a week. After this, Ferry retired to a suite at the Ritz ("the TV broke down at home," he apologised) to immerse himself in the tracks and come up with suitable lyrics. In the producer's chair at Air Studios was John Punter, whom Ferry extolled to Nick Kent as "a veritable Titan amongst engineers/big-time producers," adding mischievously: "Please print that. He's always complaining about the lack of press he receives."

And, where *Stranded* had benefited from a Ferry-Manzanera composition and another credited to Ferry-Mackay, the new album would feature two of each. Ferry referred to this as "part of the new policy," also noting that "it's been incredibly easy and straightforward doing these sessions. No anti-vibes whatsoever."

"We're only just past the sketch stage at present," Manzanera informed Steve Lake at the end of July. "The tracks are gradually being built up with overdubs until the picture emerges complete. But with Roxy, the style or the sound is always very difficult to pinpoint. I mean, I'd love to be able to tell you that there's five up-tempo rockers and four laid-back country tunes, but it's never that easy ... [We] keep sifting, putting synthesiser here, or violin there, and it's just a continual growing process, until you realise you've finished."

Despite the lack of "anti-vibes," elaborating the *Country Life* backing tracks proved problematic, with the finished product so delayed that it had yet to be released when Roxy's accompanying autumn dates got underway. "We were in the studio constantly up until the beginning of our British tour," Ferry admitted. "We just finished it by the skin of our teeth. About three-quarters of the way through it I just had to get out of town, so I went to Portugal for two weeks to try to finish off some of the songs. I went with Eric Boman, the photographer, and that's where we did the album cover, about a hundred yards from the ocean at 3.00 am."

Ferry had hit upon the album's title, *Country Life*, as an affectionate joke at the expense of the slightly fusty high-society magazine of the same name. "I'm an avid reader of glossies and that's one of the great eccentrics," he maintained. "The cover contrasts with the usual *Country Life* photography, where you normally have characters shooting ducks or jumping over fences in top hats." Ferry might have added that the title page of each edition tended to feature a portrait shot of some winsome landed debutante, with whom the two brazen Valkyries featured on the album cover couldn't have formed a more shocking contrast. With pubic hair on show this time, it's also safe to say that the title's first syllable was intended as a double-entendre in line with Hamlet's reference to "country matters."

"I've always been intrigued by the Profumo affair," Ferry added, and it's easy enough to see *Country Life*'s Constanze Karoli and Eveline Grunwald as Teutonic counterparts to government-wrecking call-girls Christine Keeler and Mandy Rice-Davies, disporting themselves in front of a hedge at Lord Astor's country estate, Cliveden, circa 1963. The "two nearly naked wild things caught in mid-panty raid," as *Circus* magazine described them, were passed off by Ferry as just "two German girls on holiday." Maybe so, but the managerial hand of Dr Puxley is detectable here, given that Constanze (the bare-breasted girl on the right) was the sister – and Eveline (the "mid-panty raid" girl on the left) the girlfriend – of Michael Karoli, guitarist with Krautrock giants Can and a client of Puxley's.

Describing their remit as having to look like "two ladies being surprised in a delicate situation," Constanze remembered in 1990 that "Bryan liked our shoulders and German outlook, so [he] proposed just for fun to make this photo session. We didn't think it would actually be used! We didn't talk much about it, we just had to look weird and surprised." According to Eveline, "People thought we were lying down and masturbating, but that was never the intention! Neither did we choose the photo, but Bryan did ask us if we were d'accord with it. We didn't think it was scandalous anyway." As for Antony Price, his role was less central this time around; as he put it himself, "Well, there wasn't much going on in the clothes department..."

Pausing only to have Constanze and Eveline translate a section of his lyric for *Bitter-Sweet*, Ferry then headed back to London, where he was disappointed to discover that economy demanded an abandonment of the sprawling gatefold sleeves common to Roxy's first three albums; "our gesture for ecology," he later quipped. The luscious laminate was retained, however, and Ferry further appeased the fans with the claim that "to make up for only having an ordinary single cover we've got two girls on it instead of one." On the eventual release of the album, however, the cover image was to stir up a controversy extending well beyond the grumblings of gatefold-hungry Roxy fans.

During the album sessions, the familiar press attention on Ferry was diverted briefly to Manzanera, who was interviewed by Steve Lake for *Melody Maker* on 3 August then twice more on the 24th, by Pete Makowski in *Sounds* and Nick Kent in *NME*. Ferry wrested the focus back again in no uncertain terms when Roxy's autumn dates finally came around, though, as it turned out, the focus would take the form of outright ridicule. Ferry's omnipresence in the media had led to a widespread suspicion that he was beginning to believe his own publicity, and with the *Country Life* tour he played directly into the hands of rock journalists eager to set in motion that time-honoured British tradition, the press backlash.

Ferry's stage costumes (tended, as they would be even in the 21st century, by his French-Trinidadian dresser, Christian Wainwright) were by now the source of intense media scrutiny. In a doomed bid to reverse the enormous, and potentially damaging, impact made by the white tuxedo, Ferry had concocted with Antony Price two new 'looks' for the tour. The first – roughly speaking a jackbooted militaristic look – was thought merely tasteless in its overtones of 'Nazi chic', but the second – a Gaucho costume modelled on Rudolph Valentino's appearance in the 1920 film *The Four Horsemen of the Apocalypse* – was laughed to scorn from every conceivable quarter. For *Sounds*, the stormtrooper look made Ferry look more like "a Spanish traffic warden," while, to *Melody Maker*, he resembled "Ronald Coleman [sic] as *The Prisoner of Zenda*." The Gaucho get-up, meanwhile, saw the *Daily Mail* branding him as a "refugee from *The Horse of the Year Show*," while to *NME* he was merely the "George Lazenby of the Argentinian corned-beef market."

The author of that last barb, Nick Kent, showed his good humour, as well as a sense of historical perspective, in conceding that "it's not as if this was the first gauchoid outbreak in rock. Paul Revere and the Raiders, Sam the Sham and the Pharaohs, Dave Dee, Dozy, Beaky, Mick and Tich, they've all made complete klutzes of themselves trouping around like extras from *Blood and Sand* at one time in their careers and they're all ugly varmints anyway so they only did it for larfs." Kent wasn't to know it, but Ferry's ludicrous get-up – Hamlet shirt, velvet pantaloons, sombrero, suede bootees and all – wasn't to be rock's last 'gauchoid outbreak'; some six years later it would re-emerge courtesy of the New Romantics. Roughly speaking, Duran Duran would resurrect the Gaucho look, while Spandau Ballet would do the same for the Gestapo enforcer.

The Gestapo had supplanted the Gaucho by the time Roxy arrived in London, and was certainly more appropriate to the grandiloquent theatrics of the band's climactic four-night tenure of the Rainbow. Indeed, Allan Jones headed his *Melody Maker* report 'Achtung Roxy!' in acknowledgment of the set's yards of red plush and giant mechanised eagle. "It was regal and splendid, almost militaristic," Ferry enthused. "It looked like a coronation was about to take place."

The effect owed something to Leni Riefenstahl's filmed records of National Socialist rallies, a potentially worrying tendency that would become all the more so with David Bowie's ill-advised Nazi salute at Victoria Station in May 1976, prior to becoming the subject of clod-hopping satire in Pink Floyd's bombastic double album *The Wall*. For his part, Ferry blandly dismissed any objections with the observation that "The Nazis had a great sense of visuals. What we were doing with all that theatre was to create a style which matched the music. It was vital that the act should be visually interesting."

Even as formidable a look as this, however, was achieved on a cottage-industry level; the red and gold hangings, showily embossed with the acronym 'RM', were hand embroidered by the wife of designer Nick de Ville. The threatening ambience was defused, in any case, by Ferry's first notable attempts at audience interaction, though Allan Jones, present at the first of the Rainbow dates, would quibble with this latest development: "I can remember when he hardly spoke a word to his audience, and that distance was destroyed on Saturday [5 October]. Ferry just doesn't make it on that level. He looks strained and uncomfortable even acknowledging the presence of an audience."

Rather unfairly, the backlash even turned its sights on the fashion-conscious audiences whom Ferry had such trouble acknowledging, with one critic anatomising the "heavy-booted waterfront B-girls with scarlet slashes for mouths and pug-nosed palookas for protectors, sixth-formers fresh from raiding their grandma's wardrobe and fresh-faced fops in white ties and tails." The other band members were subject to sartorial inspection too, with Manzanera resembling "Victor Mature playing Antonio des Mortes" and Mackay "dressed to kill in a powder-blue drape jacket, matching drainpipe trousers and winkle pickers ... like a surreal Billy Fury."

For the ever-available role of bass guitarist, the EG stable hit upon John Wetton, sometime member of Family and latterly the vocalist-cum-bassist with King Crimson in its scary *One More Red Nightmare* manifestation. Initially recruited merely to supervise auditions at the Rainbow, Wetton was eventually persuaded to take on the role himself. The support act was also close to home, vocalist Jess Roden (backed on stage by Iguana) having recently put out a solo LP on Island.

Backlash or no backlash, Roxy were an instant sell-out wherever they went. Having kicked off at Cardiff on Saturday 21 September, the tour took in Bristol, Stoke, Birmingham, Leicester and Sheffield prior to the Rainbow, then Bournemouth, Liverpool, Manchester, Leeds, Edinburgh, Glasgow and Newcastle after it. The Newcastle dates, Sunday 27 and Monday 28 October, would provide much of the material subsequently included on the *Viva! Roxy Music* album. In the meantime, Ferry informed *Disc*'s Ray Fox-Cumming on the 26th that the new LP "is much better than the last album – but then I say that with every album. I think, though, that the playing has shown a marked improvement and we've got some interesting textural collages. I think too that it's a more direct album than the last."

Initially set for the last week of September, *Country Life* finally emerged in mid-November, the delay meaning that Ferry's plan to include lyric sheets for all four Roxy LPs was ditched in favour of an inner sleeve showcasing lyrics only for the album in hand. The LP entered the UK chart on 30 November, streaking straight to number three but remaining in the list for only ten weeks. The press response graciously dispensed with all thoughts of a backlash; "make no mistake," asserted *Melody Maker*, "*Country Life* is a great album." And, according to Nick Kent in *NME*: "I can't seem to recall a display of instrumental kineticism executed in the recording studio with such inspired finesse this year."

Country Life also marked an American breakthrough by reaching number 37 on the *Billboard* chart. *Billboard* itself noted that "Roxy Music requires some listening, so do yourself a favour and listen. As far as rock goes, they are far above most." In *Rolling Stone*, Jim Miller alluded to the continuing 'is he kidding or isn't he?' dilemma ("Ferry oscillates unpredictably between camping it up and sounding dead serious – and when Roxy Music gets serious, they can be scary, even repugnant"), but concluded that "Thanks to the glossy production and direct lyrics, *Country Life* makes about as accessible an introduction to Roxy Music as Ferry is likely to cut."

* * *

Your Application's Failed
(Thompson) 4:45

Dramatising a luckless pre-Roxy bid to get a job on the London Underground, *Your Application's Failed* was Paul Thompson's one-and-only writing credit during his time with the band. The jaunty result displays some of the same schizoid tendencies as more vaunted Roxy tracks, alternating between a pleasantly rinky-dink melody and heavy, hard-driving 'choruses'.

The pleasant bits seem to mirror Thompson's carefree journey to his assignation (in this the track resembles *Walking the Whippet* on Mackay's recently released solo album), while the raging band work-outs that follow presumably reflect his nervous anticipation at the interview and simmering frustration at the result. From the delightfully lugubrious Gustafson-Thompson dialogue at the beginning, through Mackay's fruitily expressive sax solos and the wholly unexpected heavy-duty attack of Manzanera's guitars, the track immediately arrests the listener's attention. Thompson himself embroiders the mix with humorous little paradiddles, while equally droll keyboard noodlings give way to a cheesy organ riff and finally great looping washes of synth at the fade-out.

Though Mackay and Manzanera go great guns in attempting to outdo each other here, this final 'wall of sound' thrash rather outstays its welcome. Earlier, Thompson has followed the example of Mackay (on *The Pride and the Pain*) and Manzanera (on *Hula Kula*) in literally adding his own voice to the mix; indeed, everything stops briefly for his doleful, Geordie-accented interjection of "Your application's failed." After this unquestioned high point, the band would have been well advised to wind things up a bit quicker and quit while they were ahead.

"I'm not into drummers' music," Thompson had claimed back in 1972. "I'm into group music, something that comes out of a unit." Appropriately then, *Your Application's Failed* boasts a really sparkling band cohesion, by turns witty and well-muscled, with no gangbusting 'look at me' theatrics from Thompson to compromise it. "Although Paul Thompson wrote the energetic B-side to *All I Want is You*," noted Jonh Ingham in *Sounds*, "he doesn't feel qualified to record an album for a couple of years, until his writing ability is cognizant [ie, commensurate] with his playing ability. Musically, Thompson is probably the keystone of Roxy. Certainly Ferry would feel lost without him."

Though relegated to doing duty as the flip-side to *All I Want is You* (and to Roxy's first US single release, *The Thrill of It All*), Thompson's one-and-only Roxy writing credit had no trouble maintaining the band's tradition of high-quality B-sides.

The Thrill of It All
(Ferry) 6:24 / single edit [US] 3:20 / *Greatest Hits* edit 4:20

Once again, a Roxy LP opens with an in-your-face flourish of instrumental pyrotechnics, a hard-rock epic so shatteringly visceral that new listeners are likely to be exhausted, spent, wrung out by the album before getting even a tenth of the way in. "When compared to *Stranded*'s cool, clean lines of sound, *Country Life* is cluttered, tempestuous," noted Wayne Robins in *Creem*. "The password is tension, which sometimes transmutes to 'intensity'. It shows itself most splendidly in *The Thrill of It All*, a long, whiny, excessive, frightening song that is the antithesis of the blues ... Behind Ferry's pop Gothic vision here, there is real emotion, and Roxy's idiosyncratic musicians are the ideal complement."

Despite the track's prevailing 'wall of sound' bombast, the tone is savage, cynical, even violent, with Ferry offering a jaundiced portrait of 1970s decadence that radically updates the street-smart attitude of his own recent solo hit, *The 'In' Crowd*. "It's probably the blackest track that one's ever done," he informed a correspondent from US magazine *Circus*. "It was incredibly difficult to mix, there are so many things wailing away."

After a keyboard opening in redirected *Editions of You* mode, the track resounds for well over six minutes to an awesome juxtaposition of Manzanera's coruscating guitar, the synthetic shimmer of Jobson's violins, Gustafson's gymnastic bassline and the truly pile-driving propulsion of Paul Thompson. Ferry's vocal is one of his most memorable performances, invested with something of the demonic force of his *Sympathy for the Devil* makeover but with the camp theatrics stripped remorselessly away. The instrumental chaos rising around him puts the listener in mind of some colossal, runaway juggernaut, sleek and inexorable, with Ferry sitting securely astride it as Manzanera strikes sparks that graduate from merely dazzling to positively lethal.

Ferry's opening salvo is uniquely ominous, conjuring a lowering sky, a keening wind, and an inflexible determination to submit to whatever decadent extremes the night may bring. The self-destructive potential of the high life is everywhere apparent, from Ferry's facetious inclusion of Dorothy Parker's celebrated one-liner re suicide – "You might as well live" – to a couple of smoochy refrains that temporarily arrest the headlong rush. Here, against the submerged finger-clicking of what sounds like an early drum-machine, Mackay's saxophone putters absent-mindedly through the mix alongside a tremulously camp backing vocal. Ferry, meanwhile, raises the spectral shade of *Strictly Confidential* in a reference to "preying shadows," scarily undercutting all the thoughtless hedonism celebrated elsewhere. It's the leering insinuation of an embodied conscience as sung by a mellifluous speakeasy crooner.

The sardonic twist that concludes the song reveals this devil-may-care hedonist as just another love-sick reject, encountering painful reminders of his lost love everywhere he goes and reduced to a stoned stupor that seems like a dark twin to the tipsy nonsense of *Bitters End*. Ferry's final anguished cries are similar to his panicked outbursts in the opening section of *Mother of Pearl*, tumbling recklessly over the soundstage while Jobson's string section and Manzanera's repeated guitar riff fade into a kind of apocalyptic delirium. Manzanera, in particular, throws down a gauntlet here that would arouse great interest in his forthcoming solo album; his contributions to *Country Life* are breathtakingly inventive throughout, displaying what Nick Kent called an "omnisustained polished ferocity that would make a whole brace of killer axemen – particularly those boastfully adept in the heavy metal regions – break down and weep at their comparative impotence."

The wall of sound complexity of the song made it a daunting one to attempt on stage, as Ferry acknowledged in Cardiff on the opening weekend of the *Country Life* tour. "There's one track called *The Thrill of It All* which has strings and the band going at full blast as well," he fretted, "and it sounds a bit thin when we do it at the moment. We'll do it if we can. I'd just like to go out and mime it to the tape." The track was attempted on some of the tour's US dates, but only became a permanent fixture on the band's *Siren* schedule, subsequently reappearing on the *Flesh + Blood* tour of 1980.

For Ferry, perhaps the deeper joke behind this swollen epic of upmarket sleaze and excess was his acquisition of its title from a squeaky-clean Doris Day vehicle of 1963. Pre-release, he had suggested to Kent that *The Thrill of It All* could well turn out to be the *Country Life* album's 'magnum opus'. It was a characteristic act of careless bragadoccio, then, to lead off the whole set with what Ferry believed to be its strongest asset. The beauty of *Country Life*, however, is that the dizzyingly high standard set by *The Thrill of It All* is maintained pretty much throughout.

Three and Nine
(Ferry-Mackay) 4:04

With much of Ferry's inspiration – never mind the band's name – derived from the celluloid glamour of yesteryear, it's appropriate that *Three and Nine* should offer a nostalgic look at adolescent fumblings in a provincial picture house. Perhaps Roxy's most engaging ballad to date, it also takes decimalisation as a governing theme. Sounds improbable, but through a wistful meditation on the old three shillings and ninepence ticket charge to get into the movies Ferry acknowledges, and grudgingly accepts, the inevitability of change. Setting the stakes very high, he told *Circus* that "It has to do with the passing of old England."

Mackay's offbeat melody, based on an original fragment entitled *Roman Blue Eyes*, is a lovely one and the arrangement more than does it justice. A brightly piping oboe solo gets things moving, feeding into Ferry's mournful harmonica break and his opening reminiscence about the breathtaking lure of Technicolor and 3-D. Given that the latter gimmick had its heyday around 1953, Ferry is reaching back a long way here, to a pair of pre-rock'n'roll teens entranced by the gaudy effusions of Hollywood but, comfortably ensconced in the back row, content to snog their way through the cheesy, and presumably British, second feature. Cradled in the warm embrace of his own multi-tracked backing vocal, Ferry shrugs his shoulders at the compromises involved 20 years on in a "decimal romance" (45 pence being the going rate at the 1974 box-office, it seems), conceding whimsically that anyone who's got his head around the fahrenheit/centigrade changeover should just about get by.

Mackay throws in a charming sax break (note for note the same as his first solo on *A Song for Europe* but beautifully smooched up for the occasion), Thompson offers typically inventive variations on his customary 4/4 beat, Manzanera contributes twinkling rhythm guitar and Jobson's synths burble woozily below. Ferry winds things up by painting a touching picture of star-crossed misfits huddling for security in the stalls, and the song ends on a gorgeously indefinite glissando from Thompson.

With no trace of *The Bogus Man*'s metallic sheen, here is a quite different Ferry, warm, self-amused, gently philosophical, even slipping in a nicely self-mocking allusion to his own appetite for nostalgia. Like much of the material on *Country Life*, the lyric is beautifully crafted, conjuring a mood with the simplest of brushstrokes.

After his experiences on *These Foolish Things* and *Another Time, Another Place*, covering erudite standards written by others, Ferry seemed more alive than ever to the importance of the words he attached to his own songs. Significantly, *Country Life* was the first Roxy album to come complete with an inner sleeve featuring Ferry's lyrics. In 1972, he had been quoted in the *Guardian* to the effect that he refused to provide lyric sheets because "there is a great joy in listening to an old record and discovering new lyrics." Two years on, he'd changed his tune. "I feel the lyrics should always stand up to reading," he told Max Bell of the *NME*. "I take a tremendous amount of care with them. It's very rarely that I leave a verse unaltered from inception."

All I Want is You
(Ferry) 2:53

All I Want is You was Roxy's fourth single and the first to miss out on the Top Ten, stalling at number 12. Phil Manzanera had given it a tantalising preview on 24 August, calling it "our best single since *Virginia Plain*" in conversation with *Sounds'* Pete Makowski. Well, he would say that, given the Manzanera-heavy mix. But perhaps it was the track's hard-rock 'wall of sound' quality that put singles buyers off. A touch less radio-friendly, this was no longer the idiosyncratic Roxy of previous singles; there were no revving motorbikes as per *Virginia Plain*, no crazy *Pyjamarama*-style Morse Code signals, no 'what the hell is that?' outbreaks of perspex violin as on *Street Life*. Instead, it sounded somehow less congenial – more like a heavy metal group fronted by a rapidly fragmenting Noël Coward.

None of which is to suggest that *All I Want is You* is anything less than Roxy close to their best. Ferry's lyric and vocal performance are stunning, and the band's ensemble instrumental cacophony jaw-dropping in its sustained impact. The narrator here is a man so irretrievably bound to an erring lover that he's happy to overlook any whispers of her possible indiscretions, ignore the temptations provided by one-night stands and spurn the empty blandishments of the jet set. In the course of this impassioned plea, Ferry throws in a couple of hi-falutin' asides in which the instrumental assault lets up a little, with only Manzanera's agonised guitar chords to echo the prevailing din. In one of these,

Ferry slips briefly into the French stylings familiar from *A Song for Europe*, the lyric elsewhere containing an explicit reference to the kind of society rag satirised in the album's title – though Ferry's claim to be uninterested in etiquette no doubt raised a few eyebrows among commentators convinced that he'd become café society's resident rock star.

The whole thing is founded on an Axminster-thick carpet of heavily treated saxophones, with Manzanera's clangorous guitar describing awesome arcs over the soundstage and reaching stratospheric proportions during an extended instrumental break. Here, the combination of Thompson's thunderous hoof-beats with Manzanera's careening guitar suggests what *Ladytron* might have sounded like with its apocalyptic outro shifted to its middle section. There's also a sublime moment when, Manzanera having shifted to an even higher register, Mackay's sax briefly soars free of the surrounding backbeat.

The final section is irresistible, with Ferry's archly camp trilling of the title phrase setting up a final realisation similar to the mind-blowing one that concluded *In Every Dream Home a Heartache*. Ferry's claim to have lost his head over his love object is followed by a muttered, sotto voce "Yeah" from someone lurking in the backbeat, emphasising the fact that a seed of madness has been present in the narrator's obsessive love all along. Hence the crazed ferocity of the instrumentation.

As vanguard to the upcoming album, *All I Want is You* spent eight weeks on the singles chart, coming in just as Carl Douglas' infectious disco anthem *Kung Fu Fighting* relinquished the top spot and passing out while the David Essex hit *Gonna Make You a Star* was holding prolonged sway. Arriving on 8 October at number 49, *All I Want is You* had vaulted to 17 the following week but then struggled its way to a high of 12 on 5 November. Though this was a somewhat disappointing result, the song at least came in as eighth best single of 1974 in *Sounds'* annual Readers' Poll.

Though featured in the band's contemporaneous tour, *All I Want is You* would, surprisingly, never be played live again. In 1984, it was covered by Tommy Keene on his four-track EP *Back Again (Try…)*, recorded live at the 'Rat' in Boston Massachusetts; it joined a live rendition of The Rolling Stones' *When the Whip Comes Down* in support of two Keene originals.

Out of the Blue
(Ferry-Manzanera) 4:46

The concluding blast of Mackay's saxophone on *All I Want is You* is succeeded by a half-heard shudder of violins, heralding the spectral oncoming swirl of *Out of the Blue*. The join is seamless, as if the two tracks were integral parts of some greater tapestry, and the shock of the new song fading up from the abandoned melody of the old echoes disconcertingly through what remains. For here is an apparently warm and optimistic lyric joined to the eeriest musical backdrop imaginable, the tone set by Mackay's oboe as it repeatedly spells out a uniquely sinister three-note riff.

That otherworldly riff will return in spine-freezing style twice more, expertly complemented by Johnny Gustafson's limber and funky bass-line. (His finest hour as far as the *Country Life* album is concerned.) Complemented and yet not complemented: like a funked-up replay of the *Ladytron* intro, the mood of disorientation is much enhanced by the fact that the bass and oboe seem to be playing entirely contrapuntal melodies. Ferry, meanwhile, sings of the transformative power of love against a racing piano figure and jaggedly riffing guitars. He claims that all the anxieties attendant on love have been suddenly swept aside but nevertheless goes into disquieting detail about what they were like – doing so, what's more, in a voice at once beatific and faintly threatening.

A crashing middle section then equates the arrival of love with the sudden emergence of the sun from a bank of clouds. Manzanera's guitar soars over the top of all this with exhilarating precision, then it's back to the circling oboe and pulsing bass and a final section in which Ferry admits that, transfiguring though it is, this feeling may be just another transient romantic fancy. A few piercing Manzanera bird-cries later and Jobson is off, unleashing an incandescent violin solo that tears unchecked through the mix until disappearing back into the clouds, leaving only a scudding vapor trail behind it. The effect is like the electrical fuzz conclusion to a previous Manzanera composition, *Amazona*, though where the older track suggested the monolithic motion of the Pacific Railroad, *Out of the Blue* hints at a journey altogether more celestial, even stratospheric.

Either way, what we have here is another inexorable juggernaut, with Ferry on top form and the band polishing up the sleek and steely bodywork to a dazzling kinetic sheen. In the memorable phrase "throwaway lines often ring true," Ferry seems to offer a teasing summation of the whole mixed Roxy Music metaphor – "part false part true," as he'd put it in *For Your Pleasure*. And in conceiving of love on a virtually cosmic plane, the song harks back to the unattainable goddess of *Mother of Pearl* and forward to the airborne euphoria of *Angel Eyes*.

Unsurprisingly, *Out of the Blue* rapidly acquired the status of fan favourite, later becoming one of only two *Country Life* tracks routinely included on compilation albums (the other being *All I Want is You*) and finally the only *Country Life* track to make it onto Roxy's latterday live sets; it missed out only in 1980, when its place was taken by a surprise resurrection of *The Thrill of It All*. With Jobson absent, his melodramatic final solo would generally take the form of a galloping Manzanera-Mackay excursion, until in 2001 Lucy Wilkins provided one of the highpoints of the reunion tour with a hair-raising recreation of Jobson's original. Having presaged Roxy's comeback with the observation that *Out of the Blue* is "one of those songs that features strong rock'n'roll violin and strong rock'n'roll oboe," Mackay proceeded to replace his oboe on the tour with an electronic clarinet, the Yamaha WX7, the results sounding almost as eerie.

Around the same time, Manzanera preserved three live renditions of the song through his own Expression label, the first a notably funked-up version from 1985, included as a hidden extra on *The Explorers Live at the Palace (Camden)*. (It makes its surprise appearance just before the final track, *Venus de Milo*, and follows the template of Roxy's own live version from the *Manifesto* tour.) The other versions were both from 1977, one on *The Complete 801 Live at Manchester University* (featuring Mackay and Thompson) and the other on *801 Live at Hull*, this one showcasing Eddie Jobson himself in full flight – and in his home town.

At the time of *Country Life*'s release, *Out of the Blue* may have seemed a slightly second-hand title, John Lennon having used it for one of the tracks on his 1973 album *Mind Games*. It was Roxy's *Out of the Blue*, however, that was covered by Wishplants on their 1993 EP, *Tortoiseshell*.

If It Takes All Night
(Ferry) 3:12

A big, bold and bluesy 12-bar swingalong, *If It Takes All Night* would join several other *Country Life* tracks – *Three and Nine, A Really Good Time*, even *All I Want is You* – in being performed live only during the album's accompanying tour. It remains, nevertheless, one of Roxy's most engaging pastiches, hilariously juxtaposing Ferry's business-as-usual lyric with a truly rumbustious performance from the band. Taking the 'country' in *Country Life* literally, Manzanera's whingeing guitar is joined by honky-tonk piano to introduce Ferry's memorable opening ode to an encroaching ennui.

Ferry's world-weary pose here is no different from that of later tracks like *Spin Me Round*, even *Avalon*, yet here it's set against a wildly incongruous saloon-bar backdrop. Gustafson's bass rolls gymnastically below, Ferry indulges in a charmingly unbuttoned harmonica break, and Mackay's phalanx of multi-tracked saxes are joined to a thoroughly camp backing chorus. Ferry's pouting stylisations are equally so, as is Mackay's storming tenor solo, which is splendidly done in his ritziest raunch mode. And at the end, Ferry's philosophical cowpoke, searching for the meaning of life inside a frontier cathouse, makes a deliciously incongruous call for further supplies of champagne.

For all its throwaway larkishness, the song connects back to one of the defining moments on the *Stranded* album; the absurdity of Ferry's deep and meaningful questions being asked during a night of drunken debauchery is in much the same vein as his self-mocking equation of life's inner meaning with his latest fling in *Mother of Pearl*. It could be argued that, after the cotton pickin' first phase of *If There is Something*, the more conventional song structures assuming dominion on *Country Life* turn what was once a generic fragment of a larger canvas into a track all by itself; presumably for this reason, *If It Takes All Night* has come in for more than its fair share of critical derision. It's superbly done, however, and confirms the promise of the various country flavourings featured on Ferry's *Another Time, Another Place* and Mackay's *In Search of Eddie Riff*.

Mackay in particular – inspired in part by his wife – was intrigued by country music, boldly emulating Roy Rogers, no less, in his solo cover of *A Four Legged Friend*. "Blatant sentimentality compensated by really good musicianship [is what] makes Country & Western work," was how he'd explained it to *Disc*'s Caroline Boucher back in January. Rounding off Side One, the cod-country stylings here would be echoed, in a seamless move from the ridiculous to the sublime, on the climactic track on Side Two, *Prairie Rose*.

Bitter-Sweet
(Ferry-Mackay) 4:50

In another splendid stroke of Roxy dualism, the second side of *Country Life* opens

127

with a Mackay soundtrack redolent of Bertolt Brecht but with a title swiped by Ferry from Brecht's polar opposite, Noël Coward. Brecht of the Number One haircut and theatrical 'alienation' effect, Coward of the brilliantined hair and minutely crafted 'well-made play'; Brecht of *Aufsteig und Fall der Stadt Mahagonny* (1929), Coward of a very different piece of musical theatre from the same year, *Bitter-Sweet*. Both collide here to disorientating effect.

Bitter-Sweet itself turned on a similarly irreconcilable collision, dramatising the clash between a fast-receding old world and a brash, upcoming new one, in effect the contest between operetta and jazz. The closing lines of its closing number – "Though my world has gone awry / Though the end is drawing nigh / I shall love you till I die / Good-bye!" – carry a mordant lyricism echoed in Ferry's fatalistic verses here, which could have been written for the clipped, emotionally constipated tones of Coward himself. As for Ferry's indebtedness to Brecht, he had included Lotte Lenya's rendition of *Alabama Song* (from *Mahagonny*) among his 11 selections for the *NME*'s 'Whatever Turned You On' column back in August 1972, commenting tartly that "It was covered horribly by The Doors – probably on the instigation of their pianist, who's a European."

The funereal mood of *Bitter-Sweet* is created by means of the metronomic time-keeping of a piano, the hesitantly thrummed musings of a bass guitar, the sad glissando of Mellotron strings, the angular circling of a guitar. Ferry is at his most affectingly resigned and the whole thing has a bewitching grace that hardly prepares the listener for the Sturm und Drang that follows. Powered by Thompson at his bludgeoning best, and resounding to some scarily metallic flourishes from Manzanera, the choruses have the feel of a Teutonic 'oom-pah' military band, a hard-faced Hitlerjunge knees-up in the vein of Brecht and his musical collaborator Kurt Weill. And, in conflating goose-stepping stormtroopers with high-kicking chorus girls, Ferry acknowledges a debt to the most recent populist manifestation of the Brecht-Weill mode, Kander and Ebb's *Cabaret*.

Before the next outbreak, Ferry returns to his introspective mood with a slightly laboured analogy comparing the consumption of wine with a parallel consumption of lovers; even so, these lines seem to equip Coward-style imagery with vampire's teeth. Any lingering doubts that what we have here is *A Song for Europe* transposed to inter-war Berlin are then dispelled as Ferry breaks into full-blown German, the words translated for him, not by Dr Puxley as on the earlier song, but by the buxom überfrauen pictured on the album sleeve, Constanze Karoli and Eveline Grunwald. Ferry grimaces his way through this Teutonic tirade, offering further thoughts on the dilemma of being "stranded between life and art" ("gestrandet an Leben und Kunst") before Mackay interposes the second of two discreet oboe meditations, the sparkling clarity of which lift the track briefly to sublime heights.

Bitter-Sweet remains an under-rated song if only because of its 'the sequel is always inferior to the original' connection to *A Song for Europe* (also a Ferry-Mackay collaboration). Beautifully arranged and mournfully song, it preserves the familiar Roxy tension between camp affectation and sincere emotion, as well as conjuring through its soundstage a lost world of George Grosz canvases, the silent films of G W Pabst, the popular songs of Friedrich Holländer, the placid beauty of Louise Brooks, the demonic intensity of Conrad Veidt. In other words, it encapsulates in under five minutes, as Wayne Robins noted in *Creem*, what "it took Lou Reed a whole album [the 1973 release *Berlin*] to get out of his system."

Triptych
(Ferry) 3:09

Having dispensed with the band's quasi-sequel to *A Song for Europe*, we come to perhaps the most outré cut on the *Country Life* LP, which in its turn plays like a tighter, more poker-faced replay of *Psalm*. In *Triptych*, Ferry abandons all trace of camp in treating Christ's crucifixion and hoped-for resurrection in the three-paneled form common to church altar-pieces.

To this end, the band invest themselves in the sombre solemnity of mediaeval church music, and, according to the *NME* estimate of Nick Kent, the result is "a short bout of ersatz-olde English pageantry ... which is very strange, and in the final analysis should have been left to the likes of Steeleye Span." Kent's judgment notwithstanding, this peculiar hybrid has a strangely bewitching authority, coupled with a beautiful arrangement and some of Ferry's briefest but most exquisite lyrics.

The track opens on a stately flourish of faux-harpsichord and Thompson's court-ceremonial drum beats, shifting into a blaring oboe fanfare from Mackay (in the circumstances, maybe we should make that a blaring hautboys fanfare) and the thoughtful circling of Manzanera's guitar. A coldly fluting synth underlies Ferry's opening observations, in which he seems to be an onlooker at Golgotha, while Mackay's oboe provides the shrill accompaniment to the song's double-tracked centre panel. Here, Ferry's explicit reference to Christ's crucified body causes the harpsichord and guitars to curdle into one in best Roxy style. The third section closes on a tremulously poetic note which nevertheless contains one of Ferry's most outrageous puns, his speculations on divine resurrection incorporating a play on 'sun' and 'son', both of which he hopes to see rising in the near future.

If the spiritual solemnity of the song sits uneasily amid the dazzling and frequently abrasive textures of *Country Life*, the decision to include such an off-kilter item is characteristic, nevertheless, of a band at the height of its powers. Though quick to refute it, Ferry was tickled by contemporary press speculation that the album's title was a veiled reference to John Donne, the 17th century metaphysical poet who had begun life as a libertine and all-round rakehell before dedicating himself to the worship of God. "It's a very interesting process, isn't it?" he said to Nick Kent during the *Country Life* sessions. "All these gay blades getting up to this incredible hanky-panky when they were young – but who at the same time wrote very moving love poetry until they ultimately approached religion with the same fanatical zeal. I could see myself perhaps falling into that."

Despite these musings, Roxy would leave explicitly religious themes to others once Ferry had got the epic sweep of *Psalm* and concentrated beauty of *Triptych* out of his system. It fell to Mackay to maintain the tradition; preparatory to becoming a student of theology, he used his 1980s Manzanera combine The Explorers to record tracks like *Sacrosanct* and *Many Are the Ways*.

Casanova
(Ferry) 3:27

If Ferry was serious in his attraction towards the dualistic John Donne template, the sequencing of *Casanova* directly after *Triptych* was surely no accident. Here, Ferry rounds vengefully on the kind of reckless libertine Donne had once been – the kind of reckless libertine certain sections of the press depicted Ferry himself as – and offers a character assassination unsparing in its detail, withering in its contempt. "The album's real ace is *Casanova*," Allan Jones raved in *Melody Maker*. "It's probably the single most powerful song that Roxy have ever produced."

The musical backing to this vitriolic diatribe is appropriately crazed and unrelenting, founded on the heavily treated, stop-start wheezings of an apparently asthmatic bass guitar. Jobson's faux-harpsichord from *Triptych* mutters dejectedly away in one corner while Ferry points an accusing finger at a hard-hearted Lothario who, for all the success of his 'love 'em and leave 'em' philosophy, is little more than a zero. Curdling organ figurations swirl in to augment the night-marish power of the backdrop, while Mackay's strangulated sax offers sneering asides in support of all Ferry's most pointed jibes. But the condemnation of this updated Bogus Man is not so single-minded that it can't take in Ferry's familiar bouts of word-play; as well as confusing 'courting' with 'caught in', he spins a remarkable tripartite pun on 'second hand', 'hand in glove' and 'second rate'.

At Ferry's allusion to the protagonist's heroin flirtation, Manzanera's guitar suddenly rouses itself from its lethargy, a moment later going absolutely nuts on a further reference to cocaine. After Ferry's final salvo, Manzanera goes further, bringing a genuinely apocalyptic edge to his metallic improvisations, suggesting the terminal thrashings of a body mortally wounded by Ferry's deadly barbs.

If Ferry's brief in *Country Life* was, as he claimed, merely to satirise the upper echelon leisure pursuits of that magazine's target demographic, *Casanova* reveals the moral corruption suppurating behind the well-bred inanities of your average 'Jennifer's Diary' column. Sporting a typically English double standard at least as strong as his victim's, however, Ferry not only reveals the corruption but revels in it, repudiating his target with such remorseless brio it verges on a kind of cannibalistic gloating. As Jim Miller, shaken to the core by the album's exposé of old-country decadence, put it in *Rolling Stone*: "It is as if Ferry ran a cabaret for psychotics, featuring chanteurs in a state of shock. The words, which speak only of l'amour, tumble effortlessly, but the Novocained lips smack of dementia."

Despite the shatteringly visceral attack of *Casanova*, Ferry was obviously dimly aware of untapped potential, soon afterwards crafting a radically different cover version of his own. This found its way onto his 1976 grab-bag solo album *Let's Stick Together*, prior to doing duty as the B-side to *What Goes On?* two years later. In it, Ferry comes on like the insidious tempter of *Strictly Confidential*, crooning his acidulous observations against a gently funky backdrop distinguished by Thompson's measured percussion and Neil Hubbard's understated rhythm guitar. Ferry's stanzas are separated by bluesy soprano interjections from saxman Mel Collins and the end result remains an excellent reading in its own right. It was this lower-tempo interpretation which Roxy themselves would follow when performing *Casanova* on their 1979 comeback tour.

A Really Good Time
(Ferry) 3:45

Country Life's Side Two proliferation of *Stranded* re-workings continues with *A Really Good Time*, which picks up the basic melody of *Just Like You* and applies it to one of Roxy's most honeyed performances, topped off with Ferry's most direct and unaffected lyric to date. The uncluttered gravity of the arrangement is particularly fine; with Jobson's string synthesiser well to the fore, the self-effacing Manzanera appears to sit this one out.

Jobson's strings (reportedly layered through the mix no fewer than 18 times) lower mournfully over the song's opening phrases in tandem with Mackay's beautifully slurred and soulful saxophone, conjuring visions of overcast skies and an atmosphere of resigned melancholy. In this mood, Ferry's vocal – disarmingly vulnerable, refreshingly unmannered – is addressed to another errant lover in terms, despite the prevailing melancholia, of some asperity. She's callous, stupid and, above all, self-destructive. Not only that – she lives in a vacuous and self-absorbed world in which the people around her care for nothing but maintaining their high-living façade. This carefree creature, patently a model judging from hints dropped elsewhere in the song, would clearly be right at home beside the LA pool depicted on the cover of *Another Time, Another Place* – or, five years later, as one of the braindead mannequins thronging the *Manifesto* sleeve.

From here Ferry shifts into a genuinely touching mode of naked introspection – referring frankly to his habit of talking to few people other than himself – before snapping back to life with a final attempt to get his point across. This plea evidently cuts no ice – hardly surprising, given the judgmental litany preceding it – and the song's final phase is given over to a nostalgic soliloquy in which he recollects the now departed lover through heavily rose-tinted spectacles.

After the jaded tone of the earlier stanzas, this final section is doubly effective. Though delivered without a trace of irony, Ferry's last-minute volte-face is obviously chock-full of it, underlining the 'love-hate' unpredictability of a person caught in the toils of infatuation. Thompson and Gustafson add understated rhythmic grace notes, Jobson sugars the mix with a twinkling agglomeration of keyboard sounds, and the song ends as it began, with Mackay offering a plaintive cameo over Jobson's fading strings. The effect is exquisitely nostalgic, and *A Really Good Time* stakes its claim to be among Ferry's most accomplished ballads.

"It's the ultimate flattery, being covered," Ferry told the *NME*'s Max Bell shortly after *Country Life* came out; more to the point, shortly after Mike McGear's *Sea Breeezes* cover came out. "On the new album I could see *If It Takes All Night* and *A Really Good Time* being done by others; I'd like that." The latter finally received 'the ultimate flattery' 22 years later. Having had two very Roxy-sounding hits in 1982 (*Icehouse* and *Hey Little Girl*), Australian band Icehouse, by this time styling themselves Iva Davies and Icehouse, covered *A Really Good Time* on their 1996 all-covers LP *The Berlin Tapes*. Among the other artists given the Davies treatment were XTC, The Psychedelic Furs, David Bowie, Talking Heads, Roxy's sometime EG stablemates Killing Joke and (via *Blank Frank*) Brian Eno. Eno himself had guested on two previous Icehouse albums, *Measure for Measure* (1986) and *Great Southern Land* (1989).

Prairie Rose
(Ferry-Manzanera) 5:12

As *Country Life* began, so does it end. *Prairie Rose* is splashed recklessly across the same epic canvas as *The Thrill of It All*, but the cynicism and savagery are replaced by a starry-eyed, windswept euphoria that sends the album out on a scalp-tingling high. It also inspired one of Nick Kent's most dazzling analogies in the *NME*: "*Prairie Rose* is more Manzanera-thick strident Technicolor chords," he wrote, "while Ferry in full Randolph Scott drag evokes the memory of 'Texas – the Big Country'. Vague echoes of *Giant* here, while Manzanera's 12-string Rickenbacker solo zeroes in momentarily on the spectre of a thousand and one cacti on the rampage. Barbara Stanwyck, eat your heart out!"

Speaking to Kent during the *Country Life* sessions in August, Manzanera was pleased as punch with his latest achievement: "I used a 12-string Rickenbacker and tuned the strings in such a way as to pretty much get that actual sound [Roger] McGuinn worked out for The Byrds' *5D* album." ("The thing is, though," he added, "I had to hire one. They're impossible to get these days.") This, then, is the unearthly jangle that supplies *Prairie Rose* with its nagging rhythmic pulse, flanked by the killer rhythm section of Thompson and Gustafson, meaty and inexorable, and the blazing introductory fanfares of Mackay's ranked saxophones. Punctuating the saxes are mushrooming Manzanera chords that impel the whole racing juggernaut to a hair-raising crescendo even before Ferry's vocal arrives.

A ghostly sigh of "Texas..." and Ferry is off, extolling the state's wide open spaces from under a ten-gallon hat and referencing two classic Westerns (*Lone Star* and *The Big Country*) in the space of a single stanza. Intoxicated by his beautiful prairie rose, Ferry tosses off another of his trademark puns – Texas is the state he's in, all right, but untrammeled ecstasy is also the state he's in – prior to the band letting rip once more on his anguished cue of "Texas ... You're tantalising me."

Against a dazzling phantasmagoric chaos of competing instruments, Mackay detonates arguably his most incandescent solo of all, careening through a heart-quickening array of seemingly unrelated notes in genuinely demented fashion. Manzanera takes over for a wildly untrammeled solo of his own, the shattering metallic build-up finally undercut by another ghostly breath of "Texas..." Ferry's panegyric then attains an almost religious intensity, invoking both "a crown of thorns" and "a scented flower" in describing his simultaneously spiky and fragrant lover, and finally responding to her irresistible call by means of a truly exhilarating outro. Powered by Thompson at his tub-thumping best, an inspired piano motif accompanies Ferry's heartfelt peals of "Prairie rose" and hypnotic background repetition of "hey-hey."

With stirring CinemaScope expanses of this sort, the song was inevitably appropriated by the more anthemic perpetrators of 1980s pop-rock. Big Country's choice of the song was an apposite one, given that Ferry had predicted their name in his reference to William Wyler's 1958 film. Their version accordingly appeared as the B-side to the 1984 single *East of Eden*, later appearing on a reissue of the band's *Steeltown* LP. Another version, this time from the short-lived Then Jerico, was featured on a 1987 EP prior to its inclusion on their *First (The Sound of*

Music) album. Manzanera's *Prairie Rose* Rickenbacker, meanwhile, would be passed on, via John Porter, to Johnny Marr, who used it most notably on The Smiths' 1985 track *The Headmaster Ritual*.

The Roxy original remains unassailable, however. "I always dreamed about Texas," Ferry claimed in US magazine *Creem*. "Basically it's because of movies, and even now the modern Texas has a big, Gold Rush feel to it, as if fortunes are being made." Not much more than six months after the release of *Prairie Rose*, life would imitate art when Ferry encountered a Texan belle of his own. Accordingly, he would sometimes dedicate the song to *Siren* cover girl Jerry Hall during the Roxy tour of 1975.

In the meantime, so confident of their effects were Roxy by this stage that they selected *Prairie Rose* as the opening number for their 1974 shows; though the song is seemingly tailor-made for use as a climactic rabble-rouser, Roxy had sufficient firepower in reserve to get it out of the way early. US critic Ron Ross was well aware of its roof-raising potential when he observed in *Phonograph Record* that "it's a driving roadrunner of a song that must inspire riots in perform-ance." He also put *Prairie Rose* in the proverbial nutshell with the incontrovertible statement, "It's regal and it's pop – nobody makes 'em any better these days."

Nine: *The Show's in Full Swing*

"Just as I would never have been able to make these records without great musi-cians, I wouldn't have been able to do any of the covers without great photogra-phers ... Having given up the idea of ever exhibiting visual art works, it would have been crazy to me to let some record company art department do an album cover when I knew that advertising images were what had intrigued me as much as anything."

Bryan Ferry, quoted in Street Life 29 November 1975

You see far worse

Having wound up their latest UK dates at the end of October 1974, Roxy then plunged into a continental schedule encompassing Germany, Sweden, Italy, Holland and France. In the course of this came another *Musikladen* performance, broadcast from Bremen on Wednesday 13 November and showcasing *All I Want is You* alongside *If It Takes All Night*.

Germany, however, was one of several countries that objected to the band's latest album sleeve, the auto-erotic suggestiveness of Constanze's breast-squeezing and Eveline's provocatively positioned middle finger proving too much for many. For German fans, a (rather effective) close-up of Eveline's face was substituted, while in America Atlantic packaged the album in a tantalising green shrink-wrap. In Canada, meanwhile, came the masterstroke of erasing the girls altogether in favour of the verdant Algarve hedge behind them, a tactic later adopted in the US too. The cover was also banned in Spain and South Africa. In the UK, by contrast, the design was voted "second best-dressed album" in *NME* and won a *Music Week* award as album cover of the year.

"While I'm pleased with the controversy, I don't think the picture's depraved," commented Ferry. "A bit seedy perhaps, but you see far worse things than that." By this time, Ferry was right, given that other rock artists were busily de-ironising the Roxy template and producing cover images frankly ripped from the pages of 1970s porn. The sweaty phallic symbolism of The Ohio Players' priapic album covers were tongue-lolling fantasies unleavened by Ferry's sardonic postmodernism, while others went further, adding outright humiliation to the basic charge of exploitation. Even *Country Life* is mild by comparison to Scorpions' *Lovedrive* or Whitesnake's *Lovehunter*, both from 1979. By 1982, the Spinal Tap pastiche cover, *Smell the Glove*, seemed so effective because so close to the truth; with an oiled-up girl tethered at the neck and cowering from the gloved fist of a male aggressor, it transformed *For Your Pleasure*'s lordly dominatrix into a simpering floozy at the other end of the leash.

Roxy's covergirls, by contrast, were required, in Antony Price's words, to be "buxom, powerful women," and they delivered in spades. As Kari-Ann put it, "I felt like I could eat somebody up. I felt strong enough to take someone on." Or Amanda Lear: "I was looking fierce." The *Country Life* girls, too, are anything but submissive dollies; indeed, Constanze's adamantine stare is better calculated to deflate than to arouse the more craven male voyeurs. In *Creem* magazine, Wayne Robins caught the intended mood exactly: "these ladies in *Penthouse* masturbatory pose dare one to fantasise – perhaps it's the red lipstick but they seem to come from the *National Lampoon* productions of *Chained Women* or *Big Bad Mama*. You know, sex is a joke."

Sensibly, however, Ferry appears to have realised that he'd now pushed the envelope about as far as he decently could, drastically reducing the flesh quotient for the piscine vampire featured on the *Siren* cover and finally eliminating it altogether for the Arthurian fog of *Avalon*.

In the early 1970s, perhaps it wasn't so much the fleshly excesses of *Stranded* and *Country Life* that raised hackles but the strangely sophisticated gloss with which they were presented. Ferry's decadent fantasies certainly provided a puzzling contrast with the sniggering true-Brit smut characteristic of the sex comedies swamping the nation's cinemas. Indeed, for a remarkable collision of the sublime with the ridiculous, look no further than *Confessions of a Pop Performer*, shot early in 1975 as the second in a four-strong series sponsored, astonishingly, by the mighty Columbia Pictures. Here, Robin Askwith's naïve ne'er-do-well Timmy Lea, forever getting his leg over almost by accident, encounters nubile Sally Harrison in a poky Elstree record shop, its walls plastered with shimmering *Stranded* and *Country Life* covers as their fumbling behind-the-counter congress causes a stack of 7" singles to come cascading down on top of them. Elsewhere in the film, incidentally, Timmy is shanghaied into playing the drums for pub band 'Kipper', one of whose songs is a loutish transposition of *Do the Strand* called *Do the Clapham*.

Ferry's next enterprise was about as un-loutish as could be imagined. "It was a weird situation to be in, two gold albums which were selling without live promotion," he said of his solo career, correcting this omission in the run-up to Christmas by finally taking to the stage as a performer in his own right – and, for the last of the three dates, no ordinary stage either.

A show at the Royal Albert Hall on Thursday 19 December featured selections from his two solo LPs (including side two of *These Foolish Things* in its entirety) together with Roxy's recently released, and rarely performed, *A Really Good Time*. The band, attired in Ferry's trademark white tuxes and red cummerbunds, comprised John Porter, Phil Manzanera, John Wetton, Paul Thompson and an unannounced Eddie Jobson, with the full might of the 55-piece Martyn Ford Orchestra in support. Of these, Chris Mercer (tenor sax), Martin Drover (trumpet), Morris Pert (percussion), Ronnie Ross (baritone sax), plus vocalists Vicki Brown, Helen Chappell and Doreen Chanter, were all past or future contributors to Ferry recordings.

Opening with *Sympathy for the Devil*, the event was a success, endorsed even by interested spectators Mackay, Eno and Robert Fripp, though Ferry would later confide to the faithful Puxley that "I'd never been so nervous in my life." Even so, he was able to offer up a few between-songs witticisms ("Nice place you've got here"), together with the cheeky touch of using a crib sheet during the massively convoluted *A Hard Rain's a-Gonna Fall*. Longtime Roxy supporter Allan Jones was unconvinced, however, recalling in 1977 that "The prospect of a solo Ferry per-formance was inviting, but the reality of that particular concert was profoundly disappointing: Ferry himself seemed utterly nervous that night and his apprehension was communicated to his band and the intrusive and unnecessary orchestra that supported them."

Sick! Sick! Sick! But, oh-h-h, it feels so good!

At the end of 1974, the *Sounds* Readers' Poll saw a healthy roster of Roxy names in prominent positions: Mackay top in the woodwind section (coming third in the international section), Ferry third best vocalist and eighth best composer, Thompson fourth best drummer (seventh internationally), Jobson fifth best 'miscellaneous', and Roxy eighth best British band (tenth internationally). Mackay could also bask in the estimation of America's *Creem* magazine, which had recently rated him second best rock saxophonist in the world. But, given his scorching contributions to the *Country Life* album, Manzanera's absence from the *Sounds* poll was a major mystery, the man himself telling Roxy's fan club that "I guess I'll just have to be content to continue as a cult figure!"

His cult status brought with it a sizable workload, however, much of it in tandem with the indefatigable Eno. "None of his motives are self-interest, you know," the latter said of him in the *NME*. "He's quite an amazing person to actually be in a band like Roxy and to be not obsessed with self-projection."

In September, with the *Country Life* album still in train and its promotional tour looming, Manzanera had collaborated on Eno's second solo LP. In San Francisco, Eno had stumbled across a set of cards promoting Tieli Xie's 1970 film *Zhi qu wei hu shan*, a staple of the Cultural Revolution also reproduced as a novel, stage play and opera. Enthused by the combination of ideas suggested by its US title, Eno cajoled Manzanera into a brain-reeling process of organising his enormous archive of musical doodlings into a coherent whole. As Eno explained in *Circus* magazine, the title exemplified "the dichotomy between the archaic and the progressive. Half *Taking Tiger Mountain* – that Middle Ages physical feel of storming a military position – and half *(By Strategy)* – that very, very 20th century mental concept of a tactical interaction of systems."

Taking Tiger Mountain (By Strategy) was recorded at Island Studios with a core band comprising Eno, Manzanera, Freddie Smith, Robert Wyatt and The Winkies' Brian Turrington. The aptest critical response came, again, from *Circus*: "Sick! Sick! Sick! But, oh-h-h, it feels so good!" – the anonymous reviewer insisting that it was "guaranteed to be put on the 'Most Wanted' list by psychopaths everywhere."

Less engaging than its predecessor, *Taking Tiger Mountain* is nevertheless a richly shambolic collision of disparate musical elements, with Eno's lyrics providing a dazzlingly Absurdist stew against which Manzanera's jagged machinations provide an even stronger foretaste of punk than was provided by *Here Come the Warm Jets*. The apotheosis of the style – abrasive, confrontational, almost cheerfully psychotic – is the extraordinary *Third Uncle*, where Eno's stream-of-consciousness approach to lyric writing is taken to sublime extremes. With the profound import of their lyrics being a major shibboleth of the windier Prog Rock groups, Eno's poker-faced delivery of apparent gibberish was a revolutionary step in itself. "I've developed new systems of writing lyrics," he told *Melody Maker*'s Allan Jones. "One of which is *panic*. I'd just start writing ideas, just from phonetics, and then in the studio I'd have to finalise them. Practically all the lyrics were written in about 15 minutes but they are based on suspicions which existed for some time."

Some of Eno's words are more organised than others, however. The hilarious *Back in Judy's Jungle* depicts a ramshackle squadron of *It Ain't Half Hot Mum* no-hopers struggling their way through a Monsoon, the lyrics displaying Eno's pawky wit at its strongest. The platoon members are itemised one by one just as the *Seven Deadly Finns* once were, and a final burst of *Bridge on the River Kwai* whistling is set against a rollicking singalong refrain. There are numerous other delights, ranging from the skewed pop textures of *Burning Airlines Give You So Much More* and *The True Wheel* to the typewriter percussion of *China My China* and Mackay's sinister sax breaks on the insane espionage drama *The Fat Lady of Limbourg*. Eno's old chums, The Portsmouth Sinfonia, provide a horribly out-of-tune backdrop to *Put a Straw Under Baby*, and Polly Eltes intrudes into *Mother Whale Eyeless* to trill further bits of Eno doggerel.

Best of all are the tracks chosen to close each side. Side Two winds down on the gorgeous drift of the title track, in which the clownish expeditionaries who trudged through *Judy's Jungle* have become a heroic band of snowbound, starry-eyed mountaineers. In complete contrast, Side One closes with a lurid fantasy of robot rape in which "the mechanical bride" falls prey to *The Great Pretender*. The tone is similar to that of *The Bogus Man*, with metallic percussion echoing the kitchen utensils with which the hapless Monica seeks to defend herself. There's also an awesomely monolithic Manzanera solo and finally a mesmerising cricket chorus that runs on inexorably into the play-out grooves.

Typically mercurial, in 1975 Eno would abandon the pioneering sounds perfected here and head into yet stranger territory, ascending into the ether from the rough-and-tumble of proto-punk just as the sticky morass of *Judy's Jungle* melds into the windswept heights of *Tiger Mountain*.

Dalai Llama lama puss puss

With Manzanera having acted as his inspirational right-hand man on *Taking Tiger Mountain (By Strategy)*, Eno returned the favour in January 1975 when Manzanera ventured into Island's London studio to cut his first solo LP.

Assembled in support was a veritable galaxy of star instrumentalists: Mackay, Jobson, Thompson, Eno, Robert Wyatt, John Wetton, to name but a few. Also present, on an alluring instrumental called *East of Echo*, were Manzanera's former Quiet Sun associates, Bill MacCormick, Dave Jarrett and Charles Hayward. In a very Roxy touch, Manzanera added clothes designer Wendy Dagworthy to the rogues' gallery of photographic portraits within, in addition to his wife Sharon Targett-Adams, credited with "love and inspiration." The result, *Diamond Head*, was touted by Island's PR department as "a veritable El Dorado of rock'n'roll."

"The main reason for recording solo albums for me was just as an excuse to get together with a whole load of friends and have some fun," Manzanera recalled in 2000, a rationale very similar to the one expounded by Mackay re *Eddie Riff*. And the finished album splendidly bears out the fun that was had during the 26 days it took to record, ranking as much the best solo LP from a Roxy member thus far. Released in May and charting at number 40 on the 24th, the album was garlanded with praise from just about every quarter, the plaudits ranging from "worth its weight in gold" (*Cashbox*) to "a must for Roxy Music devotees" (*Disc*). The *NME*, meanwhile, headed its review "Nice One Peruvian Pedro."

Typically self-effacing, Manzanera put a famous shot of a Union Pacific juggernaut rocketing through Utah's Echo Canyon on the cover, recalling the steam-powered train journey dramatised in his own *Amazona*. Similarly retiring, he shared out vocal duties between Eno, Robert Wyatt, John Wetton, Doreen Chanter and Bill MacCormick; not until 1999 would he venture to sing his own songs. The soundstage resonates to an exotic and consistently beguiling fusion of latterday psychedelia, tricksy Prog Rock, sultry Latino rhythms, touches of jazz-funk, sunny Beatles-type melodies and a side-order of vintage Eno-isms. Having just been voted fifth best guitarist in the world in *NME* (a nice riposte to his inexplicable omission from the earlier *Sounds* poll), Manzanera made *Diamond Head* an impeccably tasteful tour of his eclectic talents, reserving macho grandstanding for the wall-of-sound climax of the touching closer, *Alma*.

The opener, *Frontera*, is a delight, with a sparkling froth of massed guitars overlaid onto the Hispanic warblings of Robert Wyatt; roughly translated, the lyric comes across as a nonsensical saga about a race for the border, an actor missing his cue, a visit to the Aviation company and a libel case conducted in a crowded theatre. The song would be revived in May for Wyatt's *Ruth is Stranger than Richard* album, on which *Team Spirit* is an inspired jazz transcription of it. "*Frontera* was a Quiet Sun song, Phil wrote most of it, Ian [MacDonald] and I had contributed parts," Bill MacCormick later told Stephen Yarwood. "For one reason or another I didn't get any credit for it on *Diamond Head* despite the fact that I'd written the top line ... Robert remembered this and thought it would be a good idea to do it again, but this time I would get a credit."

Having "ooh-ed" and "aah-ed" his way through *Frontera*, Eno assumes lead vocal duties on the should-have-been-a-single *Big Day*, a euphoric vignette in which a dejected Peruvian struggles his way through a London winter to the rippling accompaniment of Manzanera's tiplé. According to *Time Out*, "The Eno song ends on 1975's best line to date, 'Oo-poo-Peru.'"

For Manzanera, the vocal tracks were all co-writing projects with the lead vocalists in each case. *Same Time Next Week* is a very droll battle-of-the-sexes dialogue between John Wetton and Doreen Chanter, who had previously contributed to John Cale's *Fear* and the *June 1, 1974* album and would later become one of two Sirens featured on Roxy's autumn tour. A kind of down-in-the-dumps riposte to the Frank and Nancy duet *Somethin' Stupid*, it benefits from the bluesy wailing of Wetton and Chanter, the dejected drone of Mackay's baritone sax and a curdling guitar extemporisation from Manzanera in the fade. The standout vocal track, however, is the staggering Manzanero-Eno collaboration *Miss Shapiro*, a churning six-and-a-half-minute monolith with echoes of Pink Floyd, a chattering organ sound, blistering guitar breaks from Manzanera and some classic examples of Eno word-juggling like "Dalai Llama lama puss puss / Stella maris missa nobis."

The instrumentals range from the limpid beauty of *Diamond Head* itself, which has a lovely treated guitar offset by Jobson's elegant string section (and which would be showcased on Roxy's upcoming UK tour), to the crazed jazz-funk freak-out that is *The Flex*, in which Mackay's squealing soprano compares favourably to any Stateside funketeer of the period. Transferring to oboe, Mackay duets to gorgeous effect with Manzanera's backwards Spanish guitar on the lachrymose fragment *Lagrima*, while the full might of Quiet Sun is brought to bear on the hypnotic, and severely fuzzed-up, Prog stylings of *East of Echo*.

Seemingly tireless, Manzanera made his first solo album at the same time as the ironically titled *Mainstream*, a fleeting reunion of Quiet Sun made possible by Manzanera's Roxy celebrity. Recorded after dark, it provides an appropriately murky nocturnal twin to the radiant textures of *Diamond Head*. The result was ecstatically received, displaying, according to *NME*, "considerable quantities of intense manic energy" and, for *Sounds*, "a sense of feverish excitement and utter dedication." In *Melody Maker*, meanwhile, it was hailed as "The most manic and passionate rush of music that has been committed to vinyl so far this year."

The virtuosity on display remains awe-inspiring over a quarter of a century later, and, listened to back to back, *Diamond Head* and *Mainstream* throw up numerous nuggets of déjà vu. From the former, *Frontera*, *East of Echo*, *Lagrima* and *Alma* all turned out to be re-tooled off-cuts from an epic 1971 Manzanera-Quiet Sun piece called *Corazon y alma* (Heart and Soul). Further mix-and-matching would see *East of Echo* and Bill MacCormick's *Mainstream* composition, *Mummy Was an Asteroid, Daddy Was a Small Non-Stick Kitchen Utensil*, reshaped in 1976 into the 801 track *East of Asteroid*.

Self-parody…

If Manzanera was busy, Jobson hadn't been idle either. During 1974 he had worked with Mike (Incredible String Band) Heron's Reputation, appeared on Amazing Blondel's *Mulgrave Street* album and King Crimson's *USA*, and worked on a Flash Gordon-themed concept album alongside Elkie Brooks, Alice Cooper, John Entwistle, Bill Bruford and Maddy Prior. He had also contributed to Dana Gillespie's aptly titled *Ain't Gonna Play No Second Fiddle* album and on Roger Glover's *Butterfly Ball* LP. On top of all this, he earned the distinction of being courted by Steve Harley, Yes and David Bowie in the space of a single week, turning down all such overtures in favour of sticking with Roxy Music.

Indeed, Roxy were now committed to a renewed assault on the US, the band's spring dates in 1975 moving from Detroit, Milwaukee and Toledo to Cleveland, Chicago, Boston, New York and finally Los Angeles. The Chicago engagement threw up a showcase on NBC's *Midnight Special* programme, with the band performing *Out of the Blue* and *A Really Good Time*, and after this itinerary Roxy decamped to Tokyo as a prelude to their first Antipodean tour, taking in Auckland, Wellington, Sydney, Melbourne, Brisbane and Adelaide. John Wetton remained in place as bass guitarist throughout.

The American dates showed encouraging signs of growth; though still largely confined to tight-knit clusters of fans in Detroit and Cleveland, there were occasional eruptions of the kind of Roxymania the band were used to in Europe. The reviews were similarly positive; a gig at New York's Academy of Music, where Roxy had been fêted the previous summer, was hailed in *Record World* as "stunning", with an appreciative nod to "the band's musically masterful performance and Ferry's own on-stage presence." In the house journal of the Massachussetts Institute of Technology, Neal Vitale noted that "The act [at Boston's Orpheum] was curiously unfocused visually," adding that "the set, though, was indeed marvellous … [and] the show's climax was truly astounding."

Some Americans remained unmoved, however. "I was told that I'd fully believe in Bryan Ferry's 'seriousness' once I'd seen him live, which I did, and I still don't," observed Peter Laughner in the June issue of *Creem*, ostensibly while commenting on the *Country Life* album. "Without synthesizer, sax and Manzanera, there would be little if anything to interest an audience, 'cause face it, the guy not only can't sing so hot, he's not even a very interesting stylist, and his attempt to establish a persona has persisted to the point of irritation. If the records don't sell he can always become the new P J Proby."

Unfortunately, Ferry's latest solo effort seemed to lend validity to Laughner's theory. In April, Ferry had cut a stand-alone solo 45, his fourth, that would rise in July to a not particularly impressive 33, spending a meagre three weeks in the singles chart. A revamp of a 1938 song previously recorded by Dinah Washington and Ella Fitzgerald, *You Go to My Head* sounded sufficiently like a kitsched-up version of Ferry's earlier *Smoke Gets in Your Eyes* to smack of self-parody. With Chris Spedding's discreet guitar licks borrowed from *Shaft*, plus a chintzy infestation of twinkling vibes and a thickly cloying brass section, it's redeemed to some extent by the stately sweep of Jobson's Philly soul-flavoured strings. "Bryan sings the venerable song as straight as he can," commented *Sounds*, "delivering such lines as 'You intoxicate my soul with your eyes' as though he really meant them."

Both *You Go to My Head* and its flip, an intriguing solo rendition of *Re-make/Re-model*, would fetch up on the US-compiled *Let's Stick Together* album the following year. In the meantime, Ferry had put together a little-seen promo film of the song (this in the months preceding Queen's apparent 'creation' of the rock video with *Bohemian Rhapsody*), in which he's shown, again in self-parodic mode, slumped on a sofa at his Holland Park home, conspicuously wearing a black DJ rather than the trademark white. Kari-Ann, no less, shimmies around him in a shocking-pink sheath dress, a framed reproduction of her image on the original *Roxy Music* album peering down from above the fireplace, the whole thing "circling and encircling in a retinal daze," as Dr Puxley characteristically put it.

... and sombre reptiles

Ferry's latest waxings, and indeed Roxy's forthcoming ones, were made to look pretty paltry by the astonishing album Eno was starting work on as *You Go to My Head* puddled about in the lower reaches of the Top 40. Made during July and August at Island Studios while his erstwhile bandmates were grinding out *Siren* at Air, *Another Green World* would prove at least as influential as the first two Roxy albums. With no fewer than nine instrumental fragments among its 14 tracks, the album represents a beguiling fusion of the insanely idiosyncratic Prog Rock of Eno's previous LPs with the ambient atmospherics he was beginning to perfect through his recently established record label, Obscure.

Though the *Siren* sessions prevented Eno's Roxy confreres from contributing to *Another Green World*, Mackay had managed to play oboe on Eno's second Obscure release, a collaboration between avant-garde composers Christopher Hobbs, John Adams and Gavin Bryars called *Ensemble Pieces*. *Another Green World* featured instead names like John Cale, Robert Fripp, Phil Collins, Paul Rudolph, Kilburn and the High Roads' Rod Melvin, former Winkie Brian Turrington and Brand X bass guitarist Percy Jones. Eno's imaginative cues to these disparate musicians were as outré as ever; Fripp, for instance, is credited on *St Elmo's Fire* with "Wimshurst Guitar," in reference to the kind of antiquated electrical generators only used by 1975 in Frankenstein films.

The album had its genesis in a near-death experience Eno had undergone on the evening of Saturday 18 January, immediately after completing work with Manzanera on the *Diamond Head* track *Miss Shapiro*. Returning on foot to his Maida Vale apartment, he had been seized by presentiments of death and was promptly knocked down by a black cab. While recuperating, his feeling of woozy disorientation combined with a faulty stereo system to make him start "hearing this record [of classical harp music] as if I'd never heard music before. It was a really beautiful experience, I got the feeling of icebergs ... And I began to think of environmental music – music deliberately constructed to occupy the background. And I realised that Muzak was a very strong concept and not a load of rubbish, as most people supposed."

The first fruits of this epiphany took the form of Eno's *Discreet Music* album, recorded in May with the soothing, slow-motion drift of the half-hour title track occupying Side One and 'Three Variations on the Canon in D Major by Johann Pachelbel' comprising Side Two. (The Pachelbel original was the same piece used, at Eno's suggestion, to set the mood for Roxy's 1972 live shows.) Further fruits were the 'Oblique Strategies' cards he concocted with artist Peter

Schmidt, a set of "worthwhile dilemmas" designed to "help you to outguess yourself and return fluidity to a situation that might be getting rigid and pathological by suggesting lateral moves, little exercises for the brain, and so on."

The first of these aphorisms, Eno reported, had been concocted way back in his Roxy days and read "Honour thy error as a hidden intention." Oblique Strategies received their first credit on *Another Green World*, Eno having entered the studio with nothing prepared and only the cards to suggest a way ahead. Such gnomic hints as "Repetition is a form of change," "Don't be afraid of things because they're easy to do," "Use fewer notes" and "What are the sections sections of? Imagine a caterpillar moving" helped to create a subdued sonic tapestry that still ranks as Eno's greatest achievement.

With titles like *Becalmed* and *Spirits Drifting*, some of the album's oneiric instrumental fragments speak for themselves. Another, *Sombre Reptiles*, has Eno on "Hammond Organ, Guitars, Synthetic and Peruvian Percussion, Electric Elements and Unnatural Sounds," and in its funky corkscrew rhythms recalls the overheated lizards referred to in David Bowie's 1974 track *Rock'n'Roll with Me*. Most fleeting of all is the Farfisa-heavy title track, subsequently appropriated for use as the theme of the BBC arts programme *Arena*. There's also the by turns sinister and euphoric coupling of *In Dark Trees* and *The Big Ship*, both pieces powered by Eno's so-called "treated rhythm generator." The first was based, as Eno told Lester Bangs, on an image "of a dark, inky blue forest with moss hanging off and horses off in the distance all the time, kind of neighing, whinnying ... It was just what the rhythm box suggested."

The vocal tracks are few. The first of them, *Sky Saw*, juxtaposes Cale's scarily atonal viola with a skeletal lyric that precisely articulates Eno's dismissive attitude towards words in the ethereal realm he was now exploring. Indeed, as a tribute to the nonsense-lyric tradition of which he was an up-to-date extension (perhaps also as a sardonic reference to Ferry's mania for cover versions), Eno put out a non-LP single during the album sessions, a delightful yodelling makeover of The Tokens' Christmas 1961 smash *The Lion Sleeps Tonight (Wimoweh)*.

The B-side, *I'll Come Running (To Tie Your Shoes)*, was included on the upcoming album and is arguably the most swooningly effective of all Eno's pop songs. Tripping along to the rolling piano figures of Rod Melvin, Fripp's "Restrained Lead Guitar" and Eno's own "Castanet Guitars," it's a gorgeously unconventional melody that perhaps should have been given a go as an A-side. "As a singer Eno betrays the cutest English accent since Syd Barrett: true, he's almost invariably flat, but charmingly so," commented John Mendelssohn in *Phonograph Record*. "*I'll Come Running*, to commend my personal favorite vocal number, would be a bigger single than *Love Will Keep Us Together* in a better world than the one in which it's my and your cruel fate to be living."

Ten: *The Fifth Roxy Music Album*

"The fifth album ... sees a further drift towards centre field. Exit the cathedralic perspective of Psalm *and the mirror-multiplicity of* Mother of Pearl, *similarly,* A Song for Europe *and its cancerously Venetian melancholy.* Country Life *rerouted*

Roxy onto a mainline, Aryan course: the dictatorship of the song, with verse,
middle-eight, chorus and instrumental break. A song is a song is a song. Siren
holds no other compass points."

Angus MacKinnon, Street Life 1 November 1975

The *Siren* album was begun at Air Studios in June, having been rehearsed,
according to Johnny Gustafson, in the basement of a Holland Park boutique
called Tarts and Bows. Fresh from recent well-deserved breaks in Hawaii and
Barcelona, Manzanera explained that "We did it in two sections. We took the five
tracks that Eddie, Andy and I had written the music for, rehearsed them for one
week and then recorded them. Then we took a month's break because Bryan
hadn't got his stuff together. Just before doing the second segment, I went
around to Bryan's house and he had, for the first time, actually worked out the
chords and arrangements. He'd actually written them down, which was a major
breakthrough. Other years, I'd go there and have to look where his fingers were
on the piano and write the chords down."

Recorded on 16-track rather than *Country Life*'s 24, *Siren* was conceived as a
sparser, less cluttered record, with cleaner textures and more direct lyrics.
Somewhat enervated by Roxy's recent globe-trotting live dates, and no doubt
intimidated by the 'follow that' nature of *Country Life*, Ferry found the writing
process more difficult than usual, despite taking a recuperative holiday in Antibes
halfway through.

There was also a spell closer to home, taking the form of a riotous August day
on the isle of Anglesey off the northern coast of Wales, a location Ferry had taken
note of when footage of it turned up in a TV documentary. Here the cover for the
upcoming album was shot with Antony Price and a new photographer, Graham
Hughes, in attendance – also 19-year-old Texan covergirl Jerry Hall, whom Ferry
had spotted in *Vogue*'s May issue.

Done up as a fin-de-siècle mermaid redolent of the horrifying canvases of Max
Ernst, Hall crawls slug-like across the Anglesey rocks with a more explicitly
vampiric expression than any previous Roxy model had yet mustered. She's
precisely the "pin-up done in shades of blue" predicted in *Editions of You*, though
the blue tint was an expedient decision prompted by the dazzling weather, Price
having previously determined on green during a pre-shoot reconaissance mission.
"Luckily I'd got some tins of blue car paint with me and had to respray the whole
costume blue," he remembered. "We had the sun directly overhead, 100 degrees,
the hottest day of the year. Everything was melting. We had the glue from the
costume welded into her fanny hairs, the nails were coming off. When we
finished, we immersed her in this bath of make-up removing liquid [and]
couldn't get it off her!"

Hall claimed that, having been bundled onto the train at Holyhead, she then
accepted Ferry's invitation to remove the last of the blue tint at his London pied
à terre: "He had a nice house in Holland Park. And when I came out of the
bathroom wearing a robe, he said, 'Why don't you just stay here? I have a guest
room.' So, since it was late, I stayed there. And that's the night it began!" She
later featured prominently in Ferry's videos for *Let's Stick Together* and *The Price of
Love*, the relationship coming to a very public end late in 1977.

Back in 1975, the album's back cover was given almost as much attention as the front, with Ferry himself supplying the calligraphy for the gold 'Siren' artfully scrawled above the credits list. Scheduled for release on 11 October but delayed just as the previous two had been, the album was preceded by a brief UK tour, starting at Preston on Thursday the 2nd and taking in Liverpool, Leeds, Stoke, Glasgow, Newcastle, Manchester, Wembley, Cardiff and Birmingham. The lavish tour programme contained liner notes by Paul Gambaccini (presumably having forgotten his *Rolling Stone* rubbishing of the *For Your Pleasure* album), rendering the history of the group in rather arch free verse. Example: "Bryan looked for another place / Andy searched for Eddie / Phil climbed Diamond Head / Paul got married / Everybody was a star."

Though initial dates reportedly seemed under-rehearsed, the tour proved an overwhelming success. John Wetton having migrated to Uriah Heep, Roxy's longstanding studio bassist Johnny Gustafson was retained instead. And, in a new departure, backing vocalists Doreen Chanter and Jacqui Sullivan were enlisted as resident 'Sirens', looking extremely fetching in their powder-blue, nipped-and-tucked WRAF costumes as a counterbalance to Ferry's newly perfected 'GI' look. Their vocal contributions, however, drew almost undiluted opprobrium, Allan Jones in *Melody Maker* dismissing them as "those two dopey chicks." But *Sounds'* Jonh Ingham, reporting from Glasgow, saw a deeper rationale in Ferry's recruitment of them: "Their position at times seemed a bit superfluous, but during the last numbers a gaggle of girls assembled beneath them, copying every gesture, and their role became clear: surrogate audience."

Mackay, meanwhile, adopted a beret, a look presumably intended as terrorist rather than onion-seller chic, and a Ferry-free middle section saw his storming cover of *Wild Weekend* following hard on the heels of Manzanera's delicately beautiful *Diamond Head*, a combination that drew some of the set's best reviews. According to Nick Logan in *NME*, it was at this point that "the first real signs of footsee action began to erupt in Row F. Stirring stuff indeed from axe and sax … I had half a notion that when The Baron himself huff-puffed and shoulder-shuffled his way back into the spotlight the extra aggression immediately in evidence was in some way an answer to the gauntlet laid down by the Manzanera-Mackay challenge."

Not to be outdone, Ferry included in the set, which was an unusually long one, two of his own hits, *The 'In' Crowd* and *A Hard Rain's a-Gonna Fall*. Ferry's solo records, previously vetoed for inclusion in live performances, were presumably deemed admissible thanks to Mackay and Manzanera now having wares of their own to show off.

The climactic Wembley concerts on 17 and 18 October came complete with a then-innovative giant video screen to the band's rear, broadcasting the minutiae of the performance in Brobdingnagian form to those at the back. It was at Wembley that 18-year-old Susan Ballion of the so-called 'Bromley contingent' met Steve Bailey, the latter dressed in full 'Andy Mackay as Eddie Riff' mode. Their subsequent emergence as Siouxsie Sioux and Steven Severin, lynchpins of Siouxsie and the Banshees, was inspired by a TV showing of the Vincent Price horror film *Cry of the Banshee*, though the subconscious adoption of the name of Ferry's pre-college band is certainly intriguing.

It was at Wembley, too, that future members of the fey New Romantic band Japan fell in love with Roxy's support act. This was Sadistic Mika Band, an historic booking in that they were the first Japanese group to tour the UK. Roxy had first encountered the band's leader, singer-guitarist Kazuhiko Katoh, during their recent Japanese jaunt, and Dr Puxley had since become their manager, having by now relinquished his role as Roxy's PR guru to Adrianne Hunter. The group's brilliant albums *Sadistic Mika Band* and *Black Ship*, the latter produced by Roxy's Chris Thomas, had offered a beguilingly Oriental meld of T.Rex, Carlos Santana and Pink Floyd, and a third, *Hot ! Menu*, again produced by Thomas, was due to be released during the tour.

Back in 1973, it had been suggested in *NME* that "if they were to tour Britain right now, they'd slay us." Instead, the Sadistics' set was met with widespread befuddlement by Roxy's audiences, and not just because of the language barrier. "Three Roxettes next to me in Row F spent the best part of the [group's] performance engaged in fervent gossip, virtually with backs to the stage," noted Nick Logan, "only displaying interest when Mika reappeared after a costume change in a red Suzie Wong number slashed to mid-thigh." Despite this reception, Mika Katoh herself was moved to stay behind in England and get married to Chris Thomas, while drummer Yukihiro Takahashi would form Yellow Magic Orchestra with Ryiuchi Sakamoto and Haruomi Hosono. In due course, both Mackay and Manzanera would make substantial contributions to Sakamoto's 1981 solo LP, *Neuromantic*.

After a performance at Stoke's Trentham Gardens on the 6th, Tuesday 7 October saw both groups slipping in some TV work prior to a three-night stint at the Apollo Glasgow. For Sadistic Mika Band it was a showcase on the BBC's *Old Grey Whistle Test*, for Roxy it was a stint on LWT's rather less distinguished kids' pop extravaganza *Supersonic*. Devised by Russell Harty's former director Mike Mansfield as a Saturday morning riposte to the BBC's all-conquering *Top of the Pops*, *Supersonic* would soon become embroiled in a 'payola' scandal, though an internal LWT investigation concluded that rumours of record company backhanders, in the words of industry bible *Broadcast*, "may be written off as music biz bullshit."

Mansfield would certainly make the most of the two songs Roxy performed for him at Threshold Studios, showing both of them twice and *Love is the Drug* a third time in the show's special Christmas edition. The band appeared in their touring duds, Ferry adding to his GI threads a thoroughly ludicrous eyepatch (complete with underlying bandage), while the black-clad Manzanera performed, oddly, in his stocking feet.

For *Love is the Drug*, a blizzard of soap bubbles was the chosen motif, while for *Both Ends Burning* there was enough billowing dry ice to very nearly obscure Thompson from view. A massive camera did the same for Mackay, though the cameramens' obsessive attention to Ferry was almost outstripped by their voyeuristic emphasis on Jacqui and Doreen's gyrating posteriors. Teenage whimpers of "We love you, Bryan" went up at the beginning of *Love is the Drug* – though, admittedly, this adulation was as nothing compared to the hysteria meted out in contemporaneous episodes to The Bay City Rollers, David Essex, even the tragically run-to-seed Marc Bolan.

The album was heralded by an unbridled rave from *Melody Maker*'s Allan Jones, but on its release other critics were more lukewarm. The most dismissive was *Time Out*'s Nikki Wood, who lavished a single sentence upon it: "They've hit the plateau half way up a mountain, and have stayed there, no doubt because it's more comfortable to stagnate and try for a spot at the Talk of the Town than to continue searching and blow people's little minds out." Irrespective of its iffy reviews, the LP had no difficulty in leaping straight to number four, arriving in the album chart on 8 November and departing 17 weeks later.

"Oh, hell, I admit it," confessed Peter Laughner in *Creem*, "these guys can be appealing and exciting even *without* Eno … But please, guys, next time *more* Mackay and Manzanera." Notwithstanding endorsements like this, *Siren* climbed only to number 50 in the USA, a lower score than *Country Life* despite the Stateside success of *Love is the Drug*. In his *Rolling Stone* review, British critic Simon Frith had cannily predicted this: "Ferry's great achievement has been to frame Roxy's unique sound round just one obsession – himself. He's made it as a work of art, he's made it as a product, but I guess he won't make it as an export statistic – you've got enough fetishes of your own." A few years later, however, Greil Marcus would observe in the same magazine that "*Siren* was perhaps the most perfectly crafted album of the decade."

The core band members responded to the finished product in very different ways. Ferry was, by his standards, almost bullish: "I've always thought, and said it at the time – it's what you want to say – that this record's the best one, but I'm convinced that this one is. It's just very strong. I don't know whether the songs are any better, but the playing certainly is. The way it's been put on record is very strong." Mackay sounded a warning note, however, saying that "Our concept of this album was to try and get it closer to a band playing, so that we didn't do a lot of overdubs. We set out to try and make it simpler, to get away from the infamous Roxy wall of sound. We've not wholly succeeded." Years later, he admitted that "*Siren* was our least satisfactory album, although it did give us *Love is the Drug*."

For his part, Manzanera just came right out with it. "We were just churning out stuff in a random way. That album had some tracks on it that weren't very good."

*   *   *

Sultanesque
(Ferry) 5:24

With *Sultanesque*, Roxy's tradition of putting out quality B-sides came crashing down. As printed on the label, the alluring title and healthy running time of the *Love is the Drug* flip must have suggested hidden treasure to excited Roxy fans, perhaps some exotic musical fantasy in the vein of Mackay's *The Pride and the Pain*. No such luck, however. Despite Jobson's eleventh hour addition of rhythm-box percussion and a metronomic bassline, this droning bagpipe extemporisation by Ferry is a trial to sit through.

"I did it at home in my old flat in Earl's Court," an unrepentant Ferry explained to Idris Walters in November 1975. "On the Farfisa. That was a year or so ago. I played it to myself in a lot of hotel bedrooms. Just one tape it was. And the more I listened to it the more I got into it. It was just a kind of drone thing but it had a shape to it which I thought was interesting. I thought this could be another in the series of Roxy instrumental off-the-wall B-sides. I took it into the studio, transferred it onto the 16-track. Eddie put some rhythm-box stuff onto it. Paul put a backwards gong on it and Phil a couple of guitars."

If Manzanera really did participate in this track, his contributions certainly aren't audible. And that Ferry should have imagined *Sultanesque* was in the same "off-the-wall" mode as, say, *The Pride and the Pain* or *Hula Kula* is hard to credit. Chafing with a feeling of guilt-by-association, the post-Roxy Jobson would go into some detail about the track in the February 1977 issue of *Trouser Press*: "The [B-side] I disliked most was *Sultanesque*. I think that's terrible. That's a waste of plastic. Bryan did that at home on a Farfisa organ put through some strange little effects box that made the drone thing. It wasn't even tapeloops. He made a cassette of it, put it on 16 track and gave it to me."

Jobson also noted that "People pay their money to buy the single, [so] you should give them a full quality song." Though at one time a champion of the 7" format, Ferry appeared no longer to agree, judging the track satisfactory and hustling it out before the dismayed Jobson had finished with it. By comparison to Eno's contemporaneous experiments in ambient sounds, *Sultanesque* is merely laughable; compare it, for example, with another Farfisa-led piece, Eno's title track to *Another Green World*.

Twenty years after its first appearance, *Sultanesque* finally made it to CD on the fourth disc of the *Thrill of It All* box set, pointing up one of the enduring anomalies of that compilation – the omission of Roxy classics like *Serenade* and *Spin Me Round* alongside the fan-friendly inclusion of indulgent 12" mixes like *Dance Away* and garbage like *Sultanesque*.

Love is the Drug
(Ferry-Mackay) 4:11 / single edit: 3:58

The scene-setting sound effects in *Love is the Drug* suggest a whole world of metropolitan cool – the measured crunch of shoe leather on tarmac, the opening of a car door, the catch of the ignition, the muffled roar of a high-powered engine. "It's nice using sound effects sometimes to help build a picture," Ferry pointed out. This particular sound effect was frankly filched from Düsseldorf's electronic pioneers Kraftwerk, whose epic *Autobahn* had been a hit in February 1975, still retaining its evocative 'lorry door' overture despite being relieved of some 18 minutes for its single release. But where *Autobahn* suggested a Teutonic truck driver resuming his journey after a pause at the German equivalent of a Little Chef, *Love is the Drug* conjures the image of a well-heeled man-about-town, possibly wearing a white tuxedo, setting out for some high-class society soirée.

As the vocal quickly makes clear, however, what he actually intends to do is take a tour of the nearest red-light district. The triumph of *Love is the Drug* is its translation of Ferry's sleazier preoccupations to the upper reaches of the 1975 singles chart and, three decades on, the unthreatening confines of nostalgia radio.

The song had originated as a Mackay composition intended by him as a much slower affair, possibly a B-side – initially, according to Jonh Ingham, "it had been thought of as a nautical tune, reminiscent of tea clippers." Fitted with Ferry's predatory lyric and Gustafson's killer bass line, it became something else entirely, an obsessive ode to instant gratification with shades of disco, funk, reggae – you name it. "I suppose it's a sort of disco record," Ferry confided to *Record Mirror* at the time. "I don't think it's too different to put off our regular buyers, but if people who haven't bought our records in the past are getting it too, so much the better. New customers are always welcome." And there was no shortage of them; the single hit number two in the UK and, glory be, number 30 in the USA.

'Love', of course, isn't at issue here. Indeed, it's a pleasing irony that, in a career dedicated pretty squarely to anatomising the agonies of love, the first Ferry song to feature the word in the title should address the grim and loveless charade of one-night stands instead. The narrator merely has an itch that needs scratching, and, tellingly, the language varies from that of addiction (he needs to 'score' in more ways than one) to masochism (he's 'hooked', too, in more ways than one), and then back again.

The musical backdrop is limber yet viscous, with Thompson's tightly controlled percussion, Mackay's Stax-flavoured fanfares and Manzanera's choppy jabs of rhythm guitar all borne along on that astonishing bass line, which Talking Heads' Tina Weymouth may well have recalled, consciously or unconsciously, when supplying *Psycho Killer* with its robotic pulse. And the whole thing ends on a jarringly dyspeptic clang from Manzanera's guitar, as if to point up the ultimately futile, Chinese takeaway effect of the gratification being sought.

On home ground, the track received the signal honour of being endorsed in *Sounds* by guest singles reviewer, and light entertainer supreme, Bruce Forsyth, then riding high with *The Generation Game*. "Very, very good beat to the whole thing," he mused. "Potential disco hit. This has got all the things that I think the kids want … I could hear what he was singing about, which is always a help, you know, especially for us older folk … It's the kind of thing that if I went out I would like to jig around to, and I love the line about when the lights go down and you can guess the rest. That was saucy." In *NME*, however, Charlie Gillett offered only back-handed compliments, noting that "this has the kind of depraved charm that worked so well on Lou Reed's *Walk on the Wild Side*" but also that "It's the first Roxy music which doesn't make you think that the band was looking in a mirror when they made it."

In the USA, *Creem*'s Peter Laughner insisted that *"Love Is The Drug* not only makes the best foot-to-the-floorboards cruiser to hit AM in years, it even makes me want to start hanging out in singles bars," while Ben Edmonds observed in *Phonograph Record* that "*Love is the Drug* is danceable enough to suggest that if promotion is intelligently keyed to those Midwestern markets where the band is revered, they should have their first Stateside hit single." Several months later, Ira Robbins confirmed in *Music Gig* that "The success of *Love is the Drug* (undoubtedly the weirdest thing any disco-goer ever hustled to) has broadened Roxy's audience in this country."

Ferry's mock-American phrasing (suppressing the 'h' in 'thing', for example) was no doubt intended to be tongue-in-cheek but, coupled with the track's irresistible beat, it did indeed do the trick across the Atlantic, where Roxy's off-puttingly European dramas of alienation had never previously cut any ice. Ferry was no longer slumped, impotent and forlorn, in Venice, as per *A Song for Europe*; instead, he was cruising the singles bars in search of a transitory bit of "lumber up, limbo down." This was a gritty urban ambience that felt familiar to the record buyers of Detroit and San Francisco, who obligingly went ahead and helped make it a modest hit; it peaked at number 30 in the *Billboard* chart of 22 February 1976.

It had already borne (almost) all before it in the UK charts. Entering on 7 October 1975 at number 37, the *Love is the Drug* 45, snipped of its shoe-leather-on-gravel introduction, proved to be Roxy's most successful single to date. Kept off the top spot by a reissue of David Bowie's *Space Oddity*, it reached number two on 4 November, slipping to three the following week thanks to Billy Connolly's parody of the Tammy Wynette classic *D.I.V.O.R.C.E.* and finally departing the chart on 13 December after a lucrative run of ten weeks.

The track was buoyed up, not only by the usual *Top of the Pops* stint for the BBC, but also by two appearances (on 11 and 25 October) in LWT's new pop showcase, *Supersonic*; in the first, which also included a rendition of *Both Ends Burning*, they appeared alongside Leo Sayer, Andy Fairweather-Low, Justin Hayward and Arthur Brown, in the second Gary Glitter, Marianne Faithfull, Nazareth and Pearly Gates. Unfortunately, the so-called Sirens from Roxy's contemporaneous tour almost destroyed the song on these TV appearances, with their voices overdubbed onto the song's "Oh-oh-oh" sections to pretty grim effect.

Love is the Drug was covered at epic length (8:38) by Grace Jones on her *Warm Leatherette* album in 1980, part of her halcyon period with reggae legends Sly Dunbar and Robbie Shakespeare at Nassau's Compass Point Studios. An edited version later reached number 35 in the UK singles chart when featured on the 1986 compilation *Island Life*. Seven years later, Australian pout-rock group Divinyls, famous for the masturbatory anthem *I Touch Myself*, covered the song for the soundtrack of the film *Super Mario Bros*. Released as an Australian single in November 1993, it later appeared on two Divinyls compilation albums, *The Collection* and *Make You Happy 1981-1993*. The song has also been covered by Biarritz and Ekko featuring Lisa Hunt.

End of the Line
(Ferry) 5:14

After the clangorous, disorientating close of *Love is the Drug*, *End of the Line* introduces the blander, more MOR-flavoured sound that is to recur several times on *Siren*. After a beguilingly discongruent opening – a lachrymose combination of violin, harmonica and oboe underpinned by a charmingly relaxed piano motif – it also features one of Ferry's most transparent and affecting lyrics.

Dejected from the off, Ferry begins by deciding to venture out into the rain, immediately recalling the very similar opening of The Dramatics' *In the Rain*, a Stax hit from 1971. Kicked into gear by the resounding muscle of Gustafson's bass and Thompson's drums, Ferry reflects on his lover's persistent refusal to answer his calls, whereupon Manzanera's ruminative guitar lines and a uniquely doleful double-tracked Jobson solo are added to the mix. Mackay returns to supply a discreet oboe underlay to Ferry's final decision to go out into the storm, and the whole thing winds down on a contemplative dying fall shared out between piano, violin and bass guitar.

There are beautiful touches here, the guitars and synths in particular painting a vivid picture of the starry nocturnal backdrop to Ferry's musings. It's also a strangely cosy sound, the narrator clearly having decided against that rain-swept walk and instead luxuriating in his own misery at home. The rain and storm are obvious reflections of the narrator's state of mind (and, if that sounds like a Shakespearean analogy, then Ferry will explicitly invoke *King Lear* before Side One is out), but there's a distinct feeling that his dejection is a comforting, wraparound kind of masochism that is all too willingly surrendered to.

The temptation to bring in *Sea Breezes*-style sound effects to externalise the rain and storm is stoutly resisted, however. Ferry would eventually go down this route on his 1985 solo hit *Slave to Love* in a stirring maelstrom that recalls not only *In the Rain* (where The Dramatics' producer-cum-lyricist Tony Hester famously went to town in that department), but also Barry White's 1972 Love Unlimited hit *Walking in the Rain with the One I Love*, Phil Spector's 1964 production job on The Ronettes' *Walking in the Rain*, and The Cascades' delightful 1963 smash *The Rhythm of the Rain*. But, whether larded with storm effects or not, *End of the Line* remains a clear indication that, in 1975 at least, Roxy just didn't have what it took to produce the kind of slickly commercial sound perfected by these super-smooth US forebears.

By the time of a track like *Oh Yeah* (which, incidentally, has a tremulous fade-out very similar to the one here), they would have it down pat. But not yet, and, as a result, *End of the Line*, for all its graces, sounds like neither one thing nor the other. It's here, in short, that the listener begins to detect the faint whiff of an identity crisis, making the song's title seem oddly prophetic.

In 1995, *End of the Line* would be one of several *Siren* tracks discreetly left out of the track listing for Virgin's four-disc Roxy box set. Two years earlier, Concrete Blonde, with vocalist Johnette Napolitano, included a version of *End of the Line* on their *Mexican Moon* album. The drummer, by a strange quirk, was none other than The Great Paul Thompson.

Sentimental Fool
(Ferry-Mackay) 6:14

Fading in stealthily over the sublimated heavenly choir that closed out the previous track, *Sentimental Fool* is three songs in one, at least. Here's a brief return – and, for *Siren*, an uncharacteristic one – to the many-paneled complexity of, say, *If There is Something*, together with a generous dose of the creepy sci-fi stylings of earlier records. "[Mackay's] score for *Sentimental Fool* provides the album's climactic highpoint," pontificated Angus MacKinnon in the newly inaugurated, Roxy-quoting style magazine *Street Life*. "A hazard profile intro, with mercury graft from Manzanera's guitar, is veined sinuously into the song's first verse: gathering cumuli, lightning shock but no rain."

149

The slow and superbly ominous opening is reminiscent of the psychedelic space-age landscapes of *Ladytron* and *For Your Pleasure*, but with the threat factor multiplied a hundred-fold. It would put one in mind of King Crimson's Dylan Thomas-quoting LP title, *Starless and Bible Black*, were it not for Jobson's sinister keyboard interjections that twinkle like stars in a velvety nocturnal haze. Into this haze looms Manzanera's monolithic fuzz guitar, gathering strength like some particularly persistent migraine as Gustafson's meaty bass lines and Mackay's eerie oboe patterns cluster menacingly around it. The space being conjured up here is presumably inner space, with the sleeper's incipient nightmare demanding expression in the dialogue between innocence and experience that follows.

To a backdrop of powerfully muscular percussion from the late-arriving Thompson, Ferry finally punctuates the wall of sound with a sublime falsetto plaint, questioning, yet again, the doubtful veracity of a lover. Then, nimbly wrongfooting the listener, he replaces the gathering nightmare with a call-and-response section that's equal parts lugubrious and jaunty. This split-personality tit-for-tat doesn't carry the 'suicide note' severity of similar transactions in *Strictly Confidential*, nor the life-and-death Jekyll & Hyde struggle dramatised later in *Still Falls the Rain*. It's more resigned and nonchalant than that; more a case of the 'we've been here before ... yes I know, but I can't help myself' dialogue routinely rehearsed, and more often than not ignored, before the onset of yet another déjà vu romance. Mackay's sax improvises raunchily throughout and, once each party has had its say, he finally steps forward for a solo that's robust even by his standards.

Phase three again reverses expectations, reintroducing that spectral guitar motif together with shivery cascades of piano. Slipping inexorably back into nightmare mode, Ferry reflects obsessively on the fact that a woman's love is the only thing that makes life worth living. Punctuated by Thompson's staccato hammer blows, he winds up on a disturbing note, registering the percussive beat of his lover's heart and wondering anxiously if it will ever stop. Horrifyingly, it does.

For all the surprising singalong jauntiness of its middle section, *Sentimental Fool* is classic Roxy Music, first sending threads of icy disquiet across the soundstage, then briefly lulling the listener into a false sense of security, finally delivering the coolly envenomed sting in the tail. On top of which, that mesmerising two-and-a-half minute build-up to Ferry's entrance would later be refashioned for the opening of Roxy's comeback album three years hence.

Tellingly, *Manifesto* would kick-start the band's comeback dates in 1979 in the same way that *Sentimental Fool* provided a suitably theatrical opening number in 1975. With the unerring nose for dramatic effect of a well-drilled matinée idol, Ferry actually began his *Sentimental Fool* vocal from off-stage. Reporting from Liverpool, *Melody Maker*'s Barbara Drillsma pointed out that "*Sentimental Fool*, a track from the new album *Siren*, set the pace for the gig with the emphasis on musical quality and perfection, rather than visual extravagance. Andy Mackay and Phil Manzanera laid down a thick carpet of sound for Ferry to glide across the stage on and to re-introduce himself to the crowd. And what a change in Ferry! His voice is stronger, he appears to feel freer and he actually makes the occasional impulsive movement. His control gives way at last."

Whirlwind
(Ferry-Manzanera) 3:38

In sharp contrast to the unnatural calm of *Siren*'s cover photo, Jerry Hall is depicted on the record's label in the teeth of some preternatural storm. Half-lifted from the rock to which she clings, golden hair blasted into a fluttering fright-wig, she struggles to maintain a suitably vampiric sneer against the buffeting of something much more violent than a sea breeze. This is the literally hair-raising atmosphere conjured up by *Whirlwind*, a song that brings to mind a version of *King Lear* in which Lear and his Fool encounter, not an itinerant lunatic, but a land-locked mermaid during their storm-tossed travails on the heath.

Under his Rex Balfour pseudonym, Roxy's publicist, Simon Puxley, reserved special praise for *Whirlwind* in his 1976 book *The Bryan Ferry Story*, calling it "a very squall of a track, dervish-like in both its musical shock-tactics and its lyrical convolutions (a tour de force of wordplay, the storm-imagery, for instance, making a fleeting chameleon sortie – with such finesse that it registers on a virtually subconscious level – into Conan Doyle country)." There's nothing subconscious about it, however; Sherlock Holmes references don't come much clearer than the generic phrase "Elementary, my dear."

Elementary, elemental – it makes little difference, for here is a song that depicts love as a tempestuous struggle lit by bolts of lightning. The analogy even throws up a smutty double-entendre derived from *Moby Dick* ("There she blows"), but the most sustained imagery comes from Act III of *King Lear*, with Ferry offering a neat précis of Lear's "Blow, winds, and crack your cheeks! rage! blow! / You cataracts and hurricanoes, spout / Till you have drench'd our steeples, drown'd the cocks!" With literary allusions of this sort to get his teeth into, Ferry delivers one of his wildest and most melodramatic performances, absurdly attenuating his vowel sounds, juddering his way through at least one line in the style of The Who's *My Generation* or Bowie's *Changes*, and reaching an apocalyptic crescendo on his final, panic-stricken gale warning.

Though talking up Ferry's lyric as being more subtle than it actually is, Puxley/Balfour was right on target with his description of *Whirlwind* as "a very squall." Containing traces of Manzanera's previous score for *Prairie Rose*, the soundstage here broils with a truly elemental fury, propelled by the savage assault of Thompson's drums and agitated bubbling of Gustafson's bass, pausing to accommodate a swirling keyboard riff, finally detonating into a Manzanera solo of paint-stripping ferocity. Mackay appears to have excused himself from this storm-laden cacophony, but his absence isn't felt too strongly in view of the maniacal invention Manzanera brings to bear on it.

In a canny bit of sequencing, the savagery of *Whirlwind* was positioned just ahead of the serene *Sea Breezes* on Roxy's 1975 tour. Twenty years on, however, the track surprisingly failed to make it onto the *Thrill of It All* box set.

She Sells
(Ferry-Jobson) 3:39

Opening up the decidedly hit-and-miss second side of *Siren*, *She Sells* remains

Eddie Jobson's one-and-only writing credit for Roxy Music. It kicks off with a charmingly ritzy piano figure, goes through a number of unexpected variations, and contains an unusually lighthearted Ferry vocal. But the supper-club shades of Billy Joel and Elton John gather too closely around it to make one regret its exclusion, two decades later, from Virgin's *The Thrill of It All* box set.

Nevertheless, there are numerous instrumental graces here. Jobson's jauntily energised string section does much of the work Manzanera might normally have done (he's still in there, but in his most self-effacing mode), while Thompson's supple percussion resounds to plenty of splashy cymbals. Retaining the euphoric head of steam he perfected on Manzanera's recently released *The Flex*, Mackay throws in a couple of bright and breezy sax breaks, burbling in stop-start style from what sounds like the studio next door and finally melding with Jobson's violin in trademark Roxy style. All in all, the pop sound here is much better realised than on corresponding *Siren* tracks like *End of the Line* and *Could It Happen to Me?* – but, with the bubblegum texture applied to an unusually flippant Ferry lyric, the song doesn't attain sufficient identity to qualify as more than a throwaway.

"Without a lyric sheet the significance of the song is elusive," commented Allan Jones in *Melody Maker*. "What can be gleaned from listening with an ear to the speaker sounds fairly ominous, and the lyrics have a definitely cynical edge." Like *Whirlwind*, the lyric teems with Ferry's patented wordplay yet remains strangely impenetrable. He had complained about press intrusion, in noticeably bitter terms, in *Street Life*, and this provides the springboard for *She Sells*' mordant commentary on tabloid tittle-tattle. Along the way, Ferry's tirade gives rise to a dazzling triple-entendre in which a reference to the 1928 Hecht-MacArthur newspaper comedy *The Front Page* is succeeded by a paraphrase of Hamlet's "hold the mirror up to nature" speech and through to a well-aimed sneer at Britain's ultimate tabloid, the *Daily Mirror*.

There are a number of other verbal felicities, and even the title enshrines a hoary old tongue-twister ("She sells sea shells on the seashore") that relates neatly to the beach scene adorning the album cover. But the cynicism embodied in *She Sells* is somehow too lightweight to make much of an impression; an infusion of genuine bile would do wonders for Ferry's similarly themed *Kiss and Tell* single in 1988. By that time, of course, Roxy covergirls Marilyn Cole and Kari-Ann Moller had both gone public with their salacious recollections in – what else? – the *Mirror*.

She Sells formed part of Roxy's 1975 live set (usually sandwiched between *Nightingale* and *Street Life*) but has not been revived since. Though Roxy's upcoming 'devolution' apparently put an end to further Ferry-Jobson collaborations, another one did sneak out some 16 months after *She Sells*, *As the World Turns* being used as the B-side to Ferry's *This is Tomorrow* single.

Could It Happen to Me?
(Ferry) 3:36

The identity crisis heard on *End of the Line* intensifies with *Could It Happen to Me?* – a lovely lyric and enchanting melody that would work a treat given a suitably detailed and saccharine-heavy soundstage, but here, through a combination of the band's overly astringent asides and Chris Thomas' starkly unadorned production job, sounding merely half-arsed.

Wondering dolefully if true love will ever come his way, Ferry sets out his stall in simple terms, and brings a fatalistic grace to the verses that contrasts powerfully with the hectic gaiety of the choruses. Pursued by a jaunty keyboard melody, he tears off some exquisitely self-ironising couplets before modulating down to the touching gravity of the coda. And here the song provides a pleasing through-line in that Ferry's tentative query as to whether he should rekindle the flames of love seems to get an immediate riposte in the manic, swirling release of *Both Ends Burning*.

This is all very fine, but the uptempo swing of the middle section never really swings; the band seem too heavy-footed to do it justice, and Manzanera's guitar breaks are of the granitic kind that would later be airbrushed out of the radio mix of *Dance Away*. Similarly, despite some aptly smoochy sax sounds elsewhere, Mackay's opening fanfare seems to get more sternly militaristic on its every reappearance. The whole thing seems out of kilter; a gaily energised throwaway love song is made to sound a bit of a plod.

This is not to say that the band members couldn't keep up with the new demands Ferry was placing upon them; indeed, matching style to content was a knotty problem for all concerned, a problem that perhaps demanded the upcoming three-year sabbatical for the band to get a handle on. Some of the material on the resultant *Manifesto* album might sound bland, but none of it sounds as strangely compromised and broken-backed as this. What it doesn't sound like, in short, is Roxy Music; Mackay and Manzanera's contributions are distinctive enough, but an anaesthetic MOR gas finally smothers even them.

But in 1975, unfortunately, Ferry's priorities lay firmly with tracks of this sort. Commenting on the band's *Siren* tour, he pointed out that "I'd really have liked to be able to play the whole of the new album, but the two best tracks didn't sound quite right in rehearsal so we decided to leave them out." By "the two best tracks," he meant this and the better but still somewhat anodyne *End of the Line*. Perhaps unsurprisingly, no further attempts would be made at either track in future years, though Ferry himself, in his solo dates early in 1977, had a go at *Could It Happen to Me?*

Both Ends Burning
(Ferry) 5:16 / single edit 3:58

With the electrifying introduction to *Both Ends Burning*, Ferry proved that his familiar reliance on puns didn't even require words to make an impact. Sound effects alone could manage it, with Jobson's synth zapping alarmingly across the soundstage like the kind of siren attached, not to a blue-tinted seashore, but a fire engine. Once the rhythm section has crashed in on Jobson's heels, Mackay, too, unleashes a gorgeous four-note motif that is presumably the same "slinky siren's wail" long since referenced on *Editions of You*. If nothing else, these opening alarm signals, together with the miasmic swirl of string synthesisers against which they're set, will give a much-needed jolt to any listener succumbing to the lethargic strains of *Could It Happen to Me?*

153

The opening siren effect perhaps marks *Both Ends Burning* as a kind of psychotic riposte to The Move's 1968 single *Fire Brigade*, with its cheerful introductory jangle of old-style fire engines and catchy refrain concerning a girl who is equal parts bewitching and incendiary. The suspicion is perhaps underlined by Ferry's 1973 admission to *Melody Maker*'s Roy Hollingsworth that "When I was a DJ I had a habit of playing *Fire Brigade* every night."

But the picture painted in *Both Ends Burning* is darker, more obsessive, altogether more troubling. The disco-flavoured conflagration cooked up here shows Ferry as a sacrificial victim, subject not only to inexplicable and combustible desires but also to an intoxicating woman who is herself characterised as an unquenchable flame. The drive to fan this insatiable fire devolves into an irresistible plunge towards self-destruction, Ferry burning the candle at both ends in the futile effort to exorcise her incandescent appeal. Come the fade-out he's lost his grip on reality altogether, shrieking repeatedly over one of Manzanera's most unhinged guitar breaks.

The overwhelmingly lush wall of sound is equal parts sublime and nightmarish, as well as seeming totally out of place in the lacklustre setting of *Siren*'s second side. Driven onward by the powerhouse propulsion of Thompson's drums, together with a skittering rhythm of electronic tom-toms, the instrumentation creates a hypnotically swirling maelstrom in which the narrator is irretrievably engulfed. Gustafson's athletic bass line (lifted wholesale, he's since claimed, from Martha & the Vandellas' *Dancing in the Street*) provides the flickering pulse, with the tension expertly maintained through Mackay's piercing sax break under the first chorus and Jobson's archly plucked strings under the second. Manzanera's guitar signals the narrator's final lapse into amphetamine-fuelled dementia, and the track flies apart in a wildly out-of-control finale.

'Smouldering passion,' 'moth to a flame' – these are just two of the romantic clichés thrown up in the listener's mind, but Ferry busily chucks in a few more of his own. And into this verbal maelstrom comes a reference to sheep that's at least as off-the-wall as his previous namecheck for badgers in *Editions of You*. Further cross-referencing sees Ferry pointing out that "jungle red's a deadly shade," an unmistakable nod to the incarnadined jungle maiden of *Stranded*, just as *Editions of You* had contained the seeds of the *Siren* cover in its mention of "a pin-up done in shades of blue." And jungle-red really is the appropriate palette for *Both Ends Burning*; the cold hues of earlier Roxy tracks are replaced here by a flaming intensity from Ferry as well as the band.

Dazzling achievement though it is, *Both Ends Burning* turned out to be an unwise choice for single release, especially when abbreviated by a DJ-friendly minute or more. In December, emboldened by the phenomenal success of *Love is the Drug*, Island went ahead and issued it anyway, backed by an unavailable-elsewhere live rendition of *For Your Pleasure* to offset fan indifference to an A-side they already owned. A 16mm promo film, with the studio version rather artlessly synchronised against footage of the same song performed live, was presumably intended as another safety measure, but neither tactic did any good.

Having already appeared on Mike Mansfield's LWT programme *Supersonic* as far back as 11 October, the same *Both Ends Burning* footage was recycled for the edition of 20 December, Roxy sharing the bill this time with Melanie, Kiki Dee,

Cliff Richard and arch Roxy imitators Sailor. This didn't help much either, maybe because the horrendous caterwauling of resident Sirens Doreen Chanter and Jacqui Sullivan was overdubbed onto the song's choruses. The *Supersonic* showcase was followed three days later by the single's chart debut at number 40. It then took four weeks to reach a pretty lowly high of 25, slipping away altogether on 3 February. Tellingly, in the US it was consigned to B-side status in support of *Love is the Drug*.

Normally following the contemplative strains of *Sea Breezes, Both Ends Burning* was a highlight of Roxy's 1975 tour, a recording of it from Wembley's Empire Pool being preserved on the following year's *Viva! Roxy Music* album. (The Sirens' wail that sounded so ghastly on *Supersonic* works somewhat better in a live context, though Dave Marsh of *Rolling Stone* was still moved to insist that "Roxy should never, never use those women to sing with Ferry again.") The song cropped up intermittently in the band's 1979 set and consistently thereafter, with an intriguingly sultry, slowed-down version gracing their 1980 dates.

In 1986, Ghost Dance, a Goth-rock band featuring refugees from both Sisters of Mercy and Skeletal Family, covered *Both Ends Burning* as one of four tracks on their *River of No Return* 12" single. (They had reportedly picked up the sheet music in a charity shop for a mere ten pence.) The song was later recorded by Dutch band Fatal Flowers as the final track on their 1990 album *Pleasure Ground*. The producer was David Bowie's sometime guitarist Mick Ronson and the result, perhaps unsurprisingly, was described by Ira Robbins of *Trouser Press* magazine as "Bowie-styled". New Zealand garage-punk combo Terminals also covered the song, as B-side to their *Black Creek* single.

Nightingale
(Ferry-Manzanera) 4:11

Yet more in the ho-hum vein of *End of the Line* and *Could It Happen to Me?*, *Nightingale* puts forth florid heart-cries akin to *If There is Something*'s notorious reference to potatoes but does so with poker-faced seriousness. Ferry's update of Keats' *Ode to a Nightingale* posits a kind of transmigration of souls, with the narrator proposing to his befeathered opposite number that they should sing a duet by the light of the moon. But the lyrical substance is meagre (and Ferry is occasionally indistinct in singing it, as if even he were unconvinced) and the crash-bang-wallop of the musical backdrop disastrously wrong.

Manzanera's strummed opening, gently augmented by Gustafson's pensive bass line, hints of bucolic charms that never materialise, because Ferry's unusually strident vocal and the bludgeoning heft of Thompson's percussion knock subtlety for six the moment the song proper kicks in. Here's an instance where a touch of sotto voce sobriety might not have gone amiss; instead, Ferry's overpitched performance strains after sublimity and misses by a mile. Indeed, he hasn't sounded as dangerously close to doing himself a mischief as this since the more winceable moments of *The Bob (Medley)*.

Having previously contributed only some heavily treated subtextual burbles, Mackay's oboe comes briefly to the rescue, providing a spine-chillingly sombre hiatus with delicate rhythm accompaniment from Manzanera. But then it's back to the grind again, with Jobson's shimmering, multi-tracked violins introducing a climactic din that hammers song and listener into dazed submission. Even Ferry gets buried in the racket, though it lets up at the end for the arrival of the kind of over-literal sound effect resisted on *End of the Line*. Ferry concludes with a plaintive appeal for the nightingale to start singing, whereupon it does exactly that, twittering gently as the track fades away. Actually, though predictable, the half-heard birdsong here remains a memorable touch, contrasting nicely with the spidery guitar intro to *Just Another High*.

Again, Roxy just aren't ready to underpin this track with the delicacy it requires – and, in this instance, requires badly, for Ferry's lyric is the kind of thing he once would have played for a queasy mixture of humour and pathos, rather than the straight-faced profundity he attempts here. In the thoroughly preposterous *Bitters End*, Ferry had appreciatively observed the airborne flutterings of a raven. Three years on, the straight-faced shift from Poe's bird of ill omen to Keats' chirruping nightingale results in mere bathos.

The track was one of seven from *Siren* featured on the band's accompanying tour, Barbara Drillsma indicating in *Melody Maker* that maybe it came alive on stage in a way it stubbornly resists doing on record. "Ferry and Manzanera," she wrote, "created a tour de force with *Nightingale*, a haunting emotional number which contrasted sharply with *Both Ends Burning*, a real classic rocker."

Just Another High
(Ferry) 6:31

Melody Maker's Allan Jones went overboard about this one, calling it "as supreme an achievement as either *In Every Dream Home a Heartache* or *Mother of Pearl*. It is, in fact, *Heartache* which the mood of this song initially evokes, with Manzanera's guitar creating a similar menacing tension as Ferry half recites the opening lines with an air of disenchantment. He's addressing another lost love, this time with a suggestion of cruelty..." Well, maybe Jones overstated the case in his pre-release estimate, but there's little doubt that *Just Another High* is in the classic Roxy mould and, after the occasional mis-steps heard previously on the *Siren* album, sends the set out on, appropriately enough, a high.

Here, the sparse severity of the Chris Thomas soundstage reaps dividends, lending a chilly, monolithic grandeur to one of Ferry's most impressive performances. Manzanera's skeletal opening phrases give his guitar the stately sonority of a harpsichord, providing the perfect introduction to Ferry in his best sprechgesang mode. He feigns resigned indifference to his interlocutor's aching heart and wilting spirit, whereupon Thompson's drums crash in – and here, unlike *Nightingale*, their thunderous assault is perfectly placed – and the mask of insouciance is instantly dropped.

Simplicity is the keynote here, the song restating, in exhilaratingly grandiloquent terms, Ferry's immersion in a romantic agony so intense it becomes a masochistic source of comfort. Life has recently become an empty and meaningless charade, he seems to say, but apart from that I'm not doing too badly. Despite the prevailing mood, Ferry can still indulge in occasional cross-referencing, not to mention submerged double-entendres. While the narrator has irretrievably blown his cool, his absent lover has replied in kind by blowing out the candle – which simultaneously gives the nod to a song from two years back (*In Every Dream Home a Heartache*) and a song from two tracks back (*Both Ends Burning*). The 'candle' analogy, meanwhile, was last invoked in the third album's *Serenade*.

The instrumentation remains spartanly distributed throughout, with occasional keyboard embellishments but mainly driven by Gustafson and Thompson, together with a sensitive Manzanera guitar break that revisits the cool precision of Mackay's oboe section on *Nightingale*. Here, though, Mackay ventures in only to add staccato oboe flares to the second and third choruses, which eventually spiral into an inspired fade in which Ferry can afford to laugh self-mockingly at his own inclination to treat love as a game. The transcendant effect aimed at in the previous track's convoluted ode to a nightingale is effortlessly achieved here by the gorgeous interlocking of Ferry's ruminative vocal with his 'other self' providing a falsetto response in counterpoint.

Just Another High seems to have caused trouble as a live proposition, joining *Pyjamarama*, *A Really Good Time* and *Strictly Confidential* in only being played occasionally on the *Siren* tour and never resurfacing thereafter. According to Manzanera, its importance lay, in any case, in how it originated rather than in how it was reproduced on stage, for it apparently occasioned a sudden volte-face in Ferry's working methods. As well as noting that making *Siren* was "like getting blood out of a stone," Manzanera also observed that "One of the nicer tracks, *Just Another High*, had the lyrics *and* the music done for the first time. The lyrics are usually written after he's got the backing tracks. This was the first time he had an actual complete song, which is great. Most people write the music and lyrics simultaneously; I hope Bryan does more like that."

Maybe he would – but not, for the time being at any rate, with Roxy Music.

PART THREE

Inter-regnum

Eleven: *End of the Line*

*"There's been a lot of uncomfortable talk over the last 18 months about
dissention within the Roxy ranks. Specifically, Andy Mackay and Phil Manzanera
are said to be so unsatisfied with the emphasis placed on Bryan Ferry that they're
constantly on the verge of filing their walking papers. If this talk has even the
remotest basis in reality, somebody had better take it upon themselves to slap
some sense into these bozos."*

Ben Edmonds, *Phonograph Record* December 1975

Everyone's got their solo things to do

In the wake of *Siren*, Roxy made two further visits to the USA, in December 1975
and March 1976. The bass guitarist this time around was Rick Wills, later to collaborate with Steve Marriott on a reconstituted Small Faces prior to joining MOR
monoliths Foreigner and Bad Company.

Reflecting on Roxy's US progress in the brief pause between these two stints,
Manzanera observed that "We started out playing 1800-seaters, then got to doing
two nights at each venue. Later we graduated to one and then two shows in
3000-seaters and on the last tour we did just before Christmas we were playing in
10,000 capacity venues in some places. We had planned to do a European tour in
February, but now we've cancelled that so that we can go back to America. Last
time we concentrated on the eastern side of the country and it went so well that
we felt it would be stupid not to go back and follow it up, so this time we'll be
doing the west coast and consolidating in some places where we've been
recently."

As well as mounting renewed assaults on the USA, Roxy could reflect
indulgently on the emergence of numerous imitators, the most brazen of whom
were Sailor, who, ironically, had supported Cockney Rebel on tour in 1975. Ferry
had been off-handedly dismissive of the latter group on their emergence in 1974
with classic Roxy-inflected singles like *Judy Teen* and *Mister Soft*. "I thought their
song *Catch a Falling Star* was interesting, though I thought Perry Como's version
had the edge," he told Nick Kent, also pointing out airily that "they need a good
tailor." He was more tolerant of Roxy's Island stablemates Sparks, whose *This
Town Ain't Big Enough for the Both of Us* had stirred memories of *Virginia Plain*:
"No, I wouldn't put them down. They've worked very hard for their success –
Island have done a magnificent job I think. Actually I'm very flattered by them."

The openly imitative hit singles put out by Sailor, however, were another
matter; as Manzanera put it, "We felt a bit weird about those." A vehicle for

half-Finnish singer-songwriter Georg Kajanus, Sailor stirred half-digested elements of Kurt Weill and Jacques Brel into a song called *Glass of Champagne* – "which was, I suppose, sort of derivative of Roxy Music," admitted keyboard player Phil Pickett. With its unmistakeable echoes of *Virginia Plain*, the single was only kept off the Number One spot in late 1975 by Queen's unavoidable *Bohemian Rhapsody*, after which *Girls, Girls, Girls* hit number seven the following year.

Sailor would sink into oblivion soon afterwards, but at the beginning of 1976 there was widespread speculation that Roxy were likely to do the same. Quizzed on the subject, Manzanera was candid: "You read things that other members of the band are supposed to have said and you wonder if they might actually have said them. It can easily build up mistrust within the group. As far as I am concerned there is no question of the group splitting," he added. "I've no intention of leaving – unless, of course, I were to be provoked beyond endurance, which is a thing that could happen in any group at any time. I'm not expecting that though." For his part, Ferry claimed that "It would be nice to do one [a new Roxy album] – but Roxy Music will probably ease up a little in '76, because everyone's got their solo things to do."

So it proved. After the band's latest Stateside itinerary (a tour obviously designed to exploit the breakthrough chart success of *Love is the Drug*), Roxy opted to cool their heels for a while; for over two years, as it turned out.

Tiger-skin rug love

Prior to the announcement of the band's so-called 'devolution', the individual members were far from idle. Having met fledgling New Zealand group Split Enz during Roxy's recent Antipodean dates, Manzanera was invited to produce their first album, *Mental Notes*; he also played on the world premiere of Stomu Yamashta's 'Go' project at the Royal Albert Hall alongside Steve Winwood and Mike Shrieve. In addition, he was setting up a studio of his own with Eno and Robert Wyatt (the so-called Immaculate Conception Studio) and pondering his next move after an abortive attempt to get together a 'supergroup' comprising himself, Eno, Bill MacCormick, Bill Bruford and Eddie Jobson.

Mackay was riding high on his first foray into writing music for TV, *Rock Follies*, and the astonishing success of the resultant album, a success equalled in Roxy's own oeuvre only by *Stranded*. (More on this in Chapter 12.) Jobson, meanwhile, had worked with Rainbow and Frank Zappa during Roxy's US dates, as well as smarting slightly over the failure of his solo single *Yesterday Boulevard*, on which he'd been partnered only by drummer Simon Phillips. Undaunted, he informed *Record Mirror* that "I've certainly got an album's worth of material ready, but I keep finding so many new influences that I can never make up my mind about what kind of album I want to do."

Like Jobson, Thompson was embroiled in Ferry's most recent solo recordings, the first of which took the form of an exuberant cover of Wilbert Harrison's *Let's Work Together*, here redubbed *Let's Stick Together*. This track represented a peak of commercial success for Ferry's solo career that would not be repeated for nearly a decade. "*Let's Stick Together* … was just a fun record," he would maintain in the grimmer climes of 1978. "But it's not really the kind of thing I'd like to be remembered for. I'm capable of more subtle things than that. But of course subtlety doesn't sell a million records. It's the obvious that sells, not the subtle."

Let's Stick Together may be obvious, but as a take-no-prisoners R'n'B rocker it's hard to beat. Familiar with the song since his days in The Gas Board, Ferry larded it with a blazing Chris Mercer brass section, a thickly clotted bass line, a towering tub-thumping fusillade of The Great Paul Thompson, even a "reeba-reeba"-style outbreak of Jerry Hall backing vocals, making it one of the most inescapable dance tracks of the summer of 1976. John Wetton, however, has since recalled how Ferry and producer Chris Thomas insisted on no fewer than 48 takes of his bass line, indicating that even in as uncomplicated a 'dancer' as this lay disturbing signs of the obsessive perfectionism that was to undo Ferry in the 1980s and 90s.

Backed with a solo cover of Roxy's *Sea Breezes*, *Let's Stick Together* entered the UK singles chart on 8 June, reaching a high of number four on the 29th – The Real Thing's *You to Me are Everything* was in the top spot – and in all spending ten weeks in the listings, half of them in the Top Ten. At the beginning of this triumphant progress, Ferry appeared on *Top of the Pops* on 10 June as part of an eclectic bill encompassing Archie Bell & the Drells, The Sensational Alex Harvey Band, The Real Thing, Slik, Osibisa, The Surprise Sisters and The Wurzels. By November, *Let's Stick Together* had even managed a US high of 160, making it Ferry's first solo single to make any impression Stateside.

The accompanying video featured Ferry, Spedding, Thompson, Rick Wills et al ranged against gold drapes, with a late entrance from a tail-twirling, tiger-skinned siren played by Jerry Hall herself. Ferry's look here – white suit, red polka-dotted tie and, worst of all, a ferrety Ronald Colman moustache – is without question his sleaziest, and to add insult to injury a notably greasy and unappealing still from it would be used by Atlantic for the opportunistic US album subsequently spawned by the track.

A *particularly polite group*

With Ferry's most successful solo 45 approaching its chart peak, on Saturday 26 June came the ambiguous announcement that Roxy Music were going to 'devolve' for a while. The title of Ferry's latest single immediately acquired a heavy admixture of irony, particularly because his solo ambitions were widely seen as the spur that convinced him Roxy should *not* stick together. "We have all decided to go our separate ways," Ferry claimed, "for the rest of the year at least, to have a rest from Roxy Music for a while. And this seemed like a good time to stop."

"I think that this is a particularly polite group," Jobson had recently observed, and his opinion was borne out by Ferry's later, more candid account of the band's 'devolution'. "Being in a group year in year out is rather like going on holiday with friends – tension builds up through people being too close together and you fall out," he told the *Sun*. "With Roxy there was never a major row that I can remember, never a night when people stormed out shouting that they would never work with each other again. It just became obvious that the time had come for a natural break. There were a lot of reasons. There was a bit of bad feeling about my solo career being so successful. Nothing was said, but I could feel it."

Saturday 25 November 1972: Roxy Music performing *The Bogus Man Part II*
on the live BBC arts showcase, *Full House*

The *Virginia Plain* line-up, 1972 – back: Mackay,
Thompson, Manzanera, Kenton; front: Ferry, Eno

Bizarro warp factor – Eno in performance, 1972

Preparing to assault the USA, Eno already drifting off at right; 1972

Performing *In Every Dream Home a Heartache* on the 3 April edition of *The Old Grey Whistle Test*, 1973

Ferry with new recruit Eddie Jobson in July 1973

Stranded on tour, autumn 1973: another short-stay bass player, Sal Maida, is on Manzanera's right

Now you see them now you don't: bowdlerised *Country Life* cover, 1974

'Roxy sax object' Andy Mackay on stage in October 1975

Both Ends Burning at Wembley, Saturday 18 October 1975: Ferry and Mackay
with Sirens Doreen Chanter and Jacqui Sullivan

GI boy howlin' out for more: performing *Love is the Drug*, autumn 1975

End of the line: with bass guitarist Rick Wills (on Manzanera's right) just prior to 'devolution', 1976

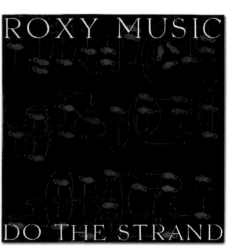

Arresting cover art for the belated
but non-charting
Do the Strand single, 1978

A stellar line-up for
Roxy Music Greatest Hits, 1977

Three years later and yet another bass player: Ferry, Mackay and Manzanera with Gary Tibbs, 1979

Antony Price's celestial mannequins, 1979

Ferry, lurid in lime-green, backed by
Mackay and Tibbs, 1979

Phil Manzanera in action during the
Flesh + Blood tour, 1980

Back in the white tuxedo: *Avalon*-era Ferry, 1982

Thareta de Oliveira on the back cover of the
very nearly posthumous live collection,
The High Road, 1983

1985 promo disc for The Explorers,
with vocalist James Wraith in the centre;
note Manzanera's bug-eyed spectacles

The classic axe and sax combination: Manzanera and Mackay performing *Ladytron* at Wembley, Friday 22 June 2001

Monday 24 October 2004: Thompson, Manzanera, Ferry and Mackay at the Grosvenor House Hotel to receive their Q Lifetime Achievement Award

The bad feeling Ferry referred to was presumably not just a case of the schoolboy sulks. It was more likely a genuine concern about the way in which Ferry's solo ambitions had seriously distorted the group's media profile and perceived achievement, muddying the waters to the point where the *Supersonic* cameramen had photographed *Love is the Drug* and *Both Ends Burning* as if Ferry were the only person that mattered, leaving Mackay, for instance, at least as invisible as Eno had inadvertently been back in the days of *The Old Grey Whistle Test*.

Mackay himself graciously issued a statement of his own, though a none too convincing one, claiming that "Roxy Music, as a group, has a life of its own. The group has an identity which has grown stronger and is nourished by the fact that we are able to pursue separate projects." Perhaps Mackay's emphasis on other projects was intended to indicate to the fans that all was not lost – and, incidentally, to stem the flow of hate mail that Ferry, in particular, immediately became prey to once the split was known. Whatever the reasons for Mackay's show of exaggerated diplomacy, Manzanera was having none of it, claiming unequivocally (albeit 20 years later) that "We were sick of the sight of each other."

Even so, Manzanera was the prime mover behind a long-planned live album sporting the engagingly ironic title *Viva! Roxy Music*. "It'll be quite easy," Ferry had blithely observed in a New Year's Eve interview with *Record Mirror*. "It's just a question of getting it mixed." According to contemporary fan club bulletins, the process wasn't quite so straightforward. The band members spent numerous hours sifting through Manzanera's exhaustive archive of live recordings, immersing themselves in seven gigs ranging from November 1973 to October 1975, pondering 39 songs in 127 different versions, and finally drawing up their own personal short lists. Mackay was outvoted on the matter of putting the record out as a single disc; he would have preferred a warts-and-all double-LP without studio sweetening, of which the final product reportedly received quite a lot. "It was overworked," he grumbled in 2003. "Didn't sound like Roxy."

Despite Mackay's misgivings, the album seemed an apt enough memento mori to grief-stricken Roxy fans, starting a 12-week chart run on 31 July and reaching number six. It was also enthusiastically reviewed. "It's a genuinely exciting, often thrilling record," reported Allan Jones in *Melody Maker*, "which captures precisely the flash and bravado of an impressive and intelligent band." For *Rolling Stone*'s Dave Marsh, meanwhile, the instrumentalists were the thing: "Drummer Paul Thompson, as single-mindedly rocking as anyone this side of Charlie Watts, shapes the sound," he wrote. "Phil Manzanera can play guitar with any of the big guns of the post-Hendrix school, Eddie Jobson has a more melodic touch on synthesizer than most and sax-man Andy Mackay is rarely less than terrific."

For *Viva! Roxy Music*, Ferry came out of the rear-sleeve shadows of *For Your Pleasure* and put himself on the front cover, albeit not looking particularly recognisable and upstaged, in any case, by the bejewelled forms of backing vocalists Doreen Chanter and Jacqui Sullivan. The video-striped images here and throughout the lavish *Viva!* package were culled from the filmed record of Roxy's October 1975 Wembley shows, though only one of the eight tracks within – *Both Ends Burning* – came from the same source. Two others, *Pyjamarama* and *Chance Meeting*, were recorded at the Glasgow Apollo in November 1973, but the lion's share of the album was recorded at Newcastle's City Hall in November 1974.

Whether, as Mackay put it, the album does or does not "sound like Roxy," it's certainly true that, with the tracks representing a stir-fry of three different tours and the LP itself clocking in at only 46 minutes, it gives no very powerful impression of a contemporaneous Roxy show in its full glory. Though brilliantly performed (and just as brilliantly sequenced), the eight tracks here seem like rather thin gruel compared to the menu a double album might have served up, with the omission of anything from the *Stranded* album seeming a particularly grievous oversight.

The album nevertheless gets off to an impressive start with *Out of the Blue*, in which Mackay's ominous opening motif is backed up by a heady synthetic swirl from the entire band and Jobson's violin solo streaks through the mix in truly scalp-tingling fashion at the end. The live version of *Pyjamarama* included here represented the song's first-ever appearance on an album, garnished by heavenly voices, wildly energised percussion from Thompson, a heavily treated, burbling sax break from Mackay, and a dazzling burst of last-minute guitar from Manzanera.

The Bogus Man is ponderous but genuinely sinister, benefiting from the discreet interpolation of the demonic laughter last heard in Ferry's version of *Sympathy for the Devil*, and *Chance Meeting* supplants the musique concrète of the original with a delicate, airy interplay between oboe and strings. (This would be recalled in Roxy's 2001 dates by the meshing of soprano sax and violin on *Tara*.) *Both Ends Burning* is subjected to a powerhouse hard-rock makeover, Mackay's alto blazing thrillingly through the choruses and Manzanera's guitar merging with Jobson's synths to stunning effect at the climax. Here, too, preserved on disc for posterity, is what Paul Stump has called "the jaw-dropping horror of the Sirens, whose backing vocals would be acceptable if they could (a) hit a note and (b) not sound vile."

Side Two consists of epic-length versions of *If There is Something* and *In Every Dream Home a Heartache*, the latter retaining its Crimson-quoting grandeur and accommodating gorgeous solo spots for Mackay, Manzanera and Jobson, the latter distinguished by the creepy frisson of Jobson's violin, the stately heft of Thompson's drums (somehow recalling *For Your Pleasure* more than *Dream Home*), and a staggering Manzanera freak-out to conclude. The album itself concludes with the inevitable *Do the Strand*, a fairly workaday version but graced by a reverberating climactic klang that leaves the listener feeling thoroughly winded.

Despite the posthumous gift of *Viva! Roxy Music*, bereaved Roxy fans were left wondering what had become of a valedictory single announced by Island in June. This had even been granted a catalogue number (for the record, Island WIP 6308) and was to have coupled the perennial favourite *Do the Strand* with *War Brides*, presumably an instrumental version of the boogie-woogie number Mackay had written with Howard Schuman for the concluding episode of Thames TV's *Rock Follies*. It never came out.

Extended pleasure

Though the broiling summer of 1976 saw Ferry taking possession of a capacious Sussex pile designed by Sir Clough Williams-Ellis, his procession of solo cover versions continued unabated. In July came the release of an Everly Brothers makeover, *The Price of Love*, as lead track on a nostalgic resurrection of the EP format called *Extended Play*.

Ferry's EP-reviving thunder may have been stolen by the gargantuan Demis Roussos (whose multi-track *The Roussos Phenomenon* had hit Number One earlier the same month), but *The Price of Love* remains one of his more energised and imaginative covers. Resounding to Martin Drover's trumpet fanfares, Chris Spedding's churning guitar lines and Ferry's own strident harmonica sound, it was further augmented by a stylish video in which the grisly Ronald Colman 'tache had happily been given the chop but the castanet-flickering Jerry Hall was still in place.

The EP's other tracks comprised an anodyne reading of *It's Only Love* from The Beatles' *Help!* album, a chunky remake of Jimmy Reed's *Shame, Shame, Shame* (in the words of *NME* enfant terrible Julie Burchill, "a humourless caricature that could possibly sound like the real thing to a 15-year-old whose experience of black music extends no further than Billy Ocean"), and a winsome rendering of Gallagher & Lyle's *Heart on My Sleeve*. This last had been recorded alongside *You Go to My Head* back in April 1975, long before Gallagher & Lyle themselves had a hit with it; though an unprecedented instance of Ferry recording a contemporary song rather than a time-honoured one, it can hardly be called a cutting-edge selection.

Such a pleasant but essentially pointless clutch of covers wasn't likely to appease hardcore fans bereft of Roxy Music, but the *Extended Play* package nevertheless entered the Top 40 on 3 August. Climbing to number 7 on the 31st, six places behind Abba's all-conquering *Dancing Queen*, it enjoyed a chart run of nine weeks. At this stage, Ferry can have had few qualms about 'devolving' Roxy Music, given that these two latest forays into the singles chart had scored higher than all but two of Roxy's own 45s.

And as if to urge the fans to look upon Ferry and Roxy as interchangeable commodities, the EP's liner notes impudently appropriated recent Roxy imagery. These were credited to one Sam Bertorelli, but it's hard not to detect the florid pen of Dr Puxley in the concluding paragraph: "Backing vocals are delivered by – who else? – the Sirens. Can you resist their call any longer? Need you try? To be sure, pleasure is dangerous, and especially Extended Pleasure, but ... it's fun. Cast your cares to the winds, wreck yourselves on these rocky shores of delight – in other words, place this disc on the turntable right now and ... PLAY IT LOUD!!"

In the USA, Atlantic, unwilling to risk confusing American record buyers with such an antiquated conceit, declined to release the EP, instead packaging its component parts alongside various other singles and B-sides as a rag-bag LP called *Let's Stick Together*. Initially only available as an import, the record was eventually released in the UK too (shabby frame-grab artwork and all), reaching a chart high of number 19 in October. Unfortunately, as 1976 made way to 1977, the album's roster of needless Roxy remakes and equally meaningless cover versions made it very clear that Ferry was not the all-conquering solo artist he perhaps imagined; on the contrary, with Roxy in retirement and punk rock on the horizon, he was looking increasingly like the wrong man in the wrong place at the wrong time.

A precious relic

In retrospect, it was perhaps lucky that Roxy 'devolved' when they did; inoperative during the bloodier skirmishes of the punk explosion, they were able to acquire iconic status as departed heroes, unscathed by the kind of responses any brand-new recordings might have been subjected to. As a solo artist, still plugging away in the fruitless quest for MOR acceptance in America, Ferry was not so fortunate. The *NME* review of *Roxy Music Greatest Hits* in November 1977, penned by the paper's teenage queen bitch Julie Burchill, contained the following panegyric: "This music is a precious relic, not relevant any more. But at their best Roxy Music were better than David Bowie, than The Supremes, than The Doors, than The Sex Pistols, than anyone I imagine I will ever hear." But this only came after a vitriolic denunciation of Ferry himself in the review's opening paragraph.

The peculiar relationship between Roxy Music, springing straight from the rarefied climes of Britain's art schools, and punk rock, springing ostensibly straight from the streets, went deeper than the proto-punk assault of *Editions of You* or the psychotic Eno-Manzanera collaboration *Third Uncle*. It had more to do with Roxy's self-confessed position back in 1972 as 'inspired amateurs', thumbing their noses at the rock orthodoxy that insisted on technical brilliance and a long hard slog round the college circuit. Where Roxy thumbed their noses, punk went right ahead and raised two fingers, but the principle was the same.

Much of punk's indebtedness to Roxy was only grudgingly admitted many years after the event. But the first major music press exposure for The Sex Pistols, courtesy of *Sounds'* Jonh Ingham on 24 April 1976, had contained an intriguing nugget to the effect that "Paul [Cook] admits to being fooled by Roxy Music for three albums." Steve Jones, too, had offered his own Roxy tribute via his fledgling group, The Strand. Sex Pistols acolyte Siouxsie Sioux, meanwhile, has since acknowledged that "In a lot of ways the Roxy Music audiences predated punk, because they were fairly large collections of misfits, freaks, anyone who dared to be different ... So my closest friends, like [Steve] Severin, were Roxy fans."

For all their arty emphasis on high fashion and elitist decadence, Roxy had always maintained a studiedly ironic distance, but it was precisely this distance that Ferry was now busily dismantling, not only in his own recordings but even his own life. To the sneering commentators of the New Wave, Ferry seemed to have bought in to the dream of glamour he once so astutely satirised, a capital crime exemplified by his model girlfriend and country squire existence in Sussex. A not insignificant addition to this combustible equation was the publication in late 1976 of a fawning chronicle called *The Bryan Ferry Story*, a slim volume ostensibly penned by one Rex Balfour but actually written by Ferry's own PR man, the redoubtable Puxley. "Things like *Smoke Gets in Your Eyes* are probably anathema to the New Wave," Ferry admitted. "Some of them would probably like to see me crucified for that. But there are other things I did with Roxy, like *Street Life*, that are probably more New Wave than the New Wave, you know."

Though he was aware that many young music fans saw him merely as "some kind of playboy who occasionally makes records," the immovable Ferry was not about to make any concessions. Having introduced his monied white tuxedo look at the height of Britain's penny-pinching Three-Day Week, he would demonstrate a similar inadvertent tactlessness throughout the punk-dominated Roxy 'inter-regnum'. As a result, the period would prove a much more rewarding one for moving targets Mackay and Manzanera.

Twelve: *The Talking Pictures*

"Eleven years after Channel 13 first broadcast this six-part Thames Television series, Rock Follies *retains all the originality and excitement that first made it a cult classic. It has grown dearer, too, for it is that rare commodity – an original [musical] work (script and lyrics by Howard Schuman, music by Andy Mackay) for television."*

Ellen Cohn, *Village Voice* **22 November 1988**

The Show Business

In October 1975, Jonh Ingham revealed to *Sounds* readers that Andy Mackay was embroiled in an extracurricular project well outside the usual round of session work and solo albums: "Currently he is providing the music for *Rock Follies*, a six-part serial to be aired in January concerning the tribulations of a three-girl rock group." He also quoted Mackay to the effect that "I rather enjoyed sitting down at the piano like Cole Porter and saying, 'How does that sound?'"

A scabrous satire on the music business (and much else), Thames TV's genre-busting *Rock Follies* was destined to raise howls of execration from the rock press yet exercise a profound influence over the course of television drama. During the summer of 1975, however, few could have predicted either of these outcomes. As Mackay remembered it 25 years on, the scene at Notting Hill's Serbian Community Centre consisted of "production assistants putting tape marks on the floor, piles of scripts, and in the corner an upright piano." Also present were the show's stars, Charlotte Cornwell, Julie Covington and Rula Lenska, Mackay putting them through their paces "whenever I could get them out of rehearsing some other part of the show." The whole thing was an exhilarating contrast to Mackay's alternative stamping grounds that summer, notably the Holland Park basement in which the *Siren* album was rehearsed and the Oxford Circus studio in which it was subsequently recorded.

Mackay's involvement in the series came courtesy of Colin Bucksey, a television cameraman and the husband of Thames TV's Head of Drama, Verity Lambert. American playwright Howard Schuman had been commissioned to write a serial about a struggling girl group called The Little Ladies, detailing their unhappy progress from bawling pub rockers to a mellifluous 1970s version of The Andrews Sisters. The original idea for the show, however, had been brought to Thames in December 1973 by the so-called Rock Bottom group, consisting of actresses Gaye Brown, Diane Langton and Annabel Leventon and their composer-cum-manager Don Fraser. The fact that these four had no involvement in the eventual series was to have serious repercussions later on; that a programme concerned in part to anatomise the cynicism of the music business should end in a 'breach of confidence' court case was perhaps the crowning irony of the whole *Rock Follies* scenario.

Mackay, though, was oblivious to these gathering storm clouds during his initial meeting with Verity Lambert at an Italian restaurant in Olympia. Having been sent the script for the first episode, he then met Schuman at the latter's home and the two clicked immediately. "Being introduced to Andy was one of the turning points, creatively, in *Rock Follies*," Schuman recalled. "He was the *real* rock music. But a wonderful musician, incredibly literate and with a fantastic sense of humour. We had an instant rapport."

Four years Mackay's senior, Schuman's writing career had started out at a pretty low level. Back in his native New York, he and his writing partner had lived a hand-to-mouth existence in Greenwich Village. "We would look at what was the idea current that week," he remembered, "write a song around it, take it down to what was left of Tin Pan Alley and get £20 for it. Nothing ever happened to it, it didn't get published, but that wasn't the point. It kept us in hamburgers." After having no luck with an Off Broadway musical revue, Schuman drifted to London in 1968 and made ends meet by writing music for both the National and Chichester Festival theatres. He was also courted by the cigar-chewing executives of American International Pictures to write a 'hip' horror-comedy for Vincent Price, but nothing came of the idea.

By 1973, he had metamorphosed, somewhat to his surprise, into a television dramatist. "I found that I reacted to things I found in English society, and was interested by it, in a way that didn't happen in America," he told the *Guardian* three years later. One of his earliest TV experiences was an unhappy one, however. His BBC play *Censored Scenes from King Kong* initially failed to be shown thanks to the privations of the Three-Day Week, but when it remained invisible thereafter Schuman realised that it had itself been 'censored'. Cynicism honed to a fine point by this experience, Schuman began developing *Rock Follies* in 1974. "Somebody asked me what my qualification was for writing *Rock Follies*," he deadpanned in *TV Times*. "It is seven years of total failure in the music business."

The Loony Tunes

Mackay's collaboration with Schuman was diametrically opposed to the work he had done with Bryan Ferry, whose collage techniques had involved musical tracks being laid down well before he even thought about lyrics. "For me it was slightly frustrating because it restricted the way in which I could actually write top lines, and chord sequences and rhythm ideas," Mackay maintained. All this changed with Schuman, who provided lyrics first and often required music to be set to them in record time. "It was a very liberating way of working. Being a great lyricist, Howard's words have inherent rhythm in them, which makes a composer's job easier."

As well as being involved in the audition process for the three actresses involved, Mackay was charged with getting together a suitable backing band for them, for on-screen as well as recording purposes. He came up with Ray Russell (guitar), Tony Stevens (bass), Brian Chatton (keyboards) and Peter Van Hooke (drums). Of these, Stevens was a particularly apt choice in that he had abandoned boogie band Foghat in order to have a go at being an actor. Ray Russell's career, meanwhile, stretched back to 1963, when he replaced the legendary Vic Flick in The John Barry Seven; he would later become a key conspirator in Mackay's second solo album. The songs were pre-recorded at Thames' own recording studio (not a sophisticated outfit, confined as it was to six-track technology) and done at what Mackay called "an exhilarating, not to say reckless, pace." Sometimes he would be lucky to have three hours in which to nail a song down.

The process was an unusual one for Mackay in that, given the satirical nature of Schuman's scripts, several of the songs were required to be purposely bad. He needed to juggle numbers like *War Brides*, "which was supposed to be the wrong direction for The Little Ladies to take," with others like *The Road*, "which was the kind of thing that expressed their inner ideas." His first duties, in fact, were to write pastiche show tunes for the ghastly touring musical, *Broadway Annie*, on which the constituent members of The Little Ladies first meet.

That the Schuman-Mackay formula was a winning one was evidenced straight away. "The songs, by Schuman and Andy Mackay, are very catchy," observed the *Sunday Times'* Peter Lennon in response to the first episode. As the series wore on, Stewart Lane of the *Morning Star* would draw attention to "some splendid numbers by Andy Mackay," while in the *Times Literary Supplement* Lorna Sage paid Mackay the ultimate back-handed compliment: "Though the songs got gradually worse, they were still good-bad songs (disillusioned tunes by Andy Mackay of Roxy Music)."

This description of Mackay's music as 'disillusioned' might be attributable, not merely to the sardonic requirements of Schuman's story, but also to his feelings regarding the gradually disintegrating Roxy Music. "He not only wrote wonderful music," observed Schuman, "but he would supply me with details about sound checks and rotten tricks that bands would do to the supporting acts. He was a mine of background information." One suspects that the name Jethro Tull, among others, must have crossed Mackay's lips during these conferences.

It was Mackay's insider knowledge, then, that put flesh on the bones of Schuman's bilious critique, accurately identifying the music scene as just another manipulative branch of showbiz. It was this, however, that would cause *Rock Follies* to become a bête noire to the music papers. Claiming in the *NME* that "being whipped with red-hot barbed wire is only fractionally more unpleasant than Thames TV's sensational smash-hit series *Rock Follies*," Tony Tyler noted with unfeigned horror that "Roxy sax object Andy Mackay" was one of its prime movers. "The hell with objectivity. I hated *Rock Follies*," he continued. "I found the plot cumbersome and the script foolish. I disliked the fundamental inaccuracy of the 'real bits', remained unentranced by the 'surreal' bits, grew increasingly irritated at the predictability of the crises and downright contemptuous of the constant attitudinising."

As late as 1979, Nick Kent would observe in the same paper, apropos the reactivated Roxy, that Mackay "made his pot of gold not from Roxy but his work as composer and part-conceptualist of the (albeit wretched) *Rock Follies* – to the point where reuniting with the very character (Ferry) with whom he'd apparently come to a most unamicable parting of the ways during the *Siren* era was a move totally bereft of financial considerations."

The sore rubbed by *Rock Follies* was the same sore that Roxy themselves had so enthusiastically aggravated back in 1972, with the fading fantasies of the late 1960s causing the more holier-than-thou musos to recoil from any suggestion that rock music was basically a capitalist enterprise. Also speaking in 1979, Mackay insisted in *Record Mirror* that the series "was one of the most original TV programmes made in the last ten years. It was made in opposition to what the TV companies wanted. It was seen here as a commercial programme, which it conspicuously was not. In the three years since *Rock Follies* there has been nothing else as exciting. It related [the] rock business to show business, which most rock'n'roll musicians find offensive, but I think it's true."

As of the show's first broadcast on Tuesday 24 February 1976, most television critics proved better disposed to the series than the music press. "*Rock Follies* is tough, funny and searching. You will love it. You don't think you will, but you will," wrote Nancy Banks-Smith in the *Guardian* the next day. "Passing one test of enjoyment at a canter, *Rock Follies* (ITV) left me eager to find friends who missed the launching episode in order to share some of its unkind yet truthful wisecracks," enthused Shaun Usher in the *Daily Mail*. "And it's good, too, to find a work in which women get the attention and are presented as sharply different, well realised, if predictable, characters."

Usher's prognostication was a simple one: "*Follies'* destiny is to become a cult success or a palpable flop: there seems no middle way." The show ran until 30 March and proved triumphantly to be the first of these, though how deep a cult impression it had made would only become clear when Mackay put out an LP of the music.

The Blitz

Getting the music onto disc wouldn't prove easy, however. The original tapes were obviously unreleasable, not only because of their six-track mono sound but also because of union restrictions. A fully fledged re-recording was called for, but Mackay found himself handling the project almost unaided. "I think I can safely say, without fear of legal action, that EG were completely useless at dealing with it," he recalled in 2002, "and they really had no experience of the theatrical or television worlds. No one – neither Thames nor EG nor Island Records – was interested."

Thames were willing to finance the recording of a single, but Mackay wasn't to be fobbed off with anything less than an LP. Only when he was poised to mortgage his home did EG finally get behind the project, whereupon Mackay repaired to Basing Street with the three lead actresses, the four on-screen musicians and his backing vocalist friend 'Countess' Sadie Mackenzie. Recorded in January and February, the album was released in the final week of March and rocketed straight to Number One, reportedly selling 55,000 copies in less than 48 hours.

Accompanied by Rula Lenska and his wife Jane, Mackay had embarked on a TV and radio tour to promote the album, and was fulfilling an engagement in Birmingham when the startling news came through. Somehow, his humble *Rock Follies* album had seen off Paul McCartney's *Wings at the Speed of Sound* and, though subsequently displaced by Led Zeppelin, would come back the following week and displace Led Zeppelin in turn.

Mackay has since interpreted EG's reluctance to make the album as a craven act of obeisance to their chief asset: "I think EG were under some pressure from Bryan Ferry, who wasn't terribly happy about the possibility of me becoming more prominent or successful." If so, the outcome was more galling than Ferry could have imagined; Mackay had effectively produced a solo album only matched in commercial terms by Roxy's *Stranded*, and not matched at all by Ferry's own solo output. As a peculiar side-effect, however, *Rock Follies* would create an upsurge in membership (albeit not at the most opportune time) for Peter Leay's Liverpool-based Roxy Music Fan Club.

The series, meanwhile, wasn't received with open arms by all the TV critics, with some replicating the contempt of the rock press. On 8 April, Richard Alton noted in the *Evening News* that "*Rock Follies*, which has fortunately come to an end, was never anything but a disaster. It was ill conceived, badly written and lamentably cast. It is hard to believe that [director] Jon Scoffield, who turned out such shows as *The Stanley Baxter Picture Show*, was also responsible for this folly ... Bad language, promiscuity and drug-taking were essential ingredients all along. And, as if they hadn't already run the gamut of bad taste, they perpetrated a song called *Glenn Miller is Missing*."

In fact, *Glenn Miller is Missing* is probably the highlight of the accompanying LP, a dreamlike lament punctuated by Mackay's lilting soprano sax and graced by some of Schuman's most plangent lyrics. *Biba Nova* is beguiling too, a gently Reggaefied elegy to two recently defunct 1960s style monoliths, a trend-setting boutique and a lifestyle magazine respectively, with a jaunty Eddie Jobson violin solo thrown in for good measure. *Stairway* has a lovely string arrangement reminiscent of a John Barry production for Adam Faith (the strings were the responsibility of Barry alumnus Ray Russell), while the honking raunch of *Talking Pictures* and the spectral introduction to *Hot Neon* are equally engaging.

Much of the rest of the LP is workaday rock'n'roll of the kind satirised in the show (some of it sounds like low-budget Meat Loaf), underlining the bizarre Pirandellian trick Mackay had pulled off – that of sending up the music of his more clod-hopping contemporaries while simultaneously selling it in impressive numbers to a public who presumably didn't see the joke.

Mackay himself appeared in the sixth episode, when The Little Ladies are forced to reinvent themselves as The Victory Gals and trill an 'austerity rock' number called *War Brides*. Dressed up like a long-haired version of Private Pike in *Dad's Army*, he plays some sterling boogie-woogie tenor prior to the venue being blown up as part of an insurance scam. (The name Schuman gave to the ill-fated club here, The Blitz, would assume greater significance at the end of the decade.) There are plenty of other titbits for Roxy fans; not only does virtually every music paper featured on screen carry a Roxy headline, but Simon Jones, as a snooty club concierge, offers the following explanation for the failure of The Little Ladies' previous incarnation as vampish 1930s torch singers: "Remember, we opened in 1974. Now that's a long time ago. It was the heyday of the elegant renaissance – Bryan Ferry in his white dinner jacket – a great era." And then a sideswipe at Ferry's most recent 'GI' look: "They're victims of an elegance backlash. We're into hard times. The tastemakers are into khaki."

"As far as I am concerned the series kept its interest, its style and its edge right up to the closing titles," claimed Bernard Davies in *Broadcast*. "Howard Schuman is one of the few people writing for TV who recognises that we live in a confused world, that sacred cows are often either funny or pathetic, and that things look different through a satirical eye ... I would very sincerely like to see *Rock Follies* again," he added, "and I trust that Thames, who generally know a good thing when they see one, will realise that they have got hold of a good thing and behave accordingly."

The Real Life

Mackay wasn't totally preoccupied with *Rock Follies* in 1976; as well as being committed to Roxy's eleventh-hour tour of the US, he also produced Eddie and the Hot Rods' first single, a roaring remake of *Wooly Bully*, and contributed to the Pavlov's Dog LP *At the Sound of the Bell*. The inevitable call had already come through, however, from *Rock Follies'* producer Andrew Brown. "Andy Mackay and I were put under the most pleasant kind of pressure," Schuman recalled. "Would we write a sequel?" This request was hardly surprising, given that the show had won a BAFTA award over the head of the BBC's hotly tipped *I, Claudius*.

While the original series had anatomised a whole host of contemporary trends (most amusingly, a group of Camden commune dwellers with reading matter like 'The Psychopathology of Imperialism in Trinidad'), Schuman identified the show's governing theme as "the tangled relationships between men and women, on both the personal and corporate level." To that end, the beautifully differentiated performances of Julie Covington, Charlotte Cornwell and Rula Lenska had been supported by the variously repulsive or merely ineffectual men around them: vacillating activist (Billy Murray), hang-dog academic (Stephen Moore), vacuous surfer dude (Michael J Shannon), calculating manager (Emlyn Price), steadily disintegrating upper-class rock journalist (James Warwick) and oily mother's boy impresario (Michael Angelis). Now, claimed Schuman, "I suddenly saw that the sequel could focus on the tests and tensions of friendships between women and women."

Enter the inimitable Beth Porter and Little Nell as The Little Ladies' new hype-fixated manager and her space-cadet PA. The new series, *Rock Follies of '77*, would also contain a monstrous cameo for Tim Curry (a veteran, like Little Nell, of *The Rocky Horror Show*), playing a paranoid quasi-punk pomp rocker who sabotages The Little Ladies' support act. (Distinct shades of Jethro Tull again.) Also prominently featured were two gay characters (one of the actors involved, Denis Lawson, based his 'cropped hair and spectacles' look on Schuman himself), prompting Keith Howes of *Gay News* to hail the show as "a flashy bouquet of barbed wire tossed into the living rooms of the nation and aimed at scratching at the surface of feminism, sexism, drugs and homophobia within the record industry and beyond."

The new series had an increased budget and erred more towards fantasy musical sequences, providing an imaginative benchmark that would inform not only future television drama but also the fledgling field of rock video. (And not just in a general sense; among the most obvious *Rock Follies* 'quotes' was Kate Bush's 1980 video for *Breathing*, which replicated the first episode's *The Band Who Wouldn't Die* sequence.) "I do not find the songs particularly distinguished: what makes the hair prickle on the back of my neck is the *technique*," remarked Peter Buckman in the *Listener*. "The producer, Andrew Brown, has employed directors to make out of Howard Schuman's marvellous scripts something that is total television. That is – pictures that are intriguing, provocative, extraordinary and, above all, memorable. The subject is tatty, sordid, and often despicable even to the participants, but it is dealt with in a style that is truly new, at least on television."

Rock Follies of '77 began transmission on Wednesday 4 May 1977 but lost some impetus when it was suspended half-way through its run by a strike of Thames production assistants. The final three episodes were accordingly delayed until November and preceded by a two-hour digest of the first three to bring viewers back up to speed. There was a small adjustment, meanwhile, in The Little Ladies' backing band (Chris Parren replacing Brian Chatton on keyboards), with whom Mackay cut a second LP, this time put out through Polydor rather than Island.

Where the original LP had been a massive hit and its attendant singles (*Glenn Miller is Missing* and *Sugar Mountain*) had flopped, in 1977 the process was reversed: the album failed to repeat its forerunner's success but a single taken from it, *OK?*, outstripped even Ferry's contemporaneous *Tokyo Joe*. Despite being excluded from the playlists of both Radio 1 and Capital Radio, *OK?* entered the singles chart on 17 May, hitting a high of number ten two weeks later, and remaining in the Top 20 for four weeks of a six-week run. Mackay and Schuman had pulled off their Pirandellian trick yet again. Even more so than the original series, *Rock Follies of '77* was about the blurring of reality and illusion, and here was a song that in the fictional fabric of the show had been a flop. Yet in what Schuman dubbed "the real life," it became a sizable hit. "I'm writing songs about hyping – and hyping at the same time," he quipped.

It was well deserving its hit status, however, with a macho metallic tapestry that exemplified both series of *Rock Follies* through the raucous plaint of "You want to do me / But I don't want to be done, OK?" And *Jubilee*, fitted by Mackay with a flavoursome Caribbean backdrop, raised several eyebrows thanks to Schuman's inclusion of unemployment figures in his caustic lyric. Elsewhere, however, the new score doesn't contain anything quite as memorable as *Glenn Miller is Missing* or *Biba Nova*.

The belligerent mantra of "You want to do me / But I don't want to be done" attracted the attention of political commentators but still cut no ice whatever in the music press. In a piece for *New Society* headed 'Rock Political', Tony Gould applauded Schuman's awareness that "record companies are not noticeably different from any other big companies … Hence the opposition to the series in the music press, which is itself so much a part of the business that it is unable to stand back and examine the innate contradiction of a potentially liberating music in the grasp of capitalist enterprise … *New Musical Express*, for instance, recently got Suzi Quatro to put the boot in. But her wilful misrepresentation of the series (how many episodes did she see?) gave one little confidence in her views."

By the end of *Rock Follies of '77*, the bitter logic of Schuman's story has had its inevitable effect: Covington's obviously talented Dee discards Anna (Cornwell) and 'Q' (Lenska), heading off to the USA with a new partner, Rox (Sue Jones-Davies).

In "the real life," of course, Covington had already scored a Number One hit of her own with the original rendition of *Don't Cry for Me Argentina*. And, as the final episode went out, an appropriate epitaph was pronounced on the series by Clive James in the *Observer*: "*Rock Follies* had its low moments, but on the whole it deserves its reputation as one of the most original television series ever made. And on top of all that, it had Little Nell."

The Divorce

Unfortunately, the aftermath of *Rock Follies* was messy and undignified. The first reports that the constituent members of Rock Bottom (remember them?) weren't going to take the series lying down came as early as March 1976. Annabel Leventon, Diane Langton and Gaye Brown, together with their manager Don Fraser, could well have adopted "You want to do me / But I don't want to be done" as their own collective rallying cry. They insisted that Schuman had met Leventon, and discussed her notion of turning Rock Bottom's trials and tribulations into a television drama, way back in January 1974. And they weren't going to keep quiet about it.

The group's grievance centred around an agreement, drawn up in October, that any such series should feature them, and that Thames had dropped them on a mere technicality – namely, that Langton had elected to take a role in the West End production of *A Little Night Music*. The case finally came to court in October 1982, with the result that Rock Bottom were awarded substantial damages in an out-of-court settlement the following July.

March 1976 didn't merely bring the first rumblings of legal action, but also the first references to a projected big-screen version of *Rock Follies* – "not a small English picture," sniffed Schuman's agent, Jenne Casarotto, "but a big American picture." Progress was slow, however, and the outcome an unhappy one. Mackay was involved in the initial stages but, by the time Schuman's screenplay was completed in October 1978, the shifting musical landscape had entailed some radical alterations.

"We are looking for peak performers with demonic charisma to play members of a New Wave band," commented producer Davina Belling in the *Evening Standard*. "We don't want to make a spin-off, we want to make a new start." And by the following spring Belling was making it clear that The Little Ladies were long gone. "We have discarded them altogether. We now have a totally different group – three boys and a girl," she informed the *Daily Mail*. "It is not a film from the TV series and was never intended to be. There was some confusion because we had initially retained the title, but now that will go too. We haven't thought up the new title yet."

When filming finally began in October 1979, the new title was revealed as *Breaking Glass*, and the result was exactly the kind of "small English picture" Schuman's agent had pooh-poohed three years earlier. It can hardly have mattered to her by this stage, however, as Schuman himself was no longer associated with the project, screenplay credit going instead to director Brian Gibson. The punkette lead singer was played by Hazel O'Connor, and of the "three boys" one was played by bass guitarist Gary Tibbs, who, ironically, was then a member of the resurrected Roxy Music. Belling's soundbites of the "we want to make a new start" variety were presumably motivated by disquiet over the pending legal action surrounding *Rock Follies*; if so, the members of Rock Bottom had taken a proxy revenge on Schuman and Thames before the case even came to court.

In June 2005 came the announcement of Polydor's plans to create a new girl group via "a *Sex and the City*-style Channel 4 drama series about the band's exploits. The 13-part series, called *Totally Frank*, will follow the travails of four 21-year-old girls – together called Frank – as they struggle their way through the music business in London, trying to find gigs and survive in a cut-throat environment." The first girl to be cast, according to the *Guardian*'s Dave Simpson, was Jah Wobble's daughter Hayley, and "the obvious historical precedent is the hard-hitting 1980 film *Breaking Glass*, which made a real-life pop star out of Hazel O'Connor."

The obvious historical precedent, of course, was actually *Rock Follies*. Mackay had long since pointed to the success of Bananarama (their name, incidentally, a deliberate allusion to Roxy's *Pyjamarama*) as proof that the rock papers' second main objection to the series – its sheer 'three girls in a rock group' improbability – was a bogus one. Now he could add any number of millenial followers, from The Spice Girls and All Saints to Girls Aloud, Atomic Kitten, Sugababes, Destiny's Child, the list goes on. He doubted, however, that *Rock Follies* had contributed to female empowerment, given that the exploitative dealings of the music business were at least as prevalent in 2005 as they had been in 1976. But he could content himself with the fact that he had been a key player in a genuine television landmark. On top of which, he had become the first Roxy Music member after Ferry to become significantly wealthy from his association with rock music.

Thirteen: *The Central Shaft*

"It would be great to see 801 become a more permanent live fixture. I almost hope Roxy's sabbatical is extended indefinitely. Who needs Roxy Music now anyway?"
Angus MacKinnon, *NME* 13 November 1976

We are the 801

In the wake of *Another Green World*, Eno had been approached to write his first feature film scores. Back in 1970 he had provided the music for Malcolm Le Grice's *Berlin Horse*, a 16mm experimental short lasting a mere eight minutes. Now he scored a 90-minute feature for director Ken McMullen called *Resistance*, funded by the BFI Production Board in 1976, and the first film directed by Ken Russell's production designer of choice, Derek Jarman. This was *Sebastiane*, a groundbreaking film not only in its full-on homoerotica but also in that its dialogue was spoken in Latin. Eno's very first feature commission, however, had been a Costa Carayiannis potboiler called *The Devil's Men*, in which Donald Pleasence and Peter Cushing connoted Good and Evil in various far-fetched rituals staged in a Spartan cave.

In 1976, the kind of limpid subtleties brought to these scores would be showcased on an Eno album initially available only as a limited edition of 500 copies, a kind of ready-made sequence of so-called 'library music' called *Music for Films*. In the meantime, he was coaxed by Phil Manzanera into an increasingly rare foray, not only into rock'n'roll, but also live performance. Vaguely reminiscent of Richard Williams' *June 1, 1974* project, this new venture would prove considerably more powerful, giving rise to an LP described by *Rolling Stone* as very probably "the most vital live album of the decade."

Manzanera's idea was a suitably Eno-esque one: to get together a bunch of disparate musicians as a live act that would have a built-in sell-by date, and then simply see what happened. Retiring to Ludlow that summer, Manzanera and Eno were joined by Quiet Sun bassist Bill MacCormick and his journalist brother Ian MacDonald for what MacCormick termed a "think tank" devoted to track selection.

Lagrima, *Diamond Head* and *Miss Shapiro* were culled from Manzanera's solo album, *Rongwrong* from the Quiet Sun LP *Mainstream*, and the Eno selections were *Sombre Reptiles*, *Golden Hours*, *The Fat Lady of Limbourg*, *Baby's On Fire*, *I'll Come Running* and *Third Uncle*. *East of Asteroid*, meanwhile, was a conflation of Manzanera's *East of Echo* with Quiet Sun's *Mummy Was an Asteroid, Daddy Was a Small Non-Stick Kitchen Utensil*. They also hit upon The Kinks' *You Really Got Me* and, at MacCormick's suggestion, The Beatles' epoch-making *Tomorrow Never Knows*, here rechristened *TNK*.

The group name, 801, was based on a line from Eno's *The True Wheel*, eighth track on his *Taking Tiger Mountain* album. As he recounted it to MacDonald, in 1974 he had been in New York for a punishing round of promotional interviews, at one point falling into a mescaline-fuelled doze and having a dream "where this group of girls were singing to this group of sailors who had just come into port. And they were singing 'We are the 801 / We are the Central Shaft' – and I woke up absolutely jubilant because this was the first bit of lyric I'd written in this new style. Because I didn't know what it meant, but I got the feeling of 'Christ – this means something, this is interesting.'" The dream itself sounds similar to the farcical premise of *Seven Deadly Finns*, while the *NME*'s Miles helpfully pointed out that "801 in geomantic terms *is* the central shaft – Eno must have heard it somewhere." On top of all this, of course, eight-nought-one in acronymic terms spells e-n-o.

In addition to Manzanera, Eno and MacCormick, the chosen performers numbered keyboard player Francis Monkman (who had preceded Eddie Jobson in Sonja Kristina's group Curved Air), blues guitarist Lloyd Watson, recipient of a *Melody Maker* award and formerly a one-man support act to Roxy Music, and a young drummer named Simon Phillips, later to become a king among session percussionists.

An exacting three-week rehearsal period at Island's premises in St Peter's Square – during which the band tried out, but abandoned, *The True Wheel* itself – quickly demonstrated that the mixture of musicians was a combustible one. According to Manzanera, "there were conflicts, and I seem to remember that the whole thing almost went down the pan." Or, as MacCormick euphemistically put it: "There were some interesting creative tensions." Typical of these was a frustrating moment while rehearsing a tricky 13/8 section in *East of Asteroid*, during which Monkman, Phillips and MacCormick tried to 'count' it and the instinctive Eno insisted upon 'feeling' it.

Eno nevertheless found the process stimulating, enshrining as it did his cherished theory of the decisive effect chance events could have in art of all kinds. "For me, projects aren't really interesting if you can predict their outcome," he claimed. "One of the most encouraging things, actually, about our recent rehearsals has been that something has been happening that none of us anticipated."

Peak after peak

After a discreet warm-up gig at the West Runton Pavilion in the Norfolk seaside resort of Cromer, the group appeared at the Reading Festival on Saturday 28 August, forming part of a Bank Holiday Weekend bash also graced by Rory Gallagher, Sutherland Brothers & Quiver, Eddie and the Hot Rods, The Enid and AC/DC, among others. The billing read "PHIL MANZANERA featuring Eno, Bill McCormack [sic], Lloyd Watson & Simon Phillips", both Francis Monkman and the collective name going unmentioned. According to MacCormick, Monkman's omission from the bill almost turned out to be a self-fulfilling prophecy, entailing a frantic last-minute redistribution of parts prior to Monkman's long-delayed arrival at the site.

Despite this, they were rewarded with a volley of praise, Mo Geller in *NME* hailing them for "the most interesting and adventurous music of the day. For a too, too short three quarters of an hour they hit peak after peak. Bright jazzy guitar runs, jaggedly staccato or sweetly mellifluous, powerhouse drumming, dazzling individual work, overwhelming unison and really rocking harder than anyone else the whole day." The redoubtable John Peel, whose early championing of Roxy Music seemed like a distant memory, pointed out in *Sounds* that "for me the musical highpoint of the weekend [was] the set played by Phil Manzanera, Eno et al. In these days, when predictability is prized above all other things, these musicians are a rare breed indeed."

Some lucrative dates in France, meanwhile, had been cancelled owing to Giscard d'Estaing's blanket ban on rock concerts in response to a Marseille riot; as a result, it was decided that the Island Mobile should be present at the band's final gig in the hope that a live album might make the whole enterprise financially worthwhile. This took place on the following Friday, 3 September, at London's Queen Elizabeth Hall, with further panegyrics ensuing. "Despite some appallingly distracting lighting effects," reported Hugh Fielder in *Sounds*, "the band showed most punk groups exactly where they should get off."

After this apotheosis, Manzanera was as good as his word and disbanded the group, moving on to share guitar duties with Chris Spedding on Bryan Ferry's upcoming *In Your Mind* tour. Phillips went on to work with Jack Bruce, Monkman returned to session work (eventually joining Sky and composing the score for the seminal British gangster movie *The Long Good Friday*), and Eno travelled to Berlin for a highly charged collaboration with David Bowie that would result in the albums *Low* and *"Heroes"*. They left behind them, however, the remarkable *801 Live* album, issued in November.

"I've only played it once," Eno remarked to Miles, "and I must admit I don't like it very much" – an estimate which was to place him in a very small minority.

A more typical judgment was Richard Williams' in *Melody Maker*: "Along with [Stevie Wonder's] *Songs in the Key of Life*, it's this winter's essential purchase."

From the eerie opener *Lagrima*, in which the original's guitar-oboe delicacy is replaced by a monolithic wedge of fuzz guitar, the set shifts into a spectacular reworking of *Tomorrow Never Knows*, graced by a mesmeric build-up of eccentric harpsichord runs from Monkman, the supple athleticism of MacCormick's bass, and the metallic upward inflection of Manzanera's guitar. The other cover version, *You Really Got Me*, is handled with real brawn, Eno's Morse Code pitter-patter and adenoidal vocal matched by the bludgeoning assault of Phillips' drums and a colossal Manzanera guitar riff. *Third Uncle* – unfortunately stripped of Eno's introductory comment that it was "the fastest song ever written" – is psychotic in its intensity, with MacCormick burbling hypnotically below a blisteringly energised guitar soundstage. *Rongwrong*, on the other hand, becomes a beautifully measured ballad with Soft Machine trimmings and Eno's voice at its most plangent.

A beautifully measured ballad *Rongwrong* certainly wasn't in its original incarnation on the *Mainstream* LP, and this remains one of the 801 album's most valuable features – all the tracks will be familiar to hardcore Roxy devotees, but not in the thoroughly transmogrified versions given here. *Rongwrong* segues seamlessly into a deliciously steamy rendition of *Sombre Reptiles*, all funkily syncopated rhythm boxes ranged against another monstrous guitar riff; from there into a quirkily lighthearted take on *Baby's On Fire*, transformed by Watson's slide guitar and certainly superior to Eno's *June 1, 1974* rendition; and finally into the climactic killer combination of *Diamond Head* and *Miss Shapiro*.

Two further tracks, *Golden Hours* and *The Fat Lady of Limbourg*, were added to Manzanera's 1999 reissue of the album, the former a winsome delight with one of Eno's most engaging vocal performances, the latter a slow-paced study in lugubrious, steadily building menace. Yet another track, *I'll Come Running*, was culled from 801's Reading performance and fetched up on an 'official' German bootleg called *Dalí's Car*, a collection otherwise given over to Eno's fascinating 1974 collaboration with The Winkies.

The 801 project raised Manzanera's prestige considerably; in *Rolling Stone* he was hailed as "one of the world's last psychedelic guitarists" and for having "created one of the last – and best – psychedelic bands in the world." Bill MacCormick's estimate of the enterprise was more down to earth. "It was great fun and the album [was] incredibly cheap to produce," he told Stephen Yarwood. "It was one of the top-selling imports to the USA that year; I could never understand why Island didn't release it over there. It still sells and the royalty cheques still come in."

Beatles through 10cc

As it turned out, the formation of 801 was merely an offshoot of the long-drawn-out gestation of Manzanera's next studio album, which he had been tinkering with since December 1975. Credited to Phil Manzanera/801, *Listen Now!!* was finally completed in July 1977, its stellar cast including all of the live 801 team bar Watson, plus Mel Collins, Dave Mattacks of Fairport Convention, Eddie Jobson, Paul Thompson and Dave Skinner. In addition, there was the 10cc team of Kevin Godley and Lol Creme, plus the Split Enz team of Tim Finn and Eddie Rayner.

"801 was a good outlet for songs that Phil and I had got together," recalled Bill MacCormick. "By this time he'd bought Manzanera Towers, as we called it, a huge house over in Chertsey. We just used to go over there and spend days working on various new ideas. *Listen Now!!* came out of a lot of half-finished things that Phil had, which Ian [MacDonald] and I took away to write lyrics and melody lines for and generally knock into shape."

Eno was roped in, too, eventually contributing to four tracks on the finished product. His diary for a slightless listless Monday in early 1977 (probably 17 January and reproduced in the *NME*'s 'Eight Days a Week' column) noted that: "In the afternoon Phil Manzanera and Bill MacCormick visit. Phil talks about his album-to-be, which shows signs of being very impressive ... Then we visit Paul Rudolph (Hawkwind's talented bass player), since I had suggested that he might be able to lend Phil a Teac four-track recorder, Phil's having exploded with surprise at his new guitar sounds ... On returning, we listen to David's new album. We talk about his continual ability to defy prediction and his ability to knot together the many disparate strings of new music."

If Bowie's *Low* album defied expectations, Manzanera's *Listen Now!!* would do the same for anyone anticipating a repeat of the savage Prog Rock propagated by the live 801. Instead, there's a peculiar clash between sunny melodies and shiny textures on the one hand, and grimly doom-laden lyrics on the other. Jon Savage's estimate in *Sounds*, that "at times the album reeks of Beatles through 10cc – it's no accident that Kevin Godley and Lol Creme appear – tempered with Manzanera quirkiness," is pretty accurate; unfortunately, it's sometimes hard to discount Ira Robbins' verdict in *Trouser Press* that the music is "radio-ready but barely sentient."

This is odd given the heavyweight talents involved. MacCormick, for example, had stood as Liberal candidate for Beckenham and had since ventured into journalism, appearing in the paper to which his brother Ian had long been a star contributor, the *NME*. A piece on football hooligans and an anti-nuclear interview with Julie Christie passed without much comment, but a negative article about the growth of the National Front garnered him a death threat from Manchester, together with Special Branch protection. All this fed into the Orwellian gloom of *Listen Now!!* "It's not a barrel of laughs," MacCormick later admitted, pointing out also that "The mid-1970s in Britain were a pretty dodgy time politically. There was a feeble Labour government and a big resurgence of extreme Right Wing politics in the case of the National Front ... The content of quite a lot of the lyrics reflected that."

The songs range from the blatantly political (*Listen Now, Law and Order, City of Light*) to gentler, more personal items like *Flight 19* and *Postcard Love*. All are dazzlingly performed, with the mournful *Postcard Love* a real standout and the brutish heft of the message songs equally striking. But the schizophrenia of the album is exemplified by the sweet but featureless vocals of Simon Ainley, another Old Alleynian who had sent a demo tape to Manzanera on spec. If the coupling of Ainley's choirboy delivery with MacCormick's bitter social commentary was meant to unsettle the listener, it doesn't quite work. The failure can perhaps be attributed to Manzanera's own vacillation about producing the kind of hard-hitting LP MacCormick had in mind. "Though the lyrics are doomy, I approached it from an optimistic point of view," he told Ian Birch at the time. "That's why I felt justified putting a very melodic instrumental in the middle, to inject my peaceful side."

The track Manzanera was referring to, *Island*, is a deliciously relaxed piece that's fully the equal of the title track to his first solo collection. *Initial Speed* is a dazzling bit of ear-misdirection, with Godley & Creme's much-touted new sampling device, the 'Gizmo', well to the fore. (Godley was Manzanera's next-door neighbour in Chertsey, and the 10cc comparisons noted by Jon Savage are most audible in the vocal fades of *Initial Speed* and *That Falling Feeling*, both of which are basically *I'm Not in Love*.) The downbeat *City of Light* resonates to the Floyd-like sound of Manzanera conducting a guitar battle with himself, and even the infectiously melodic *Flight 19* details a collapsed love affair in which 'Johnny' determines to join the titular squadron bound for the Bermuda Triangle.

Issued on 23 September, the album was preceded a fortnight earlier by a single matching *Flight 19* with the wittily titled instrumental *Car Rhumba*. (The latter turned up much later as a bonus track on Manzanera's CD reissue of *Diamond Head*.) Estimates of the album ranged from "Listen now and you're going to like it without thinking" (*Record Mirror*) to "a dark, moody canvas reminiscent of Pink Floyd" (*Rolling Stone*). In retrospect, vocalist Simon Ainley remained just as positive, insisting that *"Listen Now!!* was a great album. It had a mood to it, rather dispassionate and cold with a hard edge; it was finely crafted with lots of overdubs and fine tuning. I did loads of takes for the vocals, it all had to be note perfect."

Manzanera then took 801 out on the road again, but the band was a less super-charged one than the model that had so wowed the music press 12 months earlier. Comprising Ainley, MacCormick, Dave Skinner and Manzanera's old Roxy colleague Paul Thompson, the group also recorded a Peel session on Monday 14 November; the tracks, broadcast on the 22nd, were *Law and Order*, *That Falling Feeling*, *Remote Control* and a surprise rendition of Roxy's *Out of the Blue*. Manzanera later put out two of the concerts on CD, a Manchester University performance graced by special guests Andy Mackay and Godley & Creme, together with a Hull one featuring Eddie Jobson.

The Godley & Creme association, incidentally, was by no means confined to the *Listen Now!!* enterprise. In 1978, Mackay would contribute to their *L* album, and the following year Manzanera would play on, and partly produce, its follow-up, *Freeze Frame*.

Time and tide is on my side

If *Listen Now!!* was a long time gestating, Eno's fourth and final Progressive Rock album drove its author to a virtual nervous breakdown in the two-year attempt to produce something as groundbreaking as *Another Green World*.

He was hardly idle during this period, however, producing the first Ultravox album (released by Island in 1977 and called simply *Ultravox!*), writing three film scores, and collaborating with Manzanera on the 801 project and David Bowie on *Low* and *"Heroes"*. The latter's working methods, which would see a whole album's worth of backing tracks committed to tape in a matter of days, astonished Eno, who was simultaneously juggling with some 120 pieces intended for his new album and crashing despairingly through no fewer than three deadlines.

Something of his perfectionist vacillation is indicated by this diary entry from January 1977: "I arrange studio time with Penny Hanson at Island Studios, and breathe a sigh of relief when she says there is no time until March. If there had been time earlier, I would have taken it, but somehow I'm glad there isn't. I have just the right amount of time for preparation this way." His retrospective summary of the process was a simple one: "I was going mad."

The process of creating what would come to be called *Before and After Science* involved not only the intimidating shade of *Another Green World* but also an anxious review of his entire output so far, right back to the proto-punk stylings of *Here Come the Warm Jets*. "In talking so much about that album – in New York alone I did 48 interviews – I came to examine my methods very closely and began to see what worked and what didn't," he told Cynthia Dagnal. "In so doing I rejected about half the avenues of approach suggested in that record. *Some of Them Are Old*, for example, which really makes me squirm to hear now – the lyrics are so stupid. Although oddly enough the mood of that number seems to have come back on this new record I've just finished, *Before and After Science*."

The mood Eno referred to has been glossed by Eric Tamm as "hymn-like," a stately, sonorous wash of sound that Eno would perfect on his ambient albums, by which time he'd finally rejected the distracting lyrics he always found so troublesome. Like the Bowie records he had helped to create, *Before and After Science* is neatly divided between frenetic rockers on Side One and the woozy, pointilliste drift of Side Two. The tracks here, as Eno put it, are "sort of post-atomic tracks. They're all about the sea, in fact."

Elaborating on the notion of drift as an index to his working methods as well as the resultant sound, he noted that "*Another Green World* is like space travel in the sense of *aimed* exploration. *Before and After Science* is sea travel in the sense of putting oneself into a current and allowing oneself to drift." The pervading impression is of an intense water-borne melancholy, a kind of super-compressed version of the journey Roxy themselves underwent in the gap between *Sea Breezes* and its 1980s counterpart, *Tara*.

Though little more than refinements of his earlier work, the rockers are as bracingly off-centre as ever, with the exotic opener, *No One Receiving*, utilising the 'lost in space' ambience of Bowie's *Space Oddity* against a clanking disco rhythm. Second up, the hyperactive *Backwater* features more of Eno's trademark nonsense imagery, his expert juggling of euphonious words like logistics, heuristics and mystics being rather more engaging than his slightly tinny synthetic brass samples.

Kurt's Rejoinder is an alluring quasi-jazz fragment propelled by Percy Jones' "analogue delay bass" and a sampled vocal from the long-dead Dadaist Kurt Schwitters, *Energy Fools the Magician* is a querulous forecast of the sonorities featured on Side Two, and *King's Lead Hat* is Eno's final effort in the psychotic rocker style introduced on *Here Come the Warm Jets*. Manzanera's rhythm guitar keeps up a choppy counterpoint to Robert Fripp's obsessively circling solo, synthetic hand-claps resonate throughout, and the concluding whirlpool of synthesiser pyrotechnics seems like an updated version of *Editions of You*. The title is an anagrammatic tribute to Talking Heads, and the lyric is, again, inspired in its impenetrability.

The ambient flow of Side Two is introduced by the sparkling but overlong *Here He Comes* and includes the contemplative mood pieces *Through Hollow Lands* and *By This River*, the latter a collaboration with Achim Roedelius and Möbi Moebius of the German group Cluster. *Spider and I* is in Eno's most haunting majestic-ecclesiastical vein, and the tranquilised sound tapestry of *Julie with...* is arguably his most gorgeously evocative piece of all, its six-and-a-half-minute duration conjuring film-like visuals and graced by some of his most indelible lyrics.

Credited for the first time to Brian Eno rather than merely Eno, the album was issued in December and rapturously received. "Brian Eno," pronounced Vivien Goldman in *Sounds*, "will always continue to create the inspirational fusions that are late Seventies source music." Critical plaudits in the US were equally enthused, including "the perfect Eno album" (*Creem*), "one of the most important techno-rock albums yet produced" (*Cashbox*) and "the record Pink Floyd could make if they set their collective mind to it" (*Down Beat*).

Given the agonising birth pangs attached to *Before and After Science*, Eno was moved to change direction on finishing it. "I suspect that I've come to the end of a way of working with this record," he told Ian MacDonald in the run-up to its release. Except for his involvement with New Wave acts like Talking Heads, the evanescent drift of *Through Hollow Lands* would henceforth predominate in his work, removing him entirely from the rock landscape still occupied by his former associates in Roxy Music.

Fourteen: *Sign of the Times*

"There are so many utterly mediocre talents being acclaimed at the moment that I have no real fears for my reputation ... I know how good I am, and as long as I have faith in myself, I'll continue. And, as far as I'm concerned at the moment, everybody else can just go and fuck themselves."

Bryan Ferry, quoted in *Melody Maker* 16 September 1978

Look Ma, how unlike Bryan Ferry

With his film star looks and longtime veneration for the glamour of Hollywood, it was hardly surprising that Ferry should consider extending his dominion to the world of cinema. In July 1974, with Jack Clayton's film of *The Great Gatsby* having recently been released, he mused: "Gatsby – now there was a part I always felt a great kinship towards. Seeing the finished product was one of the great all-time tragedies, watching an utter lightweight like Robert Redford stumbling through the part of the heaviest character ever written. I always had this great desire to play Gatsby. Actually I've no time for the so-called 'new breed' of American actor – the Redfords and Steve McQueens. I've always been more enamoured by the old hands."

Among these Ferry listed Montgomery Clift, James Stewart and Humphrey Bogart, as well as homegrown heart-throbs Dirk Bogarde and Laurence Harvey.

("Really though," he added, "the best are American because the English ones are too domestic, dont you think?") In the mid 1970s, film offers did come in, but not always from the exalted likes of Jack Clayton. Britain's maverick exploitation maestro Pete Walker, the man behind skittish sex flicks like *The Four Dimensions of Greta* and unusually gruelling horror melodramas like *House of Whipcord*, tried to engage Ferry's services for at least two of his cutting-edge shockers, *Schizo* in 1976 and *The Comeback* the following year. "Well, he would have been perfect," Walker recollected in 2004. "I always felt he looked so much more like a film star than a rock star. But it's difficult with rock stars; they're always off touring somewhere and so it proved with Bryan Ferry."

The parts went in the end to John Leyton (remembered for his 1961 Number One hit *Johnny Remember Me*) and US easy-listening icon Jack Jones, the latter playing a pop star terrorised by the elderly parents of a deceased fan and described by one critic as looking like "Robert Redford with Val Doonican's teeth." Walker's choice of pop stars was clearly not always as finger-on-the-pulse as his courting of Ferry; one unrealised project around this time was a rock-opera remake of *Svengali* starring the faux-mesmeric Alvin Stardust. Walker entered a very different world in 1978, however, when another unrealised project, *A Star is Dead*, was mooted as a vehicle for The Sex Pistols.

If the emergence of aggressive new groups like the Pistols posed a problem for Pete Walker, it potentially posed an even greater one for Bryan Ferry. Bill Grundy's notorious clash with the group on the *Today* programme of 1 December 1976 was to become as seismic, in its way, as the opening night of *Look Back in Anger* on 8 May 1956. On that occasion, well-heeled dramatist Terence Rattigan, master of the 'well-made' play, commented that all John Osborne's drama amounted to was a case of "Look Ma, how unlike Terence Rattigan I'm being." With his white-tuxedoed image by now burnt irretrievably into the public mind, Ferry could well have thought something similar about the swastikaed and safety-pinned insurgents currently putting up two fingers to the complacencies of the rock establishment.

It's unlikely, however, that Ferry was as astute in assessing the threat of punk rock as Rattigan was in sensing the danger posed by the kitchen sink. "A lot of it seems manipulated and I find most of it dreadful," Ferry airily pronounced in the decidedly non-punk publication, *Miss London*. "When I look at what's going on around me I'd rather buy my own records than a lot of other people's." Twenty years later, he would confide to Michael Bracewell that "I liked the energy of punk, and the hair – but not much of the music. I was trying to be more musical at that time."

Indeed, the end of 1976 saw Ferry in typically backward-looking mode, contributing a winsome cover of The Beatles' *She's Leaving Home* to the bizarre 20th Century-Fox folly *All This and World War II*. Released in November (and pretty much buried from view ever since), Susan Winslow's film juxtaposed Movietone newsreel footage of the Second World War with all-star covers of popular Beatles tunes, frequently to spectacularly tasteless effect. The other artists involved constituted a starry roll-call at least as irrelevant to emergent punk rockers as Ferry himself: Elton John (whose version of *Lucy in the Sky with Diamonds* became a hit), Jeff Lynne, Helen Reddy, Leo Sayer, Peter Gabriel, The Bee Gees, David

Essex, The Four Seasons, Lynsey de Paul, The Brothers Johnson, Keith Moon, Rod Stewart, Tina Turner, Roy Wood, even Frankie Laine. The original double-LP soundtrack album has yet to make it to CD, presumably because of the music rights tangle represented by so many high-profile artists and so many Lennon-McCartney evergreens.

Positively Ritz

Having spent Christmas in Texas with Jerry Hall's family, Ferry kicked off 1977 with the release of his first self-penned solo single, *This is Tomorrow*. The titular reference to Richard Hamilton's 1956 ICA exhibition of the same name seems like a purely arbitrary nod to Ferry's Pop Art influences, given that the track itself is little more than an unashamed (and largely unironic) bid for US airplay.

Fading up to a benighted chorus of crickets and cicadas, the song has the bluesy feel of a nocturnal jam session conducted in a Louisiana bayou, together with some characteristically astute lyrics from Ferry. Apparently predicting the 1980s rise of MTV, he paints an evocative picture of a man marooned in a motel until jerked into life by a futuristic music channel on the television. With its engaging clod-hopping beat and corkscrew Chris Spedding guitar solo, *This is Tomorrow* began a nine-week run in the singles chart on 1 February, reaching number nine on 8 March. So far so good.

Where *This is Tomorrow* had contained a rare Ferry-Jobson collaboration, *As the World Turns*, on its flip side, a further single release, *Tokyo Joe*, rescued Ferry's version of *She's Leaving Home* from the copyright nightmare of the *All This and World War II* soundtrack. Providing a nod to Ferry's fascination with all things Eastern (a fascination predating even Roxy's adoption of Sadistic Mika Band as their *Siren* support act), *Tokyo Joe* occupied the singles chart for seven weeks, arriving on 10 May and hitting a high of 15 on 7 June. With its weedy opening swish of Oriental gongs and whingeing guitar lines, the song smacks more of TV's cartoon hero *Hong Kong Phooey* than the expected comparisons with *Virginia Plain*. The keyboards provide a stuttering reminiscence of *Pyjamarama*'s Morse Code signals, while Ann Odell's string arrangement is lifted lock, stock and barrel from Silver Convention's delightful 1976 disco smash, *Get Up and Boogie*. The bovver-boot percussion is diverting, however, and Ferry's pen-portrait of a predatory dockside Geisha is even more so.

Between these two singles came the March release of their parent album, *In Your Mind*, which reached number five in the charts but also revealed that the singles were all one really needed. As Ferry's first solo collection of original songs, it provided a depressing indication of the mediocrity into which Roxy would likely have fallen had they pressed on after *Siren*. Though Roxy personnel are included in the album's non-committal 'thanks' list (which rounds up a whopping 20 musicians in all), the *NME*'s Julie Burchill was quick to point out the telling non-appearance of arguably Ferry's most abrasive Roxy cohort. "Here we have The Great Paul Thompson," she wrote, "but my favourite (and the prettiest) Roxyperson, Andy Mackay, is conspicuous by his absence." She also slapped an entirely appropriate epitaph on the LP with her description of it as "definitely lobbyfodder Muzak, but positively Ritz."

After the opening salvo of *This is Tomorrow*, *All Night Operator* shows all too clearly the direction in which the album is headed. A pretty melody and an affecting lyric reminiscent of the William Bell-Judy Clay soul classic *Private Number* are thoroughly annihilated by a flat and flavourless production job and, in particular, the twee interjections of Mel Collins' soprano sax. *One Kiss* is a melancholic dirge with the doleful swing of an Irish folk song and a drum pattern outro swiped from, of all things, Bowie's *Five Years*. *Party Doll* is engaging enough, despite the uninspired backing, and sports a punning fusion of Greek mythology with Marcel Proust in Ferry's reference to Leda and the 'Swann'. On the evidence of this album, however, Ferry was no doubt reminding punk rockers less of Proust's Swann than Britain's dinner-suited musical duo Flanders & Swann.

The title track is a grandiloquent but windy slab of faux-stadium rock, Ferry's lyric a confusing melange of Prog Rock-style gibberish complete with incongruous references to France's nouvelle vague and namechecks for a Kubrick film (*Paths of Glory*) and a Coward play (*Present Laughter*). Only *Love Me Madly Again* and *Rock of Ages* rise above the general mediocrity, though the former devolves into a featureless instrumental outro lacking any of the familiar Roxy pyrotechnics. The remainder of the track, however – complete with eloquent strings, hectoring brass and muscular guitars – is more persuasive. *Rock of Ages*, by contrast, has a fascinating intro, over a minute of mast-creaking sound effects gradually encroached upon by throbbing synths and bass guitar. But then the workaday brass section blasts in to paste the song into predictable MOR anonymity. Even the opening, on reflection, seems like a pale shadow of its probable inspiration: the thunderous slave-ship atmosphere cooked up by Gamble & Huff for The O'Jays' 1973 epic *Ship Ahoy*.

As with *Siren*, Ferry just hasn't got what it takes here to compete with inspirational US producers like Gamble & Huff, and with the instrumental input of Roxy Music stripped away to boot, *In Your Mind* becomes a deadening plod that even Ferry wrote off as "my least successful album by a long chalk," adding "It all sounds very square to me." Worse, Ferry himself sounds sheepish and self-conscious on it, utterly belying the gritty, back-to-basics, neon-lit look of his cover photo. Though begun by Chris Thomas, production chores were eventually shared out between Ferry and Steve Nye, and the album's compromised sound is clearly a product of the pressure Ferry was under – from his own management as well as Atlantic Records – to come up with an American-sounding album.

Appropriately, *Rolling Stone*'s John Milward hailed *In Your Mind* as "by far his best solo album, and at its peaks there are indications that Ferry may well be able to pull the existential wool over the eyes of the rock audience without his steely former sidemen." The trusty Allan Jones stoutly maintained in *Melody Maker*, meanwhile, that "I'll be quite amazed if any of Ferry's contemporaries produce an album to rival its compelling excellence."

Brian Eno, however, was busy making such unguarded panegyrics seem thoroughly ludicrous, at least to the cold eye of posterity. Burying the three-year-old hatchet, he had apparently expressed an interest in being involved with *In Your Mind* but had gone off instead to Berlin, where he collaborated with David Bowie on the seismic LPs *Low* and *"Heroes"*. By comparison to albums like these, Ferry's new one looked even more threadbare.

Big in Japan ... and Australia

In the wake of several solo dates the previous autumn, EG now concocted a world tour starting on Monday 7 February with a three-day tenure of the Royal Albert Hall. Ferry's band included guitarists Chris Spedding and Phil Manzanera, plus Paul Thompson on drums and John Wetton on bass. The set list naturally favoured the current solo album, but room was found for three Roxy titles – *Love is the Drug*, *Casanova* and the never-performed-by-Roxy *Could It Happen to Me?* "Ferry appeared to tremendous applause," reported Allan Jones, "turned out like Marlon Brando in the movie of Damon Runyon's *Guys and Dolls*: cool and casually sinister." Jones also reserved high praise for Spedding, who proved "that he is, with his nonchalant pigeon-toed stance, the Hank B Marvin of the Blank Generation."

After further UK and European dates, the Ferry entourage hit Japan for two gigs, one of them at the 2000-capacity Sun Palace. Here Ferry obligingly made a horse's arse of himself by posing for the local paparazzi in Kabuki gear, appeared on the *Young Music Show* for Japanese TV, and took advantage of a two-day break to luxuriate in the punkah-walla'd colonial splendour of Singapore's legendary Raffles Hotel. He admitted, however, that Japanese record sales were "terrible". "Island's not very good over there," he told *Record Mirror*'s Sheila Prophet. "They're distributed by a big Japanese company which has a huge domestic catalogue but doesn't do much for foreign acts. But the concerts went down well – we seem to have a loyal following there."

A gruelling Australian itinerary came next (though Ferry was buoyed up by *In Your Mind*'s firm residency at Number One in the local LP charts), after which the tour was rounded off with a three-week US stint. Ferry pressed ahead with these Stateside dates despite Atlantic's pusillanimous suggestion that he cut his losses and cancel them. "I'm amazed how ineffectual they are," Ferry grumbled of Atlantic. "I thought the album would do well over here because Americans like things very punchy and it was the punchiest thing I've done." In fact, *In Your Mind* climbed to number 126 on the *Billboard* chart, hardly a world-beater but still Ferry's highest US score to date. "To be honest," he later confided, "I lost an absolute fortune on that tour. The gigs were mostly good, but there was a terrible problem with Atlantic ... They didn't think there was a suitable single from *In Your Mind*, and therefore they decided not to support the tour."

Soon afterwards, Ferry was dealt a further blow by a London Weekend documentary series called *All You Need is Love*. Directed by Tony Palmer (who four years earlier had enthused to *Observer* readers that "Only Roxy Music seems to have caught the seediness [of rock'n'roll] quite so accurately"), the series came complete with the editorial musings of *Creem* magazine supremo Lester Bangs. And in the cumbersomely titled episode *'Whatever Gets You Through the Night' – Glitter Rock*, Bangs let rip. Broadcast on Saturday 28 May, the programme intercut footage of Roxy's 1975 tour with a Bangs diatribe seemingly motivated by a mere social gaffe on Ferry's part.

"In Roxy Music you see the triumph of artifice," he began, "because what they are about is that they're not about anything. Musically they're an incredibe synthesis of a lot of different things, but I think that their vitality and their longevity will be quite limited due to the fact that the leader of the group is this fellow named Bryan Ferry, who is possibly the most vacuous excuse for a superstar that has yet been presented to us. Now, you know, I became a big Roxy Music fan when they did *Stranded*. And after that it was my unfortunate experience to meet Mr Ferry at a party, where I wanted to go up and say, 'Bryan Ferry, you're my hero, I love you! Great record!' Well, this fellow was so bland that he was standing there in this white tuxedo with a cigarette in his hand, you know, not saying anything. Somebody should've shoved him in a corner, shoved a Martini in his hand and forgotten about him.

"And he doesn't care about rock'n'roll at all," Bangs added. "The ascendance of these people is an indication of the level to which rock has sunk, because it's appearance and artifice. There's nothing, I believe, truly committed about either Bryan Ferry or David Bowie. It's much more [a] using of rock for their own ego-aggrandisement, rather than a belief in the music they're working with."

Although musings on 'artifice' and 'commitment' were sounding ridiculously old-fashioned by 1977 (and were being anatomised in satirical vein by the Schuman-Mackay project *Rock Follies of '77* at exactly the same time), Ferry might reasonably have been stung by this attack. Equally stung fans, however, could divert their attention to the programme's invaluable clips of the band performing *Sea Breezes*, *Editions of You* and *Both Ends Burning*, not to mention footage of a typically diffident Ferry accounting for his use of scantily clad covergirls. Ferry could take solace, perhaps, in the fact that Bangs didn't really have a good word for anyone featured in the programme; Elton John, Emerson Lake & Palmer, Alice Cooper, none escaped the Lester lash.

Though presumably never recovering from being 'cut' by a toffee-nosed Brit in a white tuxedo, Bangs would later become an enthusiastic supporter of Ferry's sometime collaborator, Brian Eno – though not without some initial distrust. "Me, I'm a modern guy," he had written in *Village Voice* apropos Eno's *Another Green World*, "but not so modern I don't still like music with really heavily defined *content* that you can actively *listen* to in the *foreground*." By the time of his early death in April 1982, however, Bangs had reportedly become such a convert that he was working on a book about Eno.

Out of season, out of sorts

After his *In Your Mind* exertions, a physically and emotionally exhausted Ferry retired with Jerry Hall to Los Angeles, selling his Kensington home to comic actor John Cleese and moving into a Bel Air hacienda formerly occupied by *Gigi* herself, Leslie Caron. There he played tennis with MOR producer Richard Perry, became friendly with counterculture guru Dr Timothy Leary, and earmarked Waddy Wachtel, guitar god with such artists as Linda Ronstadt and Jackson Browne, for his next solo album. By September, he was responding to the *Sun*'s queries regarding a Roxy reunion with the categorical statement, "The success of my solo tour means that Roxy is certainly dead and buried now. There would be no point in our working together again as a band. But I'm not sad about it."

In reality, Ferry was by no means as arrogant as such soundbites made him seem. Now that he was finally living the indolent poolside life depicted on the

Another Time, Another Place sleeve, the man who had written *In Every Dream Home a Heartache* found himself succumbing to the deadening emotional vacuum represented by late-1970s Hollywood. This was a town fascinated by the seamy drama of Roman Polanski's arraignment for sexual offences conducted at Jack Nicholson's dream home, which was certainly a more gripping scenario than the computerised product of its own studios. (One of which, a ghastly Robert Stigwood adaptation of *Sgt Pepper's Lonely Hearts Club Band*, was being worked on by Ferry's writer friend Henry Edwards.) "I felt terribly alien there, and the atmosphere made me, if it's possible, even more introspective than I've felt before," Ferry later admitted.

Ferry was far from idle during his enervating six-month Tinseltown spell; indeed, by November he was at the Mountain studio in Montreux with a full set of newly perfected songs to record. It was here, however, that he heard of Hall's defection to Mick Jagger, an emotional calamity since taken in tabloid circles as the defining moment of Ferry's life. This is no less absurd than the idea that the resultant LP, *The Bride Stripped Bare*, was a desolate heart-cry in direct response to Hall's betrayal. The latter assumption is hardly likely given the fact that all the tracks on it bar *When She Walks in the Room* were written before the news filtered through.

The album's executive producer, Simon Puxley, pointed out, in any case, that Ferry's relationship with Hall – begun on the night after her seaside posturing for the *Siren* cover had been photographed – had since become "a prison ship" and was likely to run aground sooner rather than later. He conceded, however, that the atmosphere in Montreux "was so depressing that I flew back to have Christmas Day in London. But Bryan refused to leave and had Christmas Day all by himself, playing up the tragedy. I remember we drove to a New Year's party at Gstaad – the usual sort of girls-and-cocaine party of those days – through blinding snow and no conversation."

Very different from Roxy's triumphal visit to Montreux in April 1973, the out-of-season ambience of the Palace Hôtel was intense to begin with, and all the more so after the news of Hall's departure. "The only thing to do there was to make music. There were no distractions. It turned out to be the strangest album I've ever done," Ferry told Allan Jones. "There was such a crazed atmosphere in Montreux. There was this band of musicians just stuck there. Like an Everest expedition or something. A real *Men Without Women* number ... It was possibly the most soulful musical experience I've ever been through. It was very remote and very lonely and very crazed."

In the early months of 1978, Ferry accordingly found himself with enough material for a double album, precipitating a crisis of confidence regarding what should go on the album and what shouldn't. As a result, there was a six-month delay in releasing *The Bride Stripped Bare*, its title offering a fairly obscure tribute to Dadaist Marcel Duchamps, whose 'The Bride Stripped Bare by Her Bachelors, Even' had been constructed between 1915 and 1923. Eno's reference to "the mechanical bride" on *Taking Tiger Mountain (By Strategy)* may have been his own obscure tribute, predating Ferry's by some four years.

Ferry's vacillation had an ominous ring about it made worse by the depressing fate of all three of the album's 45rpm trailers. Backed by Ferry's solo take on

Casanova, What Goes On entered the singles chart on 9 May at number 71, rose to 67 the following week and was then gone. *Sign of the Times* did rather better, commencing an eight-week run on 1 August and reaching number 37, but Ferry was so irritated by these worryingly low figures that he then flung the wholly inappropriate *Carrickfergus* onto the singles market in what can only be described as a suicidal gesture. Predictably, this one rated no Top 100 placing whatsoever.

Ferry was stung in particular by the rejection of *Sign of the Times*. "I thought it was a very relevant record," he complained. "It was about what's happening now. The very title indicated that." He was stung even more by the *Melody Maker* review of the single, in which Chris Brazier articulated the New Wave contempt for Ferry in notably childish and mean-spirited terms. "Very possibly the worst single Bryan Ferry has ever been involved with," he began. "The flip is worse – an abysmal facile jerkalong called *Four Letter Love*, and together they suggest he's reached his creative nadir." There was more, and worse: "Ferry seems now to have painted over his soul in contemptible jet-set gloss, to be content to live out in reality the role of 'love's anguished fool abandoned by his siren' that has so dominated his later work. But anyone who spends £397 a night on an hotel room can neither expect nor deserve to say anything of value to the rest of humanity."

In a darkly confessional interview with Allan Jones, Ferry blew his top over this spiteful broadside. "To think that *Melody Maker* has somebody like that writing for them," he fulminated. "To think they have someone with insufficient brains, who believes I'm dumb enough to pay £395 a night on a hotel room. He doesn't deserve to write the ads at the bloody back ... or even [to drive] the paper around to the bloody newsagents ... God, you try living for three months in a fucking hotel room, man, working on a new album, trying to improve upon the last record and the record before that ... My whole shirt was on the album. I don't need some ridiculous cub reporter criticising me for how much – and it was a hell of a lot less than that – I was paying to stay in a fucking hotel. He didn't write about the record. He wrote about me. And he even got that wrong. You can't get away with saying that I have nothing to say to humanity, man. That's just too heavy a thing to say about anybody."

Bryan stripped bare

Ferry's paranoia was fuelled not only by a growing awareness of his pariah status in the current rock landscape ("I've realised for a long time that I've been disliked but it's only lately that I've realised that I might actually be hated"), but also by its more practical side-effects; in this case, a mooted summer tour cancelled for lack of ticket sales. On Monday 3 July, he guested on Thames TV's *The Kenny Everett Video Show* alongside Wings, Bonnie Tyler and ELO; his blank-faced resistance to answering Everett's questions was a comic routine, of course, but all too aptly reflected his introspection and disenchantment. To make matters worse, when *The Bride Stripped Bare* was finally issued in September it rose no higher than an unlucky 13 in the album chart.

Critical reaction, however, was reasonably favourable, though acutely aware of the compromises Ferry was grappling with in his attempts to score a US hit. In *Rolling Stone*, Robert Duncan claimed that "*The Bride Stripped Bare* is better than most, and so is Bryan Ferry. If, for now, he's trying to squeeze himself into a round commercial hole, his old fans can take solace in the fact that he'll always be a hopelessly square peg." In the UK, *Melody Maker*'s Penny Valentine noted that "Ferry makes a passable job of turning into something of a 'straight' rock singer, an interesting departure. When he used to sing *It's My Party and I'll Cry if I Want To* you knew he really didn't mean it. Now you're not so sure."

The LP's rear cover featured Ryan O'Neal's ex, Barbara Allen (with whom Ferry had reportedly had a brief liaison during a New York sojourn earlier in the year), stretched out on a marble slab in Cleopatra-style rigor, a snake coiling away from her outstretched wrist. Leaving commentators to speculate on whether the snake – if not in the grass then certainly in the boudoir – might be Mick Jagger, Ferry wouldn't come up with such a necrophile cover image again until *The Best of Roxy Music* in 2001.

The running order finally arrived at saw *The Bride Stripped Bare* divided roughly 50-50 between originals and the usual run of cover versions, with several tracks consigned to oblivion. Only temporarily, as it turned out: the Ferry-penned *Four Letter Love* was used as the B-side to *Sign of the Times*, while *Feel the Need*, *Crazy Love* and Ferry's *Broken Wings* all fetched up in support of *Windswept* in 1985. *He'll Have to Go* finally appeared on *The Ultimate Collection* in 1988, prior to hitting a lowly 63 when released as a single the following year.

The covers that made the cut are as frustrating as ever. There's nothing wrong with them; Ferry's tight-knit band of ace sessionmen (Waddy Wachtel, Neil Hubbard, Alan Spenner, Rick Marotta) give a muscular account of themselves, and Ferry's vocal interpretations are no disgrace. But who would willingly listen to Ferry singing *Hold On (I'm Comin')*, *The Same Old Blues* or *That's How Strong My Love Is* when the Sam & Dave, J J Cale and Otis Redding originals are readily available? And in the context of *The Bride Stripped Bare*, these cover versions are not merely pointless but a serious distraction from the unprecedented intimacy of the album's Ferry originals.

The opening of *Can't Let Go* is sublime; the gentle interplay of acoustic guitar, hesitant percussion and a half-heard piano figure expertly conjures up the disconsolate mood that pervades the entire track. The remainder, however – described by Ferry himself, with no false modesty, as his "meisterwerk about LA … an album about Los Angeles condensed into one song" – is severely compromised by a clichéd lyric and a Ferry vocal that's merely weedy rather than affectingly vulnerable. *When She Walks in the Room* benefits from a beautiful Ann Odell string arrangement and a post-Jerry lyric that's unusually explicit in its references to Ferry's miserable Christmas. Its title taken from a lurid Universal sci-fi flick of 1955, *This Island Earth* is a mordant lament set against an appropriately creepy futuristic soundstage, and *Carrickfergus* is a highly affecting Irish folk song rearranged by Ferry with Herbie Flowers and Waddy Wachtel in support.

Of the other failed singles excerpted from the album, *Sign of the Times* certainly deserved better, resounding to a spiky New Wave klang and a bracingly cynical lyric put over with sardonic relish by Ferry. Lou Reed's *What Goes On* – incorporating fragments of another Velvet Underground song, *I'm Beginning to See the Light* – is given a virile makeover, with an uncharacteristically bearded Ferry descending neon-lit steps in the accompanying video. Not released as a single but much the most persuasive of the album's cover versions, *Take Me to the River* is a limber and funky take on a 1974 Al Green original, but even here Ferry found himself upstaged by a Talking Heads version that climbed to number 26 on the *Billboard* singles chart.

Ironically, this other *Take Me to the River* was produced by Brian Eno. Where Ferry was having the stuffing knocked out of him in the effort to lard his solo albums with radio-friendly Americanisms (and all to no avail; *Bride* reached only 159 in the US chart), Eno was simultaneously revelling in the anarchic vibrancy of New York's New Wave scene. Riding high on the sonic experimentation of *Low* and *"Heroes"*, he had since produced Devo's breakthrough album for Warner Bros, *Q: Are We Not Men? A: We Are Devo!*, as well as a cutting-edge compilation for the Antilles label called *No New York*, a showcase for The Contortions, Mars, Teenage Jesus and the Jerks, and DNA.

Now residing in a Soho loft in Manhattan, Eno's collaboration with Talking Heads would yield three startling albums (*More Songs About Buildings and Food*, 1978; *Fear of Music*, 1979; *Remain in Light*, 1980), as well as his George Martin-like position as the band's all-round eminence grise. According to David Byrne, Eno "had good ideas and genuine enthusiasm for our stuff. He 'got' it, unlike a lot of hot rock'n'roll producers ... [He] was great to work with until the others and I sensed him wanting us to be his back-up band, his source for ideas. But he wasn't really writing the stuff."

Ferry, meanwhile, could take a grim kind of solace in the fact that Eno-produced acts like Devo and Talking Heads bore unmistakeable signs of Roxy Music influence, an ironic circumstance given his increasing marginalisation by the New Wave as a whole. More pertinent to his current impasse, however, was the news from Waddy Wachtel that *The Bride Stripped Bare* was a favourite album of Elton John's.

Fifteen: *Stronger Through the Years*

"The whole point of getting on with Roxy is to get that sound that we get as Roxy. That's the good thing about working together – we incorporate the best of all the other ideas we've learned. We're learning to work together again, and we've become much more constructive than before. There's a much freer input of ideas."
Phil Manzanera, quoted in *Trouser Press* June 1979

Visions of China

Ferry's *The Bride Stripped Bare* made it into the shops at much the same time as solo LPs by his old confreres Mackay and Manzanera. Mackay's *Resolving Contradictions* is undoubtedly the most intriguing of the three, demonstrating exactly what he could have done with the film commissions that mysteriously failed to pour in after the success of *Rock Follies*.

Two further television themes had come his way, however, first for the popular Thames detective series *Hazell*, starring the rumpled Nicholas Ball and based on stories by Gordon Williams and football manager Terry Venables. For this,

Mackay cooked up a raunchy saxophone signature appropriate to the show's translation of a trenchcoated private dick from 1940s Hollywood to 1970s London. Series One began in January 1978, Series Two ended in January 1980, and in the meantime Mackay's theme, with a vocal by Maggie Bell attached, charted as a single at number 37 in March 1978. On Sunday 16 July the same year, Mackay joined Bell's backing band for a concert at the Royal Festival Hall; the other musicians were Geoff Whitehorn, Ian Paice, Jon Lord, Tony Ashton and Paul Martinez.

Also running from 1978 to 1980, *Armchair Thriller* came via *Rock Follies* producer Andrew Brown and was fitted by Mackay with a spooky soprano theme exactly matching the show's memorable title sequence: an iris shot of a plump white armchair, with a man's gangling silhouette staggering towards it and miraculously taking a seat, his shadow hands fastening on the chair's arms in time to Mackay's jarring final klang.

Also around this time, Mackay contributed to Johnny Cougar's *Biography* album and Mickey Jupp's *Long Distance Romancer*, the latter produced by Godley & Creme. Much more momentous, however, was a holiday to China conducted with his wife Jane, a trip originally mooted back in 1976 by Mackay's Deep Purple friend Roger Glover but cancelled owing to the pregnancy of Glover's wife. "I visited China in April 1978 and was very impressed – the natural beauty and splendid buildings, the huge numbers of curious but affable people, the food," Mackay noted on the occasion of the resultant album's CD debut. "And then the drab uniformity, the discipline, the palpable oppression and terror? Well, no, I can't really claim to have picked up on the last one. Was I charmed or was I conned?"

The beauty and the terror would be melded on Mackay's aptly titled solo LP *Resolving Contradictions*, which saw him briefly breaking away from the EG aegis to sign with EMI subsidiary Bronze Records. Recorded at Basing Street and the picturesque Sawmills Studios in Mackay's native Cornwall, the album roped together the band from *Rock Follies of '77* – Tony Stevens on bass, Chris Parren on keyboards, Peter Van Hooke on drums, Ray Russell on guitar – together with violinist Gavin Wright, trumpeter Michael Laird, bass guitarist Mo Foster and flautist Tim Wheater. Roxy alumnae Manzanera and Thompson were also brought on board to add distinctive touches to an epic canvas echoing Mackay's response to the socialist-realist music he had encountered in the east.

"Only a little more than a year after the great helmsman's [Chairman Mao's] increasingly shaky hand finally slipped off the tiller," Mackay commented, "we were able to visit as 'foreign friends' what seemed a different world … The music, like the culture, was a mixture of the ancient and sublime and the grandiose and vulgar. The contrasts with my world were exhilarating and irresistible. Hence the album was never really about China but about myself and that curious flat period of the late seventies."

Though Mackay's reference to the 'flatness' of the period – which by the time *The Bride Stripped Bare* came out may well have been a sentiment echoed by Ferry – gives an intriguing idea of the jaded soil from which the Roxy reunion would shortly spring, there's not a hint of flatness in *Resolving Contradictions* itself. Instead, it's bursting with life, the music conceived in sprawling CinemaScope, the soundstage teeming with incredible detail (including, of course, more multi-layered wind instruments than you can shake a stick at) and the melodies bracingly tuneful throughout.

The gorgeous opener, *Iron Blossom*, recurs as a submerged motif several times; a beguilingly low-key exchange between Mackay and Wheater, it acts here as a sort of spell-stopped introduction to the eastern flavours to follow. These are delivered in spades in the tripartite medley of *Trumpets on the Mountains*, *Off to Work* and *"Unreal City"* – with the whirling ferment of Mackay's oboe recalling *Virginia Plain* and a thickly textured martial strut running headlong into the metallic maelstrom that is *The Loyang Tractor Factory*. The dissonant crash-bang-wallop here is reminiscent of Kraftwerk's *Metall auf Metall*, but instead of portraying the dark satanic mills of the Ruhr, Mackay provides a bizarrely upbeat vision of Chinese mechanics smiling their way through some cheerfully mendacious propaganda film. Mackay's oboe buzzes bee-like over motoric drum patterns, churning synths and a vaguely ominous bass piano, bringing the most explicitly Oriental phase of the album to a close.

Rivers is exceptional. An exhilarating tapestry, over seven minutes in length, it's done in shape-shifting Roxy style, starting as a subdued lament, breaking out into a soulful Mackay solo, then modulating into a surging symphonic section that shows how different a Mackay version of Eno's *Music for Films* would have been. Co-written with Russell, *Battersea Rise* is, as its title suggests, a long way from China; a sweetly rhythmic saxophone meditation, it's presumably close kin to Mackay's earlier *Walking the Whippet* in its musical impression of his south London surroundings.

The record's second side is more diffuse, but includes the infectious sweep of *Skill and Sweat* (Mackay's tenor theatrics in another metal-on-metal middle section are hair-raisingly effective here) and the supremely smoochy sax-led ballad *The Ortolan Bunting (A Sparrow's Fall)*. *The Inexorable Sequence* is a second seven-minute epic; a mesmerising monument to Eno's old dictum "repetition is a form of change," it overlays a dazzling Manzanera solo onto a churning – and, yes, inexorable – brass backdrop. *A Song of Friendship (The Renmin Hotel)* was issued, and inevitably ignored, as a single, its genteel Sinophiliac fluting wholly unsuited to the singles chart, and *Alloy Blossom* restates the theme of *Iron Blossom* in more ominous terms, with Russell's spidery Chinese guitar flavours building up to another symphonic climax. Finally, *Green and Gold* is a brief but affecting saxophone improvisation, showcasing Mackay at his bluesy best against the twinkling of Parren's synthesiser and a pensive guitar and bass accompaniment.

The album's cover was as epic as the music within, a striking Eric Scott painting of Mackay blowing up a tenor storm in front of a bunch of mandarin-collared Chinese labourers. (His pig-tailed wife Jane is among the throng at right, rather incongruously holding the couple's pet whippet on a lead.) Scott would subsequently be used by Eurythmics for the cover of their 1987 album *Revenge*, while Mackay's absorption in Chinese culture would be replicated in the baldly titled Vangelis album *China* and Japan's swansong LP *Tin Drum*, the weakest entry in a classic triumvirate that also includes *Quiet Life* and *Gentlemen Take Polaroids*.

Resolving Contradictions is the work of a musician at the height of his powers, occasionally overblown but gorgeously performed and produced. "I found modern Chinese music really exciting," claimed Mackay, "but like my first LP it turned out to be more about me than about China, so I was a little upset when it was taken as a rather weird and escoteric record." Indeed, as a calling card for future film commissions it went predictably unnoticed, due in part, perhaps, to the opinion of at least one reviewer that it qualified as little more than Muzak for the better class of Chinese takeaway. Or, for that matter, the puzzling judgment of *Trouser Press* mainman Ira Robbins that "By the time of the Asian-oriented *Resolving Contradictions*, Mackay had banished any trace of wit: the record is a snooze."

Things could have been worse for the album's detractors, however. Out-takes included on a 1990 CD reissue indicated that early experiments in the use of pinball-effect syn-drums (the kind of thing permissible in one song and one song only, namely Rose Royce's *Love Don't Live Here Anymore*) had been sensibly removed by Mackay from the final product.

Cuban crisis

While Mackay was preparing his epic hymn to Sinophilia, Manzanera was at the Sun Park Studios in Surrey (a plush basement facility in the home of Yes bass guitarist Chris Squire) to record his second official solo album, *Listen Now!!* having been rather pedantically attributed to Phil Manzanera/801. The sessions stretched across eight weeks from March to May, much of the material having been demo'd by the 801 team that had recently toured the UK.

Presumably for this reason, Manzanera's old Quiet Sun chum Bill MacCormick, who features on bass throughout, seems to have been under the misapprehension that the project was another 801 venture. "*K-Scope*, the second 801 studio album, had no political concept and was musically a much less coherent piece of work [than *Listen Now!!*]," he told Stephen Yarwood in 1995. "It was very co-operative throughout the sessions and overdubs, then Phil rushed off and mixed the whole thing very quickly. I had nothing to do with the final mix at all, and when the album was released it didn't really come up to my expectations. The reason for the haste, it later emerged, was that Roxy were reforming so Phil was keen to get everything else out of the way."

MacCormick's dreams of a musical co-operative were clearly offended by Manzanera's apparently high-handed 'star' behaviour; after a brief collaboration with Simon Ainley in another Dulwich College-derived band, Random Hold, MacCormick would quit the music business altogether and become London organiser for the Liberal Democrats. *K-Scope*, however – despite Manzanera's expedient post-production haste – is an album that stands up very well some three decades later.

Lead vocalist on the *Listen Now!!* album and tour, Ainley was reduced to contributing rhythm guitar on two of the ten tracks, having turned up at the beginning of the sessions with a streaming cold and been replaced by Tim Finn. Finn's companions from the now disbanded Split Enz, Eddie Rayner and Neil Finn, were also on hand and, according to Manzanera, in a penurious state, the session fees helping them pay their way back to New Zealand. Notable contributions were also made by former King Crimson sax man Mel Collins and 801 drummer Simon

Phillips, with Roxy's Paul Thompson taking over for a couple of tracks. On top of all this there was a peculiar jazz-funk collaboration with vocalist John Wetton, *Numbers*, that included the now time-honoured Roxy mantra, CPL593H.

A couple of the pieces are obvious gestures to the tightly wound virility of punk rock, with the New Wave stylings of *Remote Control* resulting in a jagged hell-for-leather sprint that comes close to transcending pastiche and sounding like the real thing. *Slow Motion TV* (worked up from a Manzanera-MacCormick-Ainley original called *It Don't Matter to Me*) is less convincing, despite a melodic bass line and fancy keyboard embellishments lifted straight from Jean-Jacques Burnel and Dave Greenfield of The Stranglers.

It does, however, end on a very satisfying baritone bray from Mel Collins, whose contribution to the disco-flavoured *Hot Spot* provides a delightful reminder of the wilder woodwind histrionics of early King Crimson. The opening here – in which Collins' fluting soprano does battle with unrelenting baritone honks against the brilliantly agitated rhythm section of Phillips and MacCormick – gives place to a funky dancefloor workout graced by a typically witty lyric from MacCormick's brother, *NME* stalwart Ian MacDonald.

K-Scope itself, which opens the album, is a fabulously brawny big-band instrumental, crackling with the combined energy of Rayner's ritzy electric piano, Collins' multi-tracked riffing, the super-supple Phillips-MacCormick combo and Manzanera's own uniquely abrasive guitar parts. In addition, the track kicks off with the ominous chugging of what sounds like a steam locomotive, providing a neat thematic link to the cover of *Diamond Head* and the opening strains of *801 Live*. Here, too, is Lol Creme's trademark Gizmo, virtually the only trace on this LP of the Godley & Creme sound that was so prevalent on *Listen Now!!* The next track, however, sounds like a superior riposte to *Dreadlock Holiday*, the contemporaneous hit from Godley & Creme's former band, 10cc. *Cuban Crisis* is set to a fantastically lugubrious reggae beat, the lyric provides an agreeably droll snapshot of Fidel Castro and Rayner's piano is ranged hypnotically against Manzanera's choppy rhythmic interjections.

The album winds up with an effective juxtaposition of two instrumentals alongside two vocal tracks from MacCormick himself, whose plangent tones (last heard on the magisterial *Diamond Head* track *Alma*) are definitely preferable to the colourless plaint of Tim Finn. *N-Shift* is initially a rather workaday plod but climbs thereafter into some dazzlingly sustained Manzanera sonics, while the closer, *You Are Here*, is a sinister, limpid gem played out by Manzanera alone on synthesiser, Yamaha CS80, guitar and keyboards; this one-man-band approach would pay enormous dividends on his next solo album, *Primitive Guitars*.

Finally, the MacCormick tracks are about as good as Prog-inflected pop music gets. *Gone Flying* is a star-lit beauty, resonating to the fleet-fingered 'echo guitar' of Manzanera and Phillips' constantly surprising drum patterns. As Manzanera's personal favourite, it inspired him to an uncharacteristic, but wholly charming, bit of immodesty when writing the liner notes for the album's CD reissue, in which he drew attention to "some nifty guitar work from yours truly; am I allowed to say that? Oh what the hell!"

Walking Through Heaven's Door starts out as a delicate ballad, lushly under-pinned by the gentle throb of Manzanera and Rayner's CS80s and the bluesy soprano of Mel Collins, with MacCormick sleep-talking his way through an aeroplane-at-touchdown reverie. It then makes a startling gear change into a frighteningly funky contemplation of the city below, with traces of *Listen Now!!* in its caustic lyrical asides. Lasting close to seven minutes, it builds up a blistering head of steam as MacCormick's obsessive iteration of the title is assailed by Manzanera's lacerating punctuation marks.

If MacCormick had expected the whole album to be on the level of these two tracks, then perhaps he was right to be disappointed at the outcome. Even so, *K-Scope* more than lives up to its title in offering a mix-and-match kaleidoscope of different sounds and styles. At the height of the New Wave, however, it was predictably dismissed just as summarily as Mackay's *Resolving Contradictions*.

The Band who Wouldn't Die

The Bride Stripped Bare had been summarily dismissed too, of course, despite Ferry's assurances to anyone who would listen that it was his "first grown-up album." He also confided to Allan Jones that "I'm not utterly despondent. I haven't slashed my wrists yet. It hasn't reached that stage."

Of the failed Ferry single *Sign of the Times*, Angus MacKinnon had perceptively noted in the *NME* that "its accent on 'modernity' might have been more sensibly matched with the upcoming Roxy Music reunion." The decision to reconvene the band had been announced in August, before the disastrous reception of Ferry's latest solo recordings had made itself fully felt. Nevertheless, it was obvious that the band name had now switched from being the encumbrance it had seemed in 1976 – when everything in Ferry's solo garden seemed lovely – to a protective umbrella under which he could shelter from a press and public increasingly antagonistic to the unadorned name of Bryan Ferry.

"I thought it was probably time to make another Roxy album," Ferry recalled four years later. "I thought the New Wave was beginning to sound very much like early Roxy and also I was intrigued to see what it would be like to play with Roxy again as I'd been away for a couple of years. I wanted that built-in security of the name." On top of which, it was clear to the objective observer that *The Bride Stripped Bare* was a bit of a snooze by comparison to the fertile vibrancy of Mackay and Manzanera's parallel solo efforts. Nothing Ferry had produced since *Both Ends Burning* could match the imaginative power of *Rivers*, say, or *Walking Through Heaven's Door*. A rematch with Mackay and Manzanera was therefore the ideal way for Ferry to recharge his creative batteries.

That the Roxy name was still a viable one had been proved in spectacular style several months earlier, when Polydor (succeeding to the EG catalogue formerly licensed through Island) had put out an 11-track compilation called *Roxy Music Greatest Hits*. A catholic collection, it enshrined the original *Virginia Plain* and *Pyjamarama* on LP for the first time (albeit with the latter somewhat remixed), offered a specially abbreviated version of *The Thrill of It All* and only faltered in its omission of anything from the *Roxy Music* album. (The non-appearance of *Both Ends Burning* was more than likely an attempt to save its under-par parent album, *Siren*, from losing all glamour in the eyes of prospective record buyers.) The balance of the album was made up by *Do the Strand*, *All I Want is You*, *Out of the*

Blue, Editions of You, Love is the Drug, and – making up for the marked absence of *Stranded* cuts on *Viva! Roxy Music* – *Mother of Pearl, A Song for Europe* and *Street Life*.

The sleeve was in classic Roxy vein, cooked up by Ferry in tandem with Deirdre Morrow, Freddie Valentine and Mick Haggerty (the latter soon to win a Grammy for his design work on Supertramp's *Breakfast in America*). Here, the discreetly glimpsed gold disc of the first album now occupies centre stage, with a doe-eyed beauty whirring oneirically through its play-out grooves against a tawdry peacock-patterned background. The album spent 11 weeks in the charts, starting on 19 November 1977, and reached a very respectable high of 20.

Even better, a 45rpm trailer for the album, coupling *Virginia Plain* with *Pyjamarama*, had hit number 11, with Roxy's original *Top of the Pops* appearance getting a rerun on the edition of 10 November against a radically changed back-drop that included Boney M, Darts, Elvis Costello and the Attractions, The Tom Robinson Band and Tina Charles. A follow-up coupling *Do the Strand* and *Editions of You* failed to chart, but, with the original ferocity of punk dying down by the summer of 1978, it seemed a propitious time for Roxy Music to put their heads above the parapet once more and see if the old magic could be rekindled.

The resurrection wouldn't necessarily be an easy one, however. Nick Kent reported in the *NME* that one Roxy person, whom he left tactfully unnamed, had stated categorically that "If Bryan was the same person he'd been during the *Siren* tour I would never even have considered working with him again." Aghast, Ferry replied that "The *Siren* tour had been dreadully exhausting and uninspiring in terms of the band having reached a stage of incompatibility … I mean, everyone was getting on everyone else's nerves at that point. I don't think I can have been the main culprit. It was simply a matter of us having worked constantly, gone through all the changes that success brings and inevitably tension arises until boom! – that old human chemistry is blown. I mean, we didn't even say, 'All right chaps, this is it, goodbye forever.' The *Siren* tour was finished and we instinctively went our separate ways, figuring that we'd regroup after our extended holiday."

Talk of an "extended holiday" was certainly a long way from Ferry's airy pronouncement, as recently as September 1977, that "Roxy is certainly dead and buried now. There would be no point in our working together again as a band." Now that they *were* together again, however, who was up for inclusion? Mackay and Manzanera were obviously essential components of the Roxy chemistry, as was the less fêted but equally stalwart Paul Thompson. But what of Eno's elfin replacement, Eddie Jobson? Was he to be involved? "No," Manzanera laughed in response to Kent's query, "and he's probably rather pissed off! Not because he would have joined, but [because] we realised it was pointless to ask him. God knows, it wasn't out of any animosity."

There would have been no point in making overtures to the now 23-year-old Jobson because of his complete absorption in EG's Prog Rock supergroup UK, which united him with King Crimson alumnae Bill Bruford and John Wetton plus guitarist Alan Holdsworth. His collaboration with Frank Zappa on *Zoot Allures* and *Zappa in New York* had made Jobson a bankable name in his own right, and UK soon became a source of derision in the music press but a lasting source of fascination to the more robustly constituted Prog fans. A self-titled debut album was followed by the departure of Bruford and Holdsworth, whereupon Zappa drummer Terry Bozzio came on board for both the *Danger Money* album and the live collection *Night After Night*. Wetton would move on to form MOR supergroup Asia with Prog superstars Carl Palmer, Steve Howe and Geoffrey Downes, while Jobson would produce a solo LP (*Green/The Zinc Album*) and enjoy profitable stints with both Jethro Tull and Yes. Amid all this, a rematch with Roxy was the last thing on his mind.

As the band's Jobson-free rehearsals got under way and support musicians were selected, Ferry informed the readers of *Melody Maker* that "We're finding out, really, what exactly we have to say to each other musically. I can't be more specific. I think Roxy can still contribute something valid musically. If we were re-forming just for the money we'd have gone about it differently. But it's too early really to talk about our plans in any detail at the moment. We're just working toward making another Roxy album. I always thought we would. Roxy never really ended. And if there are some people who think we should not record together again, well, all I can say is that I'm not going to be dictated to by those people. I think the prospect of us working together is really intriguing. And so far we're all pleased."

PART FOUR

Roxy Renaissance

Sixteen: *The Sixth Roxy Music Album*

"Manifesto ... wishes to satisfy those who bought Virginia Plain *while making genuflections to present-day American radio culture. Is it compromised by its emphasis on this double-schizophrenia? Certainly it pulls some punches. But, reservations aside, this may be the first such return bout ever attempted with any degree of genuine success."*

Richard Williams, *Melody Maker* 14 February 1979

The *Manifesto* album began to take shape in September, the sessions alternating between the bucolic seclusion of Ridge Farm in Surrey and the familiar London facility at Basing Street. Though engineered by Rhett Davies, Jimmy Douglass, Phill Brown and Randy Mason, the production credit would go simply to Roxy Music. Ferry subsequently took the tapes to Atlantic Studios for a New York spit and polish, at which time several US guests added discreet, and uncredited, grace notes. These were pianist Richard Tee, percussionists Rick Marotta and Steve Ferrone, and soul stylist Luther Vandross on backing vocals.

In the UK, the core band of Ferry, Mackay, Manzanera and Thompson had been augmented by pianist Paul Carrack and bass guitarists Gary Tibbs and Alan Spenner. This was a distinguished and artfully chosen crew, Carrack, for instance, being the author of the evergreen hit single *How Long*. He had entered the music business in 1970, aged 19, as a member of Warm Dust, later forming Ace with Warm Dust bass player Tex Comer. After scoring a number 20 hit with *How Long* in December 1974, Ace broke up in summer 1977, Carrack filling in his time prior to the Roxy engagement with The Frankie Miller Band. Post Roxy, he would play for Squeeze, The Undertones, Nick Lowe, Carlene Carter, Mike & the Mechanics and Roger Waters, as well as putting out several solo albums.

Spenner was held in especially high regard by Ferry, who considered him "just the greatest English bass player." Starting out with Wynder K Frog in 1967, Spenner subsequently worked with a remarkable range of artists, from Leon Russell, Spooky Tooth, Donovan and Steve Winwood to Jim Capaldi, Ted Nugent, Whitesnake and Marianne Faithfull. He had also contributed to the original *Jesus Christ Superstar* album in 1970 and been a member of Joe Cocker's Grease Band with Neil Hubbard, who would later join him in the short-lived R'n'B group Kokomo. Most recently, of course, Spenner and Hubbard had been party to the miasmic strangeness of Ferry's *The Bride Stripped Bare* sessions.

Also contributing to *The Bride Stripped Bare* was Herbie Flowers, on whose recommendation Ferry hit upon 20-year-old bass guitarist Gary Tibbs. Formerly with punk band The Vibrators, Tibbs would prove at least as accomplished a musician as the high-powered session players being brought in to fill out the Roxy sound. For Ferry, he had the added benefit of youth, providing a visual link to the New Wave in a band that was looking increasingly patrician by the autumn of 1978. Accordingly, initial promo films of *Trash*, *Dance Away* and *Ain't That So* would dwell on the hyperactive Tibbs at least as much as the more staid Mackay and Manzanera. He would even be billed above Thompson on the album cover.

The reconstituted Roxy Music first stepped before the PR cameras in November, Ferry meanwhile consulting with Antony Price and photographer Neil Kirk over a suitable sleeve design for the Roxy relaunch. The fulsome covergirls of old were rejected in favour of a party scene recalling so many of Ferry's ongoing preoccupations, but with the sinister twist that all the partygoers appeared to be dead.

Lavishly accoutred mannequins from Price's King's Road emporium, Plaza, are seen in a 1970s dazzle of latterday Weimar decadence, their immobile stances garlanded with party streamers, sweat running down the camera lens, the monolithic typeface lending a granite inflexibility to the one-word title. (Michael Bracewell has accurately noted the similarity of this typeface to that used on the two issues of Wyndham Lewis' 'review of the Great English Vortex', *Blast*.) The eerie simulacra of Roxy's *The Bogus Man* – or, for that matter, Kraftwerk's *Showroom Dummies* – seem to have turned up here en masse, presaging the arrival of the New Romantics who would draw so much from the music within. What *Melody Maker* once characterised as Roxy's "exotic, Poe-like quality" is here translated into a scene from *The Masque of the Red Death*, except Ferry's upper-crust clubbers seem to be sheltering, not from Poe's crimson plague, but the so-called Winter of Discontent then paralysing the UK.

In a New Wave market fascinated by gimmicks of the coloured vinyl variety, the album would also be issued as a picture-disc. For this, the sleeve was cut out in peek-a-boo style to reveal the Plaza mannequins stripped of Price's lavish accoutrements, suggesting a creepy assemblage of robot naturists.

The *Manifesto* LP eventually came out in the first week of March 1979, the posters bearing the portentous legend "Three Years Later A New Album." Capital Radio DJ Nicky Horne had previewed Side One – or, to adopt the album's own terminology, the 'East Side' – in the third week of February, but was promptly silenced by an edgy Polydor before he could get around to Side Two. On top of this, a preview single, *Trash*, had been issued on 16 February and met with a rough reception. The success of *Dance Away*, however, would ensure that the album eventually clocked up an impressive 34 weeks in the album charts, its tenure beginning on 24 March and its highest chart placing being number seven.

The critical response was mixed, with old supporter Richard Williams articulating the widespread scepticism regarding the Roxy reunion in his in-depth *Melody Maker* preview on 14 February. "What good reason could there possibly be for ending the period of suspended animation begun in 1975? In other words, if *In Your Mind* and *The Bride Stripped Bare* and *Listen Now!!* and *K-Scope* and *Resolving Contradictions* had been cast in all-American platinum these past three years, who'd have chosen early 1979 as the natural time for a reunion? ... In other words, again: who really needs the follow-up to *Siren*?" Williams used this preamble, however, only as a teasing build-up to his affirmative conclusion that "*Manifesto* is a worthwhile attempt to make both form and content match its own internal preoccupations," dubbing it "a technical knockout against the odds."

"Ferry and his cohorts seem content to rely on tried and tested ethics which may pall in the context they now find themselves in," grumbled Max Bell in the *NME* (in a piece that worked an up-to-date variation on that paper's long litany of Ferry pseudonyms, calling him Bryatollah Ferrani). "Perhaps greater familiarity with *Manifesto* will reveal hidden magic," Bell added. "At present it merely comes over like an assured, modern dip into friendly territory – an entertaining, pleasant album." Conversely, in *Time Out* Steve Taylor noted that "Arrangements-wise, American influences have replaced Brian Eno's modern music input with some superb results, like the ultra-smooth *Ain't That So* or the Weather Report-ish workout which closes Side One."

Despite the American influences noted by Taylor, two especially influential US magazines were not particularly impressed, a potentially worrying sign in that Ferry's desire to crack America had actually been codified on this album into 'East' and 'West' (ie, European and American) sides. "The basic failing of *Manifesto* is its lack of adventurousness, its failure to sound like nobody else," opined Ira Robbins of *Trouser Press*. Revealing his adherence to the then-prevalent demonisation of disco, Robbins also lamented that "When the disco tracks *(My Little Girl, Cry Cry Cry*, and *Dance Away)* begin on the second side, one can't help wondering if anything remains sacred. *Love is the Drug* was a great song done to a disco beat, but done without pandering or conceding to the dreaded disco menace. This album seems to chart a course straight for it, blithely ignoring the ultimate dichotomy between disco and human music."

"Roxy Music has not gone disco. Roxy Music has not particularly gone anywhere else either," replied Greil Marcus in *Rolling Stone*, maintaining that the album "offers only embellishments on the Roxy sound and story. The new record is a lovely footnote, but it can lead nowhere." He acknowledged, however, that "The songs ending each side fade out with real grace and leave you hanging, wanting more ... So the record has its moments – moments few bands even know about – but as with the brazenly (and meaninglessly) titled *Manifesto*, they add up to little." Despite these responses, the album would reach an unprecedented high on the *Billboard* chart of number 23.

For the accompanying tour, the four key members were supplemented by Gary Tibbs and keyboard player Dave Skinner, whose association with Ferry went back to *These Foolish Things* and with Manzanera to the studio and touring incarnations of 801 Mark II. Supported by Wire on the continental leg of the tour, the new Roxy was unveiled on Saturday 24 February at Stockholm's Isstadion, the band domiciled meanwhile at the Grand Hotel and rehearsing at the Abba studio. Despite Puxley's efforts to put music journalists off the scent by suggesting Roxy were due to open in Berlin, *Melody Maker*'s indefatigable Allan Jones turned up on opening night alongside 5000 Swedish Roxy fans.

A facetious streak was detectable in Jones' subsequent report; as well as claiming to have been "surrounded by jabbering Swedes," he also wondered if Mackay's enthusiasm for the new Roxy was attributable to his "finally [being] tired of *Rock Follies* and tributes to the Chinks." Elsewhere, he described the new set, in terms reminiscent of Roxy's 1974 stage effects, as "very Nuremberg ... very stark and austere." Ferry and Price were apprehensive about it, however. "It's meant to look *epic*," complained Ferry, while Price wondered if "it wasn't too Pearl & Dean." The set would be aptly apostrophised later by the same paper's James Truman, who called it "a monstrous construction of pyramids and papier maché that looks like an RKO reject for *Antigone.*"

Reporting on the opening strains of *Out of the Blue*, Jones also offered a priceless word-picture of Ferry's now time-honoured physical awkwardness: "Thompson kicks into another volatile rhythm, and Ferry begins a curious little dance, his arse poking out beneath the hem of his jacket, his knees locked together … [reminding] me suddenly of those occasional newsreels we see of Prince Charles attempting the Watusi with dusky maidens in grass skirts somewhere on the shores of Africa."

The band's continental dates then moved on to eight days shuttling round Germany, Holland, Switzerland and France, starting on 4 March in Essen, taking in stopovers at Amsterdam, the Hague, Montreux and finally, on the 11th, the Pavillon de Paris. With the Winter of Discontent still reverberating in the UK, Mackay was quick to set the record straight regarding Roxy's comeback itinerary. "We don't see Europe as a warm-up for Britain," he pointed out in *Record Mirror*. "Not to put down our British fans but Britain is only one place to play. I find something inexpressibly dreary about driving round and round Britain and staying at those chain-owned hotels … I prefer being in Europe. Some of those old cities have kept a quality that London has lost. The feeling here [in the UK] is that everything is gradually running down. There's a general feeling of depression and decay."

Prior to the release of the album, the new Roxy had filmed three of its tracks – *Ain't That So*, *Trash* and *Dance Away* – for a 16mm *Manifesto* promo made by Eyeline Films. Now, with the accompanying tour getting under way, the band plunged into a slew of TV engagements all over Europe, notable among them a BBC extravaganza devised by future *Top of the Pops* guru Michael Hurll. This was shot in the third week of February, while Roxy were making ready for their Stockholm debut, and kept back for use as an Easter special in aid of UNICEF. On the evening of Monday 16 April, viewers fresh from *Larry Grayson's Generation Game* were accordingly regaled with a 55-minute confection called *Abba in Switzerland*. "Abba star in their first ever European television special," gushed *Radio Times*, "recorded on location in the Swiss Alps."

To be precise, the setting was the Big Top in the winter sports resort of Leysin, with Roxy joining Kate Bush as Abba's special guests. (Contrary to initial reports, Boney M and Leo Sayer did not take part.) Abba junkies got to hear such evergreen hits as *Take a Chance on Me*, *Mamma Mia*, *The Name of the Game*, *Chiquitita*, *Does Your Mother Know?* and *Thank You for the Music*. They also got to see screen legend and *The Moon's a Balloon* author David Niven clowning around in – what else? – a hot-air balloon. Kate Bush was in her purple prime for a loopy rendition of *Wow* incorporating much frankly certifiable windmilling of arms, and Roxy were given a winsome build-up by the Abba girls themselves. "Aren't we lucky having one of our favourite groups on the show?" beamed Frida. "Yes," replied Agnetha, "and I'm so happy they got together again" – whereupon Roxy, augmented by Tibbs and Skinner, offered a smoothly mimed rendition of the about-to-chart single mix of *Dance Away*.

The dress code for the new Roxy – slimline suits and equally slimline ties – was similar to that of the statuesque Kojak type featured on the album cover. It managed to accommodate the angular cool of New Wave with a classically tailored look, making the band seem like trendy and faintly forbidding bank managers. Mackay, however, went for all-out forbidding, adopting a grey Mandarin-collared ensemble – part Nehru, part early Beatles – that made it clear he was still intent on making "tributes to the Chinks." As well as being studiedly Oriental, the look was also in line with Mackay's Kraftwerk-like musings in *Record Mirror*: "It would be intriguing to *not* look like a rock band, to travel round looking like a group of computer operators or something."

Manzanera, meanwhile, was hedging his bets regarding the Roxy revival. "People mustn't think of Roxy Music as a group," he told Ira Robbins. "I've never thought of it that way. In terms of staying together, at the end of this we might go off and do something else for two years."

* * *

Manifesto
(Ferry-Manzanera) 5:29

Opening the so-called 'East Side', this first track on the new album was the last to be recorded and confirmed that the Roxy Music reunion was to be no pussyfooting cop-out of a comeback, no thing of nostalgic half-measures, but an all-out, unrepentant assault on the music scene they once dominated. From the impudent self-possession embodied in the title through to the borderline-absurd grandiloquence of Ferry's lyric, *Manifesto* is a magnificently arrogant gesture, the kind of overblown musique concrète that wouldn't disgrace a Nuremberg rally. Put more simply, given Ferry's recent travails at the hands of mean-spirited music journalists and an indifferent record-buying public, *Manifesto* is perhaps the most elaborately upholstered 'up yours' on record.

It takes a good two-and-a-half minutes for Ferry to arrive and the slowly gathering, thickly textured build-up is a spellbinding one. Tentative at first, the music soon acquires a sinister, nerve-wracking power. Anchored by the heavy pulse of Thompson's percussion, we first hear Alan Spenner's bass extemporising a wildly erratic heartbeat, then Mackay's saxes surging woozily across the soundstage and Manzanera's guitar running disconcertingly backwards. The synthesiser's raga-flavoured arabesques hint at the grandeur of the main motif to come, and finally the tension is screwed to its highest pitch by the increasingly urgent interjections of Mackay's woodwinds – "overdubbed," as the faithful Richard Williams memorably put it, "into nightmarish foghorn blares."

Finally, Manzanera spells out the metallic main theme and Ferry bursts the bubble with an almost off-handed entrance (itself an act of brazen showmanship in view of the histrionics we've been led to expect), calmly elucidating a manifesto so self-important that, as in the best Roxy tracks of old, the listener is left agreeably unsure as to whether he's kidding or not. For listeners who'd assumed the track was going to be an instrumental, Ferry throws in an arch reference to being taken by surprise in the very first line, the backdrop of improvising bass, multi-tracked guitar and swirling keyboards slowly regaining their old intensity as he warms to his theme. Even in this bombastic context, Ferry can still find room for the punning word-play of yore; there's an especially tricky conflation of floors with flaws, for example. And, once his Nietzschean expressions of self-belief have drawn to a close, the track fragments into an eerie blur of Mellotron-fuelled heavenly voices (a faint echo of *For Your Pleasure* here) and a jarring climactic klang.

Ferry's knack for disorientating his listeners – this time regarding the degree to which his tongue was in his cheek in spelling out so grandiose an agenda – had clearly not deserted him. In the *NME*, Max Bell asserted that "The mannerisms of yore are intact though the profundity barometer is not moving," an exact parallel to Greil Marcus' judgment that "Ferry ... [has] rarely traded on such banality, and he mouths the lyrics as if he hopes no one will hear them. The sound may be alive, but the story is almost silent."

"Safer to assume," concluded Bell, "that Ferry is writing his manifesto according to the standards of *My Way* – as such, the track is entertaining." But, whatever its degree of bathos, the track can hardly be accused of the self-absorbed navel-gazing of *My Way*; indeed, much of Ferry's lyric smacks more strongly of the epic sloganeering characteristic of Brecht and other socialist writers. "Ah, *Manifesto*," Ferry reflected 15 years later. "Yes. I loved that one. That's one of my favourite lyrics. Nobody ever commented on it, though, which hurt my feelings."

If a line like "I am for the revolution's coming" sounded odd in the mouth of a perceived dilettante like Bryan Ferry, he would later interpret it for *Mojo*'s Rob Chapman as meaning "there's always a revolution coming with every generation, and I'm for it. I'm for whatever the new thing is." It also transpired that, just as the opening track on the first album had been inspired by a Derek Boshier painting, so *Manifesto* took its cue from a 1961 exhibition blurb by Swedish avant-garde sculptor Claes Oldenburg. ("I am for an art that is political-erotical-mystical," etc.) If the specifics of Ferry's manifesto were indigestible, and the degree of irony underlying them difficult to call, it was at least a consolation to know that, with the 1980s on the horizon, Roxy's Pop Art credentials were still intact.

The protracted build-up to Ferry's entrance, irresistibly theatrical even on record, made the positioning of *Manifesto* at the beginning of Roxy's live dates in 1979 a foregone conclusion. The effect was obviously modelled on the opening to Roxy's previous tour, when *Sentimental Fool* had made a similar impact. The track would not, however, be revived for Roxy's remaining tours, though a radically different 'remake' would be recorded for B-side purposes during the *Flesh + Blood* sessions.

Trash
(Ferry-Manzanera) 2:13

The second track on the *Manifesto* album was also the first track from it to be released as a single, with pretty discouraging results. To indicate that Roxy hadn't been asleep during their protracted lay-off, *Trash* picks up on, and perfects, the New Wave stylings Manzanera had introduced on his latest solo album, notably on tracks like *Remote Control*. But, given that Roxy were now perceived as 30-something elder statesmen, *Trash* was never going to be a New Wave track per se; instead, it preserves the ironic distance so crucial to the early Roxy Music. On top of which, of course, there's that inescapably judgmental title.

Replete with pouting outbursts of the "uhuh-huh-huh" variety, Ferry's gaily insouciant vocal is nicely at odds with the skeletal lyric, which is very much a case of *Street Life* updated. Offering a jaundiced pen-portrait of the late 1970s teen scene, it firmly equates the song's 17-year-old subject with the showroom-dummy socialites featured on the album's front cover. To underline the point, the picture sleeve for the single release offers an unflinching close-up of the red-wigged, red-lipped central figure in that robotic tableau. To underline it yet further, there's even a name-check for Antony Price's fashionable King's Road emporium Plaza – which, of course, had provided all the clothes in which the *Manifesto* mannequins are decked out.

Though Ferry's lyric is allusive and fragmentary, his trashy protagonist is clearly identified as a model, just as his addressee in *A Really Good Time* had been in 1974. The Kraftwerk connection provided by the *Showroom Dummies* on the album cover is therefore supplemented with another echo (though no doubt inadvertent on Ferry's part), this time of *The Model*. There, the imperturbable Ralf Hütter offered a deadpan character assassination of a statuesque creature who only stirs into life when a camera is trained on her.

Manzanera gets things moving with a stand-alone sizzle of noonday-sun guitar; perhaps it's not too fanciful to imagine one of Eno's *Sombre Reptiles* basking on a rock in its warming glow. The clash of conflicting sounds as the track gears up is an exuberant one: great pluming riffs from Manzanera, Mackay's peripatetic oboe providing a fair approximation of *Virginia Plain*'s crazed bumblebee effect, and a chintzy organ sound that wouldn't have seemed out of place in a working men's club.

The central section explodes into a dazzling fusillade of what one contemporary reviewer dubbed "discorama": a riot of electronic hand-claps and frenzied guitar runs, the whole thing kicked off by a surprising outbreak of Ferry's harmonica. Actually, given that Mackay can be seen miming to this section on the accompanying promotional film, maybe that should read Mackay's oboe treated to sound like Ferry's harmonica. The track is only hamstrung by its unusual brevity; no sooner has Mackay started up again than Ferry devolves into a slightly unimaginative repetition of "Yeah, yeah" and the song is over and gone, as if the band didn't have sufficient confidence in it to give it a bit of breathing space.

Unhappily, the single was met with across-the-board derision when unveiled on 16 February. The title alone, a richly provocative one given the delicate business of relaunching an apparently passé band after a three-year hiatus, didn't fail to draw the expected jibes from the music press. Even in the USA, *Trouser Press* editor Ira Robbins would suggest that "The single from the album (*Trash*) can only have been chosen because it's the shortest of the ten tracks. In light of the clever commerciality of Roxy's previous classic English 45s (*Virginia Plain*, *Street Life*, *All I Want is You*), *Trash* hardly rates a second listen."

Having first appeared at number 43 on 27 February, the following week *Trash* entered a Top 40 dominated by The Bee Gees' *Tragedy*, Elvis Costello's *Oliver's*

Army, the Gloria Gaynor anthem *I Will Survive* and the quirky Lene Lovich classic *Lucky Number*. In this climate, *Trash* failed completely to register. Having got to number 40, it promptly slipped back to 43 again and disappeared altogether three weeks later, making it the least successful non-reissue single the band ever released. This was naturally the cause of some serious misgivings regarding the Roxy revival. "At first it looked like it wasn't going to work," Manzanera recalled on the 1994 Radio 1 documentary *The Bryan Ferry Story*. "The first single came out and it didn't do fantastically well. Then *Dance Away* ... was a big hit and it kind of saved our bacon."

Trash was covered by San Francisco band Pansy Division on their 1995 collection *Pile Up*; the song was redirected along the lines suggested by other titles on the album, among them *Ring of Joy*, *Smells like Queer Spirit*, *Cowboys are Frequently Secretly Fond of Each Other* and *Bill and Ted's Homosexual Adventure*.

Angel Eyes
(Ferry-Mackay) 3:32

Possibly feeling written out after the epic exertions of *Rock Follies*, not forgetting two further TV commissions and his own magisterial *Resolving Contradictions* LP, Andy Mackay managed only one co-writing credit on the *Manifesto* album, a score that would dwindle to nought on *Flesh + Blood*. Happily, his lone contribution, *Angel Eyes*, proved a winner, and a lucrative one, too, once it had been re-recorded as a dancefloor epic for the singles market.

In the meantime, the album version resounds to a very different klang, hard to define but, if anything, a kind of gentlemen's club version of heavy metal. Just as Manzanera provided a single oscillating note to get *Trash* under way, so *Angel Eyes* begins, very amusingly, with an isolated shrill of Mackay's alto. The rest of the band crashes in right on his heels, the chugging bass suggesting some vast but slightly antiquated machinery and Manzanera seemingly doing a hundred and one things at once, shooting out great mushrooming power chords from one channel while fiddling abstractedly away in another.

Ferry's vocal, delicate and haunting against this bone-shaking backdrop, offers up a heartfelt paean to a loved one perceived as a superior being, a heavenly body. In *Sea Breezes*, Ferry had speculated on how angels in Heaven handle the agonies of love, while in *Just Another High* he had discussed the generic idea of a 'marriage made in Heaven' with a similar lack of optimism. None of this nagging self-doubt surfaces in *Angel Eyes*, however, the tone being lifted instead from Ferry's starry-eyed assurance in *Pyjamarama* that he and his angel will be united in Heaven.

In the middle of all this, Mackay trots out two wonderfully sinister little sax breaks, wheezing eerily over the soundstage while a second sax burbles bits of a counter-melody from further back. And once Ferry's plaint is over, the band, securely anchored by Thompson's powerful drumming, takes over for an awesome and seemingly unstoppable outro. Mackay accompanies Ferry's repeated moans of "angel, angel eyes" with some of his ritziest riffs, the synths surge in and out like hellish blasts of gas escaping from whatever cumbersome machinery this is, and Manzanera continues to extemporise in any number of inventive ways. (This in the time before hired gun Neil Hubbard was called in to help out on rhythm guitar.) Pretty soon, the instrumentation sounds fit to burst, which it duly does when the pressure becomes too great, the track shuddering to a sudden stop after three-and-a-half relentless minutes.

Never revived on stage since 1979, *Angel Eyes'* one and only live outing is preserved on the numerous bootleg recordings of the *Manifesto* tour, though most of these, unfortunately, muffle Mackay's deranged alto extemporisations into virtual anonymity. As for the re-recorded disco version, the only drawback to its singles chart success in August was that it rapidly supplanted the original on subsequent pressings of the album. Excellent in its own right, the LP version was only revived in 1995 for the *Thrill of It All* box set, finally being restored to the album itself via the remastered edition four years later.

Still Falls the Rain
(Ferry-Manzanera) 4:13

After the creepy dualistic dialogues featured on *Strictly Confidential* and *Sentimental Fool*, Ferry returned to the theme with *Still Falls the Rain*, routinely introducing the song on the band's 1979 tour with "Here's one for all you people out there interested in schizophrenia," or sometimes the more inscrutable "Two in one..." That we're dealing with the simplified, populist view of schizophrenia, however, is made clear by the track's explicit evocation of those old Janus-faced favourites, Dr Jekyll and Mr Hyde.

The 'good cop, bad cop' conversation featured in *Sentimental Fool* is here restated in genuinely frightening terms. Poor Jekyll hasn't a hope in this uneven contest, contributing two plaintive verses either side of a rip-roaring Hyde chorus, but falling away completely after that as Hyde takes over untrammeled. In a classic bit of Roxy dualism, Jekyll's platitudinous appeals for mercy stand in stark contrast to the increasingly aggressive demands of his alter ego, who wants his 'share' (presumably of Jekyll's troubled soul) and insists that Jekyll remove himself from the equation altogether. The musical backing to the Jekyll sections is appropriately bland, distinguished only by some nicely melodic bass guitar, but the band crank themselves up several gears for the jazzy, hell-for-leather choruses, with Mackay's alto riffing in alarm at Hyde's every demand, Thompson offering some expertly dextrous drum fills and Manzanera sending the track on its way with a stormingly metallic solo.

With its precise division between what Richard Williams called "an anxious ballad" and "a Faustian invitation to the dance", *Still Falls the Rain* exemplifies the contrary influences endemic in Roxy's sound, influences formularised on this very album into 'East' and 'West'. Its ponderings on duality are also interesting given the fact that Ferry's most recent solo album was fatally divided between confessional originals and business-as-usual cover versions. The song also reminds one of Ferry's occasional ponderings to the effect that Librans are equally attracted to the opposite poles of good and evil. Perhaps, too, it reflects Ferry's precarious position as a working class lad who had become, as he put it, "the jet set's pet rock star," as well as dramatising the tension between the intensely shy private man and the apparently gregarious stage performer, a tension common to all the band members and, by extension, performers in general.

As long ago as 1972, Ferry had asserted, apropos of his stage persona, that "You have to be an actor, project yourself into it." Ten years later, he elaborated on this theme: "You take an aspect of yourself and either simplify it or ham it up. To some extent it's like method acting ... You say to yourself, 'How does this song go? Oh yeah,' then you get into a role for it and leave that role when the song ends." Mackay, too, would express similar sentiments: "You believe in [the music] in the same way that an actor performs his role," he explained on the DVD release of *Rock Follies*. "You know, if you're playing a bad character you don't have to be a bad person – but you have to believe."

For this song, at least, the 'bad character' remains uppermost, with the jazz-funk release of the choruses remaining much the most memorable feature of the track. Just as the villain always gets the best lines, so the Devil always gets the best tunes – and to underline the point, Ferry's concluding "woo-woos" provide an archly self-referential nod to his own hair-raising version of the Stones' *Sympathy for the Devil*.

Stronger Through the Years
(Ferry) 6:16

Despite the distant echo of *Strictly Confidential* found on *Still Falls the Rain*, it still comes as a surprise to encounter the icy gravitas of *Stronger Through the Years*, a track which plumbs the paranoid depths of the *For Your Pleasure* album much more thoroughly. Its title seems to hint at the grandiloquent self-possession of *Manifesto* itself – 'stronger through the years' carrying an obvious connotation, coming from a band that had been dormant since 1976 – but the music and lyric offer no such bland assurances.

. Stark, sombre and inscrutable, the song posed a problem for long-time Roxy supporter Allan Jones even before the *Manifesto* album was released. In Stockholm for the new Roxy's first-ever gig on 24 February, he noted that newly minted tracks like *Angel Eyes* and *Trash* readily identified themselves, but that "There followed a number – again from *Manifesto*, I supposed – which defied any attempt at identification. I'm afraid my notes refer only to a brutal solo from Manzanera, Mackay's chilling oboe and [David] Skinner's ethereal keyboard contributions."

The keyboard contributions on the album version come courtesy of either Paul Carrack or Ferry himself (Skinner was confined to the accompanying tour) and lend a coldly baleful atmosphere to the track from the start. Thompson's drums roll in (running disorientatingly backwards) and Manzanera contributes the first of several gratingly effective guitar breaks. Ferry's vocal is teasingly sinister, rising to muscular, mock-heroic heights in a disturbing refrain derived, in the opinion of at least one contemporary reviewer, from his bruising experiences in Montreux; here, Ferry vows to forsake, not merely tears, but feeling itself. The bass guitar is thickly pasted on yet amazingly fluid; forsaking the supple time-keeping characteristic of earlier albums, it conducts a highly idiosyncratic monologue of its own as Manzanera emits frenzied seagull shrieks to one side and the keyboard wends its way through the murk on the other.

Thompson's drums, limber and funky, keep up a subtly inventive underpinning to all this, but Mackay's heavily treated sax only puts in an appearance after

Ferry's final murmurs have faded away. Having slurred threateningly in and out of the mix, it finally bursts out, accompanied by weirdly wittering oboes, as a multi-layered backdrop to a stratospheric Manzanera guitar solo. The effect is not unlike the protracted conclusion of *For Your Pleasure*, but the vast psychedelic soundscape here has turned from cosmic grandeur to something more furtive and inward-looking.

The liner notes attached to the *Thrill of It All* box set attribute this track to "smoky late-night sessions in the barn at Ridge Farm" (make of that what you will), as well as giving rather fuller credits for the *Manifesto* album in general, revealing that here, as per *Stranded*, 'treatments' were handled by Mackay and Manzanera. In which case, much of the darkly textured complexity of *Stronger Through the Years* can perhaps be attributed to them.

Though future crowd-pleaser *Dance Away* was passed over for inclusion, the much more forbidding *Stronger Through the Years* was one of six *Manifesto* tracks routinely included on the accompanying tour, its six-and-a-half minute duration blending seamlessly into a much extended version of Mackay's oboe introduction to *Ladytron*.

Ain't That So
(Ferry) 5:39

Kicking off *Manifesto*'s US-flavoured 'West Side', the mesmeric laid-back funk of *Ain't That So* sounds like Roxy's belated riposte to David Bowie's 'plastic soul' stylings on the *Young Americans* album. Richard Williams must have had this comparison in mind when writing in *Melody Maker* that "*Ain't That So* is a euphoric uptown shuffle, fuelled on Thompson's cool displaced accents and an alto saxophone which sounds more like David Sanborn than Andrew Mackay."

Though generally spot-on in his assessments, Williams seems off-beam here; not only is *Ain't That So* far from euphoric, but Mackay's sulphuric saxophone sounds nothing like Sanborn's strangulated squeals on Bowie's top-selling title track. Backing vocals on both songs, however, were provided by Luther Vandross, who goes mysteriously uncredited on *Manifesto*'s rather tight-lipped credits list.

Getting into gear on a churning guitar figure accompanied by Ferry's bleating harmonica, the song brings to mind a film noir cityscape not unlike the one adorning the cover of *For Your Pleasure*. But where Amanda Lear and her tethered panther conjured fantasies of chicly metropolitan Euro-deviancy, here Ferry's lyric suggests a fagged-out private dick lolling dejectedly in an Edward Hopper-style late-night diner. Or possibly the kind of "smoky nightclub situation" memorialised in *2 H.B.* – and, of course, Humphrey Bogart would have been right at home in this kind of scenario. But take your pick – Dana Andrews in *Where the Sidewalk Ends*, Ralph Meeker in *Kiss Me Deadly*, Jack Nicholson in *Chinatown* – any of these compromised antiheroes would fit snugly into the noirish landscape of *Ain't That So*.

The liner notes for Virgin's 1995 Roxy box set apply to the long-ago *Strictly Confidential* an intriguingly gnomic summary: "Secrets ... private and personal ... private eye ... in confidence ... pulp fiction..." All of this applies equally well to the fleabitten protagonist of *Ain't That So*, whose shuttered existence in a rundown hotel is assailed by the same watchful shadows previously invoked in *The Thrill of It All*. Where Ferry's solo single *This is Tomorrow* had depicted a motel-bound narrator who was feeling kind of blue but for the most part optimistic, the ambience of *Ain't That So* is much darker, more furtive, steeped in paranoia.

Though fairly subdued elsewhere on this Americanised half of *Manifesto*, Mackay is really given his head here and responds with a virtuoso display of semi-parodic alto extemporisations, adding a sardonic aside to Ferry's every pronouncement. Sweet and soulful yet full of muscle, he weaves nimbly in and out of a heavy bass/drums backbeat with consistently inventive phrasing, rasping atonally here, smouldering suggestively there. Three years prior to the appearance of *Ain't That So*, Ron Ross of *Phonograph Record* had pointed out that "Andy Mackay ... would have been in a black jazz band in the 30s," a prescient observation given his sleek and sassy contributions here.

The measured swing of bass and percussion is briefly arrested halfway through for a dislocating wash of shuddering keyboards, flickering castanets and Manzanera's dextrously zig-zagging guitar; it's fairly safe to say that this section would have been dropped from the mix prepared, as per *Dance Away*, by Bob Clearmountain for a US single release that never transpired. Either way, it's hard to see how a 45rpm version of *Ain't That So* would have won through in America. Richard Williams' accolade – "Roxy Music can bring pictures to your head like no one else" – was seven years old by now but *Ain't That So* proved that it still applied in spades. And the picture, in this instance, wasn't a pretty one. For all its smoochy downtown sound, the song retains a chilly breath of the sinister in which that urban cityscape is positively crawling with, if not panthers, then certainly predators of one sort or another. Maybe even *The Bogus Man* himself.

Normally positioned between *Mother of Pearl* and *Stronger Through the Years*, *Ain't That So* was a highlight of Roxy's 1979 stage show, though never resurrected since.

My Little Girl
(Ferry-Manzanera) 3:17

Second in line to get the 'West Side' treatment, *My Little Girl* replaces the flyblown furtiveness of *Ain't That So* with a relaxed vibe suggestive of supper-club schmaltz rather than downtown dives. It's a slight piece but deftly played, with Ferry's vocal displaying a warmth and gentle humour as yet unheard on the *Manifesto* LP. This didn't stop it from being dropped, however, from the *Thrill of It All* box set, a fate shared by most of the cuts on this Americanised half of the album.

Another catalogue of a faltering romance, this one deals in readily recognisable dilemmas, the narrator recoiling from overly demonstrative couples whose relationships are obviously in better shape than his, and in the meantime struggling to reconcile the two sides of his loved one's personality – to him she's a girl, to the outside world she's a fully fledged woman. The seedy hotel bolt-holes of *Ain't That So* are replaced by cosy cafés populated by indolent lovers (clearly much more inviting places than the desolate café referred to in *A Song for Europe*), and a plangent note is struck on Ferry's closing admission that this is by no means the first affair to have ended in goodbye. A brief lapse into self-pity, this line would find an echo in the lachrymose canvas of the upcoming album's *My Only Love*, but the overall tone of *My Little Girl* is resigned and gently philosophical rather than angst-ridden.

The instrumentation is at first intriguingly at odds with Ferry's vocal style, opening with a heavy metronomic drum pattern in which Thompson makes no concessions to the band's increasingly airbrushed sound. Manzanera's guitar lines are just as brawny, smoothly undercut by Mackay's smoochy saxes but returning in style for a strikingly funky instrumental break. The US-accented backing vocal (Luther Vandross again, presumably) has a caressing quality at least as beguiling as Mackay's horn section, and the final melody is a lovely one, with Ferry crooning forlornly in tune to the velvet-voiced backing and Mackay trilling away on a whole phalanx of saxophones, soprano warmly to the fore.

Characteristically, a phrase from Ferry's lyric would be recycled for the title of a later song, *True to Life*. But, for all its graces, *My Little Girl* is somehow too insubstantial to seem like much more than a makeweight piece, rather like *Could It Happen to Me?* in the same position on the *Siren* album. Here, at least, the well-muscled soundstage is better adapted to the saccharine subject matter than the bludgeoning incongruity of *Siren*'s weaker tracks.

That the song was always perceived as something of a throwaway is perhaps indicated by the fact that it would later fetch up as the B-side to *Angel Eyes*, also failing to make it onto the set list of the band's 1979 tour – or, indeed, any subsequent one. As Roxy imitators began to proliferate, however, Australian band Icehouse provided an echo of it on their 1982 hit, *Hey Little Girl* – its title derived from an earlier Roxy song, *Amazona*.

Dance Away
(Ferry) 4:20 / single mix 3:48 / extended remix 6:33 ·

Issued as the second 45 excerpted from *Manifesto*, *Dance Away* was given a memorable send-off by the anonymous singles reviewer of *Melody Maker*: "A kind of midtempo ballad that cross-fertilises disco and reggae, it has a wonderfully lilting and incisive grace. Bryan sings with bags of wracked sentiment about nothing much in particular, and everyone meshes with stirring precision. Go on, give 'em a hit."

And the British public duly did, keeping *Dance Away* in the UK chart for longer (14 weeks) than any other Roxy Music single. As Phil Manzanera put it, this was the song that "kind of saved our bacon," its massive commercial success erasing the false start provided by *Trash* and confirming the Roxy reunion as a going concern.

Long gestating, it had been pencilled in by Ferry for two solo albums in succession, first *In Your Mind*, then *The Bride Stripped Bare*. Finally recorded by Roxy (supported by uncredited session players Richard Tee on piano and percussionists Steve Ferrone and Rick Marotta), it gave Ferry the prize he had sought ever since recording *These Foolish Things* in 1973. Having interpreted so many 'standards' of others' devising, he had finally written a standard of his own.

Appropriately, the song took its title, whether by accident or design, from one of the most indelible standards of all, the Frank Sinatra evergreen *Strangers in the*

Night. "Did you know I once sang *Strangers in the Night* in a talent contest in a working men's club?" Ferry had informed Ian MacDonald back in 1973. "Didn't win the prize though." In Ferry's world, however, the dance invoked by Sinatra becomes a forlorn one, marking the end of an affair rather than its starry-eyed beginning. Having chronicled the first tell-tale signs of imminent break-up, Ferry then condemns himself to a social whirl peopled by figures not only "turned to stone" but also frozen in the unnatural glare of a strobe light; these, presumably, are the clubbing mannequins featured on the album sleeve. (And, again, one of them – the heavily rouged blonde stage left – was homed in on for the picture sleeve of the *Dance Away* single.)

Sad, self-pitying stuff, and not wholly free of cliché, but sung with such style and played with such understated élan that its release as a single was surely a foregone conclusion, *Trash* notwithstanding. And just as *Trash* had indicated that Roxy were well aware of New Wave sounds, so *Dance Away* picked up a trick or two from punk's apparent polar opposite, disco. The gentle tick-tick of the rhythm-box, the treacly pulse of the bass line, the rhythmic interjections of Manzanera's guitar – all combined the familiar Roxy precision of old with studio techniques that were unmistakeably modern.

The opening sound effect – the striking of a match and Ferry sniffing his way through a disconsolate first drag on his cigarette – is agreeably self-referential, not only recalling the revving motorbike of *Virginia Plain* and departing car of *Love is the Drug* but also the whole *Smoke Gets in Your Eyes* persona of Ferry's solo career. And Roxy can still spring a few surprises, withholding a chorus after the second verse prior to interrupting the climactic chorus with a "dub-style section to create a climate of disorientation" (Richard Williams again). Mackay's alto, having previously contributed only a couple of humorous asides in the third verse, then sends the song out on some soulful wailings in tune with Ferry's swirling climactic mantra, in which he seeks to sublimate his heartache through dance. Older fans may have grumbled about the stark difference between this smoothed-down sound and the last occasion when the word heartache featured prominently in a Roxy song, but it was clear, nevertheless, that this was a band at the top of their game.

For the single version, Ferry turned for the first time to New York remix wizard Bob Clearmountain, who quickly decreed that Williams' "climate of disorientation" was surplus to requirements as far as the Top 40 was concerned. "I had worked with Chic ... so I got a reputation over at Atlantic for doing R&B stuff and dance mixes," Clearmountain recalled in *Sound on Sound* magazine 24 years later. "They said they wanted an R&B type of thing, but I remember at the time the drums weren't doing the right thing. The bass drum wasn't consistent enough, so I actually brought in a New York drummer to just play bass drum, and we added some percussion. Then the song wasn't structured right. It was verse, chorus, verse, middle eight. Ahmet Ertegun came over and he said 'Where's the second chorus? You've got to have another chorus in there.' I didn't know Roxy Music, I'd never met any of them, and I was thinking, 'How can you mess with their song?' But we put the second chorus in and they loved it."

One might quibble with Clearmountain's removal of that intriguing "dub-style section", together with his softening of Manzanera's guitars and virtual expunging of Mackay's entire contribution. But there can be little doubt that the silky-smooth result helped the single to gain its giddy chart eminence of number two. Less congenial, however, was Clearmountain's laborious 12" extended remix, six-and-a-half minutes of rhythm-box finger-clicking that contrasts starkly with Roxy's next experiment in the 12" format, *Angel Eyes*.

The *Dance Away* single was given an extra push by saturation television coverage, a multiplicity of performances made gentle fun of in the band's *Total Recall* video compendium, which wittily cuts to and fro between appearances, Ferry wearing a white leather suit here, a sober-sided grey one there, a lurid lime-green one elsewhere. Its first UK airing was on the *Abba in Switzerland* TV special on 16 April, eight days after which it arrived just outside the Top 40, at 41. The following week it rose to number 34 alongside a clutch of other durable new entries – Bowie's *Boys Keep Swinging*, The Police's *Roxanne*, *Jimmy Jimmy* from The Undertones and (effecting a disco-flavoured comeback of their own) Sparks' *The Number One Song in Heaven*.

After the band's appearance on the 10 May edition of *Top of the Pops*, the single's rise was rapid, hitting number two on the 22nd and staying there for three weeks, stalled throughout by Blondie's Number One smash *Sunday Girl*. Once Blondie's tenacious grip was finally loosened, it was by Anita Ward's *Ring My Bell* and Tubeway Army's *Are 'Friends' Electric?* rather than *Dance Away*, which slipped gracefully out of the Top 40 on 10 July.

Dance Away was a modest hit in the USA too, reaching number 44. Unfortunately, the success of the single prompted the removal of the original mix from further pressings of its parent album, the same applying to subsequent CD versions. Even the 1999 remaster followed this example, an odd anomaly given that it simultaneously reinstated the album version of *Angel Eyes*. As a result, the original *Dance Away* survives only on disc three of the *Thrill of It All* box set.

Cry, Cry, Cry
(Ferry) 2:55

Though sending *Manifesto* on its way with an echo of his energetic championing of the band in 1972, Richard Williams made no bones about this one in his lengthy *Melody Maker* preview. "The obvious failure," he wrote, "is *Cry Cry Cry*, a tiresome Stax pastiche recalling the populist histrionics of *Let's Stick Together* and including a jarringly blatant reference to the Ferry/Jerry Hall/Mick Jagger triangle."

Indeed. The B-side to *Dance Away*, *Cry, Cry, Cry* might have been forgivable if left in such a lowly slot, but somehow it found its way onto the *Manifesto* album proper. Something has gone seriously awry here, with Roxy's gifts as pasticheurs in complete abeyance as Ferry unleashes a vindictive broadside that reeks, as the lyric freely admits, of "bad blood." It's the sustained character assassination of *A Really Good Time* taken to vengeful extremes, branding its subject as cheap, mercenary and phony just for starters. Contemporary observers were bound to speculate on the identity of Ferry's target here, but it's irrelevant when a laboured R'n'B workout misfires this badly.

Along with *Both Ends Burning*, *Casanova* and *Virginia Plain*, *Cry, Cry, Cry* would be given occasional airings on the *Manifesto* tour but never form part of the consistent set list; the wonder is that Roxy bothered with it at all, given its essential blandness. In the studio version, Thompson is on great tub-thumping form, Mackay adds to a multi-layered impression of the Memphis Horns a few camp little adornments of his own, and Manzanera throws in some droll licks of the *Do the Funky Chicken* variety. Paul Carrack's piano, too, is unusually fine. But the depressing thing is that these touches add up to so little. Where once Roxy would bring their own skewed take to bear on a generic sound (on *If It Takes All Night*, for example), here the anonymity of the band makes the track indistinguishable from one of Ferry's proliferating soul cover versions.

Curiously, when faced with a fully fledged soul cover the following year – Wilson Pickett's *In the Midnight Hour* – Roxy would go right ahead and reinvent it, coming up with something fresh and sparkling. Yet, faced with a leaden Ferry parody of the same kind of song, the results are lumpen and uninspiring; in fact, the reading of *Shame, Shame, Shame* featured on Ferry's *Extended Play* EP has far more brio and inventiveness than this. With its very similar title, *Cry, Cry, Cry* could even be seen as a kind of sequel to the Jimmy Reed song, the cavalier behaviour of Reed's 'baby' being avenged with sneering thoroughness. Ferry's vocal stylings, however, are full of Americanised vibrato yodelling and are sufficiently high-camp-comical to take the sting out of some of the lyric.

The extremely irritating titular refrain, delivered at a high pitch by various unspecified caterwauling backing singers, is presumably Ferry's nod to the million-selling 1966 hit by the so-called ? and the Mysterians, *96 Tears*, fully fledged covers of which would follow from Garth Jeffreys in 1981 and The Stranglers in 1990. Ferry, in the meantime, had included *96 Tears* among the 14 tracks comprising his Radio 1 *Star Special*, broadcast on Easter Monday 1981. Whatever Ferry's inspiration, the song's epitaph was pronounced most pithily in *Rolling Stone*'s review of the *Manifesto* album. According to Greil Marcus, "*Cry, Cry, Cry* is a horrible piece of old-fashioned soul."

Spin Me Round
(Ferry) 5:15

One of Ferry's most ubiquitous preoccupations – roughly speaking the 'party's over' syndrome – here receives arguably its most bewitching interpretation, the later *Avalon* notwithstanding. There's not a lot to choose between the deserted ballroom depicted here and the deflated party atmosphere of the latter song, but *Spin Me Round* is even more inward-looking. Without the dreamy consolation of seeing *Avalon*'s last-minute partner coming out of the ether, this exhausted partygoer concludes forlornly that he's little more than "a shadow echoing on."

The song fades up on a warm wash of synthetic strings and the distant turning of a key in a music box. A ghostly tinkling sound ensues, and Ferry's exquisite vocal – reflective, hesitant, wounded – is at first accompanied only by an understated piano and some sensitive timpani from Thompson. A bashful bass guitar is added, then Mackay arrives to underscore the piano's staccato punctuation marks as Ferry characterises himself as "a netherworld dancing toy." After spelling out a gorgeous oboe theme, Mackay returns to accompany Ferry's plaintive repetition of "Spin me round" as the music box gradually winds to a halt. Manzanera meanwhile, fashionably late, sends some beautifully understated guitar runs curdling through the mix and Mackay throws in a final, receding blast of treated saxophone, sounding very like those "foghorn blares" on the title track, only sweeter-natured. The track's concluding moments, hesitant and haunting, quote the nursery motif of Brahms' *Lullaby and Good Night*, and, with that, the album winds down in time with the music box itself.

Conjuring up a dreamlike state of suspended animation, this is a truly ravishing performance in which nobody puts a foot wrong, the rhythm section in particular doing wonders during the protracted outro. The spell-stopped atmosphere takes the listener right back to, of all things, *The Bob (Medley)*, in which Ferry muttered dreamily of the magic time when the raucous sounds of a party give place to peace and tranquillity. And, in light of this closing track, the "netherworld dancing toys" pictured on the album cover suddenly appear like ghosts, vanishing at break of day only to be wound up for an identical round of empty hedonism at a later date.

In the *NME*, Max Bell reserved special mention for *Spin Me Round*, noting that it "boasts the album's one great arrangement, a hypnotic whirlpool of balletic grace and a poignant lyric to match." Perhaps unsurprisingly, Roxy omitted to add the delicate and hard-to-reproduce textures of *Spin Me Round* to their 1979 stage act, nor have they attempted it since. Much more surprising, the track failed to make it onto the *Thrill of It All* box set in 1995, though its importance had already been acknowledged from a different quarter. Given the way in which the *Manifesto* album would sink deep into the fabric of the burgeoning New Romantic movement, it's appropriate that David Sylvian should mutter the phrase "spin me round" on the title track of Japan's 1980 album *Gentlemen Take Polaroids*.

Trash 2
(Ferry-Manzanera) 3:09

Flip-side of the *Trash* single (and back-up to *Dance Away* in the US), this replaces the manic strut of its fast and furious forebear with a kind of somnambulant zombie shuffle, particularly in Ferry's vocal. An opening array of synthetic strings could have done with the kind of personal stamp Eddie Jobson would have given them, though ominous touches of bass guitar maintain interest and the mid-song break, thoroughly unhinged in the original, here becomes a funky melange of choppy guitars, 60s-style organ and a positively jaunty theme picked out on the bogus violin. To mark Ferry's departure, the strings exhale briefly in an eerily effective imitation of Mackay's oboe (or maybe Mackay's oboe exhales briefly in an eerily effective imitation of the strings) and the track fades out on an engaging repetition of that jaunty violin motif.

Trash 2 has attracted a certain amount of misplaced opprobrium over the years. "As you might expect, *Trash 2* is simply an alternate version of the album track, here rendered slower," observed Dave Connolly on his Progrography website. "Since you could probably achieve the same effect by playing *Trash* at a lower speed, I wouldn't make acquiring *Trash 2* a priority." In *Unknown Pleasures*, Paul Stump went further, dismissing it as "flaccid" and "a mimsy cop-out of a take on the original."

And yet it has a certain weight and presence, the strings in particular giving it a dense, danse macabre feel. Something about Ferry's robotic vocal, together with the sludge-like consistency of the instrumentation, suggests that the New Wave thrash of the A-side has been supplanted by something more akin to the hypnotic drone of *The Bogus Man*. And if that connection identifies the song's 17-year-old protagonist as one of the creepy, empty-handed simulacra featured on the *Manifesto* album cover, then the point is made more forcefully by *Trash 2* than *Trash* itself.

South Downs
(Ferry) 5:08

Like *Sultanesque*, this is a solo performance on synthesiser by a presumably after-hours Bryan Ferry. This one was extemporised during the *Manifesto* sessions at Ridge Farm in November 1978, finally emerging as B-side to *Oh Yeah* in July 1980. Unlike *Sultanesque*, it's reasonably listenable, in no way matching Eno's ambient experiments in similar mode but providing an agreeable aural impression of rolling countryside. But, as rock music evocations of the South Downs go (and it must be a pretty small field), it would be firmly trounced by the astonishing *Cissbury Ring* cycle concluding Manzanera's 2004 solo album, *6PM*.

Even considered as a B-side it remains a flimsy and rather token gesture; where most Roxy fans no doubt failed to sit through the appalling *Sultanesque* even once, this one was treated to maybe one airing before being forgotten about altogether. Fans would hear it again, however, when it was used as the opening theme for Roxy's contemporaneous live shows. Joining the likes of *The Pride and the Pain* before it and *India* to follow, the fog-laden strains of *South Downs* proved a suitably tantalising introductory backdrop to Roxy's 1980 tour, offering a deceptively soporific cue for the sudden percussive arrival of *The Bogus Man* and the heart-in-mouth elevation of the set's giant Venetian blinds.

The track was recycled along with another hard-to-find B-side, *Lover*, on a *Jealous Guy* CD single issued by Virgin in 1988. Seven years later, it resurfaced on the fourth disc of the *Thrill of It All* box set, bizarrely running backwards owing to a pressing error. (Another such error cropped up on the third disc, *While My Heart is Still Beating* being accidentally prefaced by the final drum-box patterns of *India*.) Ferry's original at least had a lachrymose garnishing of synthetic strings to lend glamour to the pervading fug, suggesting an oncoming pea-souper mist twinkling with drops of dew. The reverse version smothers the strings completely, leaving just an undifferentiated haze that's no doubt skipped over by discerning Roxy fans to this day.

Seventeen: *Same Old Scene*

"I didn't take to dressing up at all ... On the Manifesto *tour we started off wearing suits. No way was I going to wear a suit while playing! I wore one for the first gig and then went back to black T-shirts."*

Paul Thompson, quoted in *Mojo* December 1995

So good to be back home again

As the critical responses to the *Manifesto* album came in, Roxy took a breather lasting some two weeks before moving the accompanying tour to the USA, the itinerary starting on Wednesday 28 March in Philadelphia. The next night they performed in New York (with an enthusiastic David Bowie in attendance), after which they visited Boston, Oakland, Detroit, Chicago, Buffalo, Columbus, Milwaukee, Kansas City, Minneapolis, Omaha, Denver, Cleveland, Pasadena and San Diego. Four days later, on Thursday 26 April, they were in Japan for a three-day stint embracing Nagoya, Osaka and Tokyo.

Shortly before setting out on the US tour, Mackay informed *Record Mirror's* Rosalind Russell that "Roxy has always done well in big cities. We like playing industrial towns – the dingier the town or industrial environment, the better we do. In the big cities, like London, the first four rows are full of people who've got free tickets and who think it's not cool to clap. We do a long set and unless you get something back from the audience you wonder why you're bothering." Surprisingly, Roxy's US audiences gave back a great deal in 1979. The adulation the band received was not confined, as before, to old Roxy strongholds like Detroit and Cleveland; it was now widespread, helping the *Manifesto* album reach its encouraging high of number 23 on the *Billboard* chart.

There wasn't time for the band to rest on their laurels, however; a mere four days after performing in Tokyo, they were at Leicester's De Montfort Hall on Wednesday 2 May for the beginning of their first British tour since the autumn of 1975. Support act on these UK dates was The Tourists, a much-maligned group here making their live debut and soon to score with the singles *I Only Want to Be With You* and *So Good to Be Back Home Again*. Later to form Eurythmics, Annie Lennox and Dave Stewart were here promoting their LP *Reality Effect*, as well as being fully aware of the tensions characterising Roxy's return to their home turf; as Stewart put it at the time, "There was a lot at stake for Roxy personally and professionally."

The tour comprised two nights each at Birmingham, Manchester, Glasgow and Newcastle, with one-off dates at Liverpool, Bristol and·Southampton preceding a three-night tenure of London's Hammersmith Odeon. Just as Roxy's show in Denver Colorado would give rise to any number of audio bootlegs, so the Manchester dates were recorded by Granada TV for their *On the Road* showcase, resurfacing on video in the 1990s and on DVD in 2003, complete with one of Ferry's most memorable on-stage witticisms: "I suppose you've noticed we've got the outside broadcast unit from *Coronation Street* here tonight."

Melody Maker's James Truman was present at the final Hammersmith date on Friday 18 May, noting that Manzanera's guitar slipped out of tune in the opening minutes, necessitating an emergency switch to an untreated Les Paul for the remainder of the set, and that *Angel Eyes* and *Ain't That So* were the surprise highlights of the evening.

These two, he claimed, "underline Roxy's new approach to performing. Whereas with Eno, and to a lesser extent Eddie Jobson, the stage offered chances for pulling the songs off into unexpected tangents, the new line-up affords the opportunity of working from within, softening the music's rigid structures and applying a new sensuality." He also scrutinised the audience with a jaundiced eye: "Beside the occasional bit of moth-eaten glam tattoo, it's straight-ahead weekend crossover Ford Capris, beer guts and bomber jackets, the antithesis of the young exquisites who documented the early years." Then came the rhetorical question, "Had Roxy Music survived with more dignity than their fans?"

Plus ça change

By this time, *Dance Away* was shouldering its way up the singles chart – indeed, it would reach its high point of number two the following Tuesday – so the band's dignity was intact as far as record sales were concerned. This, in turn, presumably meant that some of the tensions noticed by Dave Stewart were now easing off. Rather than facing indifference from the record-buying public, however, Roxy found themselves faced instead with the dismissive attitude of a music press utterly transformed by the emergence of punk, a music press for whom the phrase 'sell-out' was just as bitterly talismanic as 'hype' had been to Roxy's hippie antagonists in 1972.

Mackay and Manzanera were to experience this holier-than-thou attitude at first hand. The last time Siouxsie and the Banshees attended a Roxy show was back in 1975, the occasion effectively marking the inauguration of the band. Now they were at the after-show party on Roxy's first Hammersmith date, with Steve Severin buttonholing Mackay and Manzanera to fling the 'sell-out' accusation at them, an impertinence he had cause to remember with embarrassment when recording *Happy House* and *Christine* at Manzanera's Chertsey studio the following year. "Funnily enough," he mused, "when the Banshees were recording *Juju* [their 1981 album] we did some recording in Phil Manzanera's studio. I think he probably lent us a guitar."

Mackay, in particular, had no time for the fashionable vagaries of the rock comics. When discussing the newly famous hatchet-job duo of Tony Parsons and Julie Burchill, he was prepared to be drolly facetious: "He [Parsons] interviewed Bryan and I in an Italian restaurant. He was wearing a vest, I remember. How dare he interview us in a vest? It's a wonder he wasn't mistaken for one of the cooks." Elsewhere, however, he adopted a darker tone, noting in 1981 that "I stopped reading the rock papers when they started becoming abusive. They just remind me how silly it is that the Youth Cult should have persisted for over 20 years. The reason why we're better on stage nowadays is simply because we know the importance of entertaining an audience.

"Watching a lot of new bands, I'm always disappointed by their amateurishness; the whole idea of being slightly rude to your audience and refusing to give encores simply does not work. The idea that you're at your best as a semi-competent teenager, and that you have to be horrible to be any good, is totally daft and clearly another case of promotional manipulation. That's why New Wave, insofar as there ever was such a thing, was just a manufactured myth, and *The Great Rock'n'Roll Swindle* was a great film because it recognised all the ironies and made fun of them. The mistake of the music press is to make rules and generalisations about rock music, and I don't think you can."

Mackay was well aware that the New Wave's veneration of 'integrity' was no different to that of the long-hairs who had sniffed at Roxy seven years earlier, and the barbs were just as irritating as before. Visibly chafing, he conceded that "The main accusation was that Bryan's solo records weren't selling as well as they used to, and none of us were as prosperous as we once were, and that was why we revived the band. But their mistake was to think we had any integrity in the first place – not in the sense they mean, anyway. Your ultimate aim is simply to entertain people and enjoy yourself by playing music you like. But you must never let the public lead you. Respect for your audience, in terms of giving 100 per cent and never letting them down, is not the same thing at all as just giving the public what they want."

Happily, the response to *Dance Away* indicated that one thing the public definitely wanted was the new-style Roxy Music. A follow-up was urgently called for, and, with no new material to hand, Roxy elected to revamp a track already included on the *Manifesto* album.

*   *   *

Angel Eyes ['remake']
(Ferry-Mackay) 3:07 / extended version 6:37

After the muted disco flavourings brought to the hugely lucrative *Dance Away*, it was decided that *Angel Eyes* should be given a full-on dancefloor makeover – and not just remixed to that end, but entirely re-recorded. The result is one of Roxy's most irresistible singles, with the added bonus of a smoothly imaginative 12" version to boot.

Cued by the beguilingly futuristic new sounds emanating from mainland Europe – in particular Giorgio Moroder's epoch-making production job on Donna Summer's *I Feel Love* – disco producers were soon making explicit reference to science fiction in a series of hit records that ranged from the sublime (Sheila & B Devotion's Chic-produced *Spacer*) to the ridiculous (Sarah Brightman's *I Lost My Heart to a Starship Trooper*, Crown Heights Affair's *Galaxy of Love*), with Britain's very own The Real Thing falling somewhere inbetween on the anthemic *Can You Feel the Force*. It was upon this space-age subgenre of disco that Roxy turned a sardonic eye when refashioning *Angel Eyes*, and it was an appropriate target given Roxy's own space-age plumage back in 1972. *Angel Eyes* would accordingly become the eerie 'lunar landing' prologue of *Ladytron* set to a thunderous disco beat.

The opening is hypnotic – the metronomic clatter of the rhythm box, the absurd washes of smoothly plucked harp, Ferry "woo-wooing" wordlessly to a jangling Manzanera backdrop, and finally Mackay introducing the vocal proper with a gorgeous, twice-repeated sax riff. As sci-fi synth noises skitter across the soundstage, Ferry's vocal (despite dropping the original's third verse with its suggestive line, "seems to me you fill the skies") makes it clearer than ever that the subject of the song is a being not merely unattainable but literally celestial. A breathlessly expectant middle-eight concludes with Mackay and Manzanera trading clangorous three-note riffs, and the track's metallic swing winds up with

Ferry exchanging warbled invocations to his loved one with what sounds like a fleet of ghost backing vocalists in the sky.

Dance Away having slipped out of the Top 40 only four weeks earlier, the revamped *Angel Eyes* entered the singles chart on 7 August at number 32; by coincidence, an identically titled Abba single was then in the top five. By the 28th it had reached number four, directly behind Gary Numan's *Cars* but some way short of Cliff Richard's Number One ballad *We Don't Talk Anymore*. It remained stalled at four for a further week before leaving the chart altogether on 16 October, after a run of 11 weeks.

Given the boring job applied earlier to the extended version of *Dance Away*, and the similarly uninspiring 12″ treatment accorded *The Main Thing* in 1982, Bob Clearmountain's extended *Angel Eyes* is a delight, bringing Gary Tibbs' funky bass to the fore and also foregrounding those phoney harps and skittering sci-fi flutes. And, excepting the barely seen promo films for *Re-make/Re-model* and *Both Ends Burning*, *Angel Eyes* became the first Roxy track to sport an accompanying video. Wreathed in dry ice, Ferry is seen tottering atop a Grecian pillar in lavender-coloured leather, while Mackay (still in his Oriental phase) is togged up in a mandarin-collared glitter jacket and sports a very peculiar two-pronged hunting horn. Looking back, Manzanera has nostalgically dusted off the bluebottle shades of yore, while, looking forward, the serenely unruffled lady harpist seems to be auditioning for a spot on the upcoming *Flesh + Blood* cover.

Antony Price's striking photo for the *Angel Eyes* picture sleeve – again utilising two of the *Manifesto* dummies, but this time refitting them with absurd 1940s pompadours – wouldn't have disgraced one of the band's album covers. Twenty-one years later, in fact, a slight variant of it was used for the sleeve of Virgin's *The Early Years* compilation; an odd choice, however, in that the image obviously came from the band's later years.

The revamped *Angel Eyes* provided the cue for an unusually prescient, unsigned review in *Melody Maker*'s singles round-up of 4 August. "Re-recording of the album track, from which everyone benefits," it began. "The elements of Roxy's disco appeal are laid bare – Giorgio Moroder twiddles, soul guitar, hard sax sound, Ferry's casual, cool vocals. Appropriately enough, Roxy Music enter the 1980s as a single-minded dance band."

* * *

That's your actual French

Rather in the style of middle-class theatregoers thronging the Royal Court to lap up plays lambasting the middle class, the satirical *Trash* had by now become a favourite of the young people flocking to London's Blitz Club, young people soon to be dubbed New Romantics. While the 33-year-old Mackay inveighed against the media obsession with Youth Cults, he was presumably unaware that the *Manifesto* album – together with the glamorous imagery of the *Angel Eyes* video – were to be in large part responsible for the creation of an entirely new one.

Having sought so viciously to kick over the traces of glam rock, punk had succeeded only in resurrecting it in an infinitely more effete and self-reflexive form. At the tail end of 1979, a band previously responsible for lumbering prentice efforts like *Adolescent Sex* and *Obscure Alternatives* came up with a remarkable album called *Quiet Life*, its shimmering synthetic textures helping to crystallise a new sound popularised later by the likes of Duran Duran and Spandau Ballet. These trailblazers – David Sylvian, Mick Karn, Richard Barbieri and Steve Jansen – were collectively known as Japan and their album was produced by former Roxy associate John Punter. Just listening to one track on the LP – *Despair*, with its doleful saxophone, French lyric and Ferry-inflected vocal – should be enough to indicate how deeply Roxy were embedded in the genetic make-up of the burgeoning New Romantics.

Though he would soon grow tired of being asked what he thought of Duran Duran and others, Ferry was more concerned in the autumn of 1979 with making his acting debut. The man who had once craved Robert Redford's role in *The Great Gatsby* – and been conveniently unavailable for parts in Pete Walker's proto-slasher films – now elected to appear in a Swiss-French television soap opera called *Petit Déjeuner Compris* (Bed and Breakfast). Playing a former friend of a deceased hotelier who has a fling with the dead woman's niece, Ferry was more or less playing himself, a fact which became very clear when the niece and her husband enjoyed a touching reconciliation while attending a Roxy gig at the Pavillon.

Given that *Petit Déjeuner Compris* was a Gallic counterpart to Britain's much reviled *Crossroads*, Ferry had presumably lowered his sights considerably where acting aspirations were concerned. "You have to be a bit more of a show-off than I am to be an actor," he admitted to Lynn Hanna three years later. "You really have to love yourself, and there are people who really do. I've got nothing against that because I love movies and stars. There are certain faces that you just like to see – Charlton Heston, Marlon Brando, whoever. I once played a small role in a Swiss television show and I hated watching myself. I kept thinking, Oh God, what a terrible camera angle."

Back in more familiar TV territory, Ferry had a new – well, new old – song up his sleeve for Roxy Music's final performance of the 1970s. This was broadcast on Monday 31 December as part of a bill that also included – appropriately, given the parallel lines on which their respective careers had run throughout the dying decade – David Bowie. Cliff Richard and The Boomtown Rats were also featured, along with a bizarre, one-off combination of Thin Lizzy with various stragglers from The Sex Pistols.

ITV viewers fresh from *Carry On Dick*, and before that a New Year's Eve special featuring Max Bygraves and bandleader Geoff Love (*Max with Love*), were treated at 11:00 pm to *The 'Will Kenny Everett Make It to 1980?' Show*, a special edition of *The Kenny Everett Video Show* that the Hogmanay-phobic Everett had initially wanted to call 'The Show That Saved You from Andy Stewart'. As Everett's Tharg the Wonder Computer fluted tonelessly at the top of the programme: "Boomtown Rats and Suzie Q [Quatro] / Cliff and Hot Gossip too / Roxy Music and Bowie / Will play just for you." Undaunted by Everett's anti-Hogmanay attitude, Mackay lent a Scots flavour to Roxy's appearance by wearing a tartan jacket at least as lurid as the red-and-white bathing costumes of the dancing girls semaphoring in the background. Ferry, too, wore a white leather suit and red leather tie matching that of the dancers, whose ultra-camp choreography recalled the old US TV show *Shindig* and would be replicated by the similarly costumed dancing girls in Roxy's reunion dates of 2001.

While Cliff Richard was resurrecting an old recording, *Devil Woman*, both Bowie and Roxy would release the performances originated here at the dawn of the new decade. In February 1980, Bowie's acoustic version of *Space Oddity* would fetch up as the B-side to his *Alabama Song* single, and in May Roxy's take on Wilson Pickett's *The Midnight Hour*, only slightly remixed from the track mimed to here, would lead off their *Flesh + Blood* album.

Eighteen: *The Seventh Roxy Music Album*

"Flesh + Blood is such a shockingly bad Roxy Music record that it provokes a certain fascination. The line on early Roxy (when Eno was a member) was that the band radiated high-tech decadence, and Flesh + Blood *connects with this historical interpretation by confirming the decadent part: eg, what could be more outré right now than an art-rock disco album?"*

Ken Tucker, *Rolling Stone* 4 September 1980

R eassembling in 1980, Roxy recorded *Flesh + Blood* at Basing Street and Gallery Studio, a newly inaugurated facility in the grounds of the so-called 'Manzanera Towers' in Chertsey. Having co-engineered their previous album, Rhett Davies was here promoted to producer, though his Roxy associations actually stretched back well before *Manifesto*. For Ferry, he had been an assistant engineer on *Another Time, Another Place*, while for Manzanera he had engineered *Diamond Head, 801 Live* and *Listen Now!!* More significantly, he had graduated from engineering Eno's *Taking Tiger Mountain (By Strategy)* to co-producing both *Another Green World* and *Before and After Science* with the man himself. Proving his versatility, straight after recording *Flesh + Blood* he decamped to the Bahamas in April to produce *Wild Planet*, the remarkable second album by The B-52's.

Flesh + Blood continued, and much expanded, the *Manifesto* procedure of surrounding the core Roxy members with top-flight session men. Unfortunately, these star players included three drummers, none of whom was Paul Thompson. The core of Roxy Music had now been whittled down to Ferry, Mackay and Manzanera, a self-described "board of musical directors" surrounded by variously engaged or disengaged session players.

Thompson, it transpired, had been offered up as a sacrificial lamb to Ferry's increasing drive for crossover acceptance in the USA, with Ferry's apologia for Thompson's removal reproduced in an *NME* interview with Chris Bohn in August. "His interest died a long time ago," claimed Ferry. He also cited Thompson's "inflexibility" and, worse, dismissed him as "an inspired amateur," forgetting that he had applied the same epithet to the entire band, himself included, back in 1972, and that at that time it had been meant as a compliment.

Ferry conceded, however, that "Thompson's a great live player," accordingly asking him to join the band on the accompanying *Flesh + Blood* tour. As luck would have it, Thompson was involved in a motorcycle accident in the run-up to the tour, breaking, of all things, a thumb. Andy Newmark was drafted in instead, so Thompson's final Roxy performances remained his TV spots for *The Midnight Hour* on 31 December and *Over You* on 15 May, the latter only a fortnight before Roxy's live schedule got under way.

In October, Thompson would be nominated by bereaved Led Zeppelin fans as a possible replacement for his recently deceased hero John Bonham, while in July 1983 there were similar rumours of his joining AC/DC. Instead, he teamed up with Concrete Blonde and through them garnered a US gold album for the first time – "something I never achieved with Roxy Music," as he happily points out on his personal website. Though nobody could fault the expertise of the players brought in to replace him, it remains the case that Roxy's sound was never quite the same once Thompson's dextrous 'Blooter Blatter' foundations were removed. For the band's final albums, Roxy would become a more ethereal kind of structure, founded on shifting sands rather than Thompson's rock-solid rhythms. That fans preferred the Thompson touch was amply evidenced in 2001, when his return to Roxy was in large part motivated by fan pressure, his presence lending an extra authenticity to the whole enterprise.

In 1980, however, Ferry's US-focused intentions were deep-rooted and inflexible. In July of the following year he informed Paolo Hewitt that *Flesh + Blood* "is still my favourite. It sort of feels good. I don't think it's any cleverer or that the ideas are any better. Just the playing of it is more pleasing to my ear. It swings more, because the trouble with a lot of records I've made is that they don't swing at all. And it's so depressing to listen to your old work and think, 'God, how could I have done *that*

Though most of the percussive duties on *Flesh + Blood* were undertaken by Allan Schwartzberg, it was Andy Newmark whom Ferry considered the real catch in his new-found zeal for smooth US rhythms. Newmark had come to prominence on Sly and the Family Stone's genre-busting *Fresh* album in 1973, also working with an amazing roster of star names that included George Harrison, Carly Simon, George Benson, Tom Verlaine, Grand Funk, B B King, Badfinger, Dan Fogelberg, Rickie Lee Jones, Carole King, Cat Stevens, Jim Capaldi, Steve Winwood – the list goes on. In 1974 he had played on David Bowie's US breakthrough album, *Young Americans*, only missing out on the two tracks Bowie recorded with John Lennon. Soon after *Flesh + Blood*, he would correct that omission by working with Lennon on the latter's *Double Fantasy* LP. For Ferry, meanwhile, he would become a kind of talisman, resurfacing on Roxy's *Avalon* and all six of Ferry's solo albums thereafter.

Disconcerted by the expulsion of Thompson, Gary Tibbs would end up contributing to only one track on *Flesh + Blood* – and, as Kenny Everett's New Year's Eve extravaganza made clear, the track in question, *The Midnight Hour*, was pretty much in the can while Thompson was still in place. The drums credit on the album nevertheless goes to Allan Schwartzberg, with Manzanera's former 801 associate, Simon Phillips, adding grace notes to just one track, *My Only Love*. Tibbs' duties were shouldered by Neil Jason and *Manifesto* veteran Alan Spenner, with *Manifesto*'s Paul Carrack brought in to add keyboards and strings to *Running Wild* and *Oh Yeah* respectively. Even Manzanera found himself shadowed by the rhythm guitar of Neil Hubbard, formerly of Kokomo and several Ferry solo items.

The album cover would be as bland and inoffensive as the music within, though news that Ferry and Antony Price were after living breathing models as of old, rather than the shop-window dummies of *Manifesto*, caused the expected stir. "The word went round the model agencies like a flame through petrol," Price confirmed. "They were queueing up to do it ... All the major dragons wanted the part, and it went to three little girls, complete novices."

These "little Olympian nymphs," as Price described them, are seen toting parallel javelins in a very distant echo of the Nuremberg associations familiar from Roxy's *Country Life* tour, the image coming across as an airbrushed homage to Leni Riefenstahl's notorious documentary film *Olympia*. Given these echoes, the butch Teutonic look of Constanze and Eveline wouldn't have gone amiss here. But maybe that was the joke – the drippy English debs conspicuous by their absence from the *Country Life* cover had been transplanted onto a cover more suited to the Valkyries who *did* appear on the *Country Life* cover. If so, the joke doesn't work. An old-style gatefold sleeve would have come in handy, too, given that the composition unfairly relegates one of the three nymphs to the back cover.

As well as providing Dr Puxley's one and only cover design credit, the *Flesh + Blood* sleeve retained photographer Neil Kirk from *Manifesto* and marked the Roxy debut of Peter Saville, who would later design the sombre picture sleeve for *Oh Yeah* and work with the Ferry-Price-Kirk team again on *Avalon*. The year before *Flesh + Blood*, Saville had co-founded the independent Manchester label Factory Records, his resultant cover designs, notably for Joy Division's *Closer*, having a profound impact on graphic design in the music business and beyond. "Around 1974, Roxy were the biggest single influence in my life," he later told Rick Poynor. "From hairdressing to fine art, all points were covered. I had a good grasp of pop and they were the quintessential living expression of Pop Art."

By late March Ferry was in a blizzard-tossed New York, supervising Bob Clearmountain's mixing job at the Power Station. Preceded by the Top Five single *Over You*, the finished album appeared in the last week of May, charting on the 31st and rapidly proving a major seller. Even the Our Price chain was moved to concoct an ad featuring the album's glamorous spear-carriers alongside the legend, "Note to: Roxy Music. You should see the crowds. *Flesh + Blood* is the main event." The album would spend two separate stints at Number One, totalling four weeks in all, with another 56 ensuring a marathon run in the charts that extended into the middle of 1981. By that time, it had already gone down as the UK's sixth best-selling LP of 1980.

Critical responses to the album included Paul Morley's judgment in the *NME* that "*Flesh + Blood* is at once elusive and indulgent, graceful and infuriating, technically adventurous and immensely calculated." His further description of it as "an environment not an album" was a prophetic one in that it would apply far more cogently to the upcoming *Avalon*, though Morley's observation that the album saw Roxy "selling bitterweet fantasies and seductive happy endings, making music where the nostalgic tendencies are impossibly correct" was more in line with his trademark style of postmodern impenetrability.

In *Time Out*, Steve Taylor began by characterising its predecessor, *Manifesto*, as "Definitely not a replay of the epoch-turning *Roxy Music* or *For Your Pleasure*, but neither was it a *Siren*-like paean to indecision. Its gamut of sharp turn-of-the-decade dance melodies has given way on *Flesh + Blood* to a tighter Roxy, assured of survival on the strength of Bryan Ferry's superbly apposite compositions and ear for side-men. Ferry's own keyboards, bolstered by the excellent Paul Carrack, Phil Manzanera's laterally thought guitar soloing, and a great Anglo-American rhythm section which includes ex-Kokomo Alan Spenner, realise some of the sharpest Roxy songs to date and two intriguing covers. Brilliant mainstream rock for unselfconscious enjoyment."

The LP also received an enthusiastic send-off in the *Sunday Times* from the straitlaced Derek Jewell, who claimed that "Roxy have never sounded better, with Bryan Ferry's air of debauched elegance dominating the proceedings," adding that "The ideas and arrangements are highly inventive." As author of *The Popular Voice*, a benchmark tome devoted to the kind of crooners Ferry was a latterday extension of, Jewell was well placed to draw attention to Ferry's "newly matured, totally original vocal style."

In the USA, however, the album was comprehensively savaged by *Rolling Stone*'s Ken Tucker, who, among other choice epithets, called it "shockingly bad," also noting that "if the rest of Roxy Music is as bored as they seem, Bryan Ferry sounds positively bound and gagged. The best he can do is add a little tension by muttering the lyrics through clenched teeth and a constricted throat. He seems to be trying to get his messages out to us without the other musicians hearing him." As for *Creem*, a facetious non-review by Mitchell Cohen, imagining Ferry doing a cabaret stint with comedian Rodney Dangerfield, finally yielded the judgment that *Flesh + Blood* was "bleak, arid, and yet somehow sensuous and fascinating." Irrespective of these verdicts, the American market continued to resist in any case; for all Roxy's newly mellifluous sound, plus Ferry's inclusion of two US-friendly cover versions, the album rose only to number 35, a notable drop on the position scored by *Manifesto*.

Starting at Le Mans on Saturday 29 May, the tour accompanying *Flesh + Blood* was a massive, and massively successful, one. As well as Newmark, the musicians backing Ferry, Manzanera and Mackay were Carrack, Hubbard and Tibbs. Four further French dates preceded a long trek through Belgium, Germany, the Netherlands, Denmark, Sweden, Switzerland and Italy. There were 20 engagements in Germany alone, along with further dates in France and four scheduled gigs in Spain and Portugal that had to be cancelled when Ferry collapsed after a show in Nice on 12 July.

"I was writhing in pain," he told the *Sunday Telegraph*'s Jim Crace. "I was brought back to England by ambulance plane, surrounded by drips and nurses. It was just like Howard Hughes being wheeled across the tarmac. There were photographers everywhere!" Ferry recovered from his kidney infection in record time, however, re-emerging on Wednesday the 23rd for a gig at Brighton's Conference Centre. Two performances apiece at Birmingham, Manchester and Glasgow preceded two nights at Wembley Arena on 1 and 2 August. These climactic gigs were taped by the BBC for use on Paul Gambaccini's Radio 1 programme *In Concert*, the show going out on 26 December and also being syndicated in the USA.

The support act was US band Martha and the Muffins, who had recently charted with the infectious single *Echo Beach* and, according to *Melody Maker*, "looked out of their depth in such cavernous surroundings." Roxy's stage set consisted of a towering phalanx of Venetian blinds, which only unfurled halfway through the long-unheard strains of *The Bogus Man*. With the spidery silhouettes of Ferry, Mackay and Manzanera backlit into colossal relief, the final elevation of the blinds provided a genuine coup de théâtre.

Immediately prior to their Wembley dates, the band had performed *Oh Yeah* on the 31 July edition of *Top of the Pops*. Also on the show were Northern Ireland's The Undertones, performing their hit *Wednesday Week* and reportedly clustering round Ferry for autographs in the hospitality area afterwards. Roxy's enormously protracted German itinerary, meanwhile, had thrown up a stint on *Musikladen*, the band's performance of *Over You* going out on 19 June, with *Oh Yeah* held back until 9 October. They were also billed opposite Van Halen, Styx and The J Geils Band on the 21 June edition of *Rock Pop*, appearing on the programme again on 8 November.

Given its phenomenal sales and the triumphal progress of the accompanying tour, some of the album's less-than-flattering reviews could easily be dismissed. Ferry himself accounted for the unprecedented success of *Flesh + Blood* in simple terms: "The music was more clearly defined and controlled, as opposed to the earlier stuff which was slightly more complex and not so easy on the ear. And I don't think it's necessarily a bad thing to make a record people can hear and like it instantly."

* * *

Manifesto ['remake']
(Ferry-Manzanera) 4:00

Just as Ferry had felt the need to refashion several tracks from the original *Roxy Music* album as solo B-sides, so the opening three cuts on the 'new' Roxy's debut album would be remade/remodelled, though this time under the Roxy imprimatur. While *Trash 2* was a makeover contemporaneous with its original and *Angel Eyes* a disco reimagining concocted several months later, *Manifesto* was retooled during the *Flesh + Blood* sessions and used as the B-side to *Over You*, where it would remain for 15 years until resurrected on the 'odds and sods' disc of the *Thrill of It All* box set.

The tone is noticeably more upbeat, with the nightmare advance of the original deleted in favour of an uplifting signature riff from Manzanera and plenty of thudding electronic percussion – somewhat muted, unfortunately, in the mix prepared for the box set. Ferry's vocal is as garrulous as ever but split this time into three sections, in sharp contrast to the inexorable litany poured out in one go on the LP version. This gives Manzanera the chance to restate that infectious, anthemic riff at each interval, but it also causes a bit of trouble with Ferry's trademark word-play, particularly when the phrase "all or nothing" is bisected by the instrumental break, nonsensically, after the word 'all'.

Garnished with the electronic throb of a shimmering string section, and with what sounded on vinyl like some last-minute shrills of Mackay's oboe regrettably airbrushed out on the remastered *Thrill of It All* mix, this new *Manifesto* is an intriguing experiment but by no means the blood-curdling experience provided by the original. Though just as radical a recasting as Ferry's solo versions of *Re-make/Re-model* and *Casanova*, the featureless wash of 1980s electronics in which it's smothered renders it perfectly listenable but somehow redundant. Even so, it represented better value than Roxy's preceding 45s, which had slapped album tracks *Cry, Cry, Cry* and *My Little Girl* onto songs culled from the same source.

The Midnight Hour
(Cropper-Pickett) 3:12

In May 1980, buyers of the new Roxy Music album were immediately intrigued to find two cover versions listed on the back cover – an indicator, it was surmised, of a lack of material or, worse, Ferry's desire to bring the group more into line with his largely anodyne solo recordings.

The latter concern had been voiced, albeit inadvertently, several months earlier, when the first of these covers received its debut courtesy of Thames TV's New Year's Eve special, *The 'Will Kenny Everett Make It to 1980?' Show*. Everett himself – in blackface no less – introduced Roxy's performance with the following tongue-in-cheek rap: "And now, we are going to bring you some real funky soul rhythms. We got a song here all about what night it is here currently. It's called *Gonna Wait Till the Midnight Hour*. It's by who? [scandalised:] Bryan Ferry? That man's a honky!"

Fans whose hackles had been raised by Everett's attribution of the track to Ferry rather than Roxy were perhaps mollified by the finished product, which kicks off the *Flesh + Blood* album on a mellow and engaging note. Wilson Pickett's original, recorded in 1965 at the legendary Stax studios in Memphis, had been a number 21 hit in the US prior to reaching number 12 in the UK; it was co-written by Steve Cropper, guitarist with the Stax house band Booker T and the MGs and a key architect of the Memphis 'sound'. The Roxy interpretation in no way recalls the sonic attack of previous album openers (*Do the Strand*, say, or *The Thrill of It All*) but provides an accurate index to the laid-back groove *Flesh + Blood* is to follow almost throughout.

The track opens with a subliminal nod to *Love is the Drug* – a split-second crunch of shoe leather on gravel – before Ferry counts us down to midnight and the song proper gets into gear on a dozily blurted cue from Mackay. As indicated, it's hardly a high gear, but Ferry's half-tranquilised invocation of the midnight hour is beautifully supported by Gary Tibbs' rolling bass, Manzanera's circling guitar and a simple but highly effective sax break from Mackay. The latter, incidentally, is the only part of the recording that differs from the initial track Roxy mimed to on the Everett special; there, the drums (still played by Thompson at that stage) went into a syncopated and much funkier rhythm while Mackay's sax was treated in a style reminiscent of Eno's tamperings of yore.

Just as Ferry's refined vocal couldn't be more different from Pickett's testosterone-fuelled approach in the original, so Mackay's radiant alto (treated or not) stands in stark contrast to the trademark bray of the Stax horn section. Ferry, in particular, doesn't sound like the kind of man whose love is likely to "come tumbling down" at midnight or any other time. Between them, however, Ferry and Mackay banish all memories of the former's stumbling attempts to sound black on his solo albums, instead refashioning *The Midnight Hour* as a song ideally suited to Roxy Music. The newly remade-remodelled Roxy Music at any rate.

The track clicked even with *Rolling Stone*'s Ken Tucker, who tore the accompanying album to very comprehensive shreds. "*Flesh + Blood*'s one clearheaded success, Wilson Pickett's *In the Midnight Hour*," he wrote, "is a brilliant choice for Ferry, who loves to find ready-made existentialism in such unironic styles as Sixties pop and soul. Here, he twists Pickett's howl of discrete carnality into the moan of an aesthete's orgasm."

Nitpickers take note: the song's full title – *In the Midnight Hour* – is retained on the album's inner sleeve and even the label, though it mysteriously loses the 'In' on the cover itself, which is the example followed here. The track was issued as a single in the USA and Portugal, the picture sleeve showing the band (plus semaphoring dancing girls) during their Kenny Everett performance.

Oh Yeah
(Ferry) 4:50 / single edit 4:12

If *Dance Away* achieved Ferry's long-held ambition and became accepted as a modern standard, it's hard to see why the same accolade has yet to be bestowed on *Oh Yeah*, which is perhaps the most limpidly beautiful ballad in his portfolio.

Unashamedly sentimental but performed with utter conviction by all concerned, it deals in the simplest kind of 'lost love' imagery – memories of a broken affair triggered by a familiar song on the radio – and smuggles into its delicate fabric a killer chorus to boot. On top of which, Noël Coward's dictum regarding the peculiar potency of 'cheap music' is here given a self-reflexive twist: the song that stirs all the bitter-sweet memories is called *Oh Yeah*, just like this one, so the impression that we're dealing with a song-within-a-song-within-a-song underlines the universality of the emotions involved. We've all been here, in short, and the song's power derives from the fact that Ferry is dealing for a change – straightforwardly, sincerely – in common currency.

All the instrumentation here meshes perfectly to create a spellbinding effect; even the session players sound fully engaged, with Paul Carrack's synthetic strings providing elegiac touches and Allan Schwartzberg's drums adding genuine muscle as each chorus rolls around. Mackay is more discreet, interjecting some typically idiosyncratic hiccoughs to the second chorus, droning subliminally behind Manzanera's solo, and finally adding some lovely grace notes to the song's dying fade, which is further distinguished by Neil Jason's beautifully measured bass line.

Manzanera, meanwhile, joins with Neil Hubbard to create the "rhythm of rhyming guitars" specified by Ferry's lyric, which elsewhere trades cheerfully in outright cliché – car radios, movie shows, "our song" – but nevertheless creates a moving contrast between innocence and experience in the space of two verses. Rarely has Ferry sounded more vulnerable; the melody spelled out by his piano is also suffused with resignation and regret, and the double-tracked heavenly Ferrys heard on the titular refrain pack an emotional punch of their own.

Some of the imagery seems to echo that of Ferry's *Another Time, Another Place*; the indolent lover reminiscing at home and voluntarily spinning emotionally charged discs is here discovered out and about in his car, suffering involuntary pangs when the DJ puts on a painfully nostalgic song. But the spooky atmosphere and savage release of the earlier song are missing, as is the ironic distance. Indeed, the triumph of *Oh Yeah* lies in its use of the clichés listed above, Ferry enlisting the full armoury of the traditionally manipulative love song yet somehow making a truthful and genuinely affecting statement with it.

For its single release, the song was shorn of its uniquely poignant dying fall but acquired a subtitle, becoming *Oh Yeah (on the radio)*. Taking no chances, the US version came up with the idiot-proof *Oh Yeah (There's a Band Playing on the Radio)*. (To confuse matters further, subsequent compilations have occasionally appended an entirely inappropriate exclamation mark to the basic title.) Starting at number 30 on 29 July, the single was showcased on *Top of the Pops* two days later (the band knee-deep in dry ice and introduced by Elton John, no less), leapt to nine the following week and hit a high of number five on the 12th, directly behind a startling new entry for David Bowie, *Ashes to Ashes*. It left the chart five weeks later, on 18 September. In America, however, it did nothing, despite, or perhaps because of, that extended title. Ferry had nursed high hopes for its US acceptance, and, in view of the song's vaguely transatlantic allusions to the open road and drive-in cinemas, not to mention that infectious chorus, this was a reasonable assumption.

Oh Yeah was covered by The Divine Comedy (aka Irish singer-songwriter Neil Hannon) as B-side to the aptly titled 2002 single *Perfect Lovesong*.

Same Old Scene

(Ferry) 3:57

"And the same old soundtrack," muttered the indefatigable singles reviewer of *Melody Maker*. "Richard Gere could have tripped the light fantastic to this in [Paul Schrader's film] *American Gigolo* and it would have all passed by before we even noticed. Empty, disco-orientated pap that does their once great name a disservice. In every dreamband a heartache."

Though disco was still a dirty word to *Melody Maker* and many others, the infectious rhythmic pulse of *Same Old Scene* certainly wasn't about to "pass by before we even noticed." Indeed, it would prove at least as influential as anything on Roxy's earliest albums, and in record time too. Its supercharged kinetic attack, as Paul Stump aptly puts it in *Unknown Pleasures*, "was imprinted upon every new popster's eardrum almost immediately, most notably upon Duran Duran, who first built a debut single (*Planet Earth*) and then a career upon this one brief moment of Roxy Music studio harmonisation."

Ferry's vocal, pitched high and attractively double-tracked in the choruses, gives a deceptively euphoric kick to an otherwise cynical lyric, extolling the repetitive scene even as its enervating qualities curdle nicely behind his words. This isn't quite the danse macabre conjured up by *Do the Strand*, but it still depicts a nocturnal existence devoted to non-stop clubbing and younger partners as a deadening vacuum. One phrase, in particular – a repeated mantra with which the track both begins and ends – carries a heavy weight of rueful self-knowledge, so much so that it could easily be mistaken for the song's title. Reviewing Roxy's live act on 9 August, *Melody Maker*'s Steve Sutherland did exactly that, pointing out that "Gary Tibbs' bass is always powerful and especially tasty on the disco-oriented *Nothing Lasts Forever*."

Bass guitar on the album version was handled in typically funky fashion by Alan Spenner, and, for all Ferry's plangent vocal, it's in its instrumentation that *Same Old Scene* made its most indelible impact. The breakneck energy of earlier material – *Editions of You*, say – is here wedded to the New York groove of Chic's *I Want Your Love* to produce a St Vitus Dance hybrid resonating to an awesome clatter of competing guitars, bass and synthesisers. The rinky-dink opening, with its call-and-response dialogue between a chattering drumbox and monosyllabic guitar licks, is irresistible, and Ferry's ritzy keyboard break midway through is doubly so. Manzanera's rattling chords ring out across the soundstage with scattergun virtuosity, and Mackay tops the whole thing off with the rollicking intrusion of multi-tracked saxes. A bit impersonal by Mackay's standards, these nevertheless send the track into a giddy whirlpool of a fade-out, exemplifying the frenetic circularity of Ferry's nocturnal round.

In line with the release pattern adopted the previous year, the singles excerpted from *Flesh + Blood* would graduate from a vaguely outré pop-rocker (*Over You* in the space formerly filled by *Trash*) to a wistful ballad (*Oh Yeah* doubling for *Dance Away*) and finally an out-and-out disco anthem, with *Same Old Scene* accordingly being put out in the slot previously occupied by *Angel Eyes*. Backed by the non-album track *Lover* (which could well have been a hit in its own right), it entered the Top 40, then dominated by Blondie's *The Tide is High*, on 4 November at number 29. After only a week it reached a peak of number 12 (with a new entry for Abba's *Super Trouper* on its coat-tails) and departed the chart relatively rapidly on 16 December.

Again following the release pattern of the *Manifesto* singles, *Same Old Scene* was, like *Angel Eyes*, the only *Flesh + Blood* track to be accorded a video. Here, the band are seen performing in the studio, for the most part in stylish monochrome but with nostalgic colour inserts of Ferry in white tuxedo, Manzanera in bug spectacles and Mackay in bat-collared green spangles; at the end, Ferry merely wanders off in post-vocal *A Song for Europe* style. (With split-screen adopted for some shots, Ferry hogs three of the four available sections, with the band squeezed into the remaining one top left.) Soon after its release, the song was appropriated to kick-start the Robert Stigwood production *Times Square*, a fairy tale of New York punkettes released in September. Starring *Rocky Horror* and *Rock Follies* veteran Tim Curry, its soundtrack also incorporated tracks by The Cars, XTC, The Pretenders, Talking Heads, The Ruts, Patti Smith, Joe Jackson, Gary Numan, The Cure and The Ramones.

Another one for nitpickers: continuing the title-tampering seemingly endemic to the *Flesh + Blood* album, the song acquired a definite article on its single release, an anomalous 'The' also incorporated on several subsequent compilations.

Flesh and Blood
(Ferry) 3:13

The title track of Roxy's seventh album is, strictly speaking, not a Roxy recording at all. The track-by-track personnel listings on the LP's inner sleeve made this very explicit to puzzled Roxy fans on their acquisition of the new record in May 1980. Side one track four, they learned, was effectively a Ferry solo piece with session support from Alan Spenner and two percussionists, Andy Newmark and Allan Schwartzberg.

If the mysterious disappearance of Paul Thompson from the skeleton credits on the back cover hadn't been enough of a shock, then this further discovery seemed stranger still. As US critic Dave Connolly perceptively summarises it on his Prography website, "If *Manifesto* was a Bryan Ferry album in disguise, *Flesh + Blood* drops the pretense altogether by featuring cover material (*In the Midnight Hour*, The Byrds' *Eight Miles High*) and a title track recorded without Mackay and Manzanera (Paul Thompson had already left)." Worse was to follow on the *Avalon* album, however, in which Ferry was content to recycle the solo B-side *To Turn You On*. And in 1995 both these marginal items would be preserved on the *Thrill of It All* box set in favour of superior Roxy tracks like *Running Wild* and *True to Life*.

For the record, *Flesh and Blood* at least strikes a vaguely sinister note only echoed elsewhere on the new LP by *No Strange Delight*. But the instrumentation is merely functional (Spenner's characteristically fluid bass excepted) and the impact therefore muted. The song fades up promisingly to the ominous throb of approaching synthesisers, though as the track progresses these will turn out to be essentially featureless as the similar sound Ferry employed on the throwaway instrumental, *South Downs*. For the first time since *Pyjamarama* seven years earlier, Ferry then picks up a guitar (in this case, a Gibson Flying V) and grinds out an effectively granitic riff, finally drawling an ambiguous ode to an ambitious 'friend', simultaneously commending her self-reliance while crudely objectifying her as "night size – perfect ten." The track makes a stab at disrupting the essentially bland surfaces of the *Flesh + Blood* album, but the foreboding atmosphere somehow lacks edge.

Ironically, only a month after the album's release, the accompanying European tour saw *Flesh and Blood* being given the full Roxy treatment after all. Sandwiched between *Rain Rain Rain* and *Oh Yeah* and graced by a stunningly powerful new arrangement, Mackay and Manzanera contributed thickly layered saxes and guitars to an epic musical backdrop in the vein of *Manifesto*, the whole thing lasting close to seven minutes. This version was seen on *The Old Grey Whistle Test* on 24 January 1981, the footage culled from the ZDF programme *Rock Pop* and recorded in Dortmund. A *Flesh and Blood* on this kind of grandiloquent scale would have given its parent album just the shot in the arm it needed.

My Only Love
(Ferry) 5:19

Side One of *Flesh + Blood* closes on an evanescent note, *My Only Love* acting as a trial run for the ambient stylings of *Jealous Guy* and much of the *Avalon* album. As such, it remains one of Roxy's most affecting latterday achievements.

The opening four-note keyboard motif sets the mournful tone and doesn't let up for the full five minutes plus. The build-up to Ferry's entrance is beautifully paced, with those repeated four notes joined in turn by percussion, bass, synthesiser, and finally Manzanera's delicately plucked guitar. The words are as sparse as former lyrics were dense, Ferry unafraid to flirt with bathos in his talk of flowing rivers and willow trees. The former, in fact, constitute the cornerstone of the song, describing as they do the gentle but inexorable flow of the music, an approach harking right back to *Sea Breezes* and perfected later on *More Than This* and *Tara*. And the willow tree the river flows beside is a sombre restatement of the breezily insouciant "boo-hoo willows" featured in *Serenade*.

Ferry's ponderings are interrupted by a two-part Manzanera solo with just a hint of David Gilmour's most recent Pink Floyd stylings; the second phrase dares to be about as jagged as *Flesh + Blood* gets. And finally the wash of ruminative bass and airy synths gives way to an inspired Mackay solo, again in two distinct sections and, again, achieving a dazzling purity of tone coupled with a concluding rasp that's as untrammeled as *Flesh + Blood* can manage. The serenely tranquilised sound brings the album's first side to an exquisitely indefinite conclusion, pointing the way to the more complex reveries featured on *Avalon*.

Unfortunately, this is the track that, in live performance, would go the way of *In Every Dream Home a Heartache* and become impossibly extended, that beautiful keyboard motif wearing out its welcome in an indulgent welter of Neil Hubbard (and, latterly, Chris Spedding) guitar improvisations before the last-minute arrival of Mackay's sax break, honked-up several notches for a rousing finale quite unlike the gorgeous coda to the album version. This approach wasn't so damaging in its first live go-around in 1980, but subsequent renditions (during the *Avalon* tour and the band's 21st century dates) were thoroughly hamstrung by it, the results preserved on both the *Heart Still Beating* and *Roxy Music Live* compilations.

Ironically, the elephantiasis inflicted on *My Only Love* was presumably born of Ferry's fondness for the track. "Every album that you make seems to have a central song that the rest of the album kind of pivots around," he maintained, "and *My Only Love* seems to be the central core of *Flesh + Blood* for me." A year after its release, he included it, somewhat immodestly, on his Radio 1 *Star Special* programme, adding it to a roster ranging from Frank Sinatra and The Ronettes to The Rolling Stones.

My Only Love would have made an effective single (judiciously abbreviated), but in the event was consigned to B-side status on the Japanese issue of *Same Old Scene*.

Over You
(Ferry-Manzanera) 3:27

This was the first single to be extracted from *Flesh + Blood* and also the first song recorded at Phil Manzanera's newly established Gallery Studio in Chertsey. As a refreshing change from the increasing tendency to surround the three core members with disengaged sessionmen, *Over You* was recorded by a skeleton crew of Ferry, Mackay and Manzanera backed up only by Allan Schwartzberg on drums. "Crafted as a pop song," as Manzanera put it, the result is a nostalgic Everly Brothers pastiche garnished with ultra-modern instrumental flourishes, and is a small gem.

Manzanera handles the bass here as well as the guitar, unleashing a throbbing motif that pulses almost undeviatingly throughout. There's a charming volley of percussive hand-claps (you can almost see the beaming bobby-soxers interpolating these in the video that never was), then a fetching jangle of rhythm guitar and finally Ferry's dazzling vocal, which gives a reasonably convincing impression of a lovelorn teen moping unwanted outside the Senior Prom. The lyric, too, is affecting, with the titular phrase at the end of each line subtly double-tracked and all the more engaging for it.

Commentators convinced that Roxy's latter phase saw them abandoning all the avant-garde moves that had once made them so interesting should be thoroughly confounded by what comes next. Ferry pauses suddenly for a quirky four-note motif from Manzanera, which itself introduces a repeated three-note Mackay riff replicating the bizarre sound he perfected six years earlier on the Eno track *The Fat Lady of Limbourg*. Any purely sales-fixated band would have kicked such unfamiliar sounds into touch at an early stage. But no; rasping atonally like some hitherto unknown woodwind from darkest Africa, Mackay's embellishments somehow mesh beautifully with the surging synths and fresh-faced touches of Hammond organ as Ferry resumes. A further pause for some spine-rattling Manzanera chords, then Ferry's final thoughts are succeeded by a really lovely piano melody. This in turn is picked up by Mackay, who launches into a shimmering soprano solo that pushes this throwaway confection to the point of sublimity and beyond.

Over You entered the UK chart at number 18 on 13 May, joining an eclectic clutch of new entries that included The Specials' *Rat Race*, Gary Numan's *We Are Glass*, *Mirror in the Bathroom* by The Beat, The Korgis' *Everybody's Got to Learn Sometime* and the Lipps Inc disco smash *Funky Town*. *Over You* remained in place for nine weeks, reaching a high of number five on 10 June prior to disappearing on 8 July.

Roxy followers watching the band's appearance on *Top of the Pops* on 15 May could have been forgiven for thinking that Mackay, rather than Thompson, was the longstanding member who had finally left. With Paul Carrack and Gary Tibbs miming to Ferry's keyboards and Manzanera's bass respectively, the faithful Thompson was also on hand to suffer the minor humiliation of miming to a drum track laid down in the studio by Allan Schwartzberg. Mackay, however, was on holiday at the time; a moustachioed non-lookalike was enlisted to take his place, lurking sheepishly in the background and chewing gum (not a very Roxy touch) when not miming to Mackay's tenor.

A live version of *Over You* by Canadian power-pop specialists Sloan was included on a bonus disc attached to their 1997 album *One Chord to Another*.

Eight Miles High

(Clark-Crosby-McGuinn) 4:53

Reviewing *These Foolish Things* for *Phonograph Record* in April 1974, Greg Shaw observed that "Ferry's real breakthrough lies in his recognition of classics by Dylan, Janis and The Stones as being no less absurd than any other product of an era. Time makes oldies of them all..." Shaw talked approvingly of Ferry reducing great songs "to their essential bubblegum," but it's hard to detect any such knowing postmodern rationale behind Roxy's faceless makeover of The Byrds' psychedelic classic, *Eight Miles High*. Why is it here? Merely to endear its parent album to American record-buyers? Presumably. And all, as usual, to no avail.

The original was issued as a single in March 1966 prior to its inclusion on The Byrds' *Fifth Dimension* LP the following July. Written in the main by the aeroplane-phobic Gene Clark, it was reportedly an outgrowth of his sensations during the group's transatlantic flight to the UK for their autumn tour of 1965. It has also, of course, been the subject of fierce debate regarding a drugs-related subtext. Either way, it bristles with barely suppressed paranoia, Roger McGuinn's spine-chilling guitar runs suggesting the fevered extemporisation of skeleton hands and finally reaching a crescendo of jangling madness.

Back in April 1973, Manzanera had included *Eight Miles High* among his favourite tunes in the *NME*'s 'Under the Influence' column. "I think it's taken from a John Coltrane thing," he remarked. "The harmonies were extraordinary but the guitar was simply amazing. Quite understandably, nobody's tried to get that sound before or since – although there's quite a bit of it on the *Fifth Dimension* album." As noted earlier, while embroiled in the *Country Life* sessions in August 1974, Manzanera went ahead and "tried to get that sound" by means of a 12-string Rickenbacker, the result heard to dazzling effect on the anthemic *Prairie Rose*. Sensibly, however, he elected not to reproduce it for the Roxyfied version of *Eight Miles High*, opting instead to contribute a jaggedly muscular solo to the track's extended outro. Elsewhere, he falls victim to the soporific mood induced by Ferry's vocal.

Mackay might reasonably have been expected to contribute something outstanding here, given that McGuinn's guitar sound was apparently founded on a desire to replicate a John Coltrane sax solo. Instead, Mackay's oboe only pops in, well down in the mix, to join Manzanera in spelling out the second phrase of the introductory motif, re-emerging to do the same half-way through and then disappearing altogether. As Ken Tucker put it in *Rolling Stone*, "the melody sounds like … the theme from *Hawaii Five-O*, while Ferry munches on the words, savoring only random, emotionally pointless lines and phrases." Indeed, Ferry contributes little here other than rephrasing a couple of Clark's lines, elsewhere double-tracking his vocals in a bland echo of the ghostly three-way harmonising of Clark, McGuinn and David Crosby on the original.

The track fades up from the dying fall of *Over You* in an intriguing reminiscence of the same trick on the *Country Life* album, and the hypnotic pulse of percussion, synths and guitar towards the end is agreeable enough. But the track badly misses the kind of 'bubblegum' irreverence Ferry dispensed so effortlessly on *These Foolish Things*. In its stead is a vacuous wash of 1980s production gloss, listenable but unmemorable. Perversely, the band's lengthy live version on the *Flesh + Blood* tour was far superior, Manzanera and Mackay whipping up a miasmic din of whirring guitar and oboe that suggested much more of the original's psychedelic power.

Of the several other re-interpretations of *Eight Miles High*, Robyn Hitchcock's was featured on his 1996 *Greatest Hits* collection – alongside his version of Roxy's own *More Than This*.

Rain Rain Rain
(Ferry) 3:20

After *Eight Miles High*, the somnambulant funk of *Rain Rain Rain* continues the downward slide of *Flesh + Blood*'s second half, though it's certainly preferable to *Manifesto*'s similarly titled Side Two clinker, *Cry, Cry, Cry*.

Over a charmingly sleazy Alan Spenner bass line, the opening has some nicely off-kilter dialogue, conducted in stabbing monosyllables, between Ferry's piano and Neil Hubbard's guitar. The jaded lyric – which Ferry more or less speaks, in a fashion equal parts Americanised and anaesthetised – hints of sardonic self-disgust in its skewed paean to a woman who sounds much like the subject of the earlier track, *Flesh and Blood*. It also has its fair share of winningly impenetrable lines, one of which, in its reference to the subject's designer dress, seems like a very vague echo of a similarly inscrutable lyric in *Chance Meeting*.

With Manzanera mysteriously absent, Mackay is reduced to some out-of-sorts one-note punctuation marks in the choruses, where Ferry's titular mantra seems hardly less lethargic than the rest of the track. In contrast to the effervescence of *Same Old Scene* and its fatalistic conviction that nothing can last forever, here the funereal pace is at the service, ironically, of an all-consuming passion that apparently *is* "gonna last forever." The whole thing is played out against the syncopated lurch of Allan Schwartzberg's percussion, which is the stop-start disorientation of *Sea Breezes'* middle section airbrushed into a 1980s disco sheen. At the end, Ferry throws in a last-minute interrogative not included on the lyric sheet – "Do you believe in love?" – and Spenner's viscous backdrop grinds to an inconclusive halt.

There's a forlorn echo of *Love is the Drug* here, with the seedy insinuations of the bass line well to the fore and Ferry in his familiar role of urban prowler. But the role is beginning to wear thin and Ferry knows it, sounding apathetic and half-asleep where the *Love is the Drug* protagonist was bristling with youthful expectation. And for a track like this to work it needs either the full-blooded band commitment devoted to *Drug* or the full funk arsenal thrown later at *The Main Thing*. By comparison to those two, *Rain Rain Rain* sounds merely bargain basement.

To underline its also-ran status, it was used as the B-side to no fewer than three of its companion album tracks: *Oh Yeah* in the US, *Same Old Scene* in France and *The Midnight Hour* in Portugal. It did make it onto the set list of Roxy's 1980-1 live act, however, counting as the first of seven selections from the new album, audiences having been softened up by an opening volley of *The Bogus Man*, *Trash* and *Both Ends Burning*.

No Strange Delight
(Ferry-Manzanera) 4:44

Like *Stronger Through the Years* on the *Manifesto* album, *No Strange Delight* is an out-of-kilter, though welcome, reminder of the kind of musical disorientation that was common to Roxy's earlier work. The edges are smoother, to be sure, and the impact softened. But the finished product still comes over as a kind of 1980s remake of *Strictly Confidential*, particularly via – and where, one was beginning to wonder, had it got to? – the full-fledged reintroduction of Mackay's oboe.

Ferry's ambiguous lyric is an eerie interior monologue in which friends, senses, self, soul are all yielded up to a single devouring obsession, the "strange delight" of the title. The struggle to retain a grip on reality is an unequal one, the narrator's heartbeat faltering even as he tries to recollect a time when his emotions weren't as atrophied as they are now. And the sheer effort of it causes the insomniac narrator to assume the bleary countenance of *Strictly Confidential's* would-be suicide, who also found himself tossing and turning in a sleepless haze. There are other points of contact: his alienation from a coterie of concerned friends sounds exactly like the collapse of emotional contact warned against in the earlier song, and the two narrators wind up on an identical note of existential despair. Gathered into the embrace of the spectral voices assailing him, the protagonist of *Strictly Confidential* found no illumination awaiting him on the other side, while his 1980 counterpart is well aware that he has entered Hell and that its environs contain, as the title has it, *No Strange Delight*.

Mackay's oboe is by no means as astringent as it was in *Strictly Confidential*, but it still pirouettes menacingly around Ferry's confessional verses and acquires a searing intensity on that final admission that life has become a living hell. The musical backdrop has something of the band's long-since-exorcised science fiction flavour, with robotic percussion and lurching bass lines prefacing Ferry's lyric and a veritable descent into the maelstrom once it's over. Where *Strictly Confidential* came to an abrupt end on the narrator's final tantalising query, Ferry's concluding question here is the cue for a galloping extended outro in which his piano weaves its way unmoved through a thickly clotted welter of flickering synths and Manzanera improvisations.

With its unequivocal statement that the narrator is in Hell and its spiralling descent into chaos, *No Strange Delight* also seems to echo the apocalyptic ending of *For Your Pleasure*, title track of *Strictly Confidential's* parent album. It's a chilling conclusion to an unnerving track and can't help but seem a little out of place amid the shiny textures of *Flesh + Blood*. No doubt some of the band's newest adherents, while happy to sing along to the likes of *Over You* or *Same Old Scene*, hurried past this one with something like revulsion.

A couple of minor points for trivia hounds. Whether by accident or design, the unusual phrase contained in this track's title would be replicated within a month of the album's release in the Kate Bush song *Babooshka*, issued as a single on 23 June. And a belated addition to the album's credits – only on the inner sleeve and only on later pressings – would ascribe percussion here and on *Eight Miles High* to 'Ditchum' [sic]. This presumably refers to Martin Ditcham, a Chris Rea stalwart who has also worked with Sade, Talk Talk and The Rolling Stones.

Running Wild
(Ferry-Manzanera) 5:01

This is perhaps the most underrated cut on the *Flesh + Blood* album, a magisterial coda that features on nobody's Ten Best lists, has never been played live, and somehow failed to make the grade even when the *Thrill of It All* box set was being assembled. And yet it's one of Ferry's most audacious juxtapositions of deliberately hoary instrumentation with a lyric that comes on like a sort of 'Greatest Hits' gazetteer of his trademark preoccupations, topping it all off with a sombre seriousness in the performance that, as so often in earlier Roxy songs, positively dares the listener to laugh. And yet the darkling self-absorption of the song remains powerful, even poignant.

To underline the reiteration of old obsessions, the song unashamedly recycles several motifs already heard on the *Flesh + Blood* album. After a grave and understated Spenner-Manzanera opening, Ferry invokes the 'song with bitter-sweet associations' theme of *Oh Yeah* in his very first line, later speculating on a never-ending love in a forlorn reversal of *Same Old Scene*'s insistence that nothing can last forever. Finally, the streetwise 'friend' of *Flesh and Blood* itself is now given to running amok whether her dreams come to fruition or crumble to nothing. On top of all this, the notion that love is inevitably finite and that dreams are bound to end in disappointment connects right back to *Beauty Queen*.

For the most part, the musicians follow Ferry's funereal lead, the stately sound garnished with agreeably cheesy snatches of 60s-style organ from Paul Carrack. Mackay and Manzanera, meanwhile, give the song real soul, letting rip with the kind of searing emotional outbursts Ferry is too buttoned-up to indulge in. Reversing the example of *My Only Love*, Mackay steps up first, unleashing a creamily toned solo that is at least the equal of his stellar work on *Over You*, after which Manzanera's jaggedly expressive guitar break underpins Ferry's climactic, repeated refrain.

And as the song winds down on a final muted breath of Mackay's sax coupled with a mournful piano figure from Ferry himself, we're left to ponder Ferry's earlier observation that, for all his recent unpredictable driftings, he's still essentially the same man. True enough; even in the context of this radically remodelled Roxy Music, certain time-honoured themes keep recurring like a hard-to-shake idée fixe, and *Running Wild* rounds up just about all of them.

Lover
(Ferry-Manzanera) 4:29

This gorgeous ballad fell by the wayside during the track selection for the *Flesh + Blood* album, but perhaps would have been better placed there in lieu of filler like *Rain Rain Rain* or the anodyne *Eight Miles High* makeover. It's no more of a throwaway than even the album's title track, with the added bonus of being a good deal less portentous.

With a stately rhythm-box backbeat and a hardly more than skeletal lyric, *Lover* sounds like the customary experiment in lounge-lizard atmosphere, with maybe a touch or two of Hot Chocolate pastiche thrown in, until one notices how vulnerable and subdued Ferry sounds when he makes simple appeals for his lover to hold him close. The complex word-play of old is now thoroughly abandoned, but Ferry's lyric here has a different kind of appeal, more direct and elemental.

The smooth interplay of tinkling keyboard and Manzanera's choppy rhythm guitar is seductively done, as is the rolling resonance of the bass line and the swooning wash of synthetic cymbals punctuating each of Ferry's stanzas. A vaguely ominous three-note guitar motif underscores the main theme, but the real star here is Mackay, who contributes a radiantly understated sax break over a swirling organ motif together with some lovely punctuation marks as the track winds down. The soundstage is a complex one – with any amount of rhythm guitars and percussive elements murmuring away from the wings – but the net effect is a simple one, naked, unadorned, achingly vulnerable. Though much less literal, the tinkling music-box sound of the conclusion is reminiscent of *Spin Me Round* and, as tongue-tied torch songs go, the cumulative effect is little short of hypnotic. Indeed, though never played live, the track's dying fade, and Mackay's breathy interpolations in particular, seem to have influenced the arrangement of *Oh Yeah* on the Roxy tours of both 1980 and 2001.

Having missed its chance to appear on the *Flesh + Blood* album, *Lover* fetched up instead as B-side to the third single extracted from it, *Same Old Scene*. Fans cheesed off by the dozy instrumental B-side of Roxy's previous single, *South Downs*, no doubt found this new double-bill considerably better value for money. Aside from a brief appearance in 1988 as companion piece to *South Downs* on Virgin's *Jealous Guy* CD single, the track lay forgotten until finally dusted off for the *Thrill of It All* box set in 1995. Forgotten, that is, by all but the makers of the hit US TV series *Miami Vice*, who included it on the *Miami Vice II* soundtrack album.

Nineteen: *Europe 80-1*

"Nothing surprised me more than the success of that single [Jealous Guy], and when you finally reach Number One it's kind of anti-climactic. I know I'd have liked to see Love is the Drug, *which got to number two, do the same in 1975."*
Andy Mackay, quoted in *Chronicle* 6 June 1981

Moonlighting

The tail end of 1980 found Ferry, Mackay and Manzanera engaged in various extracurricular activities. On Wednesday 12 November, Mackay was in Munich for an appearance on a Bayrischer Rundfunk-sponsored extravaganza for German TV, *Rock Meets Classic 1980*. This was a multi-faceted marathon put together by the mercurial conductor Eberhard Schoener, with whom Mackay had worked on *The Gemini Suite* seven years earlier. Also involved were Mike Batt, Alan Parsons, Gary Brooker, Jon Anderson, Morris Pert and Esther Ofarim, with Mackay on hand to lead orchestral performances of two compositions from his *Resolving Contradictions* album, *The Inexorable Sequence* and *Rivers*; 'second sax' was the ubiquitous Mel Collins.

Manzanera, meanwhile, was behind a novelty item credited to The Dumbells and widely taken to be an unofficial Roxy Christmas single. The infectious A-side was a three-minute confection called *Giddy Up (incl Sleigh Ride)*, with Manzanera's involvement confirmed by the flip, *A Christmas Dream*, which sounds like an initial sketch for the later Manzanera track *Europe 70-1*. For the record, the catalogue number of this enduring 7" enigma was Polydor/EG POSP 209.

For his part, Ferry was involved in a short-lived project featuring singer Barbara Gogan and percussionist Clive Timperley of New Wave band The Passions, who had supported Roxy on some of their recent live dates. In 1981, the band would chart with the gorgeously spectral single *I'm in Love with a German Film Star*. Here was a song with obvious Roxy affinities in its sultry haze of Berlin decadence, not to mention its beguiling word-picture of a louche heart-throb who could just as easily be Bryan Ferry as, say, Udo Kier.

The collaboration was therefore a highly intriguing one, but it seems to have foundered on Ferry's vacillation, a tendency that was to assume epic proportions in future years. "I had about half a dozen solo tracks that I wanted to finish and get out of the way so I wouldn't be thinking of them any more," he told Bill Graham of the Dublin rock paper *Hot Press*. "Then I took the tracks to New York and mixed them, just over half an album of stuff. But it's not the next album, that's definite. I don't know what they're going to be, they could be the album after next or something or they could be an EP." Predictably, nothing came of these meanderings.

During this period, Roxy could reflect on the proliferation of Roxy-inspired new acts making inroads into the charts. Back in the mid 1970s there had been Cockney Rebel, Sparks, even Sailor. Later in the decade, the first flowering of the New Wave had thrown up others who Manzanera, for one, was unconvinced by. "I don't think that Devo or Talking Heads or The Cars sound like Roxy at all," he told Ira Robbins. "The regrettable thing is that bands don't go back a bit more to their sources and get the real thing. For Roxy Music, the 'real thing' is mid-60s Tamla-Motown, John Cage, Stockhausen, and even The Beatles and The Stones."

Now, though, a whole fleet of new bands seemed to have adopted the Roxy template lock, stock and barrel. Despite an approach from Adam Ant to produce his next record, Ferry seemed no more impressed by this new generation than Manzanera had been by the previous one. "There are a lot of the New Romantic bands who were influenced by Roxy, like Japan. I suppose it's quite flattering," he suggested mildly. Elsewhere, however, he was less polite. "I suppose I have mixed feelings about the way they imitate me," he said of Duran Duran. "It makes it harder to be unique ... What do I think of Duran Duran's music? Well, I'm very critical and I don't like much." He also noted that "Spandau Ballet are not really my cup of tea. There's nothing there. It's just a kind of mince." Faced in future years with Soft Cell, ABC, The Associates and others, Ferry would wave aside all queries with stock phrases like "I'm a Libra so it's hard for me to be openly nasty."

Prior to a renewed assault on Australia, in January 1981 Roxy polished off a few UK dates as compensation for performances called off the previous summer during Ferry's illness. These began on Tuesday the 13th and incorporated two nights at Manchester and Birmingham plus a one-off appearance in Leicester on the 17th. Before this, however, they had fulfilled a German engagement that was to make a wholly unexpected impact.

*　*　*

Jealous Guy (a tribute)
(Lennon) 6:10

When news came in of the shocking murder of John Lennon on 8 December 1980, Roxy were preparing for two appearances in Dortmund as part of a colossal pan-European *Rockpalast* TV broadcast. Scheduled for 18 and 19 December by German channel ZDF, Roxy were to share the bill at the Westfalenhalle with Talking Heads, Dire Straits and Mike Oldfield. Encouraged in particular by substitute drummer Andy Newmark, who had worked with Lennon only a few months earlier on the sessions for his comeback LP *Double Fantasy*, the band decided to offer their own tribute by including a Lennon song as their Dortmund encore.

The choice wasn't a difficult one; Ferry had long considered covering the 1971 song *Jealous Guy*, "having always preferred [Lennon's] personal songs to his political," as he put it. But the emotional response from the Dortmund audience took the band completely by surprise. "They all recognised it and all lit their matches," Ferry told Bill Graham. "It was a very moving moment. It seemed a genuine thing. If that hadn't happened at that concert ... I don't think we would ever have got round to [recording] it at all."

Recorded at his Ascot home in the final week of June 1971, the original appeared on Lennon's *Imagine* album. To the strangely chilly accompaniment of his own piano, Lennon utters an emotionally naked appeal to Yoko Ono for expiation of his sins, doing so in his most emotionally naked voice. Together with a bout of Lennon's forlorn whistling in the middle eight, the warm embrace of John Barham's harmonium and Torrie Zito's dazzling string arrangement add texture to a deliberately pared-down sound. "I really like that song," Ferry commented. "I felt it was one of the best solo songs he'd done and it had never been heard that much. It had always been overshadowed by *Imagine*, which I didn't like as much."

Faced with numerous post-Dortmund requests to record the song, Ferry repaired to Manzanera's Chertsey studio in January 1981 with Rhett Davies on board as his co-producer; he also brought back Gary Tibbs on bass, whose last Roxy contribution this would be prior to his defection to the then red-hot Adam and the Ants. With Mackay and Manzanera adding powerful instrumental grace notes, the finished product was issued on 8 February and would be very different from Lennon's: no less emotional, but with the sparse instrumentation of the original replaced by a thickly textured wall of synthetic sound, and Lennon's tone of hesitant vulnerability supplanted by a considerably more grandiose romantic agony.

Ferry's vocal performance is superb, incorporating familiar tricks of inflection (note the countryfied emphasis on "inse-kewer") yet remaining straight, soulful and, above all, sincere. For all Ferry's occasional touches of vocal bravura and the tub-thumping heft of the instrumentation, we nevertheless envisage a man just as painfully exposed and spiritually broken as Lennon. Cannily, Ferry withholds Lennon's trademark whistling until the prolonged instrumental outro, the middle eight being occupied instead by Manzanera's guitar and Mackay's alto. At least as fragile and affecting as Ferry's vocal, these understated solos prepare the ground for a surging synthesiser fade lasting close to three minutes.

Here, Ferry's whistled refrain recalls not only Lennon's on the original recording but the mournful conclusion to Roxy's own *A Song for Europe*. Assailed on either side by the tuneful clang of electric guitars, Ferry perfects a swooning wash of atmospherics harking back to *My Only Love* and forward to *More Than This*. Reminiscent of the hypnotic conclusion to The Beatles' similarly extended 1968 hit *Hey Jude*, the elegiac impact is overwhelming. Lennon's murder had provoked a wave of worldwide emotion almost hysterical in its intensity; released some ten weeks later, the conclusion to Roxy's *Jealous Guy* offered a response just as deeply felt, yet at the same time more measured, reflective, even profound.

In those intervening ten weeks, no fewer than three Lennon songs had reached Number One, two – *(Just Like) Starting Over* and *Woman* – culled from his comeback album *Double Fantasy*, and the third a reissue of *Imagine* sandwiched between them. On top of this, another revival, *Happy Christmas (War is Over)*, had reached a seasonal number two. Indeed, when Roxy's *Jealous Guy* was issued on 13 February, *Woman* had only recently vacated the top spot, while *Double Fantasy* had just completed a two-week stint at Number One in the album chart. It's futile, of course, to speculate how far this necrophile enthusiasm on the part of Britain's record buyers helped propel Roxy's tribute to Number One. Its obvious sincerity helped deflect accusations of cashing in, and its extraordinary elegiac power did the rest.

Nevertheless, the danger of an adverse reaction, particularly from the ever-cynical music press, was very real as the single first hit the shops, though at least one elementary precaution had been taken. "We asked Yoko," Manzanera recalled, "and she thought it was a good idea." As for Mackay, his misgivings were related less to the potential backlash, more to the potential of the song itself: "I famously didn't want it to be released as a single. I didn't think it was going to be a hit. That shows what I know."

Indeed. Starting at number 21 on 17 February, *Jealous Guy* climbed to six in its second week before hitting the top on 10 March, where it stayed for two weeks. Though Adam and the Ants' *Kings of the Wild Frontier* was hovering expectantly at number two, it was eventually Shakin' Steven's *This Ole House* and Kim Wilde's *Kids in America* that forced it back to number three, after which it slipped to seven, 18 and finally 34 on 14 April, totting up nine weeks in the Top 40 and a further two just outside. Thankfully, the response of the British public far outstripped the enthusiasm of the rock papers. Unmoved, *Melody Maker*'s singles reviewer recommended it for "the Radio 2 playlist," adding, "I don't doubt the sincerity, but it doesn't have the edge that made Lennon's original so compelling."

The success of *Jealous Guy* would be responsible for prolonging the chart life of the *Flesh + Blood* album well into 1981, while Ferry, Mackay and Manzanera could reflect on the irony of Roxy finally reaching Number One with a song composed by someone else, following the pattern of Ferry's own solo recordings but with infinitely greater success. The accompanying video had been a vital feature of the single's impact, being almost as plain and unadorned as the picture sleeve in which it was sold. (In addition to the basic track-cum-artist attribution, nothing more than a mustard-coloured background and the handwritten words 'a tribute'). With Roxy back on the road in Australia, the promo film was shot in Sydney and presented Ferry as a self-lacerating Narcissus, emphasising the reflective nature of the song by panning up to him (immaculate in silver-blue suit and pink tie) from his mirror image in the polished surface on which he's leaning.

For no discernible reason, in November 1985 EMI issued Lennon's original as a single; it reached number 65. The following year, the Roxy version was included on the two-disc compilation album *Street Life*, chopped down to 4:35 for the occasion – a surprising move, given Ferry's conviction that the lengthy instrumental fade was crucial to his intentions.

To Turn You On
(Ferry) 4:16

First reaching the general public as B-side to *Jealous Guy*, *To Turn You On* is a melodramatic ballad in Americanised vein and chiefly a vehicle for one of Ferry's most accomplished vocal performances.

As well as an attractive arrangement, it boasts a starry-eyed evocation of a Fifth Avenue romance that is for once neither mechanistic nor doomed. The imagery – of a rainy night in New York, the twinkling lights off-Broadway, a walk through Central Park – is unusually straightforward, containing none of the spiky contradictions inherent in even the least threatening Roxy tracks. Arrangement notwithstanding, the soundstage is similarly anodyne. As Paul Stump puts it in *Unknown Pleasures*, "its progressions and resolutions just don't sound like Roxy Music, although the band do it proud. It sounds like a superior Ferry cover version of someone else's song."

The reason, as became clear in 1982 when it was included on the *Avalon* album with a full set of credits, is that it isn't a Roxy track. The 'band' don't do it proud at all; Ferry's chief collaborators here were all veterans of the highly charged *Bride Stripped Bare* sessions: Neil Hubbard (guitar), Alan Spenner (bass) and Rick Marotta (drums). Hubbard contributes a delicate guitar break, Spenner's bass is characteristically warm and fluid, and Kermit Moore's sighing cellos strike a faintly eerie note. But none of this makes it sound like Roxy Music.

The song had been conceived back in 1978, in the midst of Ferry's travails over the *Bride* album, and was tarted up, including the provision of a Paul Carrack piano track, during a break in Roxy activities in 1980. Though intended for use on some future solo project, it was dusted off when *Jealous Guy* was mooted as a single release and no Roxy B-side was to hand. By that time, its title – which quotes both from The Beatles' *A Day in the Life* and the Lennon solo track *Oh Yoko!* – made it seem a peculiarly apt companion piece to Roxy's Lennon tribute. Ferry's rationale for subsequently adding it to the *Avalon* album was merely that it was "a quality track and I don't want it to be lost." Fair enough, but instead of re-recording it with the full weight of Roxy brought to bear, Ferry was content merely to remix it a bit and add a frankly naff drum-machine intro.

For the record, a cover version of *To Turn You On* was included on *Turn Around and Look*, the 1990 debut album of R'n'B singer Wendi Slaton.

* * *

As unlike a guitar as possible

In the run-up to Roxy's phenomenal success with *Jealous Guy*, BBC2's *The Old Grey Whistle Test* rounded up three of their Dortmund performances (*Flesh and Blood*, *Oh Yeah* and *The Thrill of It All*) in a *Rock Pop* special broadcast on 24 January. Mackay, meanwhile, moved straight from memorialising John Lennon to a session with his former collaborator, playing lyricon on the Paul McCartney-Stevie Wonder composition *What's That You're Doing*. Though recorded on 26 February 1981, this would have to wait until April 1982 to be released on McCartney's *Tug of War* album. Mackay would make a more substantial contribution to its follow-up, *Pipes of Peace*, which was recorded at much the same time as *Tug of War* but delayed even longer, until October 1983. Both LPs were produced by George Martin.

Also in 1981, Mackay had a book entitled *Electronic Music* published by the Oxford imprint Phaidon. Aware that "electronics is traditionally a 'difficult' subject for the layman," Mackay went right back to basics in his Introduction: "Some of the instruments invented before the Second World War, in particular the electric guitar, form the basis of rock music: a new musical idiom and a new industry entirely dependent on electronics," he explained. "The development of the tape recorder has led to the studio playing a crucial creative role in rock. I have set out to explain some of these processes, assuming no specialised knowledge of electronics (since I possess none myself). Wherever possible, I have also tried to explain something of performance techniques from a musician's point of view."

Tracing the synthesiser back to such turn-of-the-century prototypes as the Singing Arc and the Telharmonium, Mackay also details Luigi Russolo's 'Art of Noises' and the seminal influence of composers like Karlheinz Stockhausen, John Cage and Morton Feldman. The book's final section takes the form of potted biographies of 50 crucial figures, with several rock music names making the cut – John Cale, Brian Eno, Jimi Hendrix, Jean-Michel Jarre, George Martin, Mike Oldfield, Phil Spector, Stevie Wonder and Frank Zappa. David Bowie is also included, giving Mackay the opportunity to revise his dismissive comments of 1972, calling him instead "a major myth-maker of what he has called 'this age of grand illusions.'" With no false modesty, Mackay himself appears on the book's front cover, toting a lyricon in the familiar environs of Manzanera's home studio.

Gallery was also the setting for Manzanera's latest solo album, which would make it into record shops just ahead of the next Roxy LP. "I play everything on *Primitive Guitars* except for John Wetton's bass on one track," Manzanera explained in *Trouser Press*. "I don't see any particular virtue in doing everything yourself; it just happens that the studio is ten seconds away from my house and it's easy for me to work whenever I want."

As with Mackay's solo LPs, *Primitive Guitars* was conceived as a kind of musical autobiography to mark the tenth anniversary (14 February 1982) of Manzanera signing with EG. And it was uncommonly well received. "*Primitive Guitars* bears no relation to his first solo LP, *Diamond Head* (one of the great British rock albums of the mid-seventies), but it's considerably more engaging than his last outing, *K-Scope*," remarked *Rolling Stone*'s Kurt Loder, identifying "the album's most striking aspect" as "Manzanera's ability to wrench weird and utterly unguitarlike sounds from his main instrument – one track, called *Impossible Guitar*, lives up to its title in every way."

As well as serving an autobiographical function in response to the birth of his first child, the album also sprang from Manzanera's suspicion that "if Roxy Music were starting now, perhaps we'd all be playing keyboards," and that "the guitar is going to be seen as an outdated instrument if people don't get with it. Guitar sounds exciting in a way keyboards don't if you play a chord loud. The role of the guitar is expanding incredibly. It's no longer a simple case of lead guitar and rhythm guitar."

Indeed, *Primitive Guitars* goes light years beyond the basic lead and rhythm configuration, with Manzanera conjuring whole orchestras from his instrument and the studio technology at his disposal. The latter had recently been augmented by the first Linn drums, which Manzanera snapped up as soon as they came on the market, adding this then-innovative texture to backing tracks already founded on an old-style rhythm box. The results are remarkable, with the "indigenous engineering" of Manzanera and his live-in technician Ian Little creating arguably the most inventive Roxy solo LP to date.

The album begins in thoroughly alluring style, with the Latin swing of *Criollo* founded on a bewitching tiplé motif and the sublimated plaint of Hispanic voices. The quirky hyperactivity of *Caracas*, underpinned by Manzanera's insistent keyboard needling and a lightly burbling bass, builds inexorably to a sublime guitar solo, while *La nueva ola* – as its title, 'The New Wave', suggests – is an exhilarating pastiche of the kind of synth-dominated sounds currently infiltrating the charts, everything stopping, however, for a granitic guitar interjection complete with faux-hand claps. *Bogotá* is a disorientating web of choppy guitar chords and fluttering percussion, and *Ritmo de Los Angeles* is about as straightforwardly tuneful a guitar instrumental as this album's restless experimentation permits.

The second side is bookended by the airy organ sonorities of *Europe 70-1* and the delicate guitar meditation of its mirror image, *Europe 80-1*. (Here, of course, Manzanera states not only where he was at in 1981 but also provides a backward nod to his erstwhile supergroup 801.) Sandwiched between these two are the massive percussive canvases of *Impossible Guitar* and *Big Dome*, big and brawny synthesised showcases for some of Manzanera's most inspired playing. The former would be granted a live rendition in Roxy Music's *Avalon* tour (the result fetching up on the posthumous live document, *Heart Still Beating*), while the latter would recall Mackay's *The Loyang Tractor Factory* in its unrelenting big-beat evocation of an industrial conurbation straight out of Fritz Lang's *Metropolis*.

An inveterate taper of studio as well as live sessions, Manzanera interspersed each track with fascinating 'found' fragments of studio chat, starting with a snatch of Roxy jamming their way through *The Bogus Man*, taking in what sounds like Eno's *On Some Faraway Beach* in a nascent form ("I think that's definitely the one for the single"), a rough-and-ready rehearsal of John Cale's *Gun*, and a farcical run-through of Manzanera's own *Remote Control*. There's also an intriguing burst of Eno singing a sinister refrain ("We will be teenagers casing the teenagers' scene") which isn't preserved on disc elsewhere.

"I just went in and let rip," is how Manzanera explained this astonishing burst of one-man studio creativity. More eloquently, in an uncommonly extensive set of liner notes he pointed out that *Primitive Guitars* was a response to "those who have queried an apparent absence of guitar on some of the records in which I have been involved: among my abiding interests has been the possibility of making a guitar sound as unlike a guitar as possible."

Twenty: *The Eighth Roxy Music Album*

"From numbers one to seven the Roxy Music albums go along the line of the old domino theory. Each new one extends from a part of the old one but it's usually the part you least expect. The eighth does the same. Avalon *picks up parts of* Flesh + Blood, *but twists them around a little. I'd say it was better, possibly the best since* Country Life.*"*

James Truman, *The Face* May 1982

In the wake of *Jealous Guy*, Ferry went into seclusion on the west coast of Ireland, plotting a new album and only emerging for minor engagements like Radio 1's Easter Monday *Star Special*, in which his 14 chosen tracks contained four he'd previously selected for a similar broadcast seven years earlier. All were from the 1950s and 60s with the exception of Roxy's own *My Only Love* and George McCrae's sublime disco smash of 1974, *Rock Your Baby*.

Ferry's determinedly low profile was in part brought on by a new romance, this time with Lucy Helmore, the 21-year-old daughter of a Lloyds insurance broker. Her parents' Connemara property, Crumlin Lodge, was the scene of Ferry's nascent preparations for the eighth Roxy Music album, just as the lodge's lakeside view would be the scene immortalised on the album's uniquely moody cover photo.

"I can imagine someone who didn't know me listening to my work and thinking, God, what a gloomy person," Ferry would say of the finished album in the *NME*. "But I suppose that's the side I find creative. When I'm in a light-hearted frame of mind is the last time I'd ever want to go and sit at the piano and work." He then seemed to contradict himself, saying that "Making *Avalon* was interesting in that, for a change, I wasn't going through much. But I've found that although you might think that your day-to-day life is fine and there's no great trauma going on, as soon as you start making music, all kinds of angst seems to appear out of thin air. I don't know if it's from memory or what. Perhaps it's just the introspection – asking what's the meaning of life: why am I doing this? Why does this chord sound good next to that one?"

The recording of the album was postponed till the end of the year, spilling over into the new one and divided between Manzanera's home studio in Chertsey, the Compass Point studio in Nassau and the Power Station in New York. Manzanera would take time out from mixing sessions at the latter studio, not only to publicise his own *Primitive Guitars* album, but also to assure Ira Robbins that the new Roxy LP "sounds much better [than *Flesh + Blood*] – much more interesting, with a lot more depth to it. We did a lot of demos in a lot of different styles, then whittled it down to eight tracks." In the event, there would be ten tracks in all, with Ferry smuggling an old B-side onto Side Two and

Manzanera co-writing only one of the ten, a surprisingly low score given the preponderance of Ferry-Manzanera compositions on the band's previous two albums.

The encroachment of polished session players inaugurated by *Manifesto* and *Flesh + Blood* was intensified on *Avalon*, though this time rhythm guitarist Neil Hubbard, drummer Andy Newmark and backing vocalist Fonzi Thornton formed a consistent backing band, with Alan Spenner and Neil Jason alternating on bass. An intriguing addition to the Roxy sound was provided by Jimmy Maelen, an expert in Afro-Cuban percussion whose CV included sessions for Michael Jackson, Kool & the Gang, Peter Gabriel, Pat Benatar, Barry Manilow and James Taylor. "I enjoy using all the available electronics in the studio," Maelen commented. "I've discovered some great things using digital delay effects like reverse reverb sounds, gating effects, tape loops etc. All of the basic percussion sounds updated with the new technologies, which often creates brand-new sounds."

As the band's other two musical directors, Mackay and Manzanera had decidedly mixed feelings about Ferry's all-pervading vision. "Bryan by then had a very fixed idea of how he wanted things to sound," Mackay told Michael Bracewell, "some of which was brilliant, and some of which wasn't. There was very heavy pressure on us to break in America, and somewhere along the way the more experimental material got squeezed out."

Manzanera was equally ambivalent. "If, in later years, being with Roxy was helping fulfil Bryan's fantasy," he opined, "then I was very happy to contribute to it in any way I could." He noted elsewhere, however, that the album "very much reflects [Ferry's] mood at the time. That's why it was difficult. It wasn't necessarily the way I wanted it to go, especially being a guitarist – you play through loud amps and you want a bit of angst in there." Speaking to Rob Chapman, Manzanera also pointed out a more tangible contributor to the impalpable drift of Roxy's new music: "For the last three albums, quite frankly, there were a lot more drugs around as well, which was good and bad. It created a lot of paranoia and a lot of spaced-out stuff."

Like Manzanera's own *Primitive Guitars*, the album was built up in a collage style founded on the newly available Linn drum. In perfecting this new way of working, producer Rhett Davies was reminded of his collaboration with Eno on *Another Green World*, leading to the creation of, as Paul Morley had prematurely described *Flesh + Blood*, "an environment not an album."

"We started with a blank sheet; there weren't any songs," Davies recalled in 2003. "Phil might have had some chord sequences or musical ideas, and Andy would have some tunes that he'd written, and Bryan would play around with them to see if there was any work he could do. I would then spend time with Bryan alone, writing. It didn't take that long – we'd go in in the morning and I'd get a groove going that Bryan could walk into, and hopefully he'd be inspired by it." After a month in Nassau, the backing tracks were taken to Bob Clearmountain at the Power Station, where the basic percussive exoskeleton was supplemented by Newmark and Maelen, though tracks like *India* would retain their Linn drum foundation even on the finished product.

In time-honoured fashion, Ferry would add his lyric and vocal only at the last minute. "We would cut a lot of stuff that never got used, a lot of trials that Bryan just couldn't work into songs," Davies pointed out. "If you're just starting with an instrumental, there's going to be times when you just think, 'I can't write a song for this.'" In two instances, however, this impasse was circumvented by putting the instrumentals straight onto the album unadorned. Ferry's lyrics, in any case, were becoming increasingly fragmentary, and his performance of them correspondingly evanescent; in his own words, "the lyrics kind of appear here and there as little kinds of washes of colour. They're very vague, the lyrics on this album." Indeed, referring to his growing concern with instrumentation, Ferry would come out with the startlingly Eno-like sentiment that "it's a pity to spoil it by singing over it."

The lushly textured soundscapes of *Avalon* were state-of-the-art in their day and sound little different today, especially in the context of the album's 20th anniversary SACD release, on which Davies and Clearmountain faithfully replicated the sound they had created two decades earlier. "This record probably means more to me than anything I've ever done," commented Clearmountain. "I've had more comments and compliments on this album by far than anything else I've ever done."

The album's title, *Avalon*, appealed to Ferry for its punning possibilities, relating simultaneously to a French town, a psychedelic San Francisco ballroom and the burial place of King Arthur. For his latest cover concept, however, Ferry plumped firmly for the latter interpretation, the resultant image owing a lot to his recent viewing of John Boorman's Arthurian epic *Excalibur*. Co-opting photographer Neil Kirk once more, Ferry also recruited his girlfriend, Lucy Helmore, to assume the role of the most self-effacing Roxy covergirl yet. Ferry's brief to Antony Price, meanwhile, was to concoct "a very barbaric, Macbeth-styled outfit." In horned helmet, velvet gaberdine and giant Celtic brooch, Helmore totes a hooded bird of prey on her right hand and looks out impassively over a fog-shrouded expanse of lake. The shot was taken in the sunny aftermath of a dawn drizzle, with Price sending fireworks over the lake to whip up a suitably oneiric pall of smoke.

Unlike *Manifesto* and *Flesh + Blood*, the *Avalon* cover returned to the old formula of withholding the album's title. And, in another nostalgic touch, Peter Saville's typography for the monolithic legend 'Roxy Music' is distinctly reminiscent of the spidery classicism of *Siren*, which was also the last time Ferry featured a current girlfriend and a large expanse of water on a Roxy sleeve. With Jerry Hall's man-eating Lorelei transformed into Lucy Helmore's androgynous Viking warrior, the *Avalon* cover suggested that Ferry was well aware that this album marked the end of something, just as *Siren* had.

Ferry characterised *Avalon* as "ten poems or short stories that could, with a bit more work, be fashioned into a novel," firmly refuting suggestions (based on the LP's evocative title and analogous cover imagery) that Roxy had finally got round to creating a 'concept' album. In the excitable tabloid pages of *Smash Hits*, he announced that "The album is very romantic and dreamy – good escapist stuff! I really don't know how it relates to other music at the moment. I tend to listen to Radio 4 all the time – the plays and the quizzes."

How the album related to other music in 1982 was not at all, as soon became clear when it was trailed by a beguiling Top Ten single, *More Than This*. This received two *Top of the Pops* showcases interleaved with a further BBC TV engagement for Mackay, who on Saturday 10 April was captain of the winning team on Mike Read's *Pop Quiz*. No fool, Mackay was presumably aware already that the success or otherwise of the upcoming album would be more to do with Roxy's Number One hit of 1981 than *More Than This*. Indeed, Ferry's gamble of withholding a new LP for well over 12 months after *Jealous Guy* would pay off handsomely in the form of feverish consumer anticipation. Scheduled for release on Friday 28 May, the *Avalon* album actually hit the shops several days in advance. It went straight into the UK chart at Number One in the first week of June, remaining in the listings for a whopping 57 weeks, by the end of which time Roxy had ceased to exist.

The new sound perfected by Roxy would leave most reviewers stumped, the album's sonic landscapes being so all of a piece that they apparently disarmed criticism. In *Melody Maker*, phrases like "precision-honed and upholstered with velvet" seemed to relate as much to the artfully rumpled material on the album's back cover as the music inside. In the *NME*, Lynn Hanna commented that "Avalon is actually a part of Camelot legend, a place described by Ferry as 'the ultimate romantic fantasy land,' and this record, lyrical and smooth, conjures that terrain with impressive grace. There are no rough edges whatsoever on this music. It rolls in like a glittering fog, and Ferry's shivering croon sounds downright mystical."

Strangely, the album failed, initially at least, to advance Roxy's cause in the USA, where its chart high of 53 was a full 30 places below the position attained by *Manifesto*. "Roxy Music's *Avalon* takes a long time to kick in, but it finally does, and it's a good one," wrote Kurt Loder in *Rolling Stone*. "Bryan Ferry stars as a remarkably expressive keyboard player and singer whose familiar mannerisms are subsumed in a rich, benevolent self-assurance. And reed man Andy Mackay shines in a series of cameos (his oboe meditation on Ferry's *Tara* is particularly lovely). Ten years after its debut, Roxy Music has mellowed: the occasional stark piano chords in *While My Heart is Still Beating*, for example, recall the stately mood of *A Song for Europe*, but the sound is softer, dreamier and less determinedly dramatic now. Ferry's songwriting, however, has seldom seemed stronger."

On a commercial and critical high, Ferry took the plunge and married Lucy Helmore in a quiet Sussex ceremony on Saturday 26 June. "I think marriage is worth a try," he quipped. "I believe in trying anything once." Relinquishing his 'most eligible bachelor' status no doubt focused Ferry's mind on his dictum that "The reasons that guys gravitate into and out of groups is quite often to do with the details of their domestic arrangements. Guys get married, they leave a group. Guys get divorced, they get back into a group." The first half of that equation would be amply evidenced within 12 months; the full implications of the second, however, would have to wait until the turn of the century.

* * *

Always Unknowing
(Ferry) 5:21

Where Roxy's other B-sides of 1982 – *India* and a remix of *The Main Thing* – were culled from the accompanying *Avalon* album, *Always Unknowing* was a fully developed out-take from the album sessions, ending up as the flip of *Avalon* itself in the UK and *More Than This* in the US. Like the *Flesh + Blood* out-take *Lover*, it conjures a bewitching atmosphere via Ferry's allusive lyric and some marvellously expressive touches from Mackay, but, unlike *Lover*, it finally exposes Ferry's laid-back posture as virtually horizontal.

Surprisingly, there's a very faint reminiscence of *In Every Dream Home a Heartache* here, with the nocturnal sighing of Ferry's lover providing a distant echo of the expiring sighs morbidly referenced in the earlier song. On one level this coincidence points up the stark difference between Ferry's creative muse in 1973 and its equivalent a decade later, but on another it emphasises the common ground between them. In *Always Unknowing*, the state of robotic suspended animation dramatised in *Heartache* has finally become reality. Indeed, Ferry sounds positively catatonic, his sprechgesang mode now coming over like Rex Harrison on tranquilisers.

The track starts as it means to go on, with a sleep-befuddled fog of instrumentation that sounds like a woodwind transcription of the voicebox-cum-guitar effect on tracks like Steely Dan's *Haitian Divorce*. Elsewhere, Jimmy Maelen's ambi-dextrous percussion effects rattle around the fringes of an effectively dreamlike interplay between guitar, bass and drums. Finally, Ferry drawls ditheringly into view, telling another errant lover in decidedly uncertain terms to leave him in his habitual state of hesitation and indecision. Unhappily, the clichés of old, strung together on a beguiling stream of Pop Art consciousness, now just sound like clichés. In the choruses, if such they can be called, Mackay's lachrymose sax fills are lusciously ranged against Ferry's muted heart-cries, which swirl mournfully across the stereo image and eventually usher in a bluesy, but over-extended, guitar solo: Neil Hubbard wearing his best B B King hat.

"I suppose this does sound a more polished album," Ferry maintained in *Record Mirror*. "That's inevitable as you get more sophisticated in the way you approach things. The problem is not to make it too smooth so that it doesn't have any emotional effect." Maybe *Always Unknowing* failed to make the grade when it came to put *Avalon* together because, on it, Ferry's fear of the music being "so smooth it doesn't have any emotional effect" comes close to being realised. The sound is indeed lustrous, shimmering, polished to within an inch of its life – or perhaps beyond, which is exactly the trouble.

Having previously been included on the grab-bag fourth disc of the *Thrill of It All* box set, *Always Unknowing* finally found its way onto its parent album as a bonus track on the occasion of *Avalon*'s 20th anniversary SACD release.

More Than This
(Ferry) 4:30

When the *More Than This* single appeared in March, it seemed to outdo even *Jealous Guy* in ethereal grace, discarding the last vestiges of melodrama contained in the Lennon tribute and settling instead for a sort of uninterrupted ambient haze. When it was positioned some two months later as the opening track on *Avalon*, it became clear that this was no passing sonic experiment but a sound that was to permeate the entire album. Like the tide referred to in Ferry's lyric, the music flows on undeviatingly while Ferry drifts forlornly above it, evoking a dreamlike state in which lovers are no more secure than autumn leaves.

The better to accommodate the song to the prevailing ethos, a rogue, atonal squeal of Manzanera feedback, clearly audible in the intro to the single version, has been carefully airbrushed out. As a result, the build-up to Ferry's mellifluous vocal is velvet-smooth all the way, featuring an irresistibly melodic Alan Spenner bass line and a thickly textured wash of sound in which it's hard to distinguish synth from sax or sax from synth. In a gorgeous effect, Mackay's tenor surges out of the mix with ever-increasing urgency during the choruses, prior to a prolonged outro in which layered saxes swarm woozily across the soundstage like the narcotic fumes of some slow-acting anaesthetic.

This instrumental section remains one of Roxy's most striking latterday achievements, with the dazzling extemporisations of Manzanera's guitar putting up some spikey resistance to the encroaching slumber but finally giving place to just the ghostly lilt of Ferry's synthesiser, spelling out the melody in half-heard form before the listener finally goes under.

If the instrumentation takes on the characteristics of an out-of-body experience, the relationship of which Ferry sings is just as drifting and impalpable. The mood is one of introspection and indecision, as if this kind of unknowable connection is the best any two human beings can hope for. Ferry's Byronic pose from *A Song for Europe* is here smoothed down into a resigned fatalism that mirrors the inexorable flow of the elements. The effect is akin to a famously Byronic image by Romantic artist Caspar David Friedrich, the 1818 canvas *The Wanderer Above the Sea of Clouds*, in which the dandified philosophical hero stands on a promontory above the surgings of an agitated sea. There's nothing tempestuous about this ocean, however; in *More Than This*, Roxy's sound ebbs and flows, but it no longer rages.

Romantic art of a later period would give *More Than This* its signature image, however; bypassing Friedrich, Ferry opted for a Dante Gabriel Rossetti canvas for use on the single's lustrous picture sleeve. Rossetti's 1872 painting *Veronica Veronese* – actually a portrait of ubiquitous Pre-Raphaelite model Alexa Wilding – provided a covergirl very different from Roxy's luridly accoutred vamps of yore. Robed in green velvet, the subject is seen pausing in the midst of musical composition to gain inspiration from the twitterings of a caged bird. Given that *More Than This* picks up the long-ago imagery of *Sea Breezes*, Ferry might just as well have selected a famous canvas by Rossetti's contemporary, John Everett Millais. With Rossetti's ill-fated wife, Elizabeth Siddall, for a model, Millais' 1851 rendering of Hamlet's lovesick Ophelia, floating in death among water-borne flowers, would have ideally matched the lilting flow of the music and the undertow of doomed fatalism in the lyric.

Pre-Raphaelites and High Romantics notwithstanding, the singles market into which *More Than This* was released on 22 March was one dominated by The Goombay Dance Band's *Seven Tears*, *My Camera Never Lies* by Bucks Fizz and the cloying Paul McCartney-Stevie Wonder combo, *Ebony and Ivory*. The song charted at number 18 a week later (just below another new entry, Altered Images' *See Those Eyes*) and, after the band's appearance on the 1 April edition of *Top of the*

Pops, it reached its high point of number six – this time, ironically, right behind Japan's breakthrough disc, *Ghosts*. It remained at six a further week, then departed the rundown at speed, going from seven to 14 and finally, on 3 May, 28 – totting up a total of six weeks in the Top 40 and two outside it.

Roxy's *Top of the Pops* appearance, incidentally, featured Phil Gould of Level 42 miming to Andy Newmark's drums, while Spenner's role was handled by the saturnine Tony Levin, brandishing his trademark Chapman stick and fresh from the recording of King Crimson's *Beat* album. The accompanying video, shown on the 15 April edition of *Top of the Pops*, involved a self-referential nod to the inner-sleeve imagery of *The Bride Stripped Bare*, showing Ferry slumped in a cinema with images of Roxy projected onto the screen.

On stage, however, the song would prove a problem. "*More Than This* is a hard one to do live," Ferry pointed out, "because for some reason we did it in a key which is much too high." Accordingly, it was unceremoniously dropped after the very first show of the *Avalon* tour, and would only be attempted sporadically during Roxy's 2001 reunion dates. One such attempt, however, made it onto the *Roxy Music Live* CD release – and extremely effective it is too.

"It's a very pretty song, I think," Ferry observed in 2001. "I really like that one; it's got a very good mood." That plenty of other artists agreed with him is clear from the record number of *More Than This* cover versions. Robyn Hitchcock included an acoustic version on his 1989 *Madonna of the Wasps* EP, seven years later appending it to his *Greatest Hits* collection. Atlanta band Glass Candle Grenade, and vocalist Trish Thompson, included the song on their eponymous 1996 album, and the following year 10,000 Maniacs had a hit with it, as sung by Mary Ramsey and featured on the album *Love Among the Ruins*. A dance version made Emmie a one-hit wonder in January 1999, peaking at number five in the UK, and two years later jazz guitarist Charlie Hunter employed vocalist Norah Jones to sing the song, together with Nick Drake's *Day is Done*, on his 2001 collection *Songs from the Analog Playground*.

Perhaps the most surprising interpretation is featured in Sofia Coppola's 2002 film, *Lost in Translation*, in which Bill Murray serenades Scarlett Johansson in a Tokyo karaoke bar. "We were in the karaoke place and Bill and I were just talking about how we love that album," Coppola told *indieWIRE*'s Wendy Mitchell. "I said, 'Will you sing it for me?' So he did, and I thought it was so sweet that we filmed it, and luckily we got permission to use it in the movie." The result is included as a hidden extra on the film's soundtrack album, proving, as Peter Travers remarked in *Rolling Stone*, that "Murray's version of Roxy Music's *More Than This* is one for the time capsule."

The Space Between
(Ferry) 4:30

As already noted, in 1995 Manzanera told *Mojo*'s Rob Chapman that the preponderance of drugs in Roxy's 1981-2 recording sessions contributed to the album's somnambulant atmosphere. On only two *Avalon* tracks do the band make an effort to rouse themselves from the pervading lethargy, indicating that the drugs in question might occasionally have had rejuvenating effects as well as soporific ones. Both, roughly speaking, are funk pastiches of a skewed and unpredictable sort, and the first of them is *The Space Between*.

The rhythmic relationships established by the band are placed front and centre here, with Ferry's vocal consigned to the backdrop for a change; hardly surprising, given that the lyric is virtually non-existent. The title phrase is contained in George Harrison's Beatles classic *Within You, Without You*, but cod-philosophical musings are not Ferry's concern here. Indeed, the song's title is more likely to contain a smutty double-entendre than anything to do with the human condition. Ferry states simply that he and his lover have been drifting apart and that he means to close the gap once and for all tonight. And that's about it – though, given the inscrutability of Ferry's vocal, the 'closing the gap' bit could just as easily be a psychotic threat as a bedroom-eyed promise.

The track opens to a tentative rattling of pinball guitars, acquiring an irresistible weight and pulse through the introduction of Neil Jason's meaty bass line and Andy Newmark's muscular drum patterns. The excitement is cranked up yet further with the arrival of Mackay's saxophone, blasting out a three-note riff reminiscent of similar effects on both *Over You* and *Angel Eyes*. Ferry's nonsense muttering, not included on the lyric sheet, presages the lyric proper, and something of the old Roxy dynamic is recalled by the interplay of Mackay's sax – honking lustily from one end of the soundstage – with the spiky responses from Manzanera's guitar that issue from the other. The same relationship is recalled in the instrumental middle section, where a hypnotic whirlpool of sound features the sax swirling airily against hard-edged guitar interjections. Jimmy Maelen, meanwhile, garnishes the mix with his familiar bits and pieces of comedy percussion, some of which, taken in isolation, wouldn't disgrace *The Benny Hill Show*.

The Space Between lays down a pretty awesome groove; it's tight and danceable and flavoursome, yet somehow remains a mere throwaway. This is mainly due to the fact that, in stark contrast to the band's full-blooded contribution, Ferry's performance is strictly of the phoned-in variety. Reflecting its throwaway status, the track's history in live performance was an unusually short one. Like *More Than This*, it became a very early casualty of the *Avalon* tour, being unceremoniously dropped after the opening show. Unlike *More Than This*, it was not resurrected for the 2001 reunion tour. It did, however, receive an occasional airing on Ferry's solo *Mamouna* dates in 1994.

Avalon
(Ferry) 4:16

Avalon is, as it were, Bryan Ferry bottled. The louche, world-weary persona – caught on an unending hedonistic treadmill, crushed by some unspecified ennui but showing a spark of renewed interest at sight of a fresh partner – is here distilled in its purest form. In conversation with *Smash Hits'* Ian Birch, Ferry maintained simply that "It's one of those after-the-party songs." The 'party's over' trajectory from *Re-make/Re-model* to *Mother of Pearl*, from *Spin Me Round* to *Avalon* provides a handy thumbnail sketch of the band's progress, and in this last instance Ferry's profound enervation sees him virtually refining himself out of existence. But the refinement, for this song at least, is exquisitely upholstered.

Given that *Avalon* is the umpteenth go-around for a by-now well-worn theme, the wonder of it is that Ferry avoids toppling over into self-parody. Self-parody would have to wait until his renewed solo albums of the later 1980s; for now, *Avalon* shimmers with a preternatural lustre that makes Ferry's clichés seem new-minted. Here he is again, garlanded with the sad detritus of yet another society soirée, only to flicker into life at the promise of a last dance with someone whom he sees emerging from, apparently, the ether. Though making use of the half-tranquilised delivery familiar to Roxy fans by this stage, Ferry's vocal performance is so powerful, and the soundstage so intricately built up around him, that the recycled material disarms criticism. The song conjures up an oneiric atmosphere of blurred impressions and suggests that, having arrived "out of nowhere," the narrator's dance partner is likely to whisk him, too, "out of nowhere," back into the dreamworld from which she came.

The instrumental contributions here form an appropriately hypnotic backdrop to Ferry's otherworldly dream state. This is just as well because, on closer inspection, some of Ferry's trademark wordplay is beginning to sound a bit moth-eaten. His juggling of 'motion' and 'emotion' stretches right back to *Sea Breezes*, but here it's compromised by the fact that "a motion" could just as easily refer to a bowel movement as a twirl round the dancefloor. Nevertheless, Jimmy Maelen's multi-faceted percussion resonates to an alluring samba-type rhythm, while Manzanera's guitar spirals through the mix in sublime fashion prior to a deliciously phrased soliloquy from Mackay's tenor sax. And as a heady swirl of backing vocals washes in, Mackay shifts from monologue mode to an enchanting dialogue with teenage vocalist Yanick Etienne in which he's very nearly upstaged.

Etienne's soaring climactic bird cries (somewhat reminiscent of Minnie Riperton's 1975 ballad *Lovin' You*) remain perhaps the track's most memorable feature, but were nevertheless a strictly eleventh-hour refinement – an instance, as Ferry amusingly put it, of "how fate can play into your hands if you work hard enough at it."

According to Rhett Davies, speaking to *Sound on Sound* magazine in 2003, "We were actually mixing the album, and the version of the song that we'd done just wasn't working out, so as we were mixing we recut the entire song with a completely different groove. We finished it off the last weekend we were mixing." Alone together at the Power Station that Sunday morning, Davies and Ferry were taking a coffee break when they overheard a group of Haitian musicians, Etienne among them, who had come in to cut a demo. "She didn't speak a word of English," Davies remembered. "Her boyfriend, who was the band's manager, came in and translated. And then the next day we mixed it."

"It was the most beautiful voice I've ever heard," Ferry told Ian Birch in 1982. "She created exactly the mood I wanted. A kind of surreal carnival feel. But that's a clumsy way of expressing it. When I played her the music, she knew exactly what to do with it. That sort of thing makes all the other hours when you're beating the wall with your fists [seem] worthwhile."

Ferry's addition of Etienne's vocal could have been more diplomatically achieved, however; Manzanera and Mackay arrived to find it already in place as a fait accompli. According to Manzanera, "I do remember at the time, because one was so caught up with insecurity and stress, thinking, 'How dare you put something on without asking us?' But his instinct was totally right, and it was absolutely brilliant." If nothing else, Ferry's reference to "beating the wall" with his fists and Manzanera's allusion to "insecurity and stress" give some indication of the simmering tension in which this most apparently laidback of Roxy albums was produced.

As the second single excerpted from the album, *Avalon* charted at number 33 on 15 June, two days prior to the band appearing on *Top of the Pops* to promote it. As Adam Ant's *Goody Two Shoes* succeeded Madness' *House of Fun* in the Number One spot, any prospect of *Avalon* bothering either of them was soon scotched. It vaulted impressively from 33 to 13 but then stalled, falling first to 16 and, after a further three weeks, out of the chart altogether – an indication that Roxy's three-singles-per-album strategy was finally coming up against the law of diminishing returns. The single mix was at slight variance to the album one, with Fonzi Thornton's mid-song croon of "dancin'... dancin'..." given a higher-pitched punch and Mackay's saxophone foregrounded to compete more strongly with Etienne's vocal. The *Thrill of It All* box set subsequently claimed to contain this version, but didn't.

Despite having sought to give the track "a slow, Latin American feel," Ferry per-versely larded the accompanying video with a heavy dose of Old World elegance. Sadly, the song's wraparound luxuriance falls completely flat when literalised into a high-society charade of Ferry waltzing down brocaded corridors with teenage model-cum-actress Sophie Ward (daughter of *Young Winston* himself, Simon). The album's hooded bird of prey puts in a guest appearance, Mackay and Manzanera – wearing black DJs to offset Ferry's trademark white – seem thoroughly disgruntled, and the anonymous session players look as much like painted corpses as Ferry himself. To make matters worse, The Stranglers' 1981 promo for *Golden Brown* had somehow constituted a vicious parody of the *Avalon* video a year in advance.

Like a lot of Roxy's later material, the delicately wrought atmosphere of *Avalon* proved difficult to replicate on stage, failing pretty miserably on both the 1982 tour and 2001 reunion dates, despite the fact that Yanick Etienne made a guest appearance on 13 of the latter. This didn't, however, stop other artists from attempting cover versions of the song. In 1992, veteran actor Ian McShane included it on his album *From Both Sides Now*, also releasing this version as a single; other artists covered ranged from Chris Rea and 10cc to The Police and (as per the collec-tive title) Joni Mitchell. Five years later, Mancunian dance group M People, fronted by vocalist Heather Small, recorded a version of the song for their *Fresco* album.

India
(Ferry) 1:44

Having already heard this fragmentary instrumental as the blink-and-you'll-miss-it flip-side of *More Than This*, it came as a surprise to Roxy fans to find it also included on the *Avalon* album. Previously consigned to the B-side backwater, instrumentals were a new development as Roxy album tracks, despite the elaborate instrumental work-outs included on, say, *The Bogus Man* or *Sentimental Fool* – despite, also, the increasingly skeletal nature of Ferry's lyrics on more recent albums. Stumbling across *India* seemed equivalent to finding *South Downs* included on *Flesh + Blood* or, God forbid, the horrendous *Sultanesque* on *Siren*.

India is, of course, much more sophisticated than those two, but it still seems something of a makeweight in the context of *Avalon* as a whole. Indeed, given that the album clocks in at little more than 37 minutes, maybe it's not enough of a makeweight. It feels as if it's been strangled at birth, rather as if Ferry wasn't willing to surrender himself fully to this new-fangled 'instrumentals on albums' idea and called off the further development it could well have benefited from. Roxy imitators Japan were simultaneously devoting a sizeable chunk of their *Tin Drum* album to another instrumental named after an Oriental location, in this case *Canton*, making the brevity of *India* seem all the more craven.

The Eastern flavours introduced into Western pop by George Harrison back in the late 1960s had created a flower-power vogue that reached its absurd apotheosis in John Hawkins' instrumental folly *Lord Sitar*. Any danger of a sitar turning up on *India*, however, is quickly scotched by the bizarre fusion of Manzanera's guitar and Mackay's saxophone that forms the track's dominant, raga-tinged motif. Ferry is credited here with 'guitar synthesiser', suggesting that *India* at least preserves the Eno-esque sound manipulation of old. Jimmy Maelen isn't credited at all, which is odd given the array of peculiar percussive effects included.

Whatever its personnel, *India* cooks up a beguiling sound in its brief tenure but finally serves as little more than an exotic prelude to the arresting Ferry-Mackay composition coming up. Played over the PA at each venue, it also served as an exotic prelude to Roxy's 1982-3 live set.

While My Heart is Still Beating
(Ferry-Mackay) 3:26

Reviewing the 1979-82 phase of his career, Andy Mackay glumly concluded that "I made some more Roxy Music albums and wondered what it all meant." By the time he wrote those words (for the 1990 CD reissue of his own *Resolving Contradictions* album), he had taken the plunge and enrolled on a full-time theology course at King's College London. In the meantime, something of Mackay's mood of spiritual discontent had been encapsulated in his penultimate Ferry collaboration, *While My Heart is Still Beating*, which bore the intriguing working title *Epiphany*.

Mackay's mournful melody underpins a lyric in which Ferry's familiar lovelorn posture is replaced by something quite new, a philosophical questioning that threatens to turn self-absorption into philanthropy. As well as precisely echoing Mackay's 'what does it all mean?' mood, Ferry's lyric expresses fellow feeling with the emotional needs of humanity in general. The unfamiliar tone of concern recalls nothing so much as The Beatles' most funereal song, *Eleanor Rigby*, as well as prefiguring Ferry's later solo song, *Cruel*. For the time being, however, Ferry's 'bleeding heart' questionings seem to induce in him a kind of paralysis, surrounded by well-meaning words yet half-heartedly aware that he should stop daydreaming and actually do something constructive. It's as if Ferry is surrendering to Hamlet's curse of inaction, as expressed in Shakespeare's memorable line, "The native hue of resolution / Is sicklied o'er with the pale cast of thought."

Like Ferry's lyric, the soundstage of *While My Heart is Still Beating* exudes a hesitant, probing sense of desolation that makes it the most troubling track on the album. There's a querulous question mark hanging over Mackay's peculiar little saxophone introduction and just as haunting a sense of unresolved questioning in the inconclusive arabesque he performs at the end. Elsewhere, a chilling piano motif ripples through the mix in tandem with a subdued but strangely insistent hammering of tom-toms. Manzanera's heavily treated guitar rumbles through a lowering middle section, returning at the end to be magically transmuted into an approaching wheeze of saxophone in the long-ago tradition of *Sea Breezes*. In the meantime, Mackay has contributed four-note elaborations to the choruses that are as bilious and out-of-sorts as anything in the Roxy canon. Here, too, Ferry reaches a less-than-cheering endgame with a query as to whether his poor heart, which merely skipped a beat in *No Strange Delight*, will ever stop bleeding.

A more pertinent question for cynical observers of the new Roxy was whether this track's title was an ironic reference to the band's apparent torpor throughout the *Avalon* album; if the band's heart was indeed still beating, it was only by the merest whisker. But though *While My Heart is Still Beating* is indeed the work of a unit close to death, it at least constitutes a deathbed reverie every bit as unnerving as the imagined one featured on *Strictly Confidential* nearly a decade before.

For real irony, the track's title was adapted for use on the belated 1990 live album, *Heart Still Beating*, which showcases a 1982 performance that, on record at any rate, sounds thoroughly moribund. In performance, Mackay added an extended saxophone intro to the song with an otherworldly nursery-rhyme feel to it; the *Heart Still Beating* album contrived to delete this opening, though it's thankfully preserved on Robin Nash's BBC film from Fréjus. Some 20 years later, Mackay performed the opposite trick, adding a smouldering saxophone outro to the song which can be heard on both the *Roxy Music Live* CD and the accompanying *Live at the Apollo* DVD.

The Main Thing
(Ferry) 3:54 / extended remix 7:43

Like *The Space Between*, this is another example of Roxy rousing themselves from the otherwise all-encroaching ambient haze of *Avalon* with a percussive burst of mutant funk. Ferry, too, seems to perk up for this one, delivering fabulously impenetrable lyrics with something of his old lounge-lizard venom. Indeed, for all its blistering pulse and irresistible chorus, an eerie pall of paranoia hangs heavy over the track; muttered references to "words of sand" and "a good thing gone" only add to the impression that the song's title refers to an obsessive need for gratification impelling its victim towards self-destruction. The tension built up between these two apparently opposing elements – the pulse and the paranoia – gives *The Main Thing* a queasy potency; in short, this is classic Roxy Music.

A clatter of electronic percussion and spine-jangling bass guitar gives the track a powerful undertow as synths twirl seductively above the soundstage, Ferry's vocal finally coming in on an electrifying cue from Manzanera. The ever-inventive Jimmy Maelen seemingly adds fly-zipper effects to his percussive armoury here, and the choruses are given a compulsive kick by a killer combination of Fonzi Thornton's chanted backing vocal and Mackay's molten, three-note sax flares.

A spellbinding middle section sees the entire juggernaut grinding almost to a halt, Mackay breathing stertorously in the upper reaches as Neil Jason's bass makes halting efforts to crank the machinery up again. But then the synthetic hand-claps crowd back in like a proliferating swarm of locusts, Mackay and Manzanera blaze through the mix in unison, and Ferry finally returns on a rinky-dink cue from Maelen. Only the ending disappoints; the widespread production procedure of 'if the saxophonist's started up, hit the fade button' was never one that applied to Roxy until now, with Mackay blowing some particularly smouldering and sinister lines while simultaneously disappearing into the ether.

This muffed ending at least held out hopes for a more expansive 12" version, but when it came it proved a disappointment. The single release of *Take a Chance with Me* featured a variant mix of the standard-length *Main Thing* as its B-side, a cruder, sparser cut lacking several of the album version's grace notes. Worse, the 12" release, though retaining the abbreviated *Take a Chance with Me* on its A-side, unleashed on the flip a surprisingly ineffective remix of *The Main Thing* that approaches the eight-minute mark. It's listenable enough, but never approaches the excitement of the original thanks to the choruses being stripped of Mackay's blazing punctuation marks until the closing stages.

The Main Thing provided Roxy's 1982-3 *Avalon* tour with a storming opening number: Ferry sashaying into view in full white tuxedo mode, Mackay's tenor sound at its creamiest, Manzanera and Hubbard conducting a spooky guitar dialogue mid-song, the backing vocalists chanting "on and on and on" in truly mesmeric fashion. Though this performance would be preserved in Robin Nash's BBC film from Fréjus (subsequently released to tape and, later, DVD as *The High Road*), it was mysteriously excluded from the belated live album *Heart Still Beating*, where it was supplanted by the lame-duck Ferry solo outing, *Can't Let Go*.

For foreign markets, a promotional video was shot to accompany *The Main Thing* as a potential single release, showing Ferry leering his way through the lyric in front of giant video screens – on them, the fishnet-clad legs of clearly supine but otherwise impersonal dancing girls performing all sorts of suggestive movements. Any perceived sexism contained in the *Country Life* cover pales beside this, though it too pales beside the soft-porn extremes of Duran Duran's *Girls on Film* promo. In any case, given the number of eye-popping 'splits' being performed, the video might have been better suited to promoting *The Space Between*.

Take a Chance with Me
(Ferry-Manzanera) 4:42 / single edit 3:43 / single edit [US] 2:46

Rather surprisingly, *Take a Chance with Me* begins with over a minute of vaguely disquieting instrumental scene-setting in the style of *Sentimental Fool* or *Manifesto*. Surprising not only in the context of *Avalon* as a whole but also this particular song, which, when it finally arrives, is a relatively bright and breezy affair bearing no relation to the build-up whatever.

Where earlier tracks – like *If There is Something* or, for that matter, *Sentimental Fool* itself – went through any number of peculiar gear changes, they were nevertheless made to feel organic, as if Ferry's 'three or four songs in one' approach was the most natural thing in the world. Here, the opening section is a moment of sterling weirdness but seems somehow detached, bolted on – as if thrown in by Roxy as a reassurance to their hardcore fans that they could still do 'weird' when it suited them. If so, there was really no need, given that the miasmic flow of the accompanying album was a weird enough development in itself.

With weird on the menu, Mackay's oboe was inevitably disinterred from the mothballs in which it had been languishing since the previous album's *No Strange Delight*. Here, its ethereal plaint dovetails beautifully with Manzanera's granite guitar motif, the pair of them thrown into relief by a complex mesh of swirling synthesiser, juddering bass and at least three different varieties of percussion. As the song proper kicks in, a token effort to connect the two sections is provided by the uninterrupted shrill of Mackay's oboe theme, but the dominant mood is set by the airborne riffing of Manzanera's guitar.

Ferry's vocal is in his best vulnerable mode, lamenting the sadness that love has brought him yet, in a typically schizoid twist, defiantly convinced that everyone else should approach love in the same, presumably disaster-strewn fashion. The choruses are exhilarating moments of release made doubly cathartic by Manzanera's faux-harpsichord stylings, and the extended outro is introduced by a cheesy organ figure followed by an unusually aggressive call-and-response struggle between Manzanera's guitar and Mackay's oboe.

Angel Eyes having been jostled in the charts of summer 1979 by an identically titled Abba single, Roxy were here unafraid to risk confusion with another Abba hit, *Take a Chance on Me*. The Abba song was a few years old by this time, however, so the poor showing of *Take a Chance with Me* in the singles chart was presumably not related to consumer befuddlement. Instead, it was clearly a single too far from the already well-plumbed *Avalon* album. Backed by a remix of *The Main Thing*, it was issued on 13 September, entering the chart on the 21st at number 34. Its subsequent positions oscillated unpredictably from 27 to 26 to 33, then back up to 29 but finally to 55 and gone. Towards the end of this six-week run, Culture Club's *Do You Really Want to Hurt Me?* reigned unassailable at Number One.

With a chart high of only 26, *Take a Chance with Me* brought Roxy's singles chart history to a less than stellar close. Inevitably, the single edit shaved down the opening instrumental section fairly brutally, though the no-nonsense US release went even further by ditching it, and much of the outro, altogether.

To Turn You On
see page 240

True to Life
(Ferry) 4:25

Perhaps the most extraordinary track on the *Avalon* album, *True to Life* creates a seamless tapestry of sound that is at once flowing, even featureless, yet bursting with incidental detail. Equally paradoxical, the mood is one of romantic reverie punctuated by occasional, unnerving touches of disorientation. The final paradox is supplied by Ferry's vocal – intensely wistful, almost evanescent, yet starting with the disquieting admission that his thoughts are given over to darkness.

The remainder of his tremulous vocal is dedicated to a nameless and multi-faceted "diamond lady," with engaging touches of self-pity along the way but above all the familiar anxiety regarding a soulless existence devoted to being "agitated in Xenon nightly." Towards the end, Ferry's addressee suddenly becomes "my seaside diamond," a brief reminiscence of the last time a Roxy album featured a seascape on its cover. But the disorientation is only momentary. This clearly isn't the voracious Lorelei figure crawling across the *Siren* sleeve, for in the optimistic conclusion the darkness lifts and Ferry sees light at the end of the tunnel, a conclusion to his journey, with his lover on his arm.

The virtually ambient soundstage constantly challenges the listener to identify the various instruments being deployed. No trouble identifying the huge guitar chord that gets the track into gear, nor the strange, breathy dabs of saxophone that float on the surface of the music like jewels on an agitated sea. The ever-tinkering Jimmy Maelen also brings to the track the full range of his percussive jiggery-pokery, chattering indefatigably away from every conceivable corner of the stereo image. But the synths that form a juddering underlay to the whole construction seem to hint sometimes of strings, sometimes of peripatetic woodwinds. And the staccato bursts of sound that shudder asthmatically through the mix at unpredictable intervals – are we talking Manzanera's guitar here, or Mackay's saxophone, or a woozy combination of both?

Certainly Mackay's reticence is overcome halfway through for an airy blast or two, while Manzanera throws up some magisterial lines that straddle the sound-stage in truly electrifying style. But the effort to sort this from that is ultimately a fruitless one; the slow-on-the-uptake listener finally twigs that he's been missing the point all along. For this is a track more akin to Eno's *Another Green World* than anything on, say, *Siren*. Individual contributions are not the issue here, just the conjuring of a mood in which the listener is borne unresistingly on a wave of sound even more evocative than *More Than This*.

"I like to make records that are interesting for the head," Ferry commented at the time. "There should be ideas you can relate to as well as a mood that makes you feel good. Basically it's beautiful music and it's very hard to go further than that. It's trying to make something out of nothing." *True to Life* is a triumphant exemplar of this philosophy, and, given the samey stuff that was to surface on Ferry's 1985 solo album, it's hard to resist the conclusion that he should have quit while he was ahead. From *Windswept* to *Zamba*, even unto the woozy incense fumes of the *Mamouna* LP in 1994, the *True to Life* blueprint would underpin much of his later work with ultimately debilitating results.

Though in mood and instrumentation a cornerstone of the *Avalon* album, *True to Life* has never been performed live. Given its impalpable complexities, maybe this isn't so surprising. What is surprising is that it was passed over for inclusion on the *Thrill of It All* box set to make room for the Ferry solo item and sometime B-side, *To Turn You On*.

Tara
(Ferry-Mackay) 1:38

With the instrumental fragment *Tara*, the *Avalon* album, and Roxy's studio career, is swept away on an ambient wash of the Nassau surf. According to the sleeve notes of the *Thrill of It All* box set, Mackay's gorgeously contemplative soprano solo was an improvisation providentially preserved on tape and subsequently augmented with Alan Spenner's shuddering bass line and Ferry's off-kilter piano figures. The mournful melody, coupled with the elemental sounds of the sea, make *Tara* the ideal coda to the nameless malaise that has washed over the *Avalon* album throughout.

Tara also paints an evocative portrait of the place in which the *Avalon* album was recorded; indeed, the wave sounds were taped outside the house in which Ferry was staying. Reminded by it of Tara, Scarlett O'Hara's ancestral home in *Gone With the Wind*, Ferry attached the name to this concluding track presumably in arbitrary fashion; even so, the title seems in retrospect an unusually poignant one, recalling as it does the ghostly goodbyes ("ta-ra, ta-ra") that brought the *For Your Pleasure* album to a close nearly ten years before.

The only trouble here lies in that word 'fragment'. Arguably, the track's very brevity is exactly what makes it work; but looked at another way, the piece is crying out for further development. Instead, it's wafted away after a mere minute-and-a-half on a subdued crashing of waves – "as if snuffed out," Paul Stump has aptly observed, "by some spoilsport." What that development might have been was amply demonstrated in Roxy's reunion tour of 2001, where it was transformed into a spellbinding duet between Mackay's soprano and Lucy Wilkins' equally resonant violin.

Nevertheless, the studio version remains one of Mackay's supreme Roxy moments, as well as seeming like a ten-years-on refashioning of *Sea Breezes*. The wave sounds are back, just as the soprano sax echoes Mackay's wandering oboe on the earlier song. Ferry's tortuous lyric, however, has gone. Indeed, *Tara* seems like the logical extension of Ferry's increasingly sparing use of lyrics, mirroring the abandonment of vocals their old associate, Eno, had put into practice several years earlier. By this time in Roxy's progress, no words are necessary. And the rest is silence.

PART FIVE

Roxy in Retreat

Twenty-One: *Ta-ra*

*"I never expected Roxy to last this long. It's always been a vague kind of group,
it's changed a lot over the years. I don't think I would have been able to sustain
interest if it had been the same people right through. But as for a career in music,
my interest hasn't waned at all. I don't feel I've run out of ideas and that would
be the criterion, I hope."*

Bryan Ferry, quoted in the *Observer* 19 September 1982

We are the 501s

The *Avalon* tour broke the Roxy mould in following its associated album rather
than preceding it, and would include a final sortie to the USA for which
nobody had any particular enthusiasm. By this time, Roxy's Atlantic contract had
lapsed and they had been transferred again to Warner Bros, ironically the same
label that had so badly fumbled the band's original visit to America in 1972.
"Atlantic is a great record company and I was kind of sad to leave them," Ferry
told Lynn Hanna, "but they always had us figured as a low-budget act; you know,
art music from England ... Even though we filled medium-size halls everywhere
we went, we couldn't fill really big places, and that's the only way you make any
money. It gets a bit depressing going out and working really hard then coming
home and being told, well, you only lost $50,000 on this tour."

With Roxy entering the newly corporatised world of stadium rock, the *Avalon*
tour was made possible by denim merchants Levi-Strauss, the accompanying tour
programme coming complete with a poster featuring Ferry, Mackay, Manzanera
and their session satellites on one side, and New Romantic-style models extolling
the virtues of Black Levi's and Levi's Original 501s on the other.

The programme was a lavish one, with the *Avalon* artwork on its cover (the
Viking lady's lakeside view augmented by a rather foolish funeral barge) and a
lengthy essay inside by Dr Puxley, in which he whipped up a nostalgic
approximation of the nonsense he'd composed for the *Roxy Music* album ten
years before: "What year is it, anyway? Leopard skin and sculpted quiffs, dropped
thirds and open – 1972? – Lovesick blues and padded suits, bow-ties and tape
loops – 1973? – Torch songs and tuxedos, gaucho style and Garbo – 1974? –
khaki dress and siren girls, discobeat and ... one could go on ... It's 1982. Roxy
Music's children have come of age, and would see themselves as heirs. Wherever
one looks in British pop, from avant to forefront, from New Romantic to
art-school traditional, the same thing: an idea, a detail, an aspiration that's
already familiar, that's already been done before (and better), a part of the same
legacy, the richest legacy of the 1970s."

The musicians engaged to fulfil that legacy for a 1982 audience were for the most part familiar from the *Avalon* album – Spenner on bass, Newmark on drums, Hubbard on rhythm and occasional lead guitar, Fonzi Thornton on backing vocals. Thornton was joined by Roxy newcomers Michelle Collins and Tawatha Agee, while the keyboards slot was occupied by the youthful Guy Fletcher, later to work with Dire Straits. This swollen entourage was endorsed by Ferry as "the biggest band and the most talented players. It's good to sing with a rhythm section that's as good as that. It feels like you are skating, gliding along."

For many, the *Avalon* tour involved way too much in the way of skating and gliding; the presentation and the music had attained a super-smooth slickness that numbed the mind rather than stimulated the senses. *Eight Miles High* had been dragged out of mothballs during rehearsals but didn't make the set list; nor did a projected cover of The Doors' *Light My Fire*. A still more peculiar choice of cover, apparently included at the behest of Ferry's new bride, was *Like a Hurricane*, first heard in 1977 on Neil Young's *American Stars 'n' Bars* album and here providing neat showcases for Manzanera and Mackay.

Ferry's "meisterwerk about LA," *Can't Let Go*, was included (Mackay conspicuously stalking off stage at this point), as was Manzanera's more recent release, *Impossible Guitar*. Mackay, meanwhile, had to make do with an extended version of *Tara* in the shimmer of a multi-faceted light show. Recent gossamer confections like *Dance Away* and *Avalon* obstinately refused to work in performance, while *More Than This* and *The Space Between* proved so unsatisfactory they didn't get beyond Ireland.

Roxy on the Riviera

Ireland is where the *Avalon* tour began on Thursday 12 August. Limerick's Savoy Theatre was the inaugural venue, the band moving on to two dates in Dublin and thence to Portugal (Lisbon, Faro) and Spain (Madrid, San Sebastian, Barcelona). Dates at Cap d'Agde and Reggio dell'Emilia were separated by a Fréjus event on Friday the 27th with a BBC film crew in attendance, after which there were gigs in Milan, Rotterdam, Dusseldorf, Dortmund, De Pantin, Brussels and Stockholm.

By an ironic quirk, the support band on the continental leg of the tour was none other than King Crimson, a newly funked-up incarnation very different from the Prog Rock titan that had ruled the EG roost back in Roxy's formative phase. With Robert Fripp joined by Adrian Belew, Tony Levin and old Crimson hand Bill Bruford, the group stuck with Roxy from the 20th (Lisbon) to the 30th (Milan), a further date on Wednesday 1 September at Rome's Castel St Angelo being cancelled owing to the stage set not being ready.

At Fréjus, longtime Roxy follower Allan Jones reported that the on-stage glamour was not replicated for those out front, his *Melody Maker* report aptly entitled 'Allan Jones Takes a Champagne Flight to See Roxy Music on the Riviera – and Still Complains'. "It took the best part of an hour to negotiate a safe passage into the amphitheatre," he grumbled. "Tired, dusty and threatening violence, some of us still managed to look on the bright side as we tumbled into the black claustrophobia of the teeming arena. Our protracted odyssey through the disorderly ranks of furiously gesticulating onion-heads [ie, French people] at least meant that we managed to miss most of King Crimson's support set. Not enough of it for my liking, but in such trying circumstances one must make the most of the meagrest of mercies."

The tour reached Britain with a three-night tenure of Wembley Arena from 22 to 24 September, then two nights at Birmingham's NEC, one each at Brighton and Glasgow, and finally the Playhouse in Edinburgh on Friday 1 October. Though supported by a local band, The Young Ones, at Glasgow, the support act elsewhere was Mari Wilson and the Wilsations. With a prodigious beehive outstripping even those sported by Cindy Wilson and Kate Pierson of The B-52's, Wilson was currently enjoying chart success with the single *Just What I've Always Wanted*. Ferry had caught her earlier single, *Beat the Beat*, on the radio and reportedly called it "the strangest thing I've heard in five years." On this criterion, he presumably judged her retro-recall of 1950s chanteuses like Julie London a more appropriate support act than King Crimson.

Ferry's zeal for touring, never particularly strong, was by now reaching an all-time low. "Touring is such hard work and it's a kind of work that I find somewhat destructive," he told the *NME*. "You quickly reach the point of complete mental and physical exhaustion. The last time we toured I wound up going to hospital, and we had to cancel two weeks of shows in Spain. It's not the healthiest way to live." He was keen to point out, however, that "I love performing. I get a bit of stage fright but that's quite good because it's a form of adrenaline. But the novelty of touring has worn off and I'd prefer to just go back into the recording studio. The argument is that you double your record sales by touring, but I've never seen any proof of that."

Still beating, just

In March, the *Avalon* tour was memorialised on a mini-LP archly attributed to Musique Roxy and called *The High Road*. With *Viva! Roxy Music* having seemed thin gruel as a mere single-disc album, here Ferry perversely went one better, or worse, in putting out a four-song selection that clocked in at less than 28 minutes. Recorded at the Apollo Glasgow on Thursday 30 September by Radio Clyde's Mobile 2, the songs presented were *Can't Let Go, My Only Love, Like a Hurricane* and *Jealous Guy*. With such a limited set list, the inclusion of Ferry's lumbering *Can't Let Go* was an obvious gaffe, but the band's surprisingly powerful cover of *Like a Hurricane* was well worth preserving on disc. *Jealous Guy*, too, works well enough as a reminder of the track's origins as a live performance.

Though a decidedly flimsy makeweight offering, the record charted (as an import) on 19 March, staying for seven weeks and reaching a high of number 26. The best thing about it was its Ferry-Kirk-Price-Saville cover, depicting Brazilian model Thareta de Oliveira in startling negative and with two fingers hooked, for no very obvious reason, into her outstretched lower lip. (She appeared more positively, and with the photo 'flopped' in the opposite direction, on the rear sleeve.) The same design featured on the cover of a videotape which, thankfully, qualified as somewhat better value for money.

This was derived from a BBC special produced by former *Top of the Pops* mainman Robin Nash, whose crew had been present at the band's Fréjus concert on 27 August. The result was transmitted on BBC2 under the no-nonsense title *Roxy Music* on Monday 28 February. *Radio Times* proudly pointed out that the audience at Fréjus had numbered 15,000 and, in its round-up of the songs on offer, listed something called *Both Ends Running*. The 50-minute programme was repeated on 7 August, by which time Polygram Video had issued their augmented, 74-minute version under the title *Roxy Music – The High Road*.

The Rock'n'Pop section of *Video Viewer* magazine noted that "Reunions always smell of money and, but for their [the band's] talent, this tape would be a sad, sordid affair; a band of ageing session musicians, an audience of sunburnt holiday makers and a venue on the nouveau riche side of the French Riviera – all the hallmarks of recycled past glories. But by confidently sticking to a tried, tested and effective style, Ferry and his colleagues can still put on an excellent, if unchallenging, show." In an era of prettified New Romantics bristling with arty promotional videos, the anonymous reviewer's final observation was a perceptive one: "If video had been commercially viable when Roxy Music were leaving other groups in a mire of self-indulgence it would have been a heaven-sent addition to their impact. But compared to many tapes of pre-punk pop acts this will be cherished – with one or two reservations – by anyone who remembers male make-up on *Top of the Pops* the first time around."

From its Channel 5 debut, the tape proved a durable one, being reissued by 4-Front Video some ten years later and finally making it to DVD courtesy of Universal Music International in 2004. The film's lustrous rendition of *The Main Thing* was not to make it to record or CD in any form and, though appearing right at the beginning, remains the undoubted highlight. There are other felicitous touches – the backing vocalists' skirt-billowing, which adds a tempestuous touch of *The Seven Year Itch* to *Like a Hurricane*, Mackay's always welcome duck-walk on *Editions of You*, and above all percussionist Jimmy Maelen, who is visually the star performer here, twitching away with his arsenal of percussive devices like Norman Wisdom in the final stages of Tourette's Syndrome.

In 1990, the stingey *High Road* aperitif was converted into a posthumous four-course double-album called *Heart Still Beating*, its title an ironic parallel to the 'Long Live Roxy Music' message that had characterised the band's first live album in 1976. Having been so disappointed by *Viva! Roxy Music*, Mackay would enthusiastically endorse this new package, noting that "small changes – backing singers, percussion – can make such a big difference to an idea." Ferry, however, was unable to pass comment: "It's the only album that was put together without my involvement or control, so I never listen to it."

Indeed, here is a balefully androgynous Roxy covergirl for once not stage-managed by Ferry, the photography credited to Tony McGee and the design to Michael-Nash Associates. The music inside doesn't bear out Mackay's endorsement, either, being as uncharacteristically monochrome as the cover photo. *Can't Let Go* rears its boring head once more, *Dance Away* and *Avalon* fail miserably in a live context, and only the 1982 vintage *Both Ends Burning* and *Editions of You* really come to 'beating' life in these enervated surroundings. The one and only surprise is provided by the inclusion of Manzanera's bravura solo turn, *Impossible Guitar*.

Despite the provision of a Roxy gatefold sleeve for the first time in 14 years, the album reeks of expedience and mendacity even in its credits, which claim the music was recorded at Fréjus, just as the *High Road* video was. Strange, then, that the album's versions of *Can't Let Go*, *My Only Love*, *Like a Hurricane* and *Jealous Guy* sound identical to the ones previously included on the *High Road* mini-LP. That, of course, had been recorded a long way from the French Riviera, in Glasgow.

Like the album, a single coupling *Love is the Drug* and *Editions of You* predictably failed to chart, despite the bonus inclusion of an unavailable-elsewhere version of *Do the Strand* on its 12" and CD manifestations. Unfortunately, it's a fagged-out and flavourless *Strand*, much like the *Heart Still Beating* LP in general, which could have done with that elusive version of *The Main Thing* to give it a bit of sorely needed spice.

Disgusting things

Roxy reconvened in January 1983 for an extension of the *Avalon* itinerary that began with two nights in Osaka on 1 and 2 February, moving on to a performance apiece at Nagoya, Fukoa and Kyoto, plus two in Tokyo. By the end of April, they were back in the USA for an unheralded tour that was apparently no more congenial than previous attempts. "To be a success there we'd have to tour every town in America and wake every morning in yet another Holiday Inn," Ferry had told Jim Crace in September. "It would be a nightmare. I'd rather sell fewer records and stay sane." Elsewhere, he reiterated his *Musikladen*-inspired sentiments of 1973. "I've always thought that video could accomplish what touring accomplishes," he mused, "and now that they've got that television channel in America that shows nothing but music video, maybe it will. For years I've been asking why can't we just make a video of the album and send it out?"

With MTV in its infancy, Roxy submitted themselves to Californian dates at Fresno, San Diego, Los Angeles, Santa Barbara and Berkeley, mixing these with appearances in Mesa, Chicago, Harrisburg, Baltimore and old stamping grounds Detroit and Cleveland. There were also Canadian dates in Vancouver, Edmonton, Ontario, Toronto and Montreal. Roxy Music's 20th century existence then came to a halt with two nights at New York's Radio City Music Hall on 25 and 26 May, a university gig in Boston on the 27th and, finally, a performance at Philadelphia's Spectrum on Saturday the 28th.

So Roxy Music's career ended, or so it seemed at the time, in the country that had proved so resistant to their charms for so long. By this stage the band members, fully aware in any case that the end was coming, had no great relish for their sporadic American jaunts. "We had kind of lost interest a bit, because we had much bigger audiences elsewhere in the rest of the world," explained Ferry. "And since we're not particularly fond of touring, and kind of limited the amount of touring we did, then obviously America would be the first to go." Manzanera was equally candid: "We didn't do long tours, but the ones that really put the lid on it for me were the six-week tours of America. You'd get back to the hotel and think, 'What is this?' There was nothing to stimulate the brain, you were like a performing monkey."

About the break-up, Manzanera was candid all round, putting it down to "general dissatisfaction with the management. Disgusting things were done to make us fight each other, and there came a point where I couldn't take it any more. I was in the red right up until *Avalon*. So I walked out. Andy, and then Bryan, eventually followed suit." Inclined ever since the departure of Eno to point the finger at "the people behind the scenes, the managers and agents," Manzanera went on to claim that "We'd done so much touring that me, Bryan and Andy had paid for, investing in the future. And I owed EG a lot of money, so I had to toe the line" – grimly concluding that "I didn't want any more of that manipulation."

Two years later, Ferry described the break-up to John Blake of the *Daily Mirror* in terms very similar to his pronouncements of 1976. "We were never a group for huge bust-ups or rows," he explained, "but I think finishing Roxy was best for me and my work and good for the other two – Andy Mackay and Phil Manzanera. I don't want to say anything bad about anybody because it's not my way, but I hate groups to stay together only because they share a name. I found working with the other two limiting. To be honest, the three of us never really said anything to one another about breaking up – it just happened. I think after we finished the tour that followed *Avalon* we really had drifted apart and I was closer to the session musicians ... So rather than spend the next five years squabbling with Andy and Phil, I thought it would be better just to break."

And Ferry's conclusion was an uncharacteristically final one: "I haven't spoken to them since the moment the tour ended, but then we never did speak to one another when we weren't at work ... I don't know if I'll ever see [them] again. I don't have daggers drawn against them or anything, contrary to what people might think. I just want to get on with my own career."

Ferry's reference to feeling "closer to the session musicians" may provide a clue to the dissolution of Roxy Music. However musically accomplished, these sidemen were a pretty faceless crew in the eyes of the public, for whom the notion of Ferry, Mackay and Manzanera as a triumvirate of musical directors rather than a band proper was a difficult concept to grasp. Nor can Mackay and Manzanera have found Ferry's love affair with these supposedly more 'accomplished' musicians particularly flattering. On top of this, rumours persist to the effect that drummer Andy Newmark was so venerated by Ferry that he was remunerated on a grand scale that left even Mackay and Manzanera in the shade. This shocking imbalance, so the story goes, was the proverbial straw that broke the camel's back.

Picking over the corpse

In the aftermath of the Roxy break-up, an opportunistic US compilation was rushed onto the market by Atlantic, the record also being issued in the UK. Bizarrely, *The Atlantic Years 1973-1980* gathered four tracks apiece from *Manifesto* and *Flesh + Blood* with the arbitrary inclusion of older favourites *Do the Strand* and *Love is the Drug*. As Steve Sutherland accurately characterised it in *Melody Maker*, "*The Atlantic Years* is a Christmas compilation designed to kid the Americans they've been missing out on something big by bundling together, willy nilly, some marketing person's idea of Roxy's most sellable assets. The way it stands, I doubt the band had much to do with it."

The smouldering cover – all tumbling hair, lashings of lip gloss and chicly unadorned typography – was executed by former Ferry collaborators Eric Boman and Peter Saville as a fair approximation of the airbrushed, fashion-plate glamour Ferry himself had favoured in recent years. Despite its decidedly non-essential character, the album charted on 12 November 1983, reached number 23, and remained in the chart for an impressive 25 weeks. Its blink-and-you'll-miss-it CD issue was so fleeting it now rates as a highly prized Roxy collectable.

Yet greater rewards awaited *Street Life: 20 Great Hits* in April 1986, a Number One smash that lingered in the album chart for a mighty 77 weeks. Regrettably, this was the first instance of an album mixing and matching Roxy material with Ferry's solo work, here ranging six Ferries against 14 Roxies. Not only does this procedure evince a surprising lack of faith in Ferry's own recordings (for all their patchiness, a Ferry-only hits compilation would be one hell of a record, yet nobody to this day has had the courage to try it); it also, understandably, bred further resentment in Mackay and Manzanera. The cover photo, featuring Ferry, and the rear, featuring the other band members, were both drawn from Roxy's Royal College of Art film from June 1972, a ludicrous source given the preponderance of tracks drawn from *Manifesto*, *Flesh + Blood* and *Avalon*.

A mere two-and-a-half years elapsed before the release of the so-called *Ultimate Collection*, which altered the *Street Life* ratio by pitting nine Ferry tracks against six Roxy ones. One of the Ferry cuts, *Help Me*, was a new item recorded for the David Cronenberg body-horror classic, *The Fly*; two others, *Let's Stick Together* and *The Price of Love*, were subjected to unpleasant 1980s remixes and issued as singles. Of the 15 tracks, no fewer than seven had already been included on *Street Life*, a gesture of supreme cynicism or supreme stupidity or both. Not so stupid, as it turned out: the album shouldered its way to a very respectable high of number six in November 1988.

These grubby compilations, lucrative though they were, left a nastier taste in the mouth than even the band's messy and compromised break-up. Reflecting on the final Roxy phase, Ferry observed that "luckily some really good things came out of it, thanks to some of the musicians whom I picked up in the intervening years, like Alan Spenner, who was just the greatest English bass player, and Neil Hubbard. They became part of my repertory company, if you like. Andy and Phil were still part of it, of course, but we weren't really friends, which was a shame, really. And all because of money. Or because everyone was clamouring to speak to *me* rather than them."

While Mackay discreetly kept his counsel, Manzanera's summary of the second Roxy devolution was terse and to the point. "Bryan thought he was part of the team, but in the end he realised he wasn't."

Twenty-Two: *Up in Smoke*

"A lot of the stuff that Andy and I write doesn't fit in with vocals, or it's just stylistically wrong for Roxy. That's why we do solo things."
Phil Manzanera, quoted in *Trouser Press* June 1982

Axe and sax

In the wake of Roxy Music's dissolution, Mackay decamped from Clapham Common North Side to an idyllic retreat in the Republic of Ireland, scoring the BBC TV play *Videostars* (written by his *Rock Follies* collaborator, Howard Schuman), giving a Radio 3 talk on Futurist music and getting together with Manzanera to plan a new group called The Explorers.

Signing with Pink Floyd manager Steve O'Rourke, and through him to Virgin Records, Manzanera and Mackay set to work on The Explorers in earnest in spring 1984. Their chosen vocalist was James Wraith, whom they had first met back in 1975. Formerly of Amsterdam Lil, Pete Brown's Band and Galaxis, Wraith was born in Liverpool on 18 January 1951 and had entered the music business in 1970 with the semi-pro outfits Gibbon and Rebecca. By 1977, disillusioned, he was studying dance at Merseyside Dance Centre, though he would record an album of his own two years later.

The instrumental line-up was an impressive one: Roxy veteran Alan Spenner and bald-domed King Crimson member Tony Levin on bass, Steve Gadd and Gerry Marotta on drums, and two other Roxy session men, Guy Fletcher and Paul Carrack, on keyboards. In addition to Manzanera and Mackay themselves, the producers were Keith Bessey and John Potoker; even the backing vocalists on what would turn out to be the group's second single were a stellar bunch: Eddy Grant, Justin Hayward and Eric Stewart. These last were styled 'The Blue Wavettes', much of the recording having been done at the Blue Wave Studios in Barbados; further work was done at the Park Hotel in Kenmare (near Mackay's new home), Manzanera's Gallery Studio in Chertsey and at the Townhouse in London.

Ferry was by no means unaware of all this activity, noting of Roxy's recent interment that "It's all been a bit funny since then. They [Manzanera and Mackay] knew I was making a solo album and went off and formed their new band, The Explorers." Just as he had kept a sardonic eye on the tit-for-tat proliferation of solo recordings that had followed his own *These Foolish Things*, Ferry now seemed to be suggesting that Mackay and Manzanera had only got together as a kind of schoolboy nose-thumbing exercise. (What did he expect them to do; twiddle their thumbs?) If Ferry felt obscurely that his territory was being artfully encroached upon, he was right; in its review of the eventual Explorers album, the *NME* would observe not only that *Avalon* was a touchstone of the new record but that it provided positive proof that Ferry was far from being the only creative force in the now defunct Roxy Music.

In commercial terms, however, Ferry had nothing to worry about, though the signs initially looked good when the first fruit of The Explorers' sessions, *Lorelei*, was issued as a single in June. With its titular reference to Roxy's very own *Siren* clinging to her Anglesey rock, *Lorelei* indicated that The Explorers were to be an intriguing combination of Roxy's old instrumental pyrotechnics with a canny grasp of infectious 1980s-styled pop hooks. The opening is sublime: Mackay's creamy-toned resurrection of Siegfried's call from Wagner's *Ring* (last heard on *Re-make/Re-model*) is exactly the "distant sound across the Rhine" referred to in the lyric. The soundstage echoes to the irresistible swing of Manzanera's rhythm guitar, with Mackay burbling subliminally throughout, the 'breaking glass' percussion of his long-ago *Wild Weekend* makeover worked into the agitated choruses, and Mackay and Manzanera joining forces in the middle eight for a delightful restatement of their old Roxy interplay.

The song came complete with a 12" extended version smothered in thunderous electronic rhythm-box effects, plus bizarrely doctored Mackay sax breaks that sound like nothing on earth. It was, all in all, a classic single (if a single nobody bought can be called classic), the kind of thing Roxy imitators Duran Duran had long been aiming for but failed as yet to produce.

On the flip was a stately ballad called *You Go Up in Smoke*, slightly adulterated by the choice of electric rather than acoustic piano but nonetheless working up an oboe-dominated melancholy favourably compared by one contemporary critic to *A Song for Europe*, no less. *Lorelei* failed to make an impression on the charts, however, so *Falling for Nightlife* followed in October as a second attempt to launch the group. This came with the full panoply of 1980s extra features: a 12" version (the so-called 'Kenwood Mix') and a separate picture-disc version of the 12" with a po-faced owl on one side and The Explorers themselves, looking no less po-faced, ranged across the other.

The 7" mix of *Falling for Nightlife* is rough and viscous, featuring a gorgeous 'sunrise' effect shared out between Mackay and Manzanera, yet, mysteriously, it has never made it to CD. The smoother 12" version, by contrast, would be appended to the CD issue of the group's eponymous album, complete with Lyricon owl hoots and a BBC newsreader voice – presumably in imitation of Patrick Allen's voice-over on Frankie Goes to Hollywood's contemporaneous *Two Tribes* – uttering nonsense like "All the races of tiger are now in the red book." The tiger itself, roaring from the recesses of a dripping cage, seems in some strange way a backward nod to the fearsome panther depicted on the *For Your Pleasure* sleeve. The flip was a bizarre item called *Crack the Whip*, the lyric a stream-of-consciousness volley of unrelated clichés, the music founded on the mesmeric roulades of Manzanera's guitar and concluding with a barnstorming Mackay solo in his raunchiest King Curtis vein, the kind of thing unheard on a Roxy track since *Grey Lagoons*.

It's over

Now, though, the signs weren't looking quite so good, for this single, too, failed to chart. There was a stint on Radio 1's *In Concert* on Saturday 8 December for producer Jeff Griffin, in tandem with Private Lives and introduced by Pete Drummond, who had compered Roxy's seminal appearance at Crystal Palace back in July 1972. This was followed by an LWT *South Bank Show* special devoted to electronic music. Broadcast on 27 January 1985 and called (after Caliban's wide-eyed pronouncement in *The Tempest*) *The Isle is Full of Noises*, this included a Mackay interview with Melvyn Bragg at Manzanera's Chertsey studio, as well as on-screen definitions (of digital, analogue, sine wave generator, computer etc) taken from Mackay's recently published book.

Shots of the group apparently recording *Falling for Nightlife* (but actually miming to the finished product) were intercut, to somewhat facile effect, with footage of Electric Phoenix performing a Tim Souster piece called *Mareas*. Mackay, looking 100 per cent healthier and happier than on Roxy's recent *High Road* video, was asked by Bragg about the relationship between rock and the avant-garde, and replied in unusually caustic fashion: "We want all their articles in the colour supplements and they want all our money."

A third single, *Two Worlds Apart*, was a warm and smoochy slice of blue-eyed soul that, having been showcased on the BBC's *Wogan* show on Wednesday 24 April, reached a pretty disheartening number 100 on the singles chart. (Even more disheartening, Ferry's *Slave to Love* was residing simultaneously at number ten.) A DJ-only promo disc, *Explorers Calling* (featuring Mackay's friend Rula Lenska, formerly 'Q' of *Rock Follies*, as mistress of ceremonies), paved the way for the delayed album release, which followed on 7 May. Called simply *The Explorers*, its cover was certainly peculiar, and not entirely persuasive: Mackay, Manzanera and Wraith, faces and hands daubed in gold-leaf by make-up artist Phyllis Cohen, posing with a sculpture called 'Goddess of the Void'. The sculptor was 'Alternative Miss World' guru Andrew Logan, who also supplied the outré jewellery in which the three are bedecked.

The music within ranged from the haunting opener *Ship of Fools*, a thickly curdled seascape with Manzanera at his most muscular and Mackay at his most chilling, to the bouncy singalong gaiety of *Venus de Milo*, a track that, even via the syllables of its title, plainly announced its aspirations to be a latterday *Virginia Plain*. There was also the anthemic pop of *Soul Fantasy*, the sombre luxuriance of *Prussian Blue* (with Mackay's soprano and Manzanera's guitar at the very top of their respective games), the weird mood-piece *Breath of Life*, even a rock'n'roll rave-up called, for no very discernible reason, *Robert Louis Stevenson*.

With the already familiar *Lorelei*, *Two Worlds Apart* and *You Go Up in Smoke* thrown in good measure, this was an unusually accomplished debut album. *Ship of Fools*, in particular, is an unsung classic, its dazzlingly confected soundstage the equal of anything in Roxy's lattterday canon. Press complaints that Manzanera and Mackay could have found a vocalist less obviously inclined to model himself on Bryan Ferry were not without validity, however; Wraith's voice remains the weak link in an otherwise powerful chain.

With Blair Cunningham on drums, John Mackenzie on bass and Nick Graham on keyboards, the band began a brief tour in May, culminating in two nights at the Camden Palace on the weekend of 8 and 9 June. The first of these was filmed by former *Supersonic* guru Mike Mansfield for his late-night, now-you-see-it-now-you-don't programme *Cue the Music*; the same morning, the band had taped *Lorelei*, *Venus de Milo*, *Prussian Blue* and *You Go Up in Smoke* for BBC Radio 1, the results broadcast on Tommy Vance's *Into the Music* strand on 4 July. The band's live dates trotted through most of the material on the album together with unhinged B-sides like *Voodoo Isle*, a surprise outing for Roxy's *Out of the Blue* and a grandiloquent cover of Roy Orbison's *It's Over*. Having polished off a few European dates in the meantime, Manzanera and Mackay then saw *Venus de Milo* issued as a single on 24 June; again, it sank without trace.

Seemingly undaunted, in October Mackay and Manzanera recruited their live rhythm section of Cunningham and Mackenzie, together with backing vocalists Tessa Niles and Carol Kenyon, to cut further material, material that Virgin declined to release thanks to the band's lack of success so far. The fruits of these sessions – mixed up with various cuts from the original *Explorers* album, sundry B-sides and the 12" variants of *Lorelei* and *Venus de Milo* – were finally gathered together at the end of the decade by the small US label Relativity for a couple of rag-bag albums called *Crack the Whip* and *Up in Smoke*. These were credited not to The Explorers but to Manzanera & Mackay.

Among the tracks from the unreleased second album, *Men with Extraordinary Ways* was a blistering bit of mechanised funk, *Sacrosanct* a gorgeously melancholic swirl of quasi-religious devotion, and *Dreams of the East* a multi-layered paean to the 1960s with some clever wordplay worthy of Roxy Music itself. There were also unclassifiable oddities like *Black Gang Chine*, *Built for Speed*, *Free Yourself* and *Many are the Ways*. Some of the tracks, however – notably *Every King of Stone*, *Forgotten Man* and *I Can Be Tender* – were vapid exemplars of 1980s production-line pop, though not as jaw-droppingly awful as Ferry's contemporaneous *The Name of the Game*. These tracks were an extreme instance of the dilemma dogging The Explorers throughout their short career: the unparalleled pyrotechnics of Mackay and Manzanera adding a sometimes unwarranted lustre to Wraith's unmemorable voice and some less than indelible songs.

Manzanera himself got together the later Explorers material for an album, again under the Manzanera & Mackay moniker, released by his own Expression label in 1990. As late as July 2001, he put out a double album called *The Complete Explorers*, incorporating three vocal performances apiece by Tim Hain, former Roxy support act Leo Sayer and Lenska's actor-husband Dennis Waterman – but, despite the title, still not incorporating the 7" version of *Falling for Nightlife*.

AM-PM

In response to the precipitous folding of The Explorers, Manzanera joined up with John Wetton to record an album for the David Geffen Company, sponsors of Wetton's radio-friendly supergroup Asia. Recorded at Gallery Studios between March and August 1986, the result, *Wetton/Manzanera*, is a grisly wallow in 1980s MOR pop-rock that makes the later Explorers material sound cutting-edge by comparison.

Long ago, the pair had collaborated on the delightfully lugubrious *Same Time Next Week* for Manzanera's *Diamond Head* album, while soon afterwards Manzanera had observed, apropos of Roxy's revolving bass player saga, "As far as I'm concerned, we had the right person in John Wetton, but he got a good offer [from Uriah Heep]." Ten years later, the offer to collaborate under the Geffen aegis was no doubt very good indeed, but should really have been stoutly resisted; this album does an embarrassing disservice to the man who co-wrote *Out of the Blue* and the man who sang King Crimson's horrific *One More Red Nightmare*.

A bonus track included on later pressings of the *Wetton/Manzanera* album was *Talk to Me*, a song written in collaboration with Pink Floyd's David Gilmour. Manzanera would later co-write *One Slip* with Gilmour, one of the better tracks included on Pink Floyd's first 'we can still function without Roger Waters' LP, *A Momentary Lapse of Reason*. In addition, the tireless Manzanera made an accomplished foray into the burgeoning genre of New Age instrumental with a 1988 LP credited to Nowamowa and called *The Wasted Lands*.

On top of all this, he put together an excellent 1986 compendium called *Guitarissimo*; no mere compilation, this proclaimed itself "a collocation of tracks from the albums *Diamond Head*, *801 Live*, *Listen Now!!*, *K-Scope* and *Primitive Guitars*." It also came complete with glamorous artwork by old Roxy hand Nick de Ville. An even more ambitious compilation, a two-disc affair called *The Phil Manzanera Collection*, would follow in 1995, roping together examples of his work with Roxy, Mackay, Eno, Cale, Nico, 801, Tim Finn, John Wetton, Moncada, Sergio Dias and Tania Libertad.

Mackay's reaction to the Explorers debacle was rather different. Having done session work for Duran Duran side-project Arcadia (his sax breaks on the 12" version of their *Election Day* hit are at least as bizarre as his work on the extended *Lorelei*), together with similar guest spots for Mike Oldfield, Pet Shop Boys, Masami Tsuchiya and Well Well Well, he returned to Manzanera's Gallery Studio in 1988 to cut a charming no-tech album called *Christmas*. Released under the inscrutable moniker of The Players, and available Stateside via the Massachussetts-based independent Rykodisc, it saw Mackay joining forces with gifted street musicians Chris Turner, Bob Morgan, Dirk Preston, Rachel Maloney, Simon Shepherd and Brian Barnett. With their assistance, Mackay here reshaped some 30 Christmas carols and other Yuletide tunes, providing three variants on *The Holly and the Ivy* alone. Items like *Deck the Halls* are given a rollicking, piratical flavour of *Captain Pugwash* while others, like *In the Bleak Midwinter*, a truly impressive acoustic sonority.

To publicise the album, on Saturday 16 December 1989 Mackay and his fellow musicians gave an alfresco concert at the rear of London's St Martin-in-the-Fields; in true cottage industry style, Manzanera and his small daughters were on hand with copies of the record itself. The album design was again by Nick deVille, with a typically Roxy blend of ancient and modern in John Farman's cover illustration of a snow-bound Dickensian coach-and-four, its occupants expressing consternation at a sleek 1950s automobile parked in an adjacent driveway.

In 1990, Mackay's second solo LP, *Resolving Contradictions*, finally made it to CD under the aegis of Manzanera's Expression label; ten years later, *In Search of Eddie Riff* followed suit under Mackay's own Rifff subsidiary, it and a further issue of *Resolving Contradictions* coming complete with bonus tracks. Bonus tracks turned out to be a governing theme of Manzanera's label; steadily mining his back catalogue for hidden gems, he even released a whole album of oddities under the title *Rare One*.

Oyez mi canto

In the meantime, Manzanera's fourth solo LP, *Southern Cross*, was issued by Expression in June 1990, having been recorded in scattershot fashion between 1988 and 1989. On Sunday 5 May, Manzanera and vocalist Gary Dyson previewed material from the new album, plus a shatteringly funked-up Latino rendering of Steely Dan's *Do It Again*, at a Hackney Empire aids charity gala also graced by, among others, Penguin Café Orchestra, Boy George and Sam Brown.

The album itself was a curious affair, showcasing some of the half-baked political leanings familiar from *Listen Now!!* along with schmaltzy supper-club stylings and, unfortunately, several tracks (notably *The Rich and the Poor* and *Venceremos*) bearing the baleful stamp of *Wetton/Manzanera*. The vocal duties were divided between Dyson, Manzanera's old Split Enz associate Tim Finn (by then riding high with Crowded House), and debutante chanteuse Ana María Velez, who enlivens a delightful recasting of the Hispanic standard *Guantanamera*. Manzanera had to get around to that one sooner or later, and it would have been worth a single release in preference to the pomp and circumstance of Dyson's *A Million Reasons Why*.

The title track is a characteristically enticing instrumental, done in tandem with Brazilian percussionist Bosco de Oliveira; other tracks sound like above-average Chris Rea (*The Great Leveller*) or Sade (*Astrud*), with only two tracks, *Dance (Break This Trance)* and *Dr Fidel*, acquiring real punch and weight. Both Finn collaborations, these are noticeably darker pieces. The former, as its title suggests, is a naggingly rhythmic hymn to sexual obsession, the latter a grim impression of Manzanera's Cuban childhood swept along by the backing vocalists' call of "Oyez mi canto, oyez mi voz" and the piping soprano sax of Mel Collins.

Unfortunately, as lead vocalists Dyson and Finn are no more persuasive than James Wraith, and the album lacks flavour thanks to an overly mechanised sound (only two of the 12 tracks contain a 'drums', rather than 'drum programming', credit). Manzanera touted the album as an attempt to fuse Finn's Crowded House sound with his own Latin influences, but the transplant ultimately refuses to take. It sounds like a ten-years-on retread of the *K-Scope* album, seriously hobbled by a vacuous sheen of late 1980s production gloss.

Fostering an increasingly large number of Hispanic acts under his Expression umbrella, Manzanera would eventually be chosen as MD of Seville's Guitar Legends Festival in 1991, performing there himself alongside Pino Palladino on bass and former 801 percussionist Simon Phillips. His production credits ranged from Heroes del Silencio (whose vocalist, Enrique Bunbury, he equated with Jim Morrison) to Fito Paez and the Brazilian group Paralamos do Successo. On top of all this, a March 1992 collaboration with Cuba's Grupo Moncada, recorded at Havana's Karl Marx Theatre, was finally immortalised on the 1997 CD, *Moncada and Manzanera Live at the Karl Marx*. Increasingly moved to explore his Latin roots, Manzanera would also collaborate on the excellent 1993 album *Mato Grosso* with Sergio Dias, formerly of the groups Steps of Imagination and Mutantes.

Finally, and with a pleasing inevitability, in 1999 Manzanera revised an old notion by putting together *801 Latino*, a live recording in which he teamed up again with Moncada's lead singer Augusto Enriquez. Augmented by Aldo Lopez Gavilan, Carlos 'Mosca' Valdez, Chucho Merchan and glamorous young vocalist (and covergirl) Yamile, Manzanera and Enriquez here paid tribute to Latin American heroes like Irakere, Orquestra Aragon, Benny More, Silvio Rodriguez and Antonio Carlos Jobim. "During rehearsals," Manzanera reported, "there was a lot of creatively charged Latin passion and mucho mucho talking. I don't know how we managed to get it together in such a short space of time but somehow, from the chaos, this selection of Latin music emerged." The eventual album was released by Expression in 2001, complete with a touching dedication to Manzanera's late mother, Magdalena – "my first guitar teacher, who taught me Cuban folk songs in Havana in 1958."

Mackay, by contrast, was maintaining an unusually low profile. In 1988, he had made an unexpected guest appearance on the London leg of Ferry's *New Town* tour (his first contribution to any of Ferry's solo ventures), but was otherwise preoccupied with a new role – that of mature student studying theology at King's College London. According to journalist Duncan Fallowell, Mackay had confided to Dr Puxley that he was "looking forward to taking orders and caring for a quiet country parish."

Thirteen years later, however, Mackay refuted this. "It wasn't a kind of priest training or anything," he told US journalist Melissa Giannini. "It was an academic thing. I became interested in the sort of questions that are difficult to answer, such as 'Why is there something rather than nothing?' I was a bit fed up with music at that time. I just wanted a break. It worked out very well. I was still doing some music, bits and pieces, but not a great deal." The fate of The Explorers was no doubt in Mackay's mind when he offered an explanation for his change of direction: "I think I had just been doing it [music] for a long time and there were one or two projects that I had been working on that didn't really happen, that I had put lots of work into."

By a cruel irony, Mackay's acquisition of his Bachelor of Divinity degree in 1991 was followed by the sudden death of his wife Jane. Left to bring up his two children alone, his principal musical work for much of the decade was focused on an ambitious, and as yet unreleased, setting of *Four Psalms* for voices, choir, sampled sounds, strings, saxophone and electronic instruments. As a side project, however, he wrote the theme for Carlton's 1994-5 comedy-drama, *Class Act*, at the invitation of his former *Rock Follies* associate, Verity Lambert.

Twenty-Three: *A Waste Land*

"I recently saw the clip from Re-make/Re-model, *which was the earliest film thing we did. It makes you feel slightly wistful, wishing one's youth was back. But no, I don't dwell on it much."*

Bryan Ferry, quoted in *The Face* April 1985

Tous les garçons et les filles

Asked by James Truman why he'd wound up Roxy Music, Ferry asserted in 1985 that "There were too many conflicts, really. Not musical so much as personality conflicts. Before I did *Avalon*, and while I was doing it, it felt to me that it had gone as far as it could go. It was no longer useful or stimulating to me to have that kind of friction." Sixteen years on, however, he felt rather differently: "There was no real dispute," he told *Uncut*'s Chris Roberts. "After *Avalon*, which was a tough act to follow, I wanted to do an album of my own songs and thought I'd done enough group albums. Now, I wish I *had* done that – *Boys and Girls* – with the group. It was a very painful record to make."

Having cast aside Manzanera and Mackay, Ferry regressed into a serious case of 'O'List syndrome', amassing nearly 30 top-flight session players for his first post-Roxy solo project. To replace Manzanera, only Pink Floyd's David Gilmour and Dire Straits' Mark Knopfler would do. Supplanting Mackay, meanwhile, was none other than US woodwind guru David Sanborn. Of the others, Neil Hubbard, Jimmy Maelen, Andy Newmark, Rhett Davies, Neil Jason, Yanick Etienne, Fonzi Thornton and Alan Spenner were all retained from the *Avalon* album, with Guy Fletcher and Michelle Cobbs carried over from the accompanying tour. To add a further sprinkling of studio stardust, Chic supremo Nile Rodgers and Weather Report percussionist Omar Hakim were also brought on board. Intriguingly, Ferry's cohorts here would include three double-agents; Spenner, Fletcher and King Crimson's Tony Levin were simultaneously involved with Manzanera and Mackay in The Explorers.

Whatever the details of the personnel list, it was patently obvious that it was way too long, and that Ferry's absorption in the ever-expanding vistas of recording technology – an absorption that entailed the use of six studios over a two-year period – was an ominous development in itself. "I worked with far too many musicians and in the end it was a very expensive piece of tapestry, really," Ferry lamented in 2001.

Yet, at first, nothing seemed amiss. The *Boys and Girls* LP sired a Top Ten single and went straight into the album chart at Number One, staying in the rundown for the best part of a year. But there were distinct signs of a new rigidity, as if the *Avalon* template had spun a stifling spider's web around Ferry's creative muse, leaving the music super-sleek yet ultimately vacuous. In the increasingly corporatised, 'Greed is Good' world of 1980s rock, there was a horrible suspicion that Ferry's new music was only good for yuppies to shag to. For all the top-of-the-range session stars around him, Ferry was clearly in need of the spiky resistance, the inspirational tit-for-tat, that had been provided by Manzanera and Mackay.

Few people thought this in 1985, however. OK, so the album took two years to make, but it wasn't as if Ferry had been completely idle in the interim; among other things, he'd fathered two sons. (Two more would follow in 1990.) And look at the amazing chart success of the album; you can't argue with that. Yet, in ret-rospect, the Number One status of *Boys and Girls* looks very much like a case of the *Goldfinger-Thunderball* syndrome. Watching the simultaneously bloated and enervated *Thunderball*, the viewer might wonder why it remains to this day the most commercially successful of all the James Bond films. The answer, of course, is that it followed the remarkable *Goldfinger*, a film so dazzling that it guaranteed a rapturous reception for its immediate follow-up, whatever its merits. The 007 philosophy then became set in stone: each film had to be bigger and supposedly 'better' than the one before.

In the wake of *Avalon*, Ferry became creatively constipated by just such a phi-losophy, stymied in particular by the desire (a very 007 sort of desire) for more and better gadgets. As a result, almost all his work from *Avalon* onwards seems like little more than *Avalon* reheated; creatively speaking, a kind of living death warmed up.

Some of it was quite literally *Avalon* reheated; Ferry's 1986 single *Is Your Love Strong Enough?* had originated as *Circles*, one of the many fragments consigned to

Avalon's cutting-room floor. Included on the soundtrack of Ridley Scott's fantasy folly *Legend*, this doleful exercise reached number 22 in the UK chart in March 1986, by no means matching the worldwide smash achieved the previous summer by another soundtrack item, *Don't You (Forget About Me)*, recorded by Simple Minds for the John Hughes film *The Breakfast Club*. Gallingly, the chance to record this song had originally been offered to Ferry, but his head was so full of the *Boys and Girls* project he had turned it down. The fact that Billy Idol had made the same mistake was probably small consolation.

Released in June 1985, *Boys and Girls* is saddled with a notably duff Ferry-Price-Puxley cover but contains several moments of beauty, notably the third single taken from it, *Windswept*. Though reaching only number 46 in the UK chart, this is a dream of a track, replacing the dissonant fury of the ten-year-old *Whirlwind* with a somnambulant drift that brings Ferry closer to the ambient Eno sound than ever before; even Sanborn's sleazy sax interjections are somewhat less repulsive than usual.

The two singles that preceded it are alluring too. Co-written with Rhett Davies, *Don't Stop the Dance* may have stalled at number 21 in August but it's a gently swinging exercise in blue-eyed funk, driven along by finger-poppin' drum-box effects and the metallic interplay of rhythm guitars with Sanborn's *Young Americans*-style sax squalls. As a curtain-raiser for the album, *Slave to Love* had reached number ten in April, featuring storm effects last heard in *A Hard Rain's a-Gonna Fall*, affecting details in the lyric and a meaty, countryfied backbeat.

With a brief string overture strangely reminiscent of Siouxsie and the Banshees' *Fireworks*, *Sensation* sounds like a Ferry update of the similarly titled *Fascination* (Bowie) and *Temptation* (Heaven 17), but signally lacking the urgent pulse of either. In short, it's a track that seems second-hand on several levels. *A Waste Land* is a gorgeous one-minute fragment with a mournful epigram rather than a lyric, and makes a deeper impression than any of the material on Side Two. These items, *The Chosen One* in particular, are badly dated by their reliance on contemporary percussive backdrops of a bludgeoning chart-friendly variety, though the closer, *Boys and Girls* itself, works up something of the spell-stopped weirdness of old.

Veteran Roxy follower Allan Jones was understandably disheartened in his *Melody Maker* review: "Over the nine songs here, Ferry presents himself in his familiar role of a soul in torment, buffeted by the fates, confused by love and its demands, at the mercy of his own heightened sensations. Unfortunately, very little of any of this sounds very convincing," adding cannily that "The ostensible concern and heartache of, say, *Valentine* is too refined, too neatly contrived to really move the listener. Ferry simply retains too much of a stiff upper lip in the face of disaster."

Sadly, that impeccably maintained stiff upper lip would soon solidify into a state of all-consuming paralysis.

Money changes everything

During the protracted birth pangs of the *Boys and Girls* album in 1984, Ferry made a rare TV appearance on Friday 29 June as part of Channel 4's *Midsummer*

Night's Tube. Trailed in *TV Times* as "five hours of crash-hot craw daddy," this exhausting marathon boasted an astonishing bill ranging from Paul Young, Alison Moyet, The Police and Howard Jones to Culture Club, Echo & the Bunnymen, Sade and Frankie Goes to Hollywood. Ferry was among the older artists involved, notably Hall & Oates, Nona Hendryx, Sly & Robbie, The Cramps and B B King. Though increasingly hidden from public view in recording studios, he would also be the subject of *Whistle Test Extra* on Tuesday 8 April 1986; here, an interview with Richard Skinner was padded out with plenty of old Roxy footage.

In the meantime, Ferry had formed part of the Live Aid event at Wembley on Saturday 13 July 1985, performing three of the songs from *Boys and Girls* – *Sensation*, *Slave to Love* and the title track – alongside *Jealous Guy*. The band comprised the predictable Neil Hubbard, Jimmy Maelen and Andy Newmark, plus Chester Kamen, Marcus Miller, Jon Carin and David Gilmour, no less; the backing vocalists were Michelle Cobbs, Ednah Holt and Fonzi Thornton. Ferry had dithered over committing himself to the event, and, indeed, it turned out to be a mis-step; not only was his set dwarfed by the likes of U2 and Queen, he also came under fire for his 'available at all good record shops' song selection. Johnny Marr, inspirational guitarist with The Smiths, was particularly disdainful on this score, stating unequivocally that "Bryan Ferry used the event for personal gain."

Yet in 1987 Marr's name would be attached to Ferry's *Boys and Girls* follow-up, *Bête Noire*. As Chris Roberts put it in *Melody Maker*, "as his doddering peers try everything from hapless hip-hop to whorish haircuts, Bry just ropes in some dickhead indie guitarist called Johnny Marr, knowing this will win him fifty thousand credibility units, then orders him to play Manzanera on mandrax." The Marr collaboration turned out to be the first single extracted from the new album; called *The Right Stuff*, it rose only to number 37 in September. A peculiarly uninspired Ferry lyric, complete with a reference to his old favourite *River Deep Mountain High*, is here bolted on to a backing derived from Marr's *Money Changes Everything*, the instrumental B-side to The Smiths' 1986 single *Bigmouth Strikes Again*. Coincidentally, the original had been produced by Ferry's old Newcastle friend John Porter.

"Someone [at Warner Bros] sent me a tape of the things he [Marr] had done," Ferry commented, "and I got very excited about one of them and did a version of it. And he came down and played on it and we got on really well." ("There's a kind of Northern honesty about the cut of his jib which I like," he observed quaintly elsewhere.) Unfortunately for Marr, the single emerged just as the news came through that The Smiths had split up, leading to a misapprehension among the group's fans that he had spurned Morrissey on receiving a lucrative offer from Ferry. After all that, the end product – a workaday bit of MTV-angled funk garnished with caterwauling back-up vocalists – hardly seemed to justify the fuss it caused.

Disturbingly, some of the other tracks on the album sound just as pirated as *The Right Stuff*, where the derivation was at least admitted to. With Madonna's producer Patrick Leonard taking over from Rhett Davies (who is listed this time among the labyrinthine roll-call of musicians), two of the tracks – *Day for Night* and *The Name of the Game* – sound like clumsily confected Madonna rejects. *The Name of the Game*, in particular, is an out-and-out monstrosity, aptly apostrophised by Dave Rimmer of Q magazine as "a sort of mega-MTV scarf-waver." Elsewhere, there are attempts at a less cynically commercial sound with the tremulous *Zamba* and the off-kilter *New Town*, which apparently incorporated fragments of a *Manifesto* out-take. "The chorus has a strange chord sequence," Ferry pointed out, adding unnecessarily, "the sort of thing I used to write more often."

There's also an agitated but unconvincing singalong, *Seven Deadly Sins*, co-written with bassist Guy Pratt and guitarist Chester Kamen. Were it not for the inspired title track, however, *Bête Noire* would only really be worthwhile for the two singles that followed *The Right Stuff*. These two – *Limbo* and *Kiss and Tell* – lead off the set on a bracingly powerful head of steam, making it clear that Ferry was still capable of occasionally rousing himself from his lassitude and laying down meaty dance grooves. The album itself having climbed only to number nine, these belated singles did even worse than *The Right Stuff*. *Kiss and Tell* came first, hitting number 31 in February 1988, followed by a dismal showing of 96 for *Limbo* in June. The title track, however, sends the set out on a beguiling high, with Ferry partnered by the venerable Buenos Aires troupe Tango Argentina for a Latino reverie containing agreeable echoes of Grace Jones' *I've Seen That Face Before (Libertango)*.

The front cover was a dark and moody mug-shot recalling Ferry's "You're never alone with a Strand" persona, while the back depicted him in the woody textures of a South Sea island idol, suggesting that the album had unrealised aspirations to 'world music' extending beyond the title track. The credits rounded up all the usual Ferry suspects, also bringing David Gilmour back from *Boys and Girls* and introducing such trendy names as Abraham Laboriel and Courtney Pine. As well as the expected cast of thousands, the album's credits contain a note of self-aggrandisement that would be laughable in any context, but particularly so in the reduced circumstances of *Bête Noire*. The standard credit, "Produced by Patrick Leonard and Bryan Ferry," is followed by the borderline-risible "Executive Producer: Simon Puxley" and then the Grade-A fatuous "Directed by Bryan Ferry."

Tucked away among these vainglorious absurdities is the gnomic legend, "Beat the system." This was presumably a reference to Ferry's then-current legal dispute with EG, whose insistence on retaining North American rights in his new album led to a bitter divorce from his longtime manager Mark Fenwick. This was a bruising experience for Ferry; coupled with the death in 1984 of his father, followed in 1991 by that of his mother, it made this period a peculiarly bleak one for him.

Now managed by Dire Straits guru Ed Bicknell, Ferry's appearance on NBC's *Saturday Night Live* on 5 December 1987 had helped *Kiss and Tell* reach a surprising high of 31 in the US charts. Though its parent album was nearly 12 months old and already forgotten by many, a major tour was embarked upon, with 34 US dates, plus stints in Japan, Australia and New Zealand, preceding a European itinerary that wound down in January 1989. Among the surprise Roxy revivals were *The Bogus Man*, *Ladytron* and *Casanova*.

The digital abyss

"Can a performer who appears to be so smugly a part of the Establishment continue to be a rock star? The answer in Bryan Ferry's case is, frankly, no." So wrote Mal Peachey in an unusually vindictive *Mail on Sunday* column in January 1993. "In a few weeks, Virgin Records will release a new album from the former Roxy Music star. It is not the one he's been working on for the past four years – that isn't ready yet. Instead he has compiled a collection of cover versions of American soul and pop hits, titled *Taxi*. It's hardly an inspiring comeback from the working-class Geordie brought up with a tin bath in the back yard."

Vindictive perhaps, but not untypical of the peevish reaction to Ferry's ongoing creative impasse. Simultaneously exhausted and enthused by the *New Town* tour, he had been confident in its immediate aftermath of putting out a *Bête Noire* follow-up relatively rapidly. It didn't happen. Mesmerised by the 56-track technology at his disposal, and fearful of producing anything less than his masterpiece, Ferry found the business of recording the projected *Horoscope* album an agonisingly protracted process.

This was just one more way in which his career was beginning to resemble Eno's; as well as surrendering more and more to an ambient, atmospheric fug in his music, Ferry was now trapped in a maze of indecision and vacillation that made Eno's travails over *Before and After Science* seem like child's play. The collage approach that had characterised Roxy Music, particularly in its latterday incarnation, had now become a nightmarish round of building up backing tracks in painstakingly pointilliste fashion, only to find, as Ferry put it, "the old lyrical brick wall" awaiting him on the other side. "Digital technology was an abyss for him," observed his old friend Nick de Ville. "The possibilities became so much greater. That's the reason why this album took so much longer to get under control. It was in danger of becoming a kind of cancer, duplicating itself into infinity."

In the middle of all this, the open sore that was *Horoscope* was aggravated further by the revival of past glories. In 1990, Virgin Vision put out a Roxy video compendium called *Total Recall*, its title a perplexing repeat of a contemporaneous Arnold Schwarzenegger action film. Artfully relating the story of the band without recourse to voice-over narration, the documentary contained a wealth of invaluable archive material, only stumbling in its final stages, when laborious footage of Ferry's Live Aid performance was allowed to run on and on. Later, Channel 4's *Without Walls* strand would screen a documentary called *This is Tomorrow*. Broadcast on 21 June 1992, it investigated the parallels between Ferry and his Pop Art mentor Richard Hamilton. Unfortunately, the programme only acted as a reminder of Dave Rimmer's well-aimed barb, vis à vis *Bête Noire*, that "Ferry once had a talent for inspired juxtaposition. These days the element of surprise is drowned in a rich and sophisticated aural soup."

In 1993, Ferry found himself embroiled in a minor dispute with Sylvester Stallone. Having been flown to Hollywood by director Renny Harlin, he had then shot a screen test with Stallone ("jet-lagged and terrified," by Ferry's own account) for Harlin's film *Cliffhanger*. After this, he had apparently been cast in the picture as a murderous drugs baron, only to be ousted when Stallone read an article criticising the use of rock stars in films. "Strangely enough," reported the *Daily Telegraph*, "Stallone's people have a different recollection of matters." Later, Ferry was unconcerned about this latest cinematic near-miss. "I think they saw me as a classic English villain in the Alan Rickman mould," he mused. "But it's probably a good thing it fell through – it might have sidetracked me from music."

Coming once more under the wing of David Enthoven, Ferry eventually took the traumatic decision to shelve the *Horoscope* album and, at Lucy Ferry's suggestion, return to the familiar territory of a covers LP. The idea was to record the thing quickly, on 24-track, and emerge refreshed, possibly with a view to resurrecting *Horoscope* and finally licking it into shape. *Taxi* was the result, and in March 1993, rather surprisingly, it streaked to number two in the UK chart, making it Ferry's highest placed solo LP after *Boys and Girls*. A creepy revamp of the Screaming Jay Hawkins classic *I Put a Spell on You* had already hit number 18 in the singles chart, prompting a *Top of the Pops* appearance and hopes that the strategy might yet pay off.

Given unwonted cohesion by the back-to-basics decision to record at only one studio (London's Matrix), *Taxi* was entrusted to producer, and former Procol Harum guitarist, Robin Trower. The personnel ranged from ace session players like Steve Ferrone, Nathan East and David Williams to now-familiar names like Neil Hubbard and Andy Newmark. From the most nostalgic reaches of the old EG stable came Mike Giles and Mel Collins, both early contributors to King Crimson, and even Andy Mackay put in an appearance – his first, in fact, on a Ferry solo album.

Though smothered in Ferry's trademark ambient wash, the album contains some bracingly left-field reinterpretations, notably the vaguely spooky remake of Goffin & King's *Will You Love Me Tomorrow?* that Ferry had been promising since 1973. This version is as far away from The Shirelles' original as two further soul classics, *Just One Look* and *Rescue Me*, are studiedly distanced from Doris Troy and Fontella Bass. Makeovers of the Velvet Underground track *All Tomorrow's Parties* and the Elvis Presley perennial *Girl of My Best Friend* are less successful, and Ferry's take on *Amazing Grace* is as ill-advised as his long-ago massacre of *You Are My Sunshine*. But by and large the album had exactly the effect that had been hoped for – to renew Ferry's musical visas and send him back to the abandoned *Horoscope* with a fresh slant.

While Ferry dusted off the *Horoscope* tapes, two further singles were extracted from the *Taxi* album. These were *Will You Love Me Tomorrow?* and *Girl of My Best Friend*, the latter backed by a version of *Are You Lonesome Tonight?* featured on the soundtrack of the 1992 film *Honeymoon in Vegas*. Neither charted, but the video for the former yielded a surprise appearance from the prodigiously bosomed starlet Anna Nicole Smith. "Well, we try to discover them early, you know," quipped Ferry.

Twenty-Four: *Which Way to Turn*

"Last year, when I was promoting Taxi, *this French journalist was really having a go at me about how I didn't make albums that sounded like* For Your Pleasure

*any more. He said, 'Oh, you fell in love with the sound of your Avalon album,
and now you just make it again and again.' He made me feel really awful. I felt
terrible after this interview. Am I that bad? Was he right? I don't know."*

Bryan Ferry, quoted in *Arena* September 1994

Back in the soup again

'Indecisive' had by now been nominated by music industry wags as Ferry's
middle name, and he would himself confess to the *Times* that "for the last
ten years I have had a dismal output of work." Now, though – invigorated by the
Taxi experience – he set about completing the *Horoscope* album by writing some
new pieces, getting in new musicians and engaging Robin Trower once more. He
also took to singing while stationed on a miniscule Persian rug, as well as
lighting up incense burners around a studio festooned with the erotic artworks
of John Dietrich. More importantly, he recruited Eno to add such typically
unguessable grace notes as "sonic awareness," "sonic ambience," "sonic
emphasis," "sonic distress" and sometimes just plain "sonics." The finished
album, retitled *Mamouna*, was unveiled before a less-than-breathless world on
5 September 1994, and was found to contain a bona-fide, indeed historic, first – a
track, *Wildcat Days*, credited to Ferry-Eno.

This was one of two tracks featuring Andy Mackay; Phil Manzanera, too,
would contribute to two pieces, though not the same ones. The reunion was
reportedly a stimulating one, though Manzanera would later point out that his
contributions are more or less inaudible on the finished product. This was fair
comment. Though dedicated to "making a guitar sound as unlike a guitar as
possible" – just as Mackay was no doubt dedicated to something similar with
saxophones – the painterly soundstage of *Mamouna* takes the concept to
ridiculous extremes, obliterating not only Manzanera's contribution but pretty
much everyone else's. To be fair, Ferry himself is just as occluded; eight years later
he would confess to having listened to the album again and thought, "Wow,
really interesting, but I can't hear the vocal. Where am I?" For all the noble
intentions involved in its eleventh hour resurrection, *Mamouna* sees Ferry right
back in the 'aural soup'.

Ferry has since pegged *Mamouna*, and the protracted horrors of its creation, as a
symptom of a mid-life crisis, a crisis that clearly involved a desire to hide himself
in ever more evanescent swirls of sound. "It's interesting," he mused. "When you
see an artist doing a show, which they do once every two years, they maybe have
20 pictures, and it's all really one picture. There'll be one version in pink, one in
blue – just colour variations on a theme. You can't get away with that in music.
You have to come up with ten winners every time." That *Mamouna* is conspicuously free of "ten winners" – instead floating past as ten lightly shaded variants on
"one picture" – was evidenced by its unspectacular chart placing of 11 and the
poor showing of the two singles excerpted from it, *Your Painted Smile* reaching
number 52 and the title track 57. This was a poor return on the staggering
£800,000 Ferry had reputedly spent on the whole *Horoscope-Mamouna* saga.

"The record will not have people doing pelvic thrusts on tables," admitted
Simon Mills in the *Sunday Telegraph*, "but it is extremely good and becoming for

a man approaching his half-century." *Mamouna*, in truth, is good taste taken a step too far. Ferry's netherworld voice, in particular – slurring its spectral way through a wash of half-heard phrases – is still firmly mired in *Avalon* country. There are exceptions, of course. The electronic pulse of *Wildcat Days*, the spy movie sleaze of *The 39 Steps*, the urban menace of *NYC*, the leisurely funk stylings of *Gemini Moon* – these are worthy of the Bryan Ferry who was so notably prolific before the dead hand of *Boys and Girls* settled on him.

The last of these, intriguingly, contains a fleeting sample from *Ladytron*, just as *Chain Reaction* features a rogue scrap of *The Bob (Medley)*. Another track, *The Only Face*, had reportedly been awaiting completion since 1976. Yet another carries the starkly apposite title *Which Way to Turn*. Beyond that, the most interesting thing about the album is its unprecedented use, in a Roxy-Ferry context, of a non-original cover picture – a handsome equestrian canvas by James Ward (1769-1859) from Ferry's own collection.

With BBC Radio 1 using the release of *Mamouna* as the cue for a four-part series called *The Bryan Ferry Story*, the man himself subsequently went out on tour again in support of the album, an itinerary caught up with by at least one of his old confreres. "I saw one of his Hammersmith shows," observed Manzanera. "He sang very well, but everyone around him was wrong, and he's surrounded by so much baggage. At that point, I thought I could never see the Roxy thing ever happening again." Pressed on the point, Manzanera replied: "There'd be no point in doing it unless the music sounded great. A lot would have to change before that was a serious consideration."

Manzanera's response spoke of apparently irreconcilable differences. The same year, 1995, he contributed to probably the best Roxy Music retrospective, a *Mojo* piece by Rob Chapman called 'They Came from Planet Bacofoil', pointing out ominously that "I doubt if Bryan has fully come to terms with the amount of creative input Andy and I had." Aggrieved by the latterday repackaging of Roxy's work, Mackay declined to contribute at all. Two years later, however, he would open up to the *Guardian*'s Michael Bracewell for the purposes of another excellent retrospective, 'Look Back in Languor'. "There were some serious discussions around the early nineties," he remarked of a mooted Roxy reunion. "I can't help thinking that if we did reform, it would be fantastically good. There would be no problem coming up with our late nineties solution to the same set of problems."

Limbo

For the time being, however, fans hoping for a Roxy reunion had to content themselves with a lavish four-disc box set, supervised by Ferry himself, called *The Thrill of It All*, featuring a Marcel-waved Jean Harlow clone on the cover and a pretty inclusive round-up of B-sides and oddities on its fourth disc. Its release in October 1995 coincided with another half-arsed mixture of Roxy and Ferry hits, a single-disc affair called *More Than This* that reached number 15 in the album chart. Seven years after the last such offering, the 20 tracks on this one were precisely divided between Ferry and Roxy, though its VHS companion, *Bryan Ferry & Roxy Music: The Video Collection*, included only four Roxy items among its

23 tracks, the omission of *Avalon* and *More Than This* perplexing many purists. Unsurprisingly, it was at exactly this time that Mackay expressed his "dissatisfaction with the way the Roxy back catalogue was being packaged."

The following April, a radical revamp of *Love is the Drug* made it to number 33 on the singles chart; credited to Roxy Music, it actually retained only Ferry's vocal, floating uncertainly over an instantly dated dance backdrop concocted by Rollo & Sister Bliss. Two years later came Todd Haynes' much-delayed love letter to Glam Rock, *Velvet Goldmine*, a meretricious big-screen folly that was really a thinly disguised David Bowie biopic. Of the many satellite figures fluttering round Haynes' so-called Brian Slade, Ferry and Eno were both recognisable in the composite figure of Jack Fairy. Bowie's sometime producer, Tony Visconti, dismissed the result as "a gay porn film disguised as a musical," while Bowie himself had hamstrung the film from the off by denying Haynes the use of his songs.

Among various dodges designed to get around this problem, a one-off supergroup, The Venus in Furs, was put together in which Andy Mackay rubbed shoulders with Clune, Radiohead's Thom Yorke and Jonny Greenwood, Bernard Butler of Suede and Paul Kimble of Grant Lee Buffalo, their soundtrack repertoire incorporating remakes of *Ladytron*, *2 H.B.*, *Baby's on Fire* and *Bitter-Sweet*. By this stage Mackay seemed almost to be coming out of retirement in order to participate; having remarried in 1995, he and his wife Lucinda were preoccupied with bringing up their small son, and Mackay's two older children, in the Quantock Hills in Somerset. Nevertheless, the Venus in Furs experience seems to have been a stimulating one. "It was funny," Mackay said. "I hadn't played *Ladytron* for 20 years, but it came back remarkably easily. Other stuff I'd completely forgotten."

Despite this revived interest in his Glam Rock roots, and the Roxy Music trace elements to be heard in such Britpop acts as Blur, Suede and Pulp, the post-*Mamouna* Ferry remained in thrall to writers' block, firmly rejecting Pete Sinfield's suggestion that he write some songs for other people as a kind of therapy. He had gone down this route twice in the 1980s: first, *The Way You Do*, featured in 1982 on Frida's post-Abba LP *Something's Going On*, then *Going Strong* for Roger Daltrey, included on the latter's 1985 album *Parting Should Be Painless*. But there was to be no sequel to these experiments. Instead, history was about to repeat itself in remorselessly cyclical fashion. 'Mamouna' connotes 'good luck' in Arabic, yet it wasn't to rub off on Ferry for a while yet. Indeed, there was an almost tragic inevitability about his latest all-consuming solo project. Called *Alphaville*, it would go exactly the same way as the aborted *Horoscope*, being shelved in favour of yet another stopgap covers album.

La vida moderna

Just as Ferry seemed to have mislaid his muse, Manzanera suddenly found his voice. Though virtually nobody can have been anxious to hear the follow-up to *Southern Cross*, in *Vozero* he came up with an LP that was fully the equal of *Diamond Head* and *Primitive Guitars*. Released in October 1999, the album was described by Manzanera as "a new departure on my musical journey, and it's been a great trip on all sorts of levels ... The words," he added, "are drawn from my own experiences, making it my most personal statement. It's taken me 25 years to find a way to express myself vocally as well as instrumentally."

Yes, indeed: Manzanera sings. And he reveals a sweetly vulnerable voice, fragile and hesitant in the style of his longtime associate Robert Wyatt, who duly turns up as a key collaborator on all but three of the album's 11 tracks. "In Spanish, 'vozero' means a spokesman, someone who utters words, a character singer," Manzanera told Pete Martin at the time. "Robert Wyatt had a strong presence throughout the recording. I asked him to provide the vocals, but he insisted I should sing my own words."

Manzanera's words range from relaxed New Age musings (*Mystic Moon*) to traumatic memories of a Cuban childhood, the "guerillas in the darkness" of *Rayo de bala*. There's a moving song obviously dedicated to his new love, Claire Singers (*Golden Sun*), and another track, *Hymn*, co-written by her. (Manzanera's marriage to Sharon had ended some time before, and he would finally marry Claire on 7 May 2005.) To top it all off, there's a Hispanic heart-cry delivered in the most grandiloquent fashion imaginable, *La vida moderna*, which mordantly characterises life's lottery as "una comedia negra que dura una vida entera" – a black comedy that lasts a lifetime.

The music covers a whole range of styles, with Latino sounds and Manzanera's trademark psychedelia well to the fore, but with gospel, New Age and 'world music' threaded through elsewhere. And some of the tracks are just out-and-out irresistible pop. *Mystic Moon* kicks off with an ominous trumpet fanfare from Wyatt, presumably announcing the coming of Manzanera's uniquely laidback 'vozero' figure, then works up a delightfully playful groove, Livingston Brown's liquid bass bubbling under and Manzanera crooning playfully about astral bodies and other imponderables.

Performed just by Manzanera and Wyatt, *Tuesday* is a lovely, unaffected pop song; on it, Manzanera dovetails some abrasive guitar fills with an eccentric monologue about the desirability of writing music on a Tuesday. And the gorgeous *Golden Sun* swings with a beguiling samba rhythm, a limpid love song bathed in an autumnal glow and riven by a couple of blistering guitar solos. Nigel Butler of The Audience adds an electronic lustre to *Verdadero* (which, lyrically speaking, is a kind of Spanish refashioning of *Out of the Blue*), the lugubrious *Art of Conversation* and the sole instrumental, *Vida*. *Mundo con paz* is a sprawling world music canvas, featuring snatches of the South African national anthem, a host of polyglot voices urging world peace and a guest appearance from the African Gypsies choir, with whom Manzanera had recently undertaken a WOMAD tour.

Hymn is another beauty, a particularly affecting elegy in which Manzanera's vocal is fetchingly double-tracked with Singers while Mackay's oboe keeps up a sweetly sonorous accompaniment. Finally, *La vida moderna* picks up the theme of *Vida*, transmuting it into a CinemaScope epic of shattering power. Wyatt's trumpet whinges dyspeptically throughout, Butler's synths burble unrelentingly, and Manzanera careens out of the mix in his most monolithic style. For the lead vocal, however, he wisely handed over the reins to Enrique Bunbury of Heroes del Silencio, who puts in a truly bravura performance.

Unsurprisingly, *Vozero* garnered some gratifying critical nosegays, from "a delightful album tinged with Colombian and Cuban influences" in *Classic Rock* to *Uncut*'s judgment that "Manzanera's guitar work is as tasteful and delicate as ever, and his voice is a revelation."

Time goes by

Ferry, meanwhile, had set *Alphaville* aside and repaired to Lansdowne Road Studios to record a set of cover versions under the collective title *As Time Goes By*. The result, as its attendant PR put it, was "a thoroughly urbane love letter to the standards of the Tin Pan alley era." Yet Virgin Records at first refused to release it, putting it out through their German subsidiary. Nevertheless, it climbed to number 16 in September 1999, while an accompanying tour would recharge Ferry's creative batteries in a way that was to bear remarkable fruit in 2001.

The album would also earn Ferry a Grammy nomination, the committee presumably having been beguiled by his painstaking reconstruction of 15 evergreens from the pre-rock era. Here Ferry finally made good on his 1973 promise to reinterpret Cole Porter, though the song mooted back then, *Ev'ry Time We Say Goodbye*, was passed over in favour of no fewer than three others: *Miss Otis Regrets*, *You Do Something to Me* and *Just One of Those Things*. Jerome Kern, whose *Smoke Gets in Your Eyes* Ferry had tackled in 1974, was represented by *The Way You Look Tonight*, and the Weimar decadence referenced on Roxy's *Bitter-Sweet* was manifested in Friedrich Holländer's *Falling in Love Again* and Kurt Weill's *September Song*. In addition, there was a reminiscence of *2 H.B.* in the *Casablanca*-derived title track. And, despite the prevailing pall of nostalgia, room was found for Manzanera's electric guitar on Ferry's version of *I'm in the Mood for Love*.

All these were lent a patrician allure by Ferry's matured vocal style, a huskier, smokier and altogether more intimate instrument than before, and given further distinction by producers Rhett Davies and Robin Trower. The latter was familiar from both *Taxi* and *Mamouna*, while the former was returning to the Ferry fold after a long absence. ("I drove poor Rhett Davies to semi-retirement," Ferry joked.) Just as pivotal a figure on *As Time Goes By* was Colin Good, an Oxford-educated music scholar who had been behind the retro-styled Vile Bodies orchestra and even worked with Ferry's venerated US vocal group, The Inkspots. He had first hooked up with Ferry while working on two songs for the soundtrack of Richard Loncraine's film version of *Richard III*; one of these tracks, *Sweet and Lovely*, would end up on the *As Time Goes By* album, while the other, *If I Didn't Care*, was used as support to the title track on a CD single.

Ferry went out on tour to promote *As Time Goes By*, joined briefly by Manzanera for a millennium concert at Greenwich but backed throughout by such players as Colin Good, Zev Katz, Enrico Tomasso, Lucy Wilkins, Alan Barnes and Julia Thornton. The first half of the show was unplugged and "all very Stork Club," as Caroline Boucher put it in the *Observer*, while the second was devoted to an electric rendition of various Roxy and Ferry favourites. To emphasise Ferry's by-now total detachment from the vulgar rough-and-tumble of rock'n'roll, several gigs were arranged at stately homes, with the tour winding up in September 2000 at an even more imposing venue, the Kremlin.

In the meantime, Virgin had put out yet another Roxy compilation in August, though this one, *The Early Years*, was a bit more interesting than usual in that it confined itself to a digest of the band's first three albums, with *Virginia Plain* and *Pyjamarama* thrown in for good measure. The compilation was a timely reminder of a rich musical legacy that, at the start of a new century, was in danger of stagnation. Despite the profound influence it had exercised, Roxy's music had been adulterated by way too many catchpenny compilations mixing Roxy tracks with Ferry's demonstrably inferior solo work. It was all very well for a 'happening' new band like Moloko to turn their video for *Pure Pleasure Seeker* into a sustained homage to Roxy Music, but did their fans have the slightest clue what they were going on about? In a radio culture where Roxy's back catalogue had dwindled to occasional spins of *Love is the Drug* and *Avalon,* probably not.

"We realised that there was a whole body of songs there that would never be heard again unless we played them," commented Manzanera. "I thought we'd have to be our own tribute band to celebrate these songs. You get fed up with listening to two or three of the same tracks that radio plays all the time." Ferry and Mackay were of the same mind, Ferry particularly so after the enthusiastic reception accorded the Roxy numbers on his recent tour. *As Time Goes By* had been an apt title; time was indeed passing, and for Ferry far too much of it had been wasted in the quixotic search for perfection in a series of underwhelming solo albums.

The passing of time was brought into stark relief at the turn of the century with the death of his longtime lieutenant Simon Puxley, who had graduated from writing the outré sleeve notes for Roxy's first LP to masterminding their PR machine in the glory days and finally acting as 'executive producer' on Ferry's latterday albums. A more direct brush with mortality came on Friday 29 December 2000, when Ferry, his wife Lucy and their three youngest sons were on a British Airways Jumbo Jet bound for Nairobi. When a suicidal fellow passenger broke into the cockpit at 35,000 feet, the plane and its passengers were brought within seconds of destruction. "I didn't see the fight until they actually spilled out of the cockpit," Ferry said afterwards. "Then I was thinking: 'Should I get up and get in there?' I was about one row away from having to get involved – which I would have been quite happy to do. There were three bodies grappling, it was like a movie."

Ferry adopted a charmingly flippant attitude to the whole affair (noting that "the crazy man's socks were kind of striped and I didn't really care for them much"), but it was clear that it had focused his mind in as dramatic a way as possible. "If you narrowly avoid death, I think you get a greater awareness of time," he told Marianne MacDonald. "And are you making the most of that time? – all that sort of thing. So things that you're half thinking of doing you tend to do. Like the Roxy Music reunion tour. After that, I was like, 'Okay. Let's do it!'"

Roxy Renaissance Mark Two

"People have been questioning this, as if somehow, unlike any other art form – I hesitate to call rock'n'roll an art form, let's say quasi-art form – you shouldn't revive things. No one ever says that about a Noël Coward or Shakespeare play, or Beethoven's Third Symphony … We're the people who perform those numbers best, and we hope to make them every bit as fresh and important as ever."

Andy Mackay, quoted in *Uncut* July 2001

The alchemists are back

Monday 12 February 2001 saw over 100 journalists crowding into the Lancaster Room of the Savoy Hotel, just off the Strand. Among them was Richard Williams, by then a sports writer for the *Guardian* but long before a pivotal figure in the early careers of the three men who were about to take the stage. And, at a cue from tour promoter John Giddings, in they came – Andy Mackay, Phil Manzanera and Bryan Ferry, announcing their resurrection as Roxy Music after an 18-year sabbatical. "In 2001, the alchemists are back," gushed the attendant press release. "The reconnection of these truly original spirits of British music, reinvestigating the priceless Roxy catalogue after almost two decades, is fascinating indeed."

A world tour from a long-since deactivated band was a notion fraught with potential embarrassment, and yet the result would be sensational. "Eighteen years after Roxy Music bid a fond adieu to pop's great party, they're back; dusting down their dormant muse and boarding the reunion bus for a knockout replay of the Greatest Art-Rock Story Ever Told," enthused Sarah Dempster in the *NME*. "Whatever the reasons behind their reunion, it's clear neither cynicism nor the soulless sheen of professionalism has blighted their canvas. Ferry, Phil Manzanera and saxophonist Andy Mackay still rock like demons, still sound like the bravest, smartest, strangest band that ever was. Almost two decades after they kissed their past goodnight, Roxy Music are still, effortlessly, the sound of the future."

Given the corporatised plod of the *Avalon* tour nearly 20 years before, this was a truly remarkable achievement. In the course of these 51 dates, Roxy reclaimed their own back catalogue with a youthful brio astonishing in men whose collective age was 159. The only concession to advancing years, in fact, was Mackay's well-advised deletion of his time-honoured *Editions of You* duck-walk routine. For the rest, there was a faithful replication of the band's original sound – or, rather, sounds – fostered by tour MD Colin Good, who assiduously tracked down the relevant equipment, in particular the venerable VCS3. There were even dancing girls, bringing a familiar touch of *Shindig* to *Both Ends Burning* and a breath of Las

Vegas to *Do the Strand*. To top everything, and partly at fan insistence, The Great Paul Thompson had been restored to his rightful place behind the drums.

"The promoter was very persuasive," Ferry pointed out. "And when I was touring my solo album, *As Time Goes By*, last year, I found myself singing more and more Roxy songs. The audience seemed really hungry to hear them. And people were forever asking me when Roxy are reforming. So I decided to do it again. I hope to make some money. But it's also about going back to a period I loved and resurrecting that material and bringing it to a whole new audience who would otherwise never hear it."

The band assembled in support of the key players comprised four musicians familiar from Ferry's *As Time Goes By* tour and another whose association with Roxy stretched back much further, to March 1973. This was Chris Spedding on second guitar, his bluesy extemporisations providing a perfect complement to Manzanera's psychedelic extravagance. Good himself played piano, appending a particularly gorgeous prologue to *A Song for Europe*. New Yorker Zev Katz, whose credits included work with Dr John, Annie Lennox, Suzanne Vega and Dr John, was on bass, while Julia Thornton provided percussion. Lucy Wilkins on violin and keyboards was an audience favourite, raising the roof with the violin solo concluding *Out of the Blue*. "We have a girl who combines the roles of Eno and Eddie Jobson, who plays the electric violin and the VCS3 synthesiser," commented Manzanera. "And I must say, she's a lot more pretty to look at than those chaps."

The first performance of the revitalised Roxy Music took place at Hammersmith's Riverside Studios on Wednesday 23 May, when a five-song set for BBC2's *TOTP2* programme was recorded in front of an expectant crowd that included Roxy stylist Antony Price. The songs were *Virginia Plain*, *Love is the Drug*, *Out of the Blue*, *Do the Strand* and *Jealous Guy*; the first of these had to be performed twice for technical reasons, and the last no fewer than three times. The show went out on Wednesday 6 June, garnished with *Top of the Pops* clips for *More Than This*, *Over You*, *Dance Away*, *Avalon* and *All I Want is You*, plus the long-unseen *Full House* performance of *The Bogus Man Part II*. Ferry, Mackay and Manzanera were also on hand in interview mode.

The tour began three days later at the Point in Dublin, passing through Glasgow, Newcastle, Nottingham, Birmingham, Sheffield and Manchester prior to three nights at Wembley Arena. One-day visits to Germany, Switzerland, Spain and Belgium were followed by a sustained assault on Canada and the US, starting in Toronto on 16 July. By 7 August the band were in Australia for five gigs, with three nights in Tokyo followed by further dates in Holland, Belgium, Germany, Denmark, Italy and Austria. The tour wound up where it began, with two shows on 1 and 2 October in Hammersmith. These last gave rise to a brilliantly assembled film version of the tour, issued the following year as *Roxy Music Live at the Apollo*, and the year after that came a double album called simply *Roxy Music Live*.

"We recorded just about every show on the tour, so for this live album we listened to countless versions of most songs," remarked Mackay. "I had to give up trying to choose; we all did in the end. Of course, I just started comparing the sax solos. It's hard if you're pleased with one version but the others aren't, or vice versa. So past a certain point we mainly left it to Rhett Davies: he can be objective."

The results of Davies' deliberations, like the accompanying film, provide a potent reminder of what a dazzling act of resuscitation Roxy had pulled off. In fact, were it not for the somewhat leaden versions of *My Only Love*, *Dance Away* and *Avalon* – late-period tracks that fail to ignite in performance, and which, according to Manzanera, the band would sometimes approach with a heavy heart – the *Roxy Music Live* collection is, in certain respects, the best of all Roxy albums. As Mackay put it, "Some of the versions are by far the best we ever did." Manzanera's blistering guitar solo at the end of *Ladytron* is as staggering to hear as it was to watch; Mackay's shrieking sax sound on *Both Ends Burning* is matched by his gorgeous duet with Lucy Wilkins on *Tara*; while Ferry performs with a mature twinkle throughout. Unlike the film, the CD also includes two songs only sporadically performed on the tour, both of which – *More Than This* and *If There is Something* – were well worth preserving.

The 2001 live set was an intriguing one all round, particularly for its preponderance of tracks taken from the earlier albums. Perhaps the masterstroke was the surprise inclusion of *For Your Pleasure* as a grim and spooky envoi. Coming after a predictable, though welcome, climactic volley of *Virginia Plain*, *Love is the Drug* and *Do the Strand*, *For Your Pleasure* sent the show out on an entrancing high, with the band members taking their bows and leaving the stage one by one to the ritualistic beat of Thompson's percussion, the curtains finally swaying down on the synthesiser's spectral breath of "ta-ra."

Though a self-confessed control freak, Ferry was profoundly affected by this triumphant rediscovery of his audience, not to mention his former band-mates. "Phil and Andy both turned it on every night, and I was impressed," he told Chris Roberts. "They each have their own following and a unique sound. They're very good at recapturing the mood of each song. And it's amazing how well we all got along." The man who had been buried alive for so long in the solitary contemplation of the recording studio had also been forced to the conclusion that "it's different when you're playing in a proper group in which the responsibilities are shared, because then other people feel free to debate the merits of the music a bit more. If you're simply hiring people, you don't get that frisson from playing with your equals in a band. A little bit of creative conflict can be a good thing." This, of course, was a total, and long-awaited, volte-face.

To coincide with the 2001 reunion tour, yet another compilation album was put out, though this one was the first for nearly 25 years to try to encapsulate the band's whole career, without reference to Ferry solo tracks. Issued in June, *The Best of Roxy Music* also had the intriguing distinction of playing the story backwards, starting with the fluid *Avalon* and concluding with the riotous *Re-make/Re-model*.

There was a Roxy covergirl as of old, too, with Susie Bick sprawled in an emerald glow and attended by a bejewelled raven, a whiff of necrophile glam hanging about her in that she might just possibly be dead. As well as recalling "the raven of October" from *Bitters End*, Bick's throaty familiar here is presumably croaking "Never more" to her. If Edgar Allan Poe was indeed the inspiration, it was a timely reminder of John Peel's long-ago reference to the band "tearing in like the terror of the Rue Morgue," and to *Melody Maker*'s allusion in 1973 to Roxy's "exotic, Poe-like quality."

Enotonic

When the Roxy reunion intervened, Ferry was just a few tracks away from finishing his long-deferred *Alphaville* project. Indeed, even on flight BA6029 the previous December, his thoughts hadn't been confined to "the crazy man's socks." "The plane was going to crash," he told the *Observer*'s Barbara Ellen. "We were all going to die. I just thought: 'Oh no, I've got an album to finish. Could we reschedule?'"

The album was eventually renamed *Frantic* (apparently in ironic reference to Ferry's unhurried attitude to deadlines) and released on 29 April 2002. Always fond of filmic references, Ferry had switched titles from a seminal Jean-Luc Godard sci-fi noir to a pay-the-rent Roman Polanski suspense thriller – but this turned out not to be an ominous sign. *Frantic*, in fact, emerged as his strongest solo album yet. The ambient haze and half-heard vocal style that had held sway for two decades was at last swept aside, to be replaced by a ballsy and bluesy production job and a husky vocal presence brought front and centre for a change. As Mark Edwards aptly observed in the *Sunday Times*, *Frantic* is "the unfamiliar sound of Ferry having fun."

The album is structured like *The Bride Stripped Bare* in its careful mixture of cover versions and Ferry originals. The latter are so good that the listener tends to hurry past the others with a degree of 'God almighty, Bryan, not covers again' impatience, but even here there's a new directness and brio, with *One Way Love* given a breezy pop sheen and Dylan's *It's All Over Now, Baby Blue* a bludgeoning backbeat and squalling harmonica sound. The others are more disposable, and Ferry's faux-rootsy attempt at *Goodnight Irene* is laughable in its inadvertent evocation of the Coen Brothers movie *O Brother, Where Art Thou?* But, by and large, the covers don't detract too damagingly from the originals, which are of outstanding quality.

Two of them, *Hiroshima…* and *San Simeon*, have something of the original Roxy strangeness, which in the case of *San Simeon* is unsurprising, given the lyric's origin as an off-cut from *In Every Dream Home a Heartache*. *Hiroshima…* is a doom-laden fever dream, with Ferry unconscious in Versailles, waking up in Chiang-Mai and burned-out in Berlin, assailed throughout by a sepulchral piano figure and the febrile cacophony of four guitarists, Radiohead's Jonny Greenwood among them. Ferry's explicit reference to Alain Resnais' surrealist Franco-Japanese romance, *Hiroshima mon amour*, seems straightforward enough until he wrong-foots the listener with a nod to a quite different film, namely *Blade Runner*. The track shades directly into the castellated gloom of *San Simeon*, which is Ferry in the High Weird mode fans thought he'd long since abandoned, transferring the obsessive consumer durables of *Dream Home* to a cobwebbed Hollywood mansion. The spooky backdrop, complete with spectral Alison Goldfrapp voices, conjures images of William Randolph Hearst and Marion Davies reciting a mail-order catalogue from beyond the grave.

Like *San Simeon*, *Cruel*, *Goddess of Love* and *Nobody Loves Me* are collaborations with Dave Stewart, and accordingly have something of the brassy guitars-and-drums feel of Eurythmics' 1987 album *Revenge*. Against a scorchingly powerful backdrop, *Cruel* begins with an evocation of disenfranchised Native Americans (not unlike the Talking Heads track *City of Dreams*), blending seamlessly into a plaint on behalf of the disenfranchised closer to home. Ferry singing about the dispossessed, rather than the plain possessed, is a real turn-up, but he does it with unwonted passion, particularly when appealing for an answer to a strange crew consisting of "James Bond, Jackie O, Johnnie Ray and Garbo."

The other Stewart tracks are just as strong, as is Ferry's own *A Fool for Love*, a sombre and ruminative ballad graced by Paul Thompson's percussion. The real knockout, however, is kept till last. Though a contributor to both *Hiroshima...* and *Goddess of Love*, Eno is billed as co-writer of the jaunty *I Thought*, his mellifluous background vocals giving real weight to an ineffably moving melody. The rolling bass line of Zev Katz, plus the woozy synthetic wash of the backdrop, makes the track a close relative to the soundscapes created by Eno on his 1990 John Cale collaboration, *Wrong Way Up*, while a mid-song pause for Duane Eddy-style guitar and archly plucked strings à la John Barry is delightful. And it only gets better: Ferry's coolly philosophical vocal builds to a nakedly confessional mode before fading into a sublime harmonica break from Ferry himself. For long-term Roxy followers, of course, the smooth meshing of Eno's voice with Ferry's on *I Thought* is affecting in itself.

Testifying to the album's patchy and long-drawn-out gestation, production duties on *Frantic* were shared between Ferry, Colin Good, Rhett Davies, Robin Trower and Dave Stewart. It reached number six in the UK chart, though Ferry's long-awaited return to form was somewhat overshadowed by an unusually intrusive amount of press speculation regarding his faltering marriage, which finally ended in divorce in March 2003.

Sacred days

Ferry had suddenly acquired a taste for touring, which he proceeded to indulge on a massive scale in support of *Frantic*, playing in smaller venues than Roxy could command but keeping the itinerary going throughout most of 2002 and 2003. Towards the end of this marathon stint, Roxy were reactivated briefly for gigs in Portugal, North America and Canada between 12 July and 2 August, with a one-off appearance at Bonn's Museumplatz following on Saturday 25 October.

"Before this tour," Manzanera had pointed out apropos of Roxy's 2001 reunion, "perhaps we were beginning to be considered old dogs that were about to be shot and put out of their misery, but now our tails are wagging again." They certainly were, Manzanera's in particular. With Ferry embarking on yet more solo gigs in 2004, Manzanera put out his sixth solo LP, aptly titled *6PM*, on 19 July. Gallery Studio had by now been relocated from Chertsey to London, where Manzanera gathered together a starry entourage that included friends old (longtime colleague Robert Wyatt) and new (bass player Jamie Johnson), with the original Roxy line-up represented by Mackay, Eno and Thompson. Also involved were Pink Floyd's David Gilmour and Pretender Chrissie Hynde (author 30 years earlier of a particularly notorious Eno interview). Bill MacCormick, too – by now installed as Manzanera's webmaster – came out of retirement to play bass on one track. The result was a remarkable album that dovetails a kind of autumnal serenity with ample evidence of the fact that Manzanera can still rock like hell when required.

For Manzanera, *6PM* was an opportunity to explore the formative period in which his musical tastes were developed, the result even containing a 1968 photo of him performing with Pooh and the Ostrich Feather in a Dulwich crypt. A heady whiff of psychedelia hangs over the finished product, with Floyd and Beatles influences well to the fore and a vaguely Druidical, 15-minute song cycle at the close. Defiantly free of pandering to up-to-the-minute styles, *6PM* demonstrated that *Vozero* was no flash in the pan; here was an inspired musician crafting songs of rare maturity, but with just as skewed an approach as ever.

Though presenting it in characteristically unassuming and unpretentious style, Manzanera achieves a depth of emotion on *6PM* that outdoes even *Vozero*. The opener, *Broken Dreams*, is one long sigh of regret, beginning with a uniquely ominous extended intro and building to an unadorned guitar solo that's searing in its simplicity. *Love Devotion* shows Manzanera at his most nakedly vulnerable, extolling new-found love against a portentous backdrop of synthetic strings, a caressing Claire Singers backing vocal and a doleful running commentary from Mackay's oboe. And *Wish You Well* is elegiac in the most literal sense, a forlorn envoi to MacCormick's elder brother Ian MacDonald, who had recently committed suicide. Chrissie Hynde, who worked with MacDonald on the *NME* three decades earlier, contributes wistful backing vocals and harmonica, while MacCormick himself puts in a sweetly phrased solo on bass guitar.

The tone elsewhere is more upbeat. *Green Spikey Cactus* is like a down-and-dirty flip-side to *Prairie Rose*, a stonking rock'n'roll workout powered by Hynde's fuzzed-up harmonica, Thompson's gangbusting percussion, and an extraordinary Manzanera lyric bristling with twisters, buzzards, crickets, armadillos, rattlesnakes, big fat flies and, of course, cacti. To top the whole thing off, Mackay makes a late entrance in full-on raunch mode.

Where *Green Spikey Cactus* delivers a knockout punch, *Waiting for the Sun to Shine* is more laid-back but just as infectious, with Manzanera anxious to shake a "ten-ton" depression against a deceptively sunny backdrop. There's a lovely sprinkling of so-called "Enotonic" here, plus spiralling Mackay saxes that point up the track's similarity to the old Explorers number, *Dreams of the East*. *6PM* itself has some inscrutable, muttered time-keeping from Manzanera but is otherwise a stratospheric guitar solo set against a hectoring electric viola (Brendan Jury) and Thompson's all-around-the-kit percussion. *Manzra* is a beguilingly ponderous outing for treated guitars (so treated that, in best Manzanera tradition, they're all but unrecognisable), backed up by Yarron Stavi's solemnly thrummed double-bass and wandering piano figures from Nigel Simpson.

The final stretch of the album is a 'ring cycle' collectively entitled 'The Cissbury Ring', with Robert Wyatt brought in as Manzanera's chief collaborator. Manzanera described it as a "psychedelic short story" and "a Hardyesque magical mystery tour of the South Downs with death (*Shoreline*), love (*Always You*) and final transcendence (*Sacred Days*)." And it's by no means as indigestible as Manzanera made it sound. "The essence of my music is to be able to create diverse moods and atmospheric sounds," he had said at the time of *Vozero*, and this dictum applies to 'The Cissbury Ring' in spades, recalling the filmic images routinely conjured by Roxy in their early days.

The pastoral canvas of *Cissbury Ring* itself is undercut by Wyatt's out-of-sorts trumpet fanfares as Manzanera teeters on the downs in a swirl of impressionistic images and memories of the past. Wyatt's brief brass meditation, *Porlock*, melds into the mordant *Shoreline*, in which Mackay's astringent oboe paints at least as vivid a picture as *Sea Breezes*. Manzanera, too, comes up with a lyric of remarkable, sublimated power. Doleful yet intensely beautiful (and containing an explicit Hardy reference), *Always You* blends seamlessly into the exhilarating metallic soundstage of *Sacred Days*, in which Manzanera and Dave Gilmour indulge in a ferocious guitar battle that has to be heard to be believed.

6PM was well received all round, with a capsule review in the *Guardian* providing a strikingly prophetic summary: "The chemistry here suggests that if Roxy have considered making another album, they should grasp the nettle now."

Out of the blue

On Saturday 17 July, just as *6PM* was hitting the shops, Andy Mackay could be seen performing with Badly Drawn Boy and Mick Jones of The Clash at a summer festival local to his home. There were mutterings about Mackay putting together a sax-led band of his own, not to mention an instrumental LP to be called *London, Paris, Rome* and apparently "deconstructing standards such as *Three Coins in a Fountain*." What Mackay actually came up with in September of 2004 was at least as intriguing – an album specially composed for use at the Park Hotel in Mackay's old stamping ground of Kenmare, specifically in its newly established holistic spa. Indeed, *Music for the Senses* was perhaps the most practical application yet of Eno's tireless proliferation of 'Music for' this, that or the other airport, film or whatever.

"The concept of creating music for such a defined environment posed a rare challenge," Mackay said in the attached press release. "My first thoughts were of what not to do – no waves, whales, birdsong, chanting monks. I was indeed a little apprehensive, but then I thought how fascinating it would be to approach a piece of music as someone might approach creating a perfume, or planting a garden, or choosing the colour of an interior. Music to be experienced by the body and mind." He also pointed out that "The use of such musicians as Chris Spedding, Lucy Wilkins and Julia Thornton brings a 'pop-rock-classical' influence which is fused with the controlled element of the writing [and] results in an interesting exploration of 'relaxation music'." The tracks bear such restful titles as *Sunrise, Bluebell Wood, Coral Strand* and *Valley of Seclusion*, and for the man whose first two solo LPs had been unkindly recommended for use in Wimpy bars and Chinese takeaways, *Music for the Senses* counts as a fascinating, if late-blooming, vindication.

At this late stage, Roxy began to receive the kind of awards that previously had been conspicuous by their absence. On 22 May 2003, Ferry was presented with an Ivor Novello award for Outstanding Contribution to Music, while on 4 October the following year Roxy themselves were honoured with a Q magazine Lifetime Achievement Award. Ferry also began to diversify into unusual areas. In 2004 he made his acting debut (discounting the *Petit Déjeuner Compris* nonsense of 25 years before) in the Neil Jordan film *Breakfast on Pluto*, and in 2005 he appeared as a guest on someone else's album, a previously unheard-of dispensation. Playing harmonica on the track *Hear Your Daddy*, he was joined on the Chris Spedding album *Click Clack* by Sarah Brown, the gifted vocalist who had contributed so much to Roxy's reunion tour.

On the road through much of 2004 under his own steam, Ferry reconvened Roxy for another tour in 2005, starting in Camden Town on Wednesday 8 June. The venue, Koko, was formerly the Camden Palace, where The Explorers had performed 20 years earlier to the day. "Any doubts about the band's match fitness were dispelled by a display of sustained expertise," wrote Adam Sweeting in the *Guardian*. "Manzanera's blipping and shrieking guitar was balanced by the earthier, bluesier tones of Chris Spedding, while Mackay's powerful saxophone gave many songs a lethal cutting edge ... Perhaps there's a cloning factory churning out new Bryans," he added, "but as he ran through his familiar poses and postures (not least his celebrated impression of a man digging up rhododendrons in slow motion) we could have been back in the golden age of *Stranded* or *Country Life*."

With *Chance Meeting*, *Prairie Rose*, *The Bogus Man* and *Pyjamarama* newly revived for 2005, the band played the Isle of Wight Festival on Saturday the 11th alongside Idlewild, Supergrass, Razorlight, Faithless, Nine Black Alps, Ray Davies, Babyshambles and (deputising for a non-appearing Morrissey) Travis; according to Helen Brown in the *Daily Telegraph*, despite this strong bill "it was Roxy Music who stole the show." The band then took in a continental sweep of Horsens, Goodwood, Oslo, Bonn, Amsterdam, Frankfurt, Liverpool, Tienen and Alicante. On Saturday 2 July, between the Bonn and Amsterdam dates, Roxy performed *Virginia Plain*, *Love is the Drug*, *Jealous Guy* and *Do the Strand* at the Brandenburg Gate in Berlin as part of Live 8. And on the day this book went to press, Tuesday 2 August, Roxy Music were playing the Sheraton Pines in the Algarve.

The news had since come through that Manzanera had yet another solo album due for release in October; entitled *50 Minutes Later*, it features much the same crew as *6PM*. Back in 2004, he had confided to the *Times* that "The unfinished business I have is Roxy Music. I believe we can make a new album and I keep banging on to the other guys about it, but I think I'm more optimistic than them." Now, momentously, it appeared that Ferry and Mackay had come round to Manzanera's point of view. In summer 2005 they finally ended four years of speculation and started recording again for the first time in 23 years, reckoning they'd be occupied until Christmas and have a brand-new album ready in the new year.

Early reports that Eno might be involved were soon scotched, though he, too, had returned to songwriting in 2005 with an inscrutable new album called *Another Day on Earth*. Apart from his *Wrong Way Up* collaboration with John Cale in 1990, this was Eno's first sustained attempt at putting together a sequence of songs since 1977. In Ferry-like fashion, some of the tracks, notably *Under*, were revamps of material from an LP, *My Squelchy Life*, abandoned back in 1991.

On *Another Day on Earth*, Eno's unwillingness to submit to the intimate nature of conventional songwriting remained intact; the more completely to efface himself, he would either manipulate his warm tones into a kind of electronic fudge, or else sample the voices of his Polish accountant and Lithuanian domestic help, or else hand over the vocal on the mesmerising *Bonebomb* to Aylie Cooke. "Lyrics are the only thing to do with music that haven't been made easier technically," he opined in the *Daily Telegraph*. "Lyric writing is pretty much what it was 400 years ago, whereas it's easy to throw together a piece of music using stuff you can buy in any music store. Hold down one note and you've got a career as an ambient artist." As the original non-musician and godfather of the ambient sound, he was well placed to make so pithy a judgment.

After his decades-long enslavement to the complexities of studio recording, Ferry would no doubt concur with Eno's opinion regarding the intractability of lyric writing. And yet he had shaken off the Eno-like need to occlude himself, to smother his muse in obfuscating veils of sound. *Frantic* had shown that he was back on top form, just as *Vozero* and *6PM* had done for Manzanera. Mackay, too, had obviously been stimulated by the Roxy reunion into a new burst of creativity, making one wish that his latest ambient experiments could be liberated from Kenmare and granted a commercial release. And, to judge from his powerhouse performances with the revived Roxy, The Great Paul Thompson was as Great as ever.

Roxy Music had somehow been allowed to gather dust throughout the 1990s, the band's influence duly acknowledged yet its profile strangely diminished in the eyes of posterity. That all changed, however, with the reunion tour of 2001. On those exuberant dates it was proved beyond a shadow of a doubt that Roxy's constituent members are just as mellow and mature in person as the mellifluous sound of *Avalon*, yet just as spikily unpredictable in performance as the anarchic canvas of *Re-make/Re-model*.

A new album promises, therefore, to make just as radical a statement as their eight previous ones, reasserting and redefining the most fascinating legacy in art-rock. Perhaps the party isn't over after all. Perhaps, too, the next time could be the best time. For in the 21st century, the old duality of Roxy Music, its endlessly alluring ambiguity, remains triumphantly intact. "Both ends burning," as Ferry once sang, "till the end."

Bibliography

The first book to chronicle Roxy Music was Rex Balfour's *The Bryan Ferry Story*, published by Michael Dempsey in 1976. Given that the Balfour persona screened none other than Ferry's publicist and right-hand man Simon Puxley, the result redefines the word 'biased' but is nevertheless astute in several of its observations and authoritative in its chronology of Ferry's progress up to that time.

There followed Johnny Rogan's *Roxy Music: Style with Substance – Roxy's first ten years* (Star Books 1982) and, the same year, *Bryan Ferry and Roxy Music* by Barry Lazell and Dafydd Rees, published by Proteus. Both of these are excellent straightforward histories, the former particularly good on Eno and the latter on the band's formative years. After a long gap came Paul Stump's *Unknown Pleasures: A Cultural Biography of Roxy Music* (Quartet Books 1998), which does exactly what it says on the tin, offering a fascinating sociological account of the band's rise and fall, together with an astringent analysis of their work.

More recently, David Buckley's *The Thrill of It All: The Story of Bryan Ferry and Roxy Music* (André Deutsch 2004) is essentially a Ferry biography, and an exceptionally insightful one, garnished with valuable testimony from a number of Roxy satellite figures. Other books consulted include:

Bernard, Susan – *Bernard of Hollywood: The Ultimate Pin-Up Book* – Taschen 2002
De Lisle, Tim [ed] – *Lives of the Great Songs* – Pavilion 1994
DeRogatis, Jim – *Let it Blurt: The Life and Times of Lester Bangs* – Bloomsbury 2000
DeRogatis, Jim – *Turn On Your Mind: Four Decades of Great Psychedelic Rock* – Hal Leonard 2003
De Ville, Nick – *Album: Style and Image in Sleeve Design* – Mitchell Beazley 2003
Eno, Brian – *A Year with Swollen Appendices: Brian Eno's Diary* – Faber 1996
Eno, Brian and Russell Mills – *More Dark than Shark* – Faber 1986
Frame, Pete – *Rock Family Trees* vols 1 and 2 – Omnibus 1980/1983
Gabor, Mark – *A Modest History of the Pin-Up* – Pan 1973 / Taschen 2000
Garner, Ken – *In Session Tonight* – BBC Books 1993
Goddard, Simon – *The Smiths: Songs that Saved Your Life* – Reynolds & Hearn 2004
Hall, Jerry [with Christopher Hemphill] – *Jerry Hall's Tall Tales* – Boxtree 1985
Hoskyns, Barney – *Glam! Bowie, Bolan and the Glitter Rock Revolution* – Faber 1998
Hunter, Ian – *Diary of a Rock and Roll Star* – Panther 1974
Lavers, Stephen [introductory essay] – *Roxy Music Greatest Hits* – EG Music 1978
Logan, Nick and Bob Woffinden [eds] – *The NME Illustrated Encyclopaedia of Rock* – Salamander 1977
Mackay, Andy – *Electronic Music* – Phaidon 1981
Miles [ed] – *Bowie in His Own Words* – Omnibus Press 1980
Moore, Alan F – *Rock: The Primary Text* – Oxford University Press 1992
Palmer, Tony – *All You Need is Love* – Futura 1977

Pegg, Nicholas – *The Complete David Bowie* – Reynolds & Hearn 2000
Robotham, Tom – *Varga* – JG Press 2003
Sandford, Christopher – *Bowie: Loving the Alien* – Little Brown 1996
Sheridan, Simon – *Keeping the British End Up: Four Decades of Saucy Cinema* (Reynolds & Hearn 2005)
Tamm, Eric – *Brian Eno: His Music and the Vertical Color of Sound* – Faber 1989

The internet, meanwhile, carries three exceptional Roxy websites – vivaroxymusic, roxyrama, and Phil Manzanera's own site, which contains a terrific archive under the droll editorial supervision of Bill MacCormick. Rocksbackpages.com is just as terrific, and covers the entire spectrum of popular music to boot. In addition, the BFI National Film and Television Archive is an invaluable source of vintage Roxy TV spots.

The as-it-happened history of the band is contained, of course, in the music press and other journals of the day, notably in the ace reportage of Richard Williams, Allan Jones, Nick Kent and Manzanera's friend Ian MacDonald. Without the testimony of these writers and others like them, a history of Roxy Music would be impossible to construct. The following articles and interviews are particularly illuminating:

Anon – 'Whatever Turned You On' [Ferry interview] – *NME* 5 August 1972
Anon – 'The Roxy Music File' – *Melody Maker* 14 October 1972
Anon – 'Bryan Ferry on the Swift Rise of Roxy' – *Beat Instrumental* May 1973
Anon – 'Roxy Resolutions' [Manzanera, Jobson, Ferry interview] – *Record Mirror* 10 January 1976
Anon – 'Punk Follies' – *Evening Standard* 11 December 1978
Anon – 'Why Rock Follies trio now make four' – *Daily Mail* 4 May 1979
Anon – Phil Manzanera interview – *Record Collector* June 1995
Anon – 'The bizarre career of Amanda Lear' – *Observer* 24 December 2000
Anon – 'Recording and re-mixing Roxy Music's *Avalon*' [Rhett Davies and Bob Clearmountain interviews] – *Sound on Sound* August 2003
Anon – 'Getting Roxy Music in with the 'In' crowd' [David O'List interview] – *vivaroxymusic.com* 25 April 2004
Aston, Martin – 'Cover girl Kari-Ann Moller' / 'Cover star Amanda Lear' / '*Country Life* girls' – Q February 1991
Atkinson, Peter – 'The *Rock Follies* are back' – *Evening Standard* 3 October 1977
Bangs, Lester – 'Eno sings with the fishes' – *Village Voice* 4 March 1978
Bell, Max – 'Bryan Ferry interviewed' – *NME* 21 December 1974
Birch, Ian – Phil Manzanera interview – *Melody Maker* 12 November 1977
Birch, Ian – Bryan Ferry interview – *Smash Hits* May 1982
Blake, John – 'Daddy of Them All!' [Ferry interview] – *Daily Mirror* 3 April 1985
Bohn, Chris – Bryan Ferry interview – *NME* 16 August 1980
Boucher, Caroline – 'Virginia Might Be Plain But She's Expensive' – *Disc* 16 September 1972
Boucher, Caroline – 'The Real Mackay' – *Disc* 17 February 1973
Boucher, Caroline – 'Ferry Interesting' – *Disc* 24 March 1973

Boucher, Caroline – '*Stranded* is cautious – but our first was naïve' [Mackay interview] – *Disc* 19 January 1974

Boucher, Caroline – 'Bryan the Cole Miner' – *Observer* 19 December 1999

Bracewell, Michael – 'Look Back in Languor' – *Guardian Weekend* 14 June 1997

Brown, Helen – 'Roxy Music Kick off the Summer' [Isle of Wight review] – *Daily Telegraph* 13 June 2005

Buckman, Peter – 'Television: New Frontiers' [*Rock Follies of '77* review] – *Listener* 19 May 1977

Chapman, Rob – 'They Came from Planet Bacofoil' – *Mojo* December 1995

Charlesworth, Chris – 'Roxy Music – caught in the act' [Rainbow review] – *Melody Maker* 7 April 1973

Charlesworth, Chris – 'Roxy step up the ladder' [New York review] – *Melody Maker* 15 June 1974

Clark, Pete – 'Bryan Ferry and the boys...' [Ferry, Mackay, Manzanera interview] – *Evening Standard* 14 February 2001

Clarke, Steve – 'Birmingham: Roxy Music/Sharks' – *NME* 24 March 1973

Cohn, Ellen – 'The Tube: Little Ladies Night' – *Village Voice* 22 November 1988

Coon, Caroline – 'Bryan Ferry: Putting on the Style' – *Melody Maker* 12 July 1975

Crace, Jim – 'The Ferry Tale Unfolds' – *Sunday Telegraph Magazine* 3 October 1982

Cromelin, Richard – 'Leo Sayer: The Little Clown' – *Rolling Stone* 23 May 1974

Cromelin, Richard – 'Eno Music: The Roxy Music Rebellion' [Chris Thomas and Eno interviews] – *Phonograph Record* November 1974

Cromelin, Richard – 'The Inmates Have Taken Over: Kevin Ayers, John Cale, Nico, Eno & the Soporifics' – *Creem* December 1974

Dagnal, Cynthia – 'Eno and the Jets: controlled chaos' – *Rolling Stone* 12 September 1974

Davies, Bernard – 'One Man's Television' [*Rock Follies* review] – *Broadcast* 12 April 1976

Davies, Bernard – 'One Man's Television' [*Rock Follies of '77* review] – *Broadcast* 30 May 1977

De Lisle, Tim – 'The Life of Bryan Ferry' – *Observer* 19 September 1982

De Lisle, Tim – 'Roxy is the Drug' – *Guardian* 20 May 2005

Dempster, Sarah – Glasgow review – *NME* 15 June 2001

Denselow, Robin – 'A new phenomenon in rock music' [Ferry interview] – *Guardian* 9 October 1972

DeRogatis, Jim – 'The Boys are Back' [Manzanera interview] – *Chicago Sun-Times* 27 July 2001

Dillon, Barry – 'Roxy: enjoy the luxury' [Eno, Manzanera interview] – *Sounds* 28 April 1973

Drillsma, Barbara – 'Roxy – back to the roots' – *Melody Maker* 11 October 1975

Edmands, Bob – 'Roxy doxies fail to please' [Leeds review] – *NME* 27 October 1973

Edwards, Mark – 'The Best of Both Worlds?' – [Ferry, Puxley, de Ville interview] – *Arena* September/October 1994

Ellen, Barbara – 'The Life of Bryan' – *Observer Magazine* 13 May 2001

Eno, Brian – 'Eight Days a Week' – *Melody Maker* 29 January 1977

Fallowell, Duncan – 'A Very Proper Pop Star' [Ferry, Puxley, Price interview] – *Sunday Telegraph Magazine* 1991

Fiddick, Peter – 'Saga Figure' [Howard Schuman interview] – *Guardian* 23 February 1976

Fox-Cumming, Ray – 'Solo Ferry sets sail' – *Disc* 23 June 1973

Fox-Cumming, Ray – 'The much maligned maestro of Roxy Music' [Ferry interview] – *Disc* 26 October 1974

Fox-Cumming, Ray – 'So Ferry stylish…' – *Record Mirror* 25 October 1975

Frith, Simon – 'Roxy Music's Picture Palace' – *Let It Rock* May 1974

Fudger, David – 'Not Time for Jet Lag?' [David O'List interview] – *Disc* 23 March 1975

Funtash, Dale – Eddie Jobson interview – *Trouser Press* February/March 1977

Giannini, Melissa – 'Re-make/Re-model' [Mackay interview] – *Metro Times* 24 July 2001

Gould, Tony – 'Rock Political' [*Rock Follies of '77* review] – *New Society* 9 June 1977

Graham, Bill – Bryan Ferry interview – *Hot Press* August 1981

Greenaway, Roger – 'Concepts, star trips and more foolish things' [Ferry interview] – *Record Mirror* 26 January 1974

Guarino, Mark – 'More Than This…' [Mackay interview] – *Chicago Daily Herald* 30 July 2001

Hanna, Lynn – 'Ferry's got style to burn' – *NME* 19 June 1982

Hayman, Martin – 'Roxy on a pilgrimage to Wonderland' [Ferry interview] – *Sounds* 30 December 1972

Hayman, Martin – 'The Very Physical Mr Ferry' – *Sounds* 9 June 1973

Hayman, Martin – 'Phil [Manzanera] looks to Roxy's Phase 2' – *Sounds* 13 October 1973

Hayman, Martin – 'Stylish Doyen of Rock' [Ferry interview] – *Sounds* 8 June 1974

Hoggard, Liz – 'Ferry's return trip' – *Mail on Sunday 'You' Magazine* – 24 April 2002

Hollingsworth, Roy – '*For Your Pleasure* is the title of Roxy Music's sensational second album' [Ferry interview] – *Melody Maker* 17 March 1973

Honan, Corinna – 'There's a vintage Rolex on his wrist…' [Ferry interview] – *Daily Mail* 16 April 1993

Hoskyns, Barney – 'Bryan Ferry: Melancholic of Glam' – *Independent* 16 June 2001

Howes, Keith – '*Rock Follies* à Deux' – *Gay News* 2-15 June 1977

Humphries, Patrick – 'The First 12 Months: Roxy Music' – *Vox/Record Hunter* September 1992

Hynde, Chrissie – 'Everything you'd rather not have known about Brian Eno' – *NME* 2 February 1974

Ingham, Jonh – 'Roxy Music: The Roots' – *NME* 28 April 1973

Ingham, Jonh – 'Roxy Music: Ultra Pulp Images on the Video-Cassette of Your Mind' – *NME* 9 June 1973

Ingham, Jonh – 'The Roxy Music Story' – *Sounds* 4 October 1975

Ingham, Jonh – 'If I *had* to attend a Roxy gig, I'd go to Glasgow' – *Sounds* 18 October 1975

Jones, Allan – 'Ferry turns Valentino' [Cardiff review] – *Melody Maker* 28 September 1974

Jones, Allan – 'Achtung Roxy!' – *Melody Maker* 12 October 1974

Jones, Allan – 'Eno: on top of Tiger Mountain' – *Melody Maker* 26 October 1974

Jones, Allan – 'Siren's call to the 'real' Roxy' – *Melody Maker* 4 October 1975

Jones, Allan – 'Eno – Class of '75' – *Melody Maker* 29 November 1975

Jones, Allan – 'Rockin' on the Road' [Mackay interview] – *Melody Maker* 3 July 1976

Jones, Allan – 'Darkness Falls: Ferry in the confessional' – *Melody Maker* 16 September 1978

Jones, Allan – 'Roxy's Swedish Love Night' [Stockholm review] – *Melody Maker* 3 March 1979

Jones, Allan – 'Allan Jones takes a champagne flight to see Roxy Music on the Riviera – and still complains' – *Melody Maker* 11 September 1982

Kaye, Lenny – 'Roxy shock New York' – *Disc* 15 June 1974

Kent, Nick – 'Roxy – all this and Eno too' [Ferry interview] – *NME* 18 November 1972

Kent, Nick (with Charles Shaar Murray and Ian MacDonald) – 'The Man who Put Sequins into Middle Eights' [Ferry interview] – *NME* 20 January 1973

Kent, Nick – 'A Flight of Fantasy' [Eno interview] – *NME* 3 February 1973

Kent, Nick – 'Last Tango in Amsterdam' – *NME* 9 June 1973

Kent, Nick – 'Of Launderettes and Lizard Girls' [Eno interview] – *NME* 28 July 1973

Kent, Nick – 'Tonight Southport, tomorrow the … errh … world' – *NME* 20 April 1974

Kent, Nick – 'The freewheelin' Brian Eno' – *NME* 18 May 1974

Kent, Nick – 'The sting of El Ferranti' [Ferry interview] – *NME* 13 July 1974

Kent, Nick – 'Snake-eyed Lothario goes pan-tonic' [Manzanera interview] – *NME* 24 August 1974

Kent, Nick – 'Still Raining Still Posing' [Ferry, Manzanera interview] – *NME* 19 May 1979

Kirkup, Martin – 'New look Roxy twice as tough' [Nottingham review] – *Sounds* 24 March 1973

Kleinman, Philip – '£ittle £adies, lovely lolly' – *Sunday Times* 21 March 1976

Knight, Peter – 'Strike-hit TV series dropped until autumn' – *Daily Telegraph* 10 June 1977

Lake, Steve – 'Roxy's Song for Europe' – *Melody Maker* 27 October 1973

Lake, Steve – 'Keeping Roxy fresh' [Manzanera interview] – *Melody Maker* 3 August 1974

Logan, Nick – 'GI Blues (how to get them, how to lose them)' – *NME* 11 October 1975

MacDonald, Ian – 'Foxy Roxy – a menace to society' [Ferry interview] – *NME* 12 August 1972

MacDonald, Ian – 'Roxy: kind of example we wish to set our parents?' [Manzanera interview] – *NME* 23 September 1972

MacDonald, Ian – 'Ferry Interesting Roxy: bedpan rock' – *NME* 14 October 1972

MacDonald, Ian – 'Under the Influence' [Eno interview] – *NME* 10 March 1973

MacDonald, Ian – 'Under the Influence' [Manzanera interview] – *NME* 14 April 1973

MacDonald, Ian – 'Roxy Music' [Brighton review] – *NME* 21 April 1973

MacDonald, Ian – 'Party Fun from an Old Poseur' [Ferry interview] – *NME* 8 September 1973

MacDonald, Ian – 'Accidents will happen' [Eno interview] – *NME* 26 November 1977

MacDonald, Ian – 'How to make a modern record' [Eno interview part two] – *NME* 3 December 1977

MacDonald, Marianne – 'Ferry was close to the end' – *Evening Standard* 3 March 2003

MacKinnon, Angus – Andy Mackay interview – *Sounds* 16 August 1975

Makowski, Pete – 'The two sides of Mr Manzanera' – *Sounds* 24 August 1974

Martin, Pete – 'Phil Manzanera' – *Guitarist* October 1999

McKay, Neil – ''70s is Roxy Music to the ears of many' [Thompson interview] – *Newcastle Journal* 7 May 2001

Meades, Jonathan – 'The Dream Who Made Herself Come True' [Amanda Lear interview] – *Sunday Telegraph Magazine* 1985

Miles – 'Eno: … as Thin and Serious People Gather to Make Music' – *NME* 27 November 1976

Mills, Simon – 'L'uomo vague' [Ferry interview] – *Sunday Times Magazine* 4 September 1994

Palmer, Tony – 'Shock tactics from the Roxy' [Rainbow review] – *Observer* 15 April 1973

Parade, Nicky – 'Another Time, Another Place: Bryan Ferry relives the early Roxy years' – *Rock's Backpages* June 2001

Parnes, Djuna – 'Another Glam World: Brian Eno's adventures in Roxy Music' – *Rock's Backpages* June 2001

Peachey, Mal – 'Why success has left pop star Ferry all washed up' – *Mail on Sunday* 17 January 1993

Peacock, Steve – 'The Case of the Vanishing Image' [Ferry, Eno interview] – *Sounds* 1 July 1972

Peacock, Steve – 'Eno: The Sounds Talk In' – *Sounds* 21 October 1972

Peacock, Steve – 'Roxy: What Next – a Marching Band?'[Ferry interview] – *Sounds* 27 January 1973

Peacock, Steve – 'Unease of the Bogus Man' [Eno interview] – *Sounds* 10 March 1973

Peacock, Steve – 'The Roxy Machine leaves you cold' [Rainbow review] – *Sounds* 7 April 1973

Prophet, Sheila – 'Bryan in Ferryland' – *Record Mirror* 3 September 1977

Queen, Dave – 'Music for Windows' [Eno retrospective] – *Seattle Weekly* 1-7 June 2005

Rambali, Paul – 'Brain Waves from Eno: Too Smart for Rock'n'Roll, Too Weird for Anything Else' – *Trouser Press* June/July 1977

Richardson, Michael – '£250,000 pay-off for Rock [Follies] girls' – *Daily Express* 4 July 1983

Roberts, Chris – 'Re-make/Re-model' [Ferry, Mackay, Manzanera interview] – *Uncut* July 2001

Roberts, Chris – 'Live and, er, dangerous' [Ferry, Mackay, Manzanera interview] – *Uncut* July 2003

Robbins, Ira – 'Roxy Music: Anarch-o-rock in Motion' [Manzanera interview] – *Music Gig* September 1976

Robbins, Ira – 'Manifesto Destiny' [Manzanera interview] – *Trouser Press* June 1979

Robbins, Ira – 'Phil Manzanera' – *Trouser Press* June 1982

Robinson, Lisa – 'Ferry Across the Atlantic' [Kenton, Eno, Mackay interview] – *Disc* 30 December 1972

Robinson, Lisa – 'Roxy Music: Terror in the Rue Morgue' – *Creem* May 1973

Robinson, Lisa – 'Brian Eno's last interview' – *NME* 10 August 1974

Rose, Frank – 'Scaramouche of the synthesizer' [Eno interview] – *Creem* July 1975

Ross, Ron – 'Roxy Music: *Love is the Drug* in Bi-centennial Year!' – *Phonograph Record* March 1976

Russell, Rosalind – Andy Mackay interview – *Record Mirror* 7 April 1979

Sage, Lorna – 'Three Girls in a Box' [*Rock Follies* review] – *Times Literary Supplement* 9 April 1976

Salewicz, Chris – 'The Lone Star Synthesizer Op' [Eno interview] – *NME* 7 December 1974

Sandall, Robert – 'The Quiet Man of Pop Rocks Out' [Eno interview] – *Daily Telegraph* 16 June 2005

Shaar Murray, Charles – 'Roxy Music – for your pleasure again' – *Daily Telegraph* 17 February 2001

Simmons, Sylvie – 'Ten Questions for Bryan Ferry' – *Mojo* October 1999

Simpson, Dave – 'Re-make/Re-model' [first album retrospective] – *Uncut* September 1997

Sinclair, David – 'Once more for your pleasure' [Ferry interview] – *Times* 16 February 2001

Smith, Aidan – 'Eno's Never Ending Story' – *Scotsman* [*Scotland on Sunday*] 5 June 2005

Smith, Mat – 'The Arena Confidential – Bryan Ferry' – *Arena* June 2001

Snow, Mat – 'Bryan Ferry: My Indecision is Final' – *Q* February 1993

Stevenson, Jane – 'Ready for Roxy reunion' – *Toronto Sun* 16 July 2001

Stewart, Tony – 'Roxy transfix the Swiss' – *NME* 12 May 1973

Sutherland, Steve – 'Roxy give blood' [Wembley review] – *Melody Maker* 9 August 1980

Sweeting, Adam – Koko review, Camden Town – *Guardian* 10 June 2005

Tannenbaum, Rob – 'Steadfast in Style' – *Village Voice* 28 August 2002

Taylor, John – 'Roxy Music' – *Rolling Stone* 21 April 2005

Truman, James – 'Editions of Roxy' [Hammersmith review] – *Melody Maker* 26 May 1979

Truman, James – 'Bryan Ferry Frets' – *The Face* May 1982

Truman, James – 'Bryan Ferry' – *The Face* April 1985

Turner, Steve – 'Roxy Music' [Ferry interview] – *Beat Instrumental* October 1972

Tyler, Tony – 'Roxy Music: The Answer to a Maiden's Prayer or to anyone else's' – *NME* 1 July 1972

Tyler, Tony – 'Roxy – Remade, Remodelled' [Manchester review] – *NME* 3 November 1973

Tyler, Tony – 'Schlock Jollies' [Mackay, Schuman interview] – *NME* 10 April 1976

Vilaubi, Larry – 'From Hollywood in Glorious Roxyrama' – *NME* 13 January 1973

Walters, Idris – 'The Art School Dance Goes On Forever' [Ferry interview] – *Street Life* 29 November 1975

Welch, Chris – 'Pete Sinfield has a nose for success' – *Melody Maker* 13 May 1973

Welch, Chris – 'The quiet life' [Ferry interview] – *Record Mirror* 5 June 1982

Whitworth, Ed – 'Age of Enlightenment' [Manzanera interview] – *Times T2* July 2004

Williams, Precious – 'Get Your Roxys Off' [Ferry, Mackay interview] – *Daily Mirror* 7 June 2001

Williams, Richard – 'Horizon: Roxy in the rock stakes' – *Melody Maker* 7 August 1971

Williams, Richard – 'Roxy Music' – *Melody Maker* 12 February 1972

Williams, Richard – 'This Week's Sounds' – *Radio Times* 15-21 January 1972

Williams, Richard – 'This Week's Sounds' – *Radio Times* 17-23 June 1972

Williams, Richard – 'Roxy Music: the sound of surprise' [Ferry interview] – *Melody Maker* 1 July 1972

Williams, Richard – 'Roxy Music' [band interview] – *Melody Maker* 29 July 1972

Williams, Richard – 'Crimso meets Eno!' – *Melody Maker* 4 November 1972

Williams, Richard – 'If you think Roxy Music are a hype, you should have been at the [Manchester] Hardrock last week' – *Melody Maker* 18 November 1972

Williams, Richard – 'Roxy in Paris: in which our heroes dally with Dalí' – *Melody Maker* 12 May 1973

Williams, Richard – 'Roxy split' – *Melody Maker* 28 July 1873

Williams, Richard – 'The Roxy Experiment' [Nottingham review] – *Melody Maker* 24 March 1973

Yarwood, Stephen – 'Bill MacCormick interview' – *btinternet.com/~stephen.yarwood* September 1995

Yarwood, Stephen – 'Simon Ainley interview' – *btinternet.com/~stephen.yarwood* March 1988

Song Index

*   *   *

Albums

* indicates compilation album
+ indicates live album

albums credited to Roxy Music
given in bold type